Creating a Flexible Workplace

Creating a Flexible Workplace
How to Select and Manage Alternative Work Options

Barney Olmsted and Suzanne Smith

amacom

American Management Association

This book is available at a special
discount when ordered in bulk quantities.
For information, contact Special Sales Department,
AMACOM, a division of American Management Association,
135 West 50th Street, New York, NY 10020.

Library of Congress Cataloging-in-Publication Data

Olmsted, Barney.
   Creating a flexible workplace : how to select and manage
alternative work options / Barney Olmsted and Suzanne Smith.
      p.   cm.
   Bibliography: p.
   Includes index.
   ISBN 0-8144-5919-6
   1. Hours of labor, Flexible—United States. 2. Compressed work
week—United States. 3. Part-time employment—United States.
4. Job sharing—United States. 5. Work sharing—United States.
I. Smith, Suzanne. II. Title.
HD5109.2.U5046   1989
658.3'121—dc19   88-48027
                                                          CIP

Printing number

10   9   8   7   6   5   4   3   2   1

Acknowledgments

Writing a coherent book about the subject of flexibility has sometimes seemed like performing the thirteenth labor of Hercules. We couldn't have done it if we didn't believe that the need for information was great or without the help and support of many others who also think this is an important issue. There is not room to name all those who provided information or support, but, hopefully, having the book completed will be thanks of a kind.

We do, however, want to acknowledge a few who were of particular help. The vision and patience of Adrienne Hickey at AMACOM got us started and kept us going. Editors Kate Pferdner, Sue Cohan, and Barbara Horowitz polished the material they received and tied up its loose ends. In between, we had help from friends who reviewed drafts of sections or helped us obtain needed information. For this we particularly want to thank Helen Axel, Gil Gordon, Bob Holtcamp, and all the human resources managers who shared policy models so others wouldn't have to "recreate the wheel."

Special thanks are also due our friend and colleague Dr. Stanley Nollen for his seminal work and research in the field of workplace flexibility. Because he remains an authority in the field, we have quoted liberally from his publications, particularly on the subjects of flexitime, the compressed workweek, and part-time employment, which constitute the first few chapters of our book.

Most importantly, there is the staff of New Ways to Work, past and present, whose efforts over the last 15 years made it possible for us to write this book.

Preface
Human Resources Management at a Crossroad

A not-so-quiet revolution is taking place in human resources management. Like successive shocks from an earthquake, pressures from international competition, fast-paced technological change, and projected labor force shortages are interreacting with slower economic growth and concerns about continuing balance-of-trade and budget deficits, sending private-sector employers scrambling to maintain a foothold. Regaining stability and recapturing a competitive edge through increased profitability have become primary concerns of the business community.

In trying to find some firm ground on which to stand and build for the future, managements have gone "back to basics." With much of the foreign competition's success credited to cheap labor, and with technological advances that permit work to be performed by fewer but more sophisticated employees, American companies are focusing on assessing and redirecting labor costs in order to become more profitable. Salary gains made during the expansionary years of the 1960s and early 1970s and increases in the cost of various fringe benefits and training programs are being reviewed, and considerable "downsizing" and restructuring continue.

Downsizing takes a toll, however. Battered morale has affected both managers and employees. Many managers who had to direct the cutbacks and layoffs of the early and mid-1980s feel strongly that they would never want to repeat the process. As for the workers' perspective, in one 1987 survey of corporate managers, 65 percent of the respondents indicated that worker views had worsened in the previous five years, and managers saw less interest in extra hours, job dedication, punctuality, and attendance. Another result was burnout and increased use of overtime as many companies tried to maintain the same or increased output with fewer employees.[1]

The Drive Toward Flexibility

With the worst of the layoffs behind them, employers are searching for ways to stay "lean and mean" but effective, and "flexibility" has become today's buzzword. Flexibility is increasingly viewed as providing a way to manage time, space, and people more effectively within the upswings and downturns of a global economy. It is also seen as a way to attract and retain good employees in a labor market that is steadily becoming more competitive. While there is agreement on flexibility as a goal, there is considerable difference of opinion about how to create a more flexible workplace. Two strategies have begun to emerge.

The Core/Ring Strategy

The first of these strategies would create flexibility by establishing what has been called a "core/ring configuration." A core group of primarily full-time employees is defined, and their activities are supplemented by the use of full- and part-time temporaries, consultants, and contractual workers. The employer makes commitments to core employees, providing training, fringe benefits, opportunities for career growth, and so on, while distancing the organization from the secondary rings of temporaries, consultants, and contractual employees. This configuration supposes that the peripheral components of its work force can provide the organization with an on-call flexibility. This flexibility may be illusory, however. Ironically, the existence of the outer rings sustains the stability of the core while at the same time lessening its ability to be flexible by consigning that function to nonregular employees.

Arguments against using the core/ring approach stem in part from concerns about creating a two-tiered work force and depriving a significant number of workers of the chance to achieve their full potential. A related problem is that of reducing commitment and creativity and, over the long haul, burning out the core. By narrowing the commitment of the organization, and the horizons of many of its workers, a company also minimizes the pool of potential innovation and creativity that it needs for long-range success in an increasingly complex and competitive business environment.

It is important to remember that the United States has been challenged economically not only by "emerging" countries with an abundance of cheap labor but also by foreign competitors with living standards comparable to our own. Charles Sabel and Gary Herrigel, both of MIT, note that flexible use of labor, cooperation with workers as well as other companies within the same industry, and most important, a dynamic that encouraged innovation were the factors that allowed West Germany to "innovate us out" of the textile machine industry—*not reduction of labor costs.*[2]

In a very real way, the people in our work force—their energy, ideas, and commitment to productivity and excellence—are the building blocks for all levels of our economy. The key to remaining competitive is to make certain that our labor force is as well-educated and skilled as any in the world and that our human resources policies provide a context that meets employees' needs and promotes commitment. Policies must encourage personal development and endeavor, establish an open-ended setting in which the individual is allowed to grow at his or her own rate, and reflect an understanding of the realities of global evolution.

In seeking to create a flexible organization, rejecting or limiting the scope of traditional employee-employer commitments in order to establish a core/ring organizational structure is not the only way to proceed.

The Three-Way Stretch

An alternative strategy involves making an organization more flexible by what might be called a three-way stretch—that is, creating a context that supports flexibility for the organization, the individuals within it, and the society at large and sees these aspects as being interrelated. The objectives of this human resources management scenario are long-range and proactive. The concept envisions building a totally flexible work force through a combination of tactics:

- Introducing a wide variety of integrated work schedules, many of which are offered on an optional basis.
- Using both on- and off-site space arrangements.
- Cross-training employees.

Flexibility and Organizational Viability

Management needs to formulate policies that build on the individual worker's desire for more flexibility and control in order to achieve personal objectives—for example, the balancing of work and family responsibilities. Once such policies are in place, managers can begin to encourage workers to think more creatively about taking long-range responsibility in other career-related areas, such as continuing education, training, and retraining. As uncompetitive industries are phased out, and changes in the labor force result, flexibility is a must. There is no need for workers to become "dislocated" before they start gaining new skills or interests that expand their employability, both within and outside of their present organization.

The current appeal of flexible employment policies seems to be that they can facilitate either regular or intermittent "peak-and-valley" scheduling. In the long term, their primary importance may relate to their ability to help organizations attract, retain, and retrain a work force in a rapidly changing, technologically sophisticated global economy.

The purpose of creating a flexible work force and workplace is to develop a stronger, more viable organization—with more productive, committed employees. This can only be done by identifying a means of responding to changed or changing circumstances. Although flexibility is a new concept within human resources management, small experiments to date tell us that flexibility and support breed more of the same. When it commits itself to its employees and accommodates their needs, an organization will attract quality personnel and be rewarded with enhanced employee contributions of time and energy when they are most needed.

This book provides detailed information about the various kinds of work-time alternatives that have been introduced since the early 1970s as well as guidelines on how to choose them, use them, and integrate them in a way that will allow organizations, individual workers, and ultimately, our economy and society to function more efficiently and more humanely.

Contents

Introduction: Steps Toward Workplace Flexibility

As the business world approaches the year 2000, experts in many fields are conjecturing about how to develop appropriate policies and activities to meet the challenges of the new millenium. In the same spirit, this book postulates a turn-of-the-new-century theory: By the year 2000, new ways of utilizing time and space will be human resources managers' tools of the trade; by then, management will have learned how to use them to accomplish two objectives: (1) to enable employees to be more productive, and (2) to create structural flexibility.

American managers have long held that "people are our most important resource," but as noted in the Preface, policy in recent years has not always reflected that view. For some time, human resources management strategy has focused on "streamlining" and becoming more efficient. "Lean and mean" has too often been achieved at the expense of employee morale and commitment, substituting one kind of rigidity for another in the process. In trying to find new solutions to problems posed by global competition, American management may have lost sight of a key factor: the importance of commitment—to the employee and from the employee.

If you accept the premise that organizations will need to be able to respond more flexibly to change in the future and that employee commitment to both short- and long-range objectives is essential to achieving such flexibility, then the question becomes one of process: How can flexibility and commitment be developed concurrently within an organization? Policies and practices that support the use of various interrelated options for allocating human resources are one part of the answer.

For the employer, the essence of flexibility is the ability to match the firm's labor needs with its labor supply—or put another way, it is the ability to quickly reshape the existing supply in terms of configuration, deployment, and cost. The more skills each employee has, the more scheduling and site arrangements are possible; and the more dedicated and committed the work force, the more flexible the possible response.

Flexibility falls into four separate but interrelating categories: numerical, or operational; job, or functional; financial; and structural.

1. *Numerical, or operational, flexibility.* This type of flexibility used to be assessed primarily in terms of numbers of employees, but as the use of part-time employees grows, it is increasingly discussed in terms of numbers of paid work hours. The reorganization of working time is the means by which some employers have been seeking more operational flexibility. This aspect of an organization's ability to respond flexibly is the primary focus of this book.
2. *Job, or functional, flexibility.* Job flexibility pertains to skills development, cross training, and job enlargement and enrichment. Since job restructuring often accompanies the restructuring or reorganizing of work time, it relates to numerical flexibility but is basically a separate consideration.
3. *Financial flexibility.* This type of flexibility is enhanced as a result of cost-saving strategies related to new staffing and scheduling options for regular employees as well as the strategic use of contingent, or peripheral, employees.
4. *Structural flexibility.* As new kinds of work-time and work-space arrangements are introduced and relationships within the work force become more intertwined, participative, and responsible and less hierarchical, structural flexibility increases.

In *Thriving on Chaos,* management expert and author Tom Peters talks of achieving flexibility by empowering people.[1] One aspect of this is recognizing and supporting employees' needs for flexibility. Policies that do this build employee commitment to the organization. Within all four of the categories relating to *organizational* flexibility are possibilities for expanding the opportunities for *employee* flexibility. For example, much of the original interest in new work schedules stemmed from employees' needs for more control over their work time so they could balance work with other responsibilities, such as child rearing and continuing education. By accommodating these needs, employers can also achieve some of their own objectives, such as skills expansion and increased financial flexibility. It is this kind of "win-win" approach that is discussed in detail in the succeeding chapters of this book.

A caveat should be noted here: Preserving equity for both the organization and the individual is essential to the long-range viability of a flexible organization as we are defining it. Equitable flexibility is flexibility that operates as part of a system of mutually agreeable conditions of work—conditions that combine the traditional concept of an organization's commitment to the growth and well-being of its workers with expectations of a reciprocal commitment on the part of employees to the long-range growth and well-being of the company. Intangibles such as trust are an important part of this kind of context, and the payoffs are often difficult to quantify.

Creating a Flexible Workplace

Workplace flexibility must be achieved in stages. It entails too significant a change in policy, practice, and attitude to be dealt with as a single task but should instead be considered both an overall objective and a component of all long-range, comprehensive organizational planning. Many of the tenets underlying policies that promote flexibility run counter to long-held management assumptions: Using a variety of work-time options violates the principle of standardized scheduling; telecommuting and flexiplace (working at home or off-site) arrangements are at variance with the belief that employees should be in sight and on-site; supervising and evaluating performance based on how well an employee produces or meets objectives requires different attitudes and skills than paternalistic over-the-shoulder managing. Real change in attitudes and management style will be needed in conjunction with changes in policy in order to achieve a flexible workplace.

In deciding how to proceed, it is first helpful to define some of the problems that have created the need for more flexibility. For example:

- Fluctuations in product or service supply and demand can result in changes in labor force needs. An organization may want to develop a work-sharing capacity or expand its use of regular voluntary part-time employment.
- Changes in the company's demographics—the graying of a work force or greater numbers of employees with family re-

sponsibilities—may warrant a new look at phased retirement or leave policies.

■ Technological innovation that necessitates widespread continuing training or education may encourage experimentation with sabbaticals or regular part-time employment or job sharing to allow employees the opportunity to expand their current skills.

The succeeding chapters provide a detailed overview of individual aspects of operational, or numerical, flexibility. The first two chapters deal with flexible scheduling arrangements, and the next six chapters deal with reduced work-time options; these are followed by one chapter each on flexiplace (at-home or off-site alternatives) and contingent employment. These elements of flexibility interrelate but can be implemented either separately or together. Some require extensive and complicated change at all levels within an organization; others are follow-on stages that expand on a shift away from standardized schedules that has already begun.

Each chapter describes the particular option in several overview sections, followed by an implementation section that outlines an eight-step process for introducing the option within an organization. Questionnaires and worksheets are provided to help managers identify the potential benefits of the option to their organization and outline the pros and cons of introducing it. Checklists summarizing key program design issues are also included.

The eight steps recommended as an implementation process when introducing a new scheduling or staffing option are:

1. *Gain support for the program.* The best way to build support for this kind of basic change in an organization is to initiate a system of ongoing dialog about the reasons for the change and encourage cooperation in the decision making about its implementation. Organizational change is not an issue that responds to rational analysis alone. As Dana E. Friedman, of The Conference Board, notes in a report entitled *Family-Supportive Policies: The Corporate Decision-Making Process:*

> Most managers devise organizational strategies based on the common-sense assumption that decision making is a rational process. Sometimes, however, the politics and culture of an organization foil even the most "rational" of plans. . . . These comments are not meant to suggest a loss of faith in rationality; but rather, they are an acceptance of its limits. A rational ap-

proach, executives contend, requires that all options be weighed and judgments be based on merit. But this view ignores the reality that most decisions are inherently political and that personal and political factors will always play a role.[2]

This observation is certainly true when it comes to creating a flexible workplace. Gaining support for this kind of change will require broad-based, long-term commitment from top management, middle management, and labor or employee representatives as well as input from all sectors of the work force.

A top-level planning group or task force should be appointed, with representation from all segments of the company that will be affected by the particular options under consideration. Its responsibility will be to:

■ Investigate what similar organizations have done in regard to these options. Although many of the components of flexibility are relatively new, most have been used to some extent. Having information about other companies' experience can avoid the need to "reinvent the wheel" and provide helpful hints on successful implementation.

■ Define objectives and desired results.

■ Develop a draft policy statement for review.

■ Develop an action plan and a timeline for evaluating the new program.

■ Set up a system for gathering input to the planning and implementation process and generating feedback during the initial phases of the program. Input can be gained in a variety of ways—through the use of surveys, focus groups, planning-group representation, or other appropriate information-channeling processes. Encouraging suggestions and reactions from all levels of the work force will help identify problem areas, involving both attitude and process that must be addressed. It will also begin to enlarge the base of support for the overall program.

■ Revise the policy and action plan as appropriate.

■ Determine the initial scope of the program (that is, whether it will be tested in a pilot project and then expanded to other units, instituted companywide, or introduced incrementally).

■ Set up some kind of process to provide ongoing support for those charged with implementing the change and reiterate top management's commitment to increasing flexibility. As James Taylor, of Socio-Technical Designs, Inc., noted, "In organizational change where there hasn't been the time spent for all members to buy in, middle management says, 'I'm uncertain and anxious and the only way I know to be comfortable is to get in control, to shift back to that old model of defining jobs and work.' ''[3]

2. *Set up the program's administration.* The administration will be charged with implementing the specifics of the program devised by the task force. Responsibility for overall coordination and the development of technical assistance for supervisors and employees should be assigned to a particular person. Additional project staff may be needed, depending on the scope of the program.

3. *Design the program.* Designing the specifics of a particular component of the flexibility project may be the responsibility of the task force or of a subgroup designated by the task force. In designing the program, current policy must be reviewed to determine its compatibility with the new objectives, and new policy must be framed where necessary. Such issues as eligibility, an application process, effect on employee status, and reversibility must be addressed.

4. *Develop resource materials.* Both employees and supervisors will require resource materials. In addition to a program description, educational and technical assistance materials will be needed and, in some instances, training to explain the new options and policies and also provide support and guidance in implementing them. Good resource materials will save supervisors time—since they will be well-informed and won't need to go over the same issues individually again and again with employees. Access to detailed information also facilitates planning for both managers and their employees.

5. *Announce the program.* Although this seems an obvious step, some companies have developed an alternative work-time policy and then taken a passive stance, waiting for employees to request the kind of arrangement that the policy already authorizes.

6. *Promote the program.* If an organization and its employees are to take full advantage of any of the new work arrangements, the program must be promoted on a regular basis. The concepts involved are unfamiliar. Even employees who want options like job sharing, leave time, or phased retirement need to be reassured that participating in these programs will not impact negatively on their career hopes or earning potential. From management's perspective, the benefits associated with most of the options reviewed in this book come from a

"multiplier effect"; that is, the more employees who use the program on a voluntary basis, the greater the benefits.

Although employers frequently worry that too many people will want to work part-time or will "flex" their schedules to such an extent that it is disruptive, experience has shown that this does not often occur. Furthermore, management can and should "fine-tune" the use of these options to suit the needs of the organization, as discussed below.

7. *Evaluate the program.* An evaluation process should be built into the program's design. What was the desired effect? And has the program had that desired effect? If not, why not? What are the financial ramifications? What are the problem areas? Unexpected benefits? How have the organization's employees reacted? What needs to be done?

8. *Fine-tune the program.* Information gained during the evaluation process should be used by the task force to recommend the next steps needed to fine-tune parts of the program that require adjustment. In addition, a process for obtaining feedback from supervisors and employees should be an ongoing component of the flexibility project.

These are the basic steps outlined in each chapter as a model implementation process to be followed when introducing new scheduling or off-site arrangements. Not all steps may apply to every organization or to the introduction or expansion of every option. The more extensive the change in current practice that is sought, however, the more important an in-depth, thoughtful change process becomes. Major shifts in work-time policy require longer-term, companywide efforts.

As with any new tool, implementing the alternative work time, flexiplace, and contingent employment options we describe in this book will take some effort, time, and commitment. The organization can expect at the outset to experience difficulties with supervision because of problems in such areas as scheduling and coverage as well as increased complications involving internal and external communications. As Dr. Stanley Nollen, an early expert in the field, observes, such "new work patterns are not just minor changes in work schedules. They are an adjustment in the sociotechnical system of the company."[4]

However, Jerome Rosow, president of the Work in America Institute, writing in the preface to Nollen's *New Work Schedules in*

Practice, contends that the rewards can be great: "New work schedules, when carefully chosen, designed, and executed, are among the best investments an employer can make. The cost is small, the risk is low, and the potential return is high. Best of all, they benefit all parties involved."[5] In short, the benefits of the new scheduling alternatives should warrant the development of more sophisticated skills and solutions to deal with the problems that will inevitably arise.

We hope that the information contained in the following chapters will smooth the way for those managers who want to adopt new work patterns and learn to manage time and space more effectively in their organizations.

Flexible and Restructured Full-Time Work

In his 1976 book, *The Future of the Workplace,* Paul Dickson writes:

> There are few facets to the Western way of work which are more depressing and unimaginative than the way in which work time is arranged for us. Our jobs generally demand 40 hours of service in five consecutive eight-hour clips, during which we obediently come and go at rush hours appointed by others. Except for layoffs or prolonged periods of illness, a work life is laid out in front of a person: five-day, 40-hour pieces stretch out like a seemingly endless passing train terminating abruptly at age 65 at a chicken à la king banquet, where a gold watch is presented and the boss picks up the tab for the drinks.[1]

Somewhat more than a decade after Dickson wrote those words, things have changed dramatically. The rush hours are still with us, but the gold watch has in many cases been replaced by a "golden handshake," and more than a fifth of the United States work force is employed on flexible, compressed, or reduced work schedules. The first challenge to 9–5 came in the form of flexible schedules, which for the first time gave employees some say in when they might come to and leave work. The next round of innovation restructured the 40-hour week into fewer than five days, giving employees longer workdays but larger blocks of personal time.

Part I of this book describes the emergence of flexitime and the compressed workweek, discusses what employers have identified as the pros and cons of these scheduling arrangements, and looks at the experience of some of the organizations that have used them.

CHAPTER 1

Flexitime

*F*lexitime is the generic term for flexible scheduling programs—work schedules that permit flexible starting and quitting times within limits set by management. The flexible periods are at either end of the day, with a "core time" set in the middle, during which all employees must be present. Flexitime requires a standard number of hours to be worked within a given time period, usually 40 during a five-day week.

The employer can adapt flexitime to the organization's unique needs through the decisions it makes about such issues as (1) whether flexibility is a daily or periodic choice, (2) how core time is defined (see Figure 1-1), and (3) whether credit and debit hours and "banking" of hours are allowed. Some of the possible variations in the use of flexitime are:

- Fixed starting and quitting times that are selected periodically. With this option, employees choose their starting and quitting times for a specified period (such as 12 months) and work eight hours daily, following the agreed-upon schedule.
- Starting and quitting times that can vary daily. With this option, employees are free to come to work and leave at a different time each day, providing they work a total of eight hours every day.
- Variations in the length of the day (for instance, a 6-hour day followed by a 10-hour day), with mandatory core time. With this option, credit and debit hours are allowed, as long as employees are present during the core time each day and work a specified number of hours by the end of a specified period

Figure 1-1.   Flexitime variations: company flexitime programs with core
             periods.

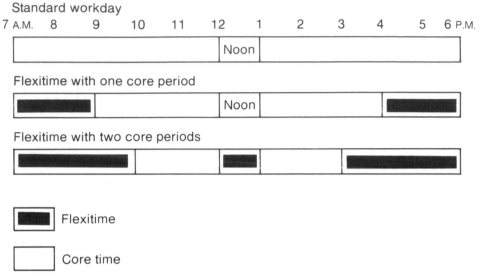

Flexitime

Core time

(such as 40 hours a week or 80 hours during two weeks). For
an example this type of variable-day schedule, see Figure 1-2.
■ Variations in the length of the day, without mandatory core
time. With this option, credit and debit hours are allowed, and
employees need not be present during a core period each day.
Employees may also bank time rather than having to work a
specified number of hours during a specified time period.
Figure 1-3 shows an example of this type of "maxiflex"
schedule.

According to a 1985 Bureau of Labor Statistics survey, the
amount of actual flexibility available to U.S. workers with flexible
scheduling options varies from as little as 30 minutes to three hours
or more.[1]

Origins of Flexitime

Flexitime was the first major divergence from the standardized 40-
hour, 9–5 workweek. The concept of allowing employees some individual choice as to starting and quitting times was first introduced in
Germany in 1967. At that time, it was seen as a means of relieving
transit and commuting time problems. Shortly thereafter, flexitime

Figure 1-2. Individual employee's variable-day schedule.

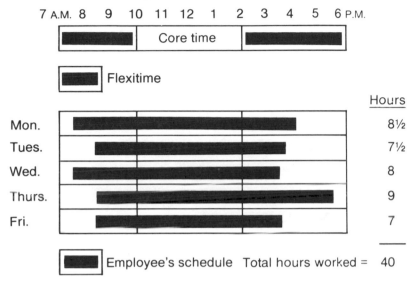

began to gain adherents in Switzerland as a way to attract women with family responsibilities into the labor force. The Hewlett-Packard Company is generally credited with introducing flexitime in the United States, using it in its Waltham, Massachusetts, plant in 1972 after having tried it first in a German division. Hewlett-Packard's rationale at the time was that since employees appeared to like having more choice over their starting and quitting times and flexitime appeared to have few or no adverse effects, it would be a low-cost, effective employee benefit.

The primary reason for flexitime's emergence would seem to have been a growing recognition that a standardized work schedule was not as appropriate as it had once been both because of the changing demographics and attitudes of the work force and because of changing management problems.

Who Uses Flexitime?

The 1985 Bureau of Labor Statistics survey cited above indicates that 12.6 percent of private-sector organizations and 11.3 percent of public-sector organizations currently use flexitime. This amounts to 9.1 million full-time workers, or 12.3 percent of the work force. The

Figure 1-3. Individual employee's maxiflex schedule with banked time.

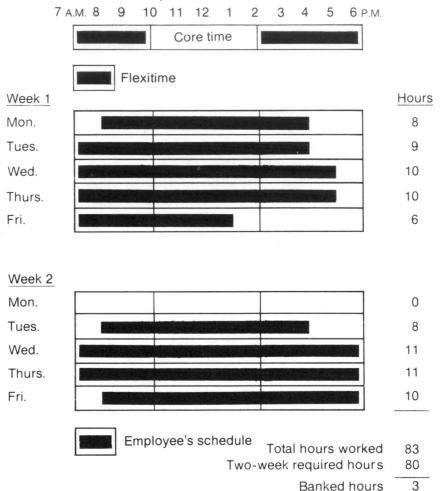

service sector of private industry has a higher proportion of use (14.5 percent) than goods-producing companies (9.8 percent).[2]

Other surveys indicate even more extensive use. A 1985 American Management Association (AMA) survey of 1,600 of its member companies found that 34.8 percent used flexitime. Of these, half said that the program had been adopted during the previous five years.[3] A 1988 survey by the Trevose, Pennsylvania-based Administrative Management Society (AMS) of 500 companies that the AMS surveys annually showed that 31 percent of the 290 respondents use flexitime and another 4 percent are considering its adoption. (Figure 1-4 shows

Figure 1-4. Flexitime usage—by region.

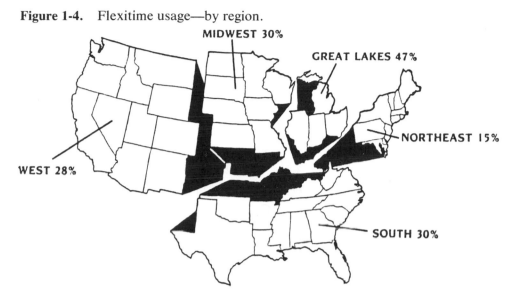

MIDWEST 30%

GREAT LAKES 47%

NORTHEAST 15%

WEST 28%

SOUTH 30%

SOURCE: Administrative Management Society, *Flexible Work Survey* (Trevose, Pa.: AMS, 1987), 5.

a geographical breakdown of the survey results.) This compares to 15 percent use reported in a similar 1977 study. AMS estimates that flexitime scheduling is currently growing at a rate of about 1 percent per year.[4]

Even when flexitime is included in personnel policy, however, it is not necessarily available in all departments or to all employees. The 1987 AMS survey indicated that 58 percent of the respondents only used it in certain departments,[5] and the AMA respondents reported that only 49 percent of the organizations with flexitime offered the program to hourly workers, while 74 percent made it available to professional and technical employees.[6]

When Is Flexitime Most Appropriate?

Most employers find that flexitime is a low-cost employee benefit that raises morale while enabling the organization to improve coverage, extend service hours, and reduce or eliminate tardiness.

Improving coverage or extending service hours. Since some employees will undoubtedly want to begin their workday earlier than the usual starting time and others will want to come in later and stay beyond the usual closing time, flexitime can enable the organization to improve its coverage or extend its service hours. This, in turn, often reduces the need for overtime.

Providing a low-cost employee benefit. Flexitime is a popular response to changing labor force needs and is particularly effective as a low-cost employee benefit. The demographics of an organization's work force may dictate the extent of the advantage that is gained by using flexitime. It is, for example, greatly valued by working parents as a way to better manage work and family time.

Enhancing employee morale. There is no doubt that flexitime boosts employee morale generally. Other positive results, such as retention of valued employees and improved recruitment, derive from this.

Reducing or eliminating tardiness. Most employers find that if tardiness is a problem, flexitime may be the answer. The reported reduction or elimination of tardiness has been attributed to several causes: In some cases, flexitime enables employees to resolve scheduling conflicts or last-minute crises (getting children off to school before leaving for work, fixing a car that won't start, finding care for a sick child), or it eases transit problems (with employees coming to work before or after the main commuting crunch).

Pros and Cons of Flexitime

Productivity and quality of work. In an article for the *Harvard Business Review,* Dr. Stanley Nollen, of Georgetown University's School of Business Administration, cites eight surveys and 30 case histories that suggest numerous reasons for flexitime's positive impact on productivity. They include:

1. Reductions in paid absences (personal business, sick leave) and idle time on the job, which result in more actual labor from the same number of hours worked.
2. Better organization of work, because meetings, telephone calls, and visits are concentrated into core hours, leaving work that requires thinking and concentration to be done at the beginning and end of the workday when there are fewer distractions.
3. People's ability to schedule work according to their own "biological clocks."
4. Improved employee morale and job satisfaction, which lead to the outcome known as "a happy worker is a productive worker."

5. Better managerial practices, including a shift from a controlling to a facilitating management style and more worker self-management.[7]

In a survey of three industries offering flexitime to clerical employees, significant numbers of respondents reported higher quality of work (banks, 54.6 percent; insurance companies, 34.6 percent; and utilities, 29.2 percent), with the remainder reporting no change.[8]

Absenteeism, tardiness, and turnover. Because employees need or prefer flexible scheduling, reductions in tardiness and turnover have also been observed in companies that use flexitime, in addition to the reductions in paid absences mentioned above. These reductions in absenteeism, tardiness, and turnover are in fact the most widely cited cost saving associated with the use of this scheduling option.

Other users of flexitime have indicated that it offers advantages in such areas as workplace coverage, overtime costs, employee skills, and recruitment.

Extended organizational workday. Since some workers generally choose to come in earlier or leave later than the norm, hours of work or service can be expanded and telephone communication with other time zones may be improved. But extending the organizational workday may in some cases also mean extra costs due to flexitime's impact on building security, heating and lighting, and other overhead expenses.

Overtime costs. Many organizations note a reduction in the use of overtime when a flexitime program is in effect. The three-industry survey mentioned earlier cited significantly lower levels of overtime, with 57.6 percent of the banks, 33.9 percent of the insurance companies, and 16.7 percent of the utilities reporting decreased overtime.[9]

Employee skills. Since in organizations using flexitime, employees often cover for co-workers on a different schedule, some employers have observed a cross-training effect that expands employee skills.

Recruitment. Most organizations that advertise scheduling flexibility find that their recruitment pool is generally expanded and improved.

Employee morale, commitment, and productivity. There seems to be little doubt that flexitime's most unassailable asset is its popularity among employees. (Even those workers who choose to retain a 9–5 schedule like the idea that they could change it if they wanted or needed to.) The popularity of this scheduling option in turn enhances employee morale and commitment. And such intangibles as employee morale and commitment are often cited as factors that have a direct impact on productivity. The ability to shift schedules to accommodate individual "biological clocks," mentioned earlier, is also regarded as a way to improve productivity.

The main problems that employers cite with flexible schedules relate to:

■ Inadequate staffing during core hours.
■ Difficulties associated with employee communication, scheduling meetings, and coordinating work among employees on different schedules.
■ Supervisors' concerns about their inability to supervise during the full range of work hours. Many supervisors are uncomfortable with anything but "line of sight" supervision and feel that with flexitime, they will have to extend their hours of work in order to be able to properly supervise employees on a variety of schedules.

A 1987 Administrative Management Society survey also lists the following problems that have been reported with the use of flexitime: accommodating employees whose output is the input for other employees, keeping track of hours worked or accumulated, and finding key people unavailable at certain times.[10]

Electronic monitoring equipment. One disadvantage of the use of flexitime can be the one-time expense of purchasing electronic monitoring equipment. However, few companies in the United States seem interested in using electronic monitoring equipment to track employee hours. Such monitoring devices tend to be unpopular with workers because they resemble time clocks. Their primary role appears to be in programs that allow banking of hours.

Employee abuse of flexitime. While such abuse has been reported, employers who cite it as a problem do not seem to consider it a major drawback.

Union attitudes. Unions remain somewhat skeptical about flexitime. There is lingering concern about whether or not it is voluntary and how it affects both overtime and the length of the workday. On the other hand, labor leaders recognize flexitime's popularity with workers and hence tend to concentrate on developing equitable ground rules for utilizing this scheduling option.

Table 1-1 summarizes the benefits and drawbacks of using flexitime, in the view of respondents to the Administrative Management Society's 1988 *Flexible Work Survey*.

Table 1-1. Advantages and disadvantages of flexitime.

	% of Companies Responding
Main advantage to companies	
Improves employee morale	40
Decreases tardiness and absenteeism	34
Increases employee productivity	26
Main advantage to employees	
Permits employees to take care of personal business	36
Accommodates the needs of employees with children	36
Allows employees to avoid rush-hour traffic	16
Expands employees' leisure time	12
Main disadvantage to companies	
Lack of supervision during all hours of work	22
Causes understaffing at times	19
Key people unavailable at certain times	19
Difficulty in scheduling meetings, coordinating projects, etc.	17
Difficulty in planning work schedules, keeping track of hours	10
Employee abuse of flextime	7
Other	3

SOURCE: Michael Cregar, "Flextime Continues to Edge Upward," *Management World* 17, no. 4 (Trevose, Pa.: Administrative Management Society, July-Aug. 1988): 15.

Should Your Organization Try Flexitime?

The tools provided in this section can help you determine whether flexitime would be an effective response to your organization's unique staffing and scheduling needs.

Let's start by taking a look at the accompanying group of profiles entitled Organizational Experience With Flexitime. These profiles show how and why a flexitime program was implemented in two organizations and with what results. As you review these profiles, pay particular attention to aspects of the companies' experience that seem particularly relevant to your own organization's situation.

Now turn to the questionnaire shown in Table 1-2, which lists the primary concerns that lead organizations to adopt flexitime programs. The more "yes" answers you have on this questionnaire, the greater the chances that flexitime is an option you should be seriously considering.

ORGANIZATIONAL EXPERIENCE WITH FLEXITIME

International Business Machines Corporation (IBM)

Description: Information-handling systems, equipment, and services company headquartered in Westchester County, New York, with 225,000 employees in its domestic operations.

Reason for Using Flexitime: The "Individualized Work Schedules" program was introduced to provide additional flexibility for employees in terms of their starting and quitting times in order to serve the interests of employees, the company, and the community. IBM piloted the program for 90 days in San Francisco and San Jose in 1981 and has been operating the program companywide since that time. The program is mutually beneficial to both the company and employees and is viewed as being particularly responsive to the needs of women, single parents, and two working parents with young children.

Implementation Process: Nearly all domestic IBM employees are eligible for flexible work schedules. In IBM's European operations, similar programs, with some country variations, have been in use since the early 1970s.

In the United States, employees can arrive at work and depart within a plus-or-minus 30-minute window. Agreement from a manager is required. Managers review jobs in their departments to determine whether and how employees will be able to participate.

Flexibility can be implemented in several ways: variable work schedules, where employees may vary their daily arrival time within established limits; staggered schedules, where employees select from a number of starting times predetermined by management; customized work schedules, where unique business or personal situations may require managers to work individually with employees to establish a special schedule for a specific time period; and fixed work schedules, which are demanded by customer or business requirements. In some units, the flexibility is not as extensive. The arrival/departure window may be only 15 minutes, for example. Carryover of time from one day to another is not permitted in any of the scheduling arrangements.

Impact to Date: A company objective is to include as many employees as possible in the program and to arrange a schedule that takes into consideration both their needs and those of the business. As part of this effort, IBM has produced a videotape to educate managers about flexitime.

The program has been extraordinarily well received by employees.

SOURCE: Director of corporate compensation and benefits, IBM headquarters, 1988.

Pitney Bowes Inc.

Description: A manufacturer of office equipment, headquartered in Stamford, Connecticut, with approximately 6,000 employees at headquarters.

Reason for Using Flexitime: The program was designed to provide a greater degree of flexibility to clerical employees. The attitude is: "You're adults, so we'll treat you like adults." The program helps with recruiting; job candidates with school-age children find it especially attractive. It also helps alleviate problems of absenteeism and lost time. If an organization has flexitime, its employees are not expected to use a lot of sick leave.

Implementation Process: Approximately 1,100 nonexempt clerical employees at corporate headquarters are eligible for the flexitime option. Although banking time is not permitted except within a given week, if an employee works 37½ hours in less than five days, then he or she is entitled to a half-day off.

The program is implemented by department, with the department head determining what core hours will be. Supervisors must ensure that phones are being covered.

Impact to Date: The program, which was instituted in the late 1970s, takes cooperation between employer and employee and requires more supervisory time. People who use flexitime like it very much, however. They seem willing to put in the extra effort to make the program work.

It's a real punishment when the option has to be taken away for disciplinary reasons. Employees fight to get back in the program. Flexitime is now an integral part of the organization.

SOURCE: Telephone interview with the manager of personnel, Pitney Bowes corporate headquarters (June 1988).

Table 1-2.   Flexitime questionnaire.

Would Flexitime Benefit Your Organization?		
	Yes	No
Do some employees prefer to come to work early while others prefer to work after regular closing hours?		
If your organization has to communicate with clients or employees in different time zones, would expanding the range of hours that employees are working facilitate this?		
Is tardiness or absenteeism a problem in your organization?		
Are the modes of transportation, particularly during commuting hours, congested in your community?		
Does your organization have a significant number of employees with family responsibilities?		
Would you like to offer your employees a benefit that is known to be popular but costs nothing?		

If your questionnaire results indicate that flexitime would indeed benefit your organization, you can use the worksheet shown in Figure 1-5 to identify your specific concerns and what you regard as the potential benefits and drawbacks of this approach.

Introducing Flexitime

The process of introducing a flexitime program starts with the appointment of a planning group to lay the groundwork for the program, followed by the appointment of a project director. In the design phase, decisions are made regarding a number of key issues. Resource materials are then developed, and the program is announced and promoted to the organization's employees. After flexitime has been in effect for a period of time, its impact is evaluated and the program is modified as necessary. In the following subsections, we will take a closer look at each of these steps.

Gain Support for the Program

In order to generate support for broad-based use of a flexitime program, your first step is to appoint a top-level planning group. The group, or task force, should have representation from all segments of the company that will be affected by a flexitime program. Its responsibility will be to:

Figure 1-5. Flexitime worksheet.

Assessing the Need for Flexitime

List the main reasons why you are considering flexitime:

1. _____

_____

_____

2. _____

_____

_____

3. _____

_____

_____

4. _____

_____

_____

List what you see as the advantages and disadvantages of flexitime:

Pros: _____

_____

_____

_____

_____

(Continued)

Figure 1-5. *(continued)*

_____

_____

Cons: _____

_____

_____

_____

_____

_____

- Investigate what similar organizations have done in regard to flexible hours.
- Develop a tentative policy statement.
- Develop an action plan. Surveys indicate that the way a flexitime plan is implemented determines whether or not it will be successful (see Table 1-3).
- Consult with labor representatives and employees.
- Set up a process for obtaining supervisors' input to the planning and implementation process as well as feedback during the initial phases of the new program.
- Revise the policy and plan as appropriate.
- Determine the initial scope of the program (that is, whether it will be tested in a pilot project and then expanded to other units, instituted companywide, or introduced incrementally).

Set Up the Program's Administration

Appoint a project director. In order to assure equity and consistent application of flexitime guidelines, responsibility for overseeing the implementation of flexitime should be assigned to someone in the human resources management or personnel area. Although departmental supervisors are generally responsible for applying the flexi-

Table 1-3. Summary of implementation steps that alleviate flexitime problem areas.

	Implementation Step			
Problem Area Alleviated	Appointed Internal Project Director	Held Meetings With Managers, Supervisors	Held Meetings With Employees	Instituted First on Trial Basis
Coverage of work situations		X		
Employee scheduling	X	X	X	
Work scheduling	X		X	
Difficulty of management job	X			
Internal communication	X	X		X

SOURCE: Stanley D. Nollen and Virginia H. Martin, *Alternative Work Schedules,* Part 1; AMA Survey Report (New York: AMACOM, 1978), 38.

time guidelines to the particular circumstances of their work unit and implementing the program there, a personnel administrator should be available to act as a resource for the supervisors and to monitor the development of the program within individual departments.

Design the Program

Some of the decisions that must be made when designing a flexitime program have to do with the parameters of flexibility. Questions must be resolved regarding the following issues:

State and federal labor laws. What affect will existing legislation have on the proposed flexitime program?

Length of company workday and workweek. What are the organization's operating hours? What are its normal workdays?

Core time. What hours of the workday or shift will be considered "core," when everyone is expected to be on the job?

Allowable starting and quitting times. What is the earliest time that an employee can start the workday, and how late can a regular, albeit flexible, schedule go? The most common span extends from 7:00 A.M. to 6:00 P.M. (In a 24-hour, continuously operating plant, these questions may have to be answered in terms of a flexible shift schedule rather than in terms of flexibility within a specified range of day-shift hours.)

Eligibility. Who will be eligible for flexitime? Will it be a companywide option, a pilot project, or a departmental option? If one of the reasons for introducing flexitime is to enhance employee morale and commitment, then eligibility should be as broad as possible. Companies should not exclude employees from participation on the basis of occupation. The key question should be function.

Special applications have been worked out by certain organizations to ensure that some kind of increased flexibility is available to all employees. For example, Hewlett-Packard is one of a very small percentage of manufacturing firms that allows flexible scheduling for production workers. In its fabrication unit, which is a continuous-shift process, individual flexitime is not possible but group flexitime is. The workers together decide what the shift changeover hours will be, subject only to the requirement that there be a 15-minute overlap between shifts.

Degree of individual flexibility. Within the established parameters, how much choice will employees have? Can they vary their hours day to day? Week to week? How much notice must they give their supervisor? If schedules are expected to remain constant for an extended period, how long a commitment must employees make to a particular schedule? What process is there for changing the schedule if it proves inappropriate?

Length of individual workday. Some companies (primarily those that allow "banking" of time, discussed later in this subsection) do not require employees to work an eight-hour day. In such cases, the core time may constitute the minimum workday period. A few states mandate eight hours as the maximum length of a workday, so you should check your state's regulations in that regard.

Length of individual workweek. If banking is allowed, can hours be carried over into another workweek? Are there minimum and maximum numbers of hours that an employee can work within a seven-day period? (State legislation may already establish this.)

Lunch hour. Is a lunch hour required each day? Of what duration?

Personal time off. How will flexitime affect existing provisions for personal time off?

Carryover hours. If your state does not have legislation prohibiting workdays longer than eight hours and workweeks longer than 40 hours, will employees be allowed to bank hours? Within what time limits (a week, a pay period, other)?

Overtime. And how will banking affect overtime? (In the General Motors Corporation flexitime policy statement, it is noted that employees electing a banking option must sign a waiver stating that premium pay and overtime will not be applied to hours that the employee has chosen to work in excess of eight hours per day in order to utilize flexitime. Some union contracts also contain language that recognizes the difference between employer-mandated overtime work and employee-chosen flexible hours that result in occasional longer-than-normal workdays.)

Coverage and work flow. How will you ensure that regular coverage continues and, if possible, is enhanced? How much lattitude will supervisors have to adjust schedules? In introducing the program, it should be clearly indicated that flexitime is a benefit—that the employees' prime responsibility is to get the work done and flexibility is secondary to the work requirements. In functions such as telephone coverage, interoffice mail, and other central communications tasks, or for employees involved in sequential work flow, the design objective is to maintain coverage while adopting flexitime.

Accountability. How will employee performance be monitored? Will regular performance evaluations be considered sufficient? If banking time is allowed, what kinds of records will be kept and how? The answers to the monitoring question range from electronic "time accumulators" to "memo ledgers" to honor systems. Unfortunately, there are always some employees who abuse any system. When an otherwise eligible employee has abused the privilege of flexitime, the easiest and most effective disciplinary tool is to deny access to the option and require that the employee work standard hours.

Enrollment process. Who will sign employees up and manage the program in the individual departments? Most flexitime programs assign the responsibility for implementing the program to departmental supervisors.

Evaluation process. How will you evaluate the effects of flexible scheduling? The program should be reviewed periodically so adjustments to existing schedules can be made if necessary.

Table 1-4 presents a program design checklist, which you can use to keep track of your progress in addressing the key design issues associated with introducing flexitime.

Develop Resource Materials

As will be discussed later in the chapter, introducing flexitime can have a significant impact on how the first-line supervisor carries out his or her responsibilities, particularly in organizations where a participatory style of supervision is not the norm. In general, the greater the change in supervisory style that is needed in order to implement flexitime, the greater the amount of resource materials that will be needed to support the implementation effort.

Memos can reinforce a sense of concern and support for super-

Table 1-4. Program design checklist: flexitime.

Key Design Issues	Notes
☐ State and federal labor laws	
☐ Company workday and workweek	
☐ Core time	
☐ Allowable starting and quitting times	
☐ Eligibility	
☐ Degree of individual flexibility	
☐ Length of individual workday	
☐ Length of individual workweek	
☐ Lunch hour	
☐ Personal time off	
☐ Carryover hours	
☐ Overtime	
☐ Coverage and work flow	
☐ Accountability	
☐ Enrollment process	
☐ Evaluation process	

visors by reassuring them that they are not expected to be available or on site during the entire time range when their employees may be working (this range is called a bandwidth). Memos can also be used to remind supervisors that time management is now a shared responsibility and that they are not expected to continually supervise all employees.

Once the flexitime program is designed, a printed *program description,* outlining the organization's objectives and detailing the program's terms and conditions, should be made available to all employees who will be affected by flexitime. (A sample program description is shown in Figure 1-6.)

Announce the Program

Once the program is in place, it should be announced companywide and information meetings held for employees. This will give them an opportunity to ask questions and enable managers to clarify the specifics of the flexitime option.

Promote the Program

Since flexitime is so popular with employees, it is generally not necessary to promote its use—only to inform employees that it is available. Any promotion is usually conducted as part of external recruitment or public relations efforts.

Evaluate the Program

Because so much of a flexitime program's success involves such relatively intangible factors as employee morale and the potential for motivating workers and enhancing their commitment, it is often difficult to evaluate specific effects. Once a flexitime program is implemented, however, a feedback process should be set up so that "glitches" can be identified.

Fine-Tune the Program

With a flexitime program, the most frequent problem areas involve management or supervision and work coverage. These problems, which can be identified through the type of ongoing evaluation process discussed in the preceding subsection, are amenable to management intervention.

Table 1-5 presents a detailed listing of problems that commonly occur with flexitime programs, together with the solutions that actual users have found effective.

Special Considerations for Supervisors and Managers

The role of first-time supervisors is radically affected by the introduction of flexitime. As Simcha Ronen observes in his book *Flexible Working Hours:*

(Text continues on page 34.)

Figure 1-6.   Sample flexitime program description.

PERSONNEL POLICY MANUAL   FEDERAL RESERVE BANK OF SAN FRANCISCO

SECTION: 400   SUBJECT: 411   FLEXTIME WORK SCHEDULE

Effective April 15, 1986
Supercedes June 30, 1982

1. Objective

The flextime work schedule allows employees latitude in scheduling their working hours within the specified limits set forth in this subject.

2. Policy

Individual departments may use a flextime work schedule, subject to the following conditions:

- The implementation, continuance, discontinuance, or modification of flextime shall be at the discretion of the management committee in consultation wth the senior officer in charge of division/branch and the personnel officer/manager.
- Adequate staff coverage sufficient to meet the operating requirements of the department shall be maintained at all times.
- The normal workweek of 40 hours and 5 days shall be retained.
- Departments wanting to implement flextime must first pilot a program for three to six months.

3. Definitions

Flextime is a schedule by which an employee may—on a daily basis and within specific limits dictated by the needs of the job—start work at a time of his/her discretion as long as the employee completes 8 hours of work per day. Time limits are placed on the amount of "flex" an employee has by establishing "core hours" and a "band width."

- *Core hours* are the hours during which all employees must be on the job (excluding regular lunch and break periods).
- *Band width* is the span of time beginning at the earliest time an employee may start work and ending at the latest time an employee may stop work.

Exempt personnel may, with management approval and as a result of business necessity, work more than or less than 8 hours in one day. This option, however, still requires that an individual work a 40-hour, 5-day workweek.

SOURCE: Federal Reserve Bank of San Francisco

The normal lunch break is 45 minutes. An employee may, however, extend his/her lunch break period within the limits of the flexible lunch period as long as management approval is obtained and the operations of the department are not disrupted.

4. Responsibilities

The personnel officer/manager ensures that flextime is administered in a consistent and equitable manner throughout the company. The personnel officer/manager also ensures that flextime schedules conform to appropriate state laws and company policy.

Department management ensures that flextime is administered in a consistent and equitable manner within the department and that flextime arrangements conform to company policy. Department management also ensures that staffing is available at all times in order to meet the operational requirements of the department.

The supervisor plans and schedules job assignments, ensuring that there is sufficient staff to meet the schedule. The supervisor informs the employees of the tasks and schedules which are to be met.

The employee plans and organizes his/her time to meet the job requirements as established by the supervisor. Also, the employee should participate in the solution of conflicts between jobs and their flextime schedules and inform the supervisor when coverage is not adequate.

One or more employees may assume coverage responsibility with the supervisor's concurrence. If a change in schedule is required, the responsible employee must find substitute coverage and inform the supervisor.

5. Procedures

Piloting Flextime

The senior officer in charge of the department wanting to pilot a program shall advise the management committee, through corporate personnel.

After management committee approval to pilot a program has been granted, the personnel officer/manager shall assist the requesting department in implementing and maintaining the pilot program.

During the pilot program, the management of the piloting department shall maintain statistical data in order to evaluate any significant effects resulting from flextime. The information shall include data regarding:

- Absenteeism
- Turnover
- Non-exempt overtime
- Relevant production statistics

(Continued)

Figure 1-6.   *(continued)*

Upon completion of the pilot program, the data collected above will be evaluated by the personnel officer/manager and the officer in charge of the piloting department to determine the feasibility of continuing with flextime. In deciding whether or not to recommend continuing the program, the opinions of management and staff of the piloting department are to be surveyed and considered.

After completing the pilot, the senior officer in charge of the department shall prepare a short report which includes statistics on absenteeism, turnover, personal business days taken, and non-exempt overtime. This report will be submitted to the management committee for review/approval for continuing with the flextime program.

Coverage Requirements

The following format should be used for the coverage plan. One copy of the plan should be returned to the officer in charge of the department; the other is to be used in coverage discussions with employees subsequent to employee briefing meetings.

Work Unit	Function	Total Employees	Employees needed for coverage		
			8:00–9:30	11:30–1:30	3:30–4:45

Time Management and Administration

Flextime involves employees as well as supervisors in the dynamic process of time planning and organization.

Each participant must organize work time to meet the policy and operating requirements for time distribution, to be accountable for the required work hours, and to prepare time cards (non-exempt staff) recording total hours worked each day and exceptions to the normal workday such as approved overtime, vacation, or other absence.

Experience and Evaluation Phase

Each supervisor is to assure that policy and operating requirements are understood and are being met within the work unit.

Computation of Vacation, Overtime, and Sick Leave

The computation of these benefits is the same for employees working flextime as for those working a standard schedule.

Shift Differential

Employees who would normally (i.e., without flextime) complete their workday during the company's regular business day and who elect to start or end their workday during the midnight or swing shift shall not be paid shift differential.

6. Guidelines*

Band width:	The time during which employees *may* be on the job.	6:00 A.M.— 7:00 P.M.
Standard service day:	The time during which normal service and functional operations must be available.	8:00 A.M.— 4:45 P.M.
Core time:	The time when all employees would be on the job, unless specifically excused.	9:30 A.M.—11:30 A.M. 1:30 P.M.— 3:30 P.M.
Flexible time:	Designated time when employees may or may not be present.	6:00 A.M.— 9:30 A.M. 11:30 A.M.— 1:30 P.M. 3:30 P.M.— 7:00 P.M.
Contracted hours:	The total number of hours which must be accounted for during the accounting period.	40 hours
Accounting period:	Time period over which contracted hours can be accumulated.	1 week
Lunch break:	The time an employee is off the job during the mid-day flex period.	Minimum ½ hour Maximum 2 hours
Daily hours:	The number of hours that must be worked daily by non-exempt employees.	8 hours†

*These guidelines are illustrated for the standard day shift.

†Existing company policies are not affected by the flextime guidelines. For example, employees who complete their assignments and receive supervisory approval may continue to leave work after having completed a 7.8 hour workday.

(Continued)

Figure 1-6.   *(continued)*

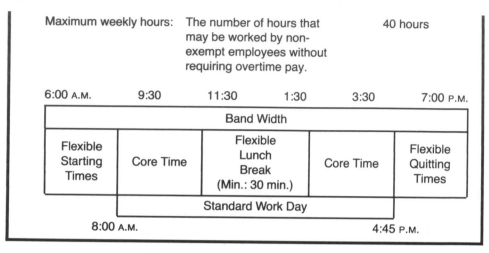

A critical factor in the success or failure of a flexible work hours system is the attitude of first-line supervisors toward the program. Flexitime, by its nature, requires a supervisory style which focuses on planning and coordination as opposed to monitoring. . . . With flexitime, supervisors should be less concerned with time-keeping functions, and should be willing to spend more time on planning, scheduling, and coordinating functions; they will have to place less emphasis on employee control and develop a more participatory style of supervision. Since this may not be an easy adjustment for some first-line supervisors, the organization must be prepared to facilitate the process through orientation beginning as soon as the decision is made to implement flexitime.[11]

As noted earlier, it is critical that supervisors be included in the initial design phases of the flexitime program. How much training the supervisors will require and how much resource material must be developed for them will depend to a great extent on the organization's existing supervisory norm.

Companies that have a generally participative style of supervision as opposed to a primarily monitoring style will probably find that their supervisors adapt with only a minimum of retraining. If a radical change in supervisory style is necessary in order for the organization to implement a flexitime program, then consideration should be given to holding a training session dealing with indirect supervisory techniques and evaluating on the basis of results rather than process.

Table 1-5. Examples of flexitime problems and their solutions.

Problem	Solution
Management or supervision problems	
First-line supervisors reluctant.	Training/education—"try it, you'll like it."
Role of first-line supervisor.	Reeducation in job.
Scheduling of meetings was made more difficult.	Earlier scheduling; most problems resolved with minor rearrangements of our own attitudes; i.e., willingness to alter inflexible habits we had gotten comfortable with.
Employees who work as a team cannot agree on a work schedule.	Company "business hours" prevail.
Coffee breaks—we had used a set time for each department, but dropped it with flexible hours. First day everyone went to coffee at the same time and we had standing room only.	We did nothing—next day problem went away. Moral: treat people as adults and they'll act as adults.
Departmental scheduling—allowing too many to use flexitime at the same time.	Require at least ⅓ staffing at all times.
Supervisors not having same degree of flexibility, sometimes required to work longer hours to cover entire workday.	Supervisors decide who will come in early and stay late; they then rotate.
Supervisory resistance—they were suspicious, insecure; doubted that employees would produce.	Launch pilot demonstration project, keep circulating testimonials.
Resistance from senior supervisors who felt loss of status and loss of control, and were unable to internalize the "Theory Y" philosophy that must accompany flexitime.	After 10 to 12 months they had adjusted.
Involvement of first-level supervisors in planning phase.	Extensive meetings on work scheduling processes and employee control procedures.
Coverage problems	
Telephone coverage by secretaries.	They established their own rotating schedule so that at least one person was available to cover phones.
Lack of agreement as to start/stop time between interfacing work groups.	Brought groups together, identified problem, and had it solved by agreement.

SOURCE: Stanley D. Nollen and Virginia H. Martin, *Alternative Work Schedules,* Part 1; AMA Survey Report (New York: AMACOM, 1978), 42–43.

(Continued)

Table 1-5. *(continued)*

Problem	Solution
Coverage problems (continued)	
Small groups unable to cover some positions if flexitime adopted.	Disallowed small groups to participate.
Receptionist does not arrive until 9:00 A.M.	Another employee had to become familiar with telephone answering and receiving visitors.
Staffing switchboard to closing time on Fridays.	Told department employees to solve it; they did.
Coverage of key desks for inside and outside contacts.	Had to ask a few people to reduce their flexitime opportunities.
Communication and coordination problems	
Coordinating two-shift operations.	Had day and evening shift make recommendations themselves, and if they couldn't solve it we just put people back on regular shift.
Had an immediate shift to an earlier workday, 7:30 A.M. to 3:30 P.M., which cut down on communication with the West Coast.	Met with department heads and employees to discuss problem and work out coverage to 5:00 P.M.
Interaction with other departments still on an 8:00 to 5:00 schedule.	Personnel from other departments had to adjust their thinking and communications to the core period.
Timekeeping problems and employee abuse of flexitime	
Minor number of abuses.	Individuals involved put on standard hours.
Employees abusing the honor system of timekeeping.	Staff meetings, constructive administration of discipline.
Not observing core hours requirement.	Talked to all employees; closer supervision.
Honor system not reliable.	Time recording devices a must.
Flexitime accumulators too expensive.	Implemented honor system.
Many employees felt no need to keep time records.	We reiterated our instructions and conducted an audit to assure compliance.
Cheating on time cards.	Peer pressure; employee taken off flexitime if necessary. The employees tend to "police" each other because they don't want to lose flexitime for all.

In all cases, however, educating supervisors and managers about the logistics of the flexitime system and its potential advantages before the program is implemented or during its initial phases will help pave the way for a smooth introduction of the system.

Summary

Flexitime, a work-scheduling approach in which starting and quitting times vary within a range established by management, was the first of the nontraditional scheduling options to gain acceptance. It was a response both to changing work force demographics and to management problems in enforcing the standard inflexible 9–5.

While surveys have indicated acceptance of flexitime by a growing number of organizations, they have also revealed that many of those organizations limit which job classifications or departments are eligible to participate in the flexitime program.

Flexitime seems best-suited to situations where management wishes to expand coverage or service hours; offer a low-cost employee benefit that not only will boost morale but also will improve recruitment efforts and help the organization retain its valued employees; and reduce or even eliminate tardiness.

In assessing the advantages and disadvantages of flexitime, the key considerations are as follows: Flexitime is highly popular with employees. It enhances productivity, employee skills, and quality of work and facilitates recruitment while reducing absenteeism, tardiness, turnover, and overtime costs. The extension of the organizational workday that comes with a flexitime program permits an expansion of coverage and service, although this benefit can be partly offset by a corresponding rise in overhead costs resulting from keeping the facility open for longer hours.

Problems with flexitime primarily involve maintaining adequate coverage, establishing effective channels of communication, keeping track of time worked, and correctly determining which employees and job functions should be eligible for flexitime. Unions are concerned about flexitime's impact on overtime and the length of the workday and about whether this option is truly voluntary. But given flexitime's popularity with workers, unions tend to concentrate on seeing that flexitime is implemented fairly rather than opposing the program altogether.

Introducing flexitime in the organization involves the same basic eight-step process that was presented in the Introduction. However, this work-scheduling approach does have a significant impact on the functions of first-line supervisors. Since flexitime is most likely to succeed in an atmosphere of participative management, steps must be taken to ensure that first-line supervisors are adequately prepared (through training and resource materials) to utilize this management style.

CHAPTER 2

Compressed Workweek

Compressed workweek refers to a workweek (usually 40 hours long) that is condensed into fewer than five days. The most common formulas are 4/10 (four 10-hour days, as shown in Figure 2-1), 3/12 (three 12-hour days, as shown in Figure 2-2), and 5-4/9 (a week of five nine-hour days followed by a week of four nine-hour days). In Figure 2-3, we have converted the nine-hour days to 9.5 hours to show an 80-hour total over two weeks; however, nine-hour days are more typically used in this type of schedule.

The first type of compressed schedule to be introduced was the four-day workweek, and it continues to be the most widely used, with the hybrid 5-4/9 being the next most popular, particularly with employees.

As organizational development experts Herman Gadon and Allan Cohen note:

> The compressed work week can be utilized in two differing ways: most commonly, the unit operates for five to seven days, more than eight hours a day (up to and including around-the-clock), but the individual employees only work three to four and one half days per week; or an entire firm or unit can operate only four days per week, with all (or most) employees in attendance for all of the four days. Under the first arrangement, days off will vary among individuals in such a way that the optimum number of employees are at work on the busiest days or at busiest periods of the day.[1]

Figure 2-1. 4/10 compressed workweek schedule.

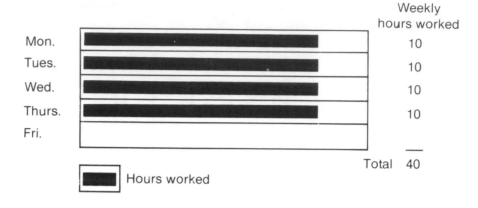

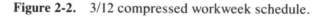

Figure 2-2. 3/12 compressed workweek schedule.

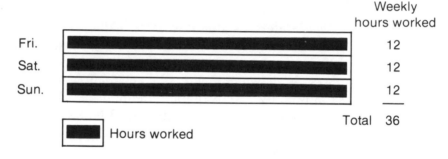

Origins of the Compressed Workweek

Introduced in the early 1970s, the compressed workweek, along with flexitime, was an effort to create alternatives to the standard five-day, 40-hour workweek by reallocating the same number of hours to fewer days. From the employers' perspective, this allowed plant facilities to be used for longer periods with fewer start-ups and shutdowns, while it gave employees longer blocks of personal time and cut down on commuting time.

The compressed workweek is probably the most controversial form of alternative scheduling. Since the mid-1970s, its popularity has peaked and waned and picked up again. While interest in it fell in the late 1970s, the Bureau of Labor Statistics noted that between 1979 and 1985, use of compressed workweeks grew four times as fast

Figure 2-3. 5-4/9.5 compressed workweek schedule.

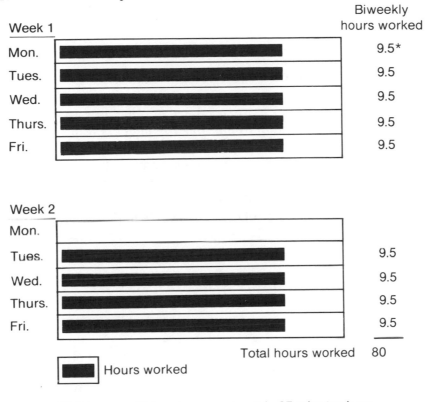

*9.5 hours with lunch approximately 37 minutes long

as overall employment growth.[2] Few employers today seem to implement a compressed schedule companywide, however, and many use a combination of several different versions, tailoring the formula to the particular type of task and work force.

Who Uses a Compressed Workweek?

A 1985 American Management Association survey conducted by Goodmeasure indicated that 15 percent of the respondents used some kind of compressed workweek schedule somewhere in the organization but not necessarily companywide. It also indicated that these schedules are most common in three industries: government (29 percent in this category reported using it), health care (31 percent), and entertainment or recreation (42 percent).[3]

Compressed workweeks are also used extensively in public agencies, especially police and fire departments and in small manufacturing companies.

When Is a Compressed Workweek Most Appropriate?

Compressed workweeks are used most often in situations where employers are attempting to *improve the allocation of labor time* or *decrease the cost of operating capital equipment.*

If their labor force favors such a schedule, it is a way to offer a *low-cost employee benefit* at the same time. Some employers have used a compressed schedule during the summer months to provide employees with longer weekends. These "summer hours" schedules are very popular.

Pros and Cons of a Compressed Workweek

Absenteeism, tardiness, and turnover. Modest improvements in these rates have been reported.

Employee morale. A compressed workweek can affect employee morale either positively or negatively. In general, compressed workweeks get mixed reviews from employees, some of whom like to work longer days in return for longer weekends, while others don't like such schedules at all.

Family time. Those employees who do like the compressed workweek often cite the opportunity for more family time as one of the reasons. On the other hand, there are working parents who cite fatigue as a negative result.

Recruitment. Most employers using a compressed workweek report improved recruitment as a result of employee interest in having more and longer blocks of personal time.

Staffing. Because the compressed workweek permits employees to have more concentrated time off, they become more willing to accept shift work and weekend assignments and work during peak periods of activity. The compressed workweek has allowed some employers to attract skilled employees to undesirable shifts.

Supervision. Because of problems with scheduling and coverage and increased complications involving internal and external communications, supervision is perceived to be more difficult with the compressed workweek. However, as noted in the Introduction, this is the case when an organization first adopts any of the new scheduling arrangements discussed in this book. Such difficulties tend to taper off as the organization gains management expertise with the particular work-time alternative.

Fatigue. Since the compressed workweek increases the length of the workday, some employees are quite tired by quitting time. This makes compressed schedules unpopular with certain employees, particularly older employees and some working parents.

Productivity. Related to the issue of fatigue is the issue of productivity. The impact of the compressed workweek on productivity gets mixed reviews, with some employers reporting an improvement and others complaining about a drop-off in productivity toward the end of long shifts—a drop-off that they attribute to fatigue.

Commuting. Many employees cite an improvement in commuting as a benefit of the compressed workweek because they are often arriving and leaving at times other than rush hours and have to travel to work one fewer day per week.

Scheduling. In a study of alternative work time conducted by Stanley Nollen and Virginia Martin, more than a third of the compressed workweek users reported rearranging shifts to improve scheduling. The report noted the following:

> The shift changes were of many varieties. For the four-day week combined with five-day operation, the simplest change is dividing the workforce into two teams, each working four days—a Monday–Thursday team and a Tuesday–Friday team. This staggering of workers keeps all functions at least partially covered during all five days. In four-day operations with two shifts, hours may be rearranged; for example, if the old hours were 7:00 A.M. to 3:30 P.M. and 4:00 P.M. to 12:30 A.M. the new hours might be 6:00 A.M. to 4:00 P.M. and 4:00 P.M. to 2:00 A.M. In computer operations two 12-hour shifts a day for two teams of workers each working three days (one on Monday–Wednesday and the other on Thursday–Saturday) is a way to achieve six-day coverage 24 hours a day. Peak workloads during one part of the day or week can also be managed through certain shift arrangements. In police work, for example, ten-hour shifts can be overlapped: a 7:00 A.M. to 5:00 P.M. shift, a 5:00 P.M. to 3:00 A.M. and a third 9:00 P.M. to 7:00 A.M. shift overlapping the busy night hours. Overloaded areas in a firm's operation can be eased by adding a Friday–Sunday team in those areas, thus adding weekend hours, or a weekend team can replace a third weekday shift. Compressed

workweeks that are four and a half days long are often accomplished by adding an hour a day to Monday–Thursday operations to permit Friday afternoons off.[4]

Utilization of plants and equipment. Extended operating times mean that facilities and capital equipment can be used more efficiently. If, for instance, capital equipment must be operated continuously because of the nature of the production process, longer and fewer shifts are generally most cost-effective, since this reduces the expense associated with start-ups and shutdowns.

Labor cost per unit. The reduction in start-ups and shutdowns that accompanies the compressed workweek translates into a corresponding reduction in the labor hours required to perform these functions. In the case of units whose employees are assigned to distant work sites, the cost of travel to and from the work site is cut when the employees work a greater number of hours per trip. The use of a compressed workweek may also result in a better match between staffing levels and peak-period activity, which may in turn reduce overtime costs.

Utility costs. If the organization is able to schedule all or part of its operations within hours when special discounts are given by utility companies, there may be a significant reduction in utility costs associated with use of the compressed workweek.

Legal considerations. In some states, wage and hours legislation creates a barrier to the use of compressed schedules. In several states, the law requires that overtime premiums be paid for hours worked in excess of eight a day, unless an industry or group of employees has been exempted in some way or unless an organization has established a compressed workweek under specified conditions. In some cases, compressed schedules of 40 hours a week are authorized if an organization's employees have been polled and two thirds are in favor of such a change and if the affected employees receive two consecutive days off within each workweek. Compensatory time in lieu of overtime is also allowed in some cases if it is used during the same pay period.

Union attitudes. Unions are generally skeptical about compressed schedules. They are concerned about the fatigue factor and the long-term effects on employee health. They are also sensitive to any encroachment on overtime or the protections embodied in the Federal Fair Labor Standards Act, particularly the 40-hour workweek. Some union contracts specify both an eight-hour day and a 40-hour week. As with other alternative work-time schedules, however, some unions whose members feel the need for such options have supported, or taken the lead in negotiating, a compressed workweek schedule.

Failure rate. It should be noted that the compressed workweek has had the highest failure rate of all the new scheduling alternatives. The survey by Stanley Nollen and Virginia Martin, cited in Nollen's *New Work Schedules in Practice,* indicated that "28 percent of one time users had abandoned it."[5] According to Nollen's *New Work Schedules in Practice,* "[T]hese failures occurred quite quickly when they happened and were usually caused by trouble with fatigue, coverage, scheduling, productivity and supervision. They were also caused in some cases by employee discontent."[6] On the other hand, many long-term users report no difficulty with the arrangement and perceive a number of benefits that have held up over a period of time.

Should Your Organization Try a Compressed Workweek?

This section provides some tools that can help you decide whether a compressed workweek would aid in solving your organization's staffing and scheduling problems.

The accompanying material entitled Organizational Experience With the Compressed Workweek profiles the program instituted by one manufacturing company. Reading this should help you focus on the major issues associated with the use of a compressed workweek.

The questionnaire shown in Table 2-1 lists the primary concerns that lead companies to try compressed workweeks. The more "yes" answers you have on this questionnaire, the greater the chances that you should be taking a serious look at this scheduling arrangement for your organization.

If your questionnaire results point to the adoption of a compressed workweek, you can use the worksheet shown in Figure 2-4 to list your specific concerns and outline what you see as the advantages and disadvantages of a compressed schedule.

Introducing a Compressed Workweek

To introduce a compressed workweek in your organization, begin by appointing a planning group to build support for the proposed program by addressing at the outset the problems that have sometimes caused such programs to fail. Depending on how complex and exten-

ORGANIZATIONAL EXPERIENCE WITH THE COMPRESSED WORKWEEK

Shell Canada Limited

Description: The Shell Canada chemical plant at Sarnia, Ontario, makes polypropylene and isopropyl alcohol. It is a continuous-process facility, operating seven days a week, 24 hours a day.

Reason for Using a Compressed Workweek: When the plant was built, a primary goal was to maximize both economic and human performance and quality of work life. The latter was defined, in part, as the creation of a learning environment, which necessitated a redesign of shift work. Another reason for reexamining existing procedures was the attrition associated with shift work. Shift scheduling was becoming increasingly unpopular with the plant's labor force because of the social dislocation it entails. The resulting costs of turnover, recruitment, and training needed to be addressed.

Implementation Process: The first step was converting from 8-hour shifts to 12-hour ones. This solved some problems (workers liked it better because it gave them three days off a week and more daytime work) but created new ones. For example, covering absences was more difficult with a compressed workweek, overtime issues had to be resolved, and paid leave time had to be recalculated.

The next stage of implementation entailed a major overhaul of work schedules, training, and management style. The objective was to obtain multiskilled workers and reduce the amount of shift work. To achieve this, the plant basically redesigned the organization. Shift work was combined with nonshift work, and training time is now part of the regular schedule.

Impact to Date: Workers have fewer nonstandard hours and are more self-managing; shift workers are multiskilled and continually trained. Both union representatives and management have collaborated to achieve the program's success.

SOURCE: Stanley D. Nollen, *New Work Schedules in Practice: Managing Time in a Changing Society,* Work in America Institutes Series (New York: Van Nostrand Reinhold, 1982), 83–93.

Table 2-1. Compressed workweek questionnaire.

Would a Compressed Workweek Benefit Your Organization?

	Yes	No
Do you have problems with recruitment or turnover for weekend coverage or for some shifts?		
Would you like to expand the use of some of your more expensive equipment?		
Do some of the workers in your work units have to travel long distances to and from work sites?		
Would it be more cost-effective to combine three shifts into two?		
Would your employees like more three-day blocks of personal time?		
Is commuting during rush hour a problem for many of your employees?		

sive the program is expected to be, it is often necessary to appoint a project administrator to oversee the program's implementation. As you move into the design phase, you will work out the details of a variety of critical issues. Supporting resource materials should then be created and the program announced to employees. Since a compressed workweek is not optional, promotion is unnecessary. It *is* necessary, however, to evaluate the program's progress and make adjustments based on your company's experience with it. The following subsections discuss this introduction process in greater depth.

Gain Support for the Program

A compressed workweek retains the 40-hour-a-week mode and the standard that everyone reports to work and leaves at the same time. Consequently, it requires less of a change in supervisory style than flexitime does for many managers. The most common reasons for introducing a compressed workweek are: (1) to improve employee morale and relations and (2) to improve production scheduling and the use of facilities and capital equipment.

Unless a companywide application is planned immediately, a full-blown task force approach may not be necessary. At a minimum, however, a planning group should be appointed.

Holding planning meetings with managers, supervisors, and employees and, where all or part of the work force is unionized, with labor groups is the most effective means of gaining support for this scheduling arrangement. The meetings have two purposes: (1) to articulate organizational objectives and (2) to solicit planning sugges-

Figure 2-4. Compressed workweek worksheet.

Assessing the Need for a Compressed Workweek

List the main reasons why you are considering a compressed workweek:

1. _____

_____

_____

2. _____

_____

_____

3. _____

_____

_____

4. _____

_____

_____

List what you see as the advantages and disadvantages of a compressed workweek:

Pros: _____

_____

_____

_____

_____

Cons: _____

tions. Since the reasons most often reported for failure of a compressed workweek have been scheduling and communications problems, fatigue, and employee dissatisfaction, it should come as no surprise that organizations that include managers, supervisors, and employees in the planning process appear to have a higher success rate than those that do not. Stanley Nollen and Virginia Martin observe that "In particular, holding meetings with managers and supervisors was associated with better productivity and work scheduling experiences, with a lower frequency of management problems."[7]

Set Up the Program's Administration

If the compressed workweek will be used in more than one form and in more than one work unit, a project administrator should be appointed to work with the planning group to coordinate the planning meetings, gather information about compressed workweek experience in other organizations, plan the program, act as a resource for supervisors during its initial phases, and monitor the program as it is implemented, evaluated, and revised.

Design the Program

The following are some of the issues that you will have to deal with in designing a compressed workweek program:

State and federal labor laws. Your first step is to review federal and state labor laws to determine what kinds of compressed scheduling options are possible. As we've noted, federal law limits to 40 the number of hours that can be worked in a week without paying overtime, and some states impose a daily maximum (usually eight hours).

Labor contracts. Existing labor agreements should also be reviewed to see whether their provisions conflict with the use of a compressed work schedule.

Once the legal parameters are established, some of the remaining design questions that must be answered are:

Extent of the program. In which areas or departments of the organization will you have a compressed schedule?

Compressed workweek model(s). What model(s) of compressed scheduling will best suit the objectives that you identified?

Operating and shift schedules. Must operating schedules be changed? (Will the organization operate fewer days? More days?) What kinds of shift changes will be necessary? (Will some shifts be combined? Will new shifts be added, perhaps on weekends or during peak periods of activity?)

Work force allocations. Will it be necessary to reallocate personnel in order to keep the organization functioning at maximum efficiency with a compressed workweek?

Holidays. Will changes in paid holidays be made? Some companies that use the 4-day, 40-hour formula, for example, alter their previous holiday plan of 10 paid holidays (8 hours each) to 8 paid holidays (10 hours each).

Duration of the program. Will the compressed schedule be in effect year-round or only during part of the year (for example, summer)?

The program design checklist shown in Table 2-2 can help you chart your progress in addressing the design issues we've just considered.

Develop Resource Materials

An information sheet detailing any changes (such as in operating schedules or holidays) occurring as a result of the introduction of a compressed workweek should be made available to all employees.

Table 2-2. Program design checklist: compressed workweek.

Key Design Issues	Notes
☐ State and federal labor laws	
☐ Existing labor contracts	
☐ Extent of the program (in terms of departments, production units, areas, and so on)	
☐ Scheduling model(s)	
☐ Operating and shift schedules	
☐ Work force allocations	
☐ Holidays	
☐ Duration of the program	

Figure 2-5 shows the guidelines that one large manufacturing company developed for the use of 12-hour shifts in its plants, together with an assessment of what the organization regarded as the benefits and drawbacks of this type of scheduling. Information of this sort would be helpful in preparing managerial and supervisory personnel for an upcoming switch to a compressed workweek.

In general, however, employers have not developed resource materials or training programs related to the introduction of a compressed workweek. Perhaps some of the problems with both internal and external communications that have been reported by certain users of this scheduling arrangement could be eliminated or minimized by the development of information materials or training sessions that focus on this aspect of the new scheduling plan.

Announce the Program

Whether the compressed workweek program is confined to particular work units or departments or is instituted companywide, a general announcement should be made when it is adopted.

Figure 2-5. A manufacturer's materials on the use of a 12-hour shift.

12-Hour Shift Guidelines

Guidelines plants have typically elected to adopt in establishing 12-hour shift schedules are:

1. No additional cost to the site (may require some adjustment in wage premiums).
2. Must not liberalize intent of current policies covering pay and benefits.
3. Comply with applicable federal (Fair Labor Standards Act and possibly Walsh-Healey) and state laws.
4. Improve employee relations (employees need prior understanding of effects).
5. Must not adversely affect safety, productivity, or attendance.
6. Preserve management's right to reestablish 8-hour system.

Typical 12-Hour Shift Schedule

Rotation:

	Mon.	Tues.	Wed.	Thurs.	Fri.	Sat.	Sun.	Hours per Week
Week 1	D	D	D	D	off	off	off	48*
Week 2	off	off	off	off	N	N	N	36
Week 3	N	off	off	off	D	D	D	48*
Week 4	off	N	N	N	off	off	off	36

D = 6 A.M. to 6 P.M.   N = 6 P.M. to 6 A.M.

A Plant's Evaluation of a Compressed Workweek Schedule

Advantages	Disadvantages
• Employees view as a positive response to request of employees working a rotating shift schedule. • Improved production-mechanical relationships. Same operating crew shuts down and starts up equipment, minimizing outages and improving safety. • Wives generally in favor. • Employee is off every other weekend.	• Brought pressure for some form of added recognition of day employees. • Some initial problem in adapting for communications. • An adjustment period was required for adapting to 12 hours of work. • Overtime scheduling is more of a problem, since the plant permits 4 hours' holdover (16-hour maximum per day).

*Federal law requires overtime rates to be paid for hours worked over 40 in a workweek. State laws may have some application.

- Has resulted in mechanics volunteering for shift assignments.
- Use of gloves, overalls, tags, etc., reduced by one third. Also, one third less shift business paperwork.
- Shift exchange time reduced.
- Trips to the plant (safety, cost, energy) reduced by one third.
- Same employees relieve each other, improving communications and relationships.

- Use of day employees to relieve shift employees is complicated.
- Now have difficulty getting volunteers to fill day assignments from shift crews.

Promote the Program

With the exception of programs in states that require an employee election before adopting a compressed schedule, these scheduling arrangements are not an employee option and do not require internal promotion. Such programs may be valuable, however, as part of a recruitment effort or a public relations promotion.

Evaluate the Program

According to the Nollen-Martin study cited earlier, about one in four users of the compressed workweek changes the way in which the organization originally used it.[8] With any new scheduling arrangement, it is important to detect problems early, and this can only be done if some kind of evaluative mechanism is built into the initial implementation process. Baseline data should be obtained and feedback from both supervisors and employees should be solicited so the impact of the program can be assessed in terms of both business results and employee reaction. In addition to the compressed workweek's effects on job performance and on the workers themselves, the effect on three cost areas (overtime, unit labor costs, and utilities) is often measured.

Fine-Tune the Program

Once the results of the evaluation are in, you will probably find that some changes are called for. Table 2-3 provides examples of some of the problems that employers have encountered in using a compressed schedule and the ways in which they have dealt with these problems.

Table 2-3. Examples of problems with compressed workweeks and their solutions.

Problem	Solution
Work scheduling problems	
Poor supervisory coverage.	Asked supervisors to work five days.
Coverage in all departments was necessary at all times.	Maintained skeleton crews and compensatory time off was granted.
Telephone coverage, Friday billing.	Cross-training; some people work five days (eight hours a day).
Customer service coverage on Friday afternoons.	Group established its own rotating coverage so a person would be present.
Customer service calls.	Rearranged shifts.
Incoming freight.	Notified local delivering carriers.
Maintaining contact with distributors, salesmen on Fridays.	Scheduled necessary contact employees on a Tuesday-Friday workweek.
Problem of service to policyholders.	Assigned 7 percent of 4-day workweek force to a Tuesday–Friday schedule with 93 percent working Monday–Thursday.
Supervisors did not like to work Friday afternoon.	We found that neither policyowners nor agents came in or called on Friday so we use an answering service for all closed hours.
Communication from one team to another.	We developed a one-hour overlap.
Communications with employees much more complex.	Required added management time.
Employee scheduling problems	
Starting times for employees under flexitime schedule were not acceptable when the ten-hour workday was instituted.	Employees were permitted to select a new flexitime schedule; lunch hours were cut to 30 minutes to shorten the day.
Office employees who contact customers also wanted a 4-day week.	We staggered their workweek; that is, half had Monday off, half Friday.
Too many wanted Mondays or Fridays off.	Each department's management simply spelled out the minimum staff required for those days and it was left up to work groups to decide who would be there.

SOURCE: Stanley D. Nollen and Virginia H. Martin, *Alternative Work Schedules,* parts 2 and 3 (New York: AMACOM, 1978), 58–60.

Employee scheduling problems *(continued)*	
Adverse effect on nonparticipating employees' morale.	Not solved.
Some married women with children find it inconvenient to arrive home late.	Solved by putting only those people who want the four-day week in that department.
Changing of daily shift hours.	Employees had to adjust and in some cases change their transportation.
Train schedules for departing employees require up to 1½ hr. wait on Friday afternoon.	Called Burlington Railroad—they are adding a train.
Babysitting and transportation.	Allowed flexibility in reporting and quitting times.
Fringe benefit reallocation problems	
How to pay for benefit such as days of vacation, holidays, funeral pay, sick days.	Generally we divided by "4" instead of "5." Everyone involved gets "1" less, but the same number of hours.
Sick days.	Had to change "sick days" to "sick hours" because of longer working day in four-day week. Now give 48 hours per year instead of six annual days previously given.
Overtime problems	
We are covered by federal law requiring overtime after eight hours.	Restructured wage schedule was developed to yield equal pay under new and old schedule.
Walsh-Healy Act requires overtime for hours over eight in day for all work on government contract.	We dropped U.S. Government as customers.
Due to Walsh-Healy, having to pay overtime for over eight hours worked.	Not solved and is why we have not expanded use of compressed workweeks.

Summary

The compressed workweek consists of a variety of scheduling options in which the standard 40-hour workweek is condensed into fewer than the standard five days. The popularity of this alternative has had

its ups and downs since the compressed workweek was first introduced in the early 1970s.

Studies indicate that compressed workweeks tend to be more
common in certain industries and that employers tend to institute the
practice in selected departments rather than companywide. Many
employers adapt the compressed workweek concept to their unique
needs by using different scheduling models in different departments
or areas, depending on the nature of the work or the workers
involved.

Employers who decide to institute a compressed workweek usually do so in order to better allocate their labor time or use their
facilities and capital equipment more effectively. And since some
employees like the compressed workweek, it can also serve as a low-
cost employee benefit.

The compressed workweek has been reported to offer the following advantages: Absenteeism, tardiness, and turnover decrease somewhat. Employee morale may be enhanced—but only if the employees
favor the compressed scheduling option—and recruitment usually
improves. Employees become more willing to accept traditionally
undesirable assignments (shifts, weekends), since longer blocks of
personal time compensate them for the inconvenience. While an
improvement in productivity is cited by only some employers, an
improvement in commuting is commonly reported. The compressed
workweek can be used to tailor shifts in a way that improves scheduling. And this work-time alternative permits more effective use of
plants, equipment, and labor and may result in decreased utility
costs.

On the negative side are problems with employee morale involving those workers who *don't* favor the adoption of the compressed
workweek and problems with supervision. Longer workdays can
result in employee fatigue and a negative impact on productivity.
Restrictions imposed by state legislation can sometimes make the
compressed workweek a less attractive option for employers, as can
the concerns of some unions and the provisions of some union
contracts. In fact, of all the new scheduling alternatives, the compressed workweek is the one that most often fails (although many
employers remain quite satisfied with this option even after prolonged
use).

The basic eight-step process for implementing a new work-time
alternative that was presented in the Introduction applies to the
compressed workweek, with the exception that because the program
is mandatory, it need not be promoted to employees. But given the

higher-than-average failure rate for compressed workweek programs, care should be taken at the outset to gain the understanding the support of all who will be involved in the program and to provide resource materials and training that address (and may help prevent) some of the commonly reported problems.

Reduced Work Time

Surprisingly, although an average of 18.6 million Americans work less than full-time, there is no agreed-upon definition of part-time employment. Employers tend to view part-time very broadly as far as hours worked are concerned. It is an umbrella term referring to anything less than the standard full-time schedule for a particular profession or industry. Thus, part-time for lawyers, teachers, federal employees, and corporate managers may each be very different in terms of hours worked per day, week, month, or year.

Until the late 1970s, anyone on a part-time schedule was regarded as belonging to a peripheral work force rather than the regular work force. Speaking to attendees at a national conference on part-time employment in 1983, Dr. Stanley Nollen—a professor at the Georgetown University School of Business Administration, a leading authority on alternative work time, and co-author of *Permanent Part-Time Employment: The Manager's Perspective*—noted the following:

> For most employers, part-time employment is simply not an issue; it is not a question; it is not a policy. By itself it does not matter. . . . [W]ork schedules, of which part-time employment is only one, are only a part of human resource management, and that is only a part of the making and selling of a product.[1]

As the economy has shifted from a production to a service orientation, however, the way in which work is scheduled, from both a service delivery and a human resources management perspective, has become increasingly important. The traditional 9–5 schedule is not necessarily the most efficient format for either one, and various new kinds of part-time schedules have begun to emerge, originally in response to employee pressures, more recently because of organizational ones.

A major barrier to learning how to use less than full-time schedules efficiently has been management's attitudes about part-time employees. In commenting on this at the conference cited earlier, Nollen said:

> My last point [is] about part-time employment: We have here really a cultural or attitudinal stereotype situation as to how managers think about part-time employment. It is not that part-time employees are less productive; no, they are probably more productive. It is not that they are less committed, less loyal; you have heard reports stating the opposite is true. Employers do not doubt those kinds of reports; you do not get any argument from employers about loyalty, commitment, dedication, quality of work, all of that is okay.
>
> The difference is that part-time employees are different. . . . [E]mployers believe that part-time employees are not career-oriented. They are not going to be there forever. They are not looking forward to the same kind of future in the company as full-time employees are looking forward to.[2]

Although there may once have been some basis in fact to this stereotype of part-timers as not being career-oriented, as the work force has changed, so, too, has the composition of the part-time segment of the labor force. According to 1986 Bureau of Labor Statistics figures, almost 2 million voluntary part-timers are managerial and professional employees.[3] Part-time is now a transition strategy for many workers; it is a way to retain partial attachment to the labor force while education is completed, children grow older, or new skills are acquired. This is particularly true of women, who currently comprise almost two thirds of the part-time labor force, most of whom are very career-oriented.

Management is now beginning to realize that most part-timers will at some point want to return to full-time employment, which is why many organizations have begun to experiment with new kinds of voluntary reduced work time and to devise processes by which employees may return to full-time employment at a later date. The emergence of permanent, or regular, part-time employment and its subsets—job sharing, phased or partial retirement, voluntary reduced work time (V-time), leave time, and work-sharing programs—has come about largely because employers want to retain good employees. There has also been a growing understanding that employees perform better if work schedules can be constructed to meet the needs of both the job *and* the worker.

Part II focuses on the various forms of *regular part-time employment* that employers have begun to use in order to create more flexibility for the organization and its employees. So that their special applications and uses can be explored in detail, a separate chapter will be devoted to each of these options, including regular part-time (discussed in Chapter 3) and its subsets of job sharing (Chapter 4), phased or partial retirement (Chapter 5), V-time (Chapter 6), leave time (Chapter 7), and work sharing (Chapter 8). Other forms of part-time (such as temporary pools and premium peak time) are covered in Part III, Chapter 10: Contingent Employment.

Regular Part-Time Employment

*P*ermanent, or regular, part-time—a term that came into common use between the mid-1970s and 1982—is part-time employment that includes job security and all other rights and benefits available to an organization's regular full-time workers.

From the mid-1970s until the 1982 recession, voluntary part-time was the fastest-growing segment of the labor force. While, according to the Bureau of Labor Statistics, the total number of people employed increased by 27 percent between 1970 and 1982, the number of part-time workers rose by 58 percent.[1] At the same time, the nature and structure of voluntary part-time work began to change. In 1982, the Bureau of Labor Statistics reported that there are 2.5 million *professional-level* part-time jobs, a number that reflected four times the rate of increase for all part-time jobs during the 1970–1982 period.

Origins of Regular Part-Time Employment

Two of the reasons why part-time employment has begun to move into the mainstream are:

1. *Changes in work force demographics.* Women have entered the work force in unprecedented numbers since the late 1970s. It is estimated that by the year 2000, approximately 47 percent of the work force will be composed of women and that they will account for almost two-thirds of the labor force growth for the previous decade.[2] Many female workers have small children, and most must work for economic reasons, whether they are married or not. This radical

change in women's employment needs and expectations has been the driving force behind the change in the dynamic of the part-time labor force and the expanded use of flexible and permanent part-time schedules.

2. *The shift from a production-based to a service-industry-based economy.* Less than full-time schedules are much more prevalent in service industries than they are in production-oriented organizations.

The impact of these two trends is in fact related, because not only do women currently make up two thirds of the voluntary part-time labor force, but 29 percent of them are in service-oriented jobs.[3] The ramifications of these two factors, particularly in terms of the inter-face between work and family responsibilities, have combined to make alternative work time, or the lack of it, a bottom-line issue for many employers, one that relates to efficient scheduling of both tasks and employees.

Traditionally, employers used part-time as an appropriate re-sponse to a staffing problem—an arrangement that would improve operations. According to Dr. Stanley Nollen:

> If absenteeism among women manufacturing employees is high because of pre-school children then job sharing is a solution to that problem. If a bank has peak loads on Monday mornings, Friday afternoons, and every mid-day then, of course, part-time tellers are a solution to that peak load problem. If creative work is the kind of work that is best done in random spurts, flexibly, then perhaps flexibly scheduled part-time employment is the answer to that kind of employment problem. That is why firms hire part-time employees in most cases I think. They have a problem to solve.[4]

The conditions of part-time employment have begun to change as employers discover organizational reasons such as those cited above to use regular part-time employees and begin to consider part-time a valuable scheduling option. Figure 3-1 illustrates how part-timers can be used to achieve various types of coverage, in contrast to the traditional full-time schedule.

With more employers starting to treat part-timers like regular employees, less than full-time schedules have become a more attrac-tive alternative for a wider group of workers. A 1983 New York State survey of 3,300 employees showed that over 30 percent of full-time employees were interested in a reduced work-time schedule.[5]

Figure 3-1. Sample part-time schedules for flexible coverage.

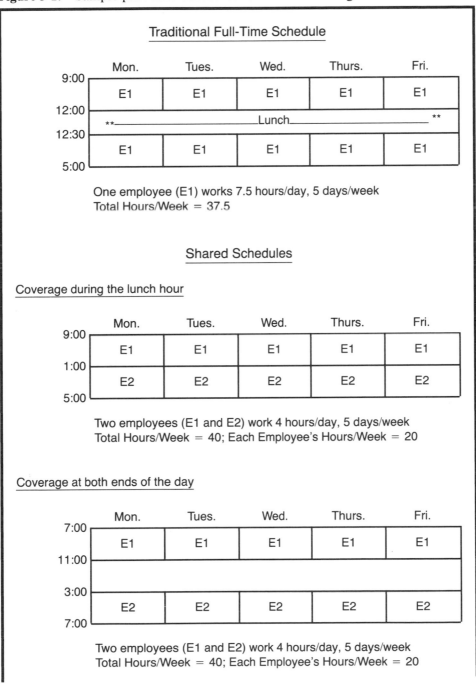

Traditional Full-Time Schedule

	Mon.	Tues.	Wed.	Thurs.	Fri.
9:00 – 12:00	E1	E1	E1	E1	E1
12:00 – 12:30	**_Lunch_**				
12:30 – 5:00	E1	E1	E1	E1	E1

One employee (E1) works 7.5 hours/day, 5 days/week
Total Hours/Week = 37.5

Shared Schedules

Coverage during the lunch hour

	Mon.	Tues.	Wed.	Thurs.	Fri.
9:00 – 1:00	E1	E1	E1	E1	E1
1:00 – 5:00	E2	E2	E2	E2	E2

Two employees (E1 and E2) work 4 hours/day, 5 days/week
Total Hours/Week = 40; Each Employee's Hours/Week = 20

Coverage at both ends of the day

	Mon.	Tues.	Wed.	Thurs.	Fri.
7:00 – 11:00	E1	E1	E1	E1	E1
11:00 – 3:00					
3:00 – 7:00	E2	E2	E2	E2	E2

Two employees (E1 and E2) work 4 hours/day, 5 days/week
Total Hours/Week = 40; Each Employee's Hours/Week = 20

(Continued)

Figure 3-1. *(continued)*

Double coverage during the lunch hour

	Mon.	Tues.	Wed.	Thurs.	Fri.
9:00 – 11:00	E1	E1	E1	E1	E1
11:00 – 1:00	E1 & E2	E1 & E2	E1 & E2	E1 & E2	E1 & E2
1:00 – 3:00	E2	E2	E2	E2	E2

Two employees (E1 and E2) work 4 hours/day, 5 days/week
Total Hours/Week = 40; Each Employee's Hours/Week = 20

Double coverage needed

	Mon.	Tues.	Wed.	Thurs.	Fri.
9:00 – 1:00	E1 & E2	E1 & E2	E1 & E2	E1 & E2	E1 & E2

Two employees (E1 and E2) work 4 hours/day, 5 days/week
Total Hours/Week = 40; Each Employee's Hours/Week = 20

Peak-time coverage

Peak-time employee (E1) works 16 hours/week
Total Hours/Week = 16

Who Uses Regular Part-Time Employees?

According to the Bureau of Labor Statistics, 20.1 million Americans were working part-time in 1985, 14.7 million of them voluntarily. The largest segment, 80 percent of voluntary part-timers, was employed in the retail and service sectors of the economy. In nonfarm occupations, 41 percent of all voluntary part-timers were in technical, sales, and administrative support positions, and 29 percent were in service jobs. Managerial and professional employees comprised 17 percent of the part-time labor force.[6]

The Work in America Institute's 1981 policy study *New Work Schedules for a Changing Society* notes that over two thirds of all companies have regular part-time employees, especially in office and clerical positions, but that they have only a few such employees— somewhere between 2 percent and 7 percent in most cases.[7] A 1985 American Management Association member study reported that 34 percent of the responding organizations were using permanent part-timers,[8] and a 1986 New Ways to Work survey of private-sector organizations in the San Francisco Bay area showed that 65 percent of the respondents were using this option.[9]

Health service providers, banking and other financial services institutions, insurance companies, and the legal profession have all experienced an increase in the use of regular part-time employment. A 1986 New Ways to Work survey of work-time options in the legal profession showed that of 141 law firms, corporate legal offices, public-interest organizations, and government entities questioned, 20 percent had a policy allowing attorneys to work part-time.[10]

When Is Regular Part-Time Most Appropriate?

Regular part-time employment has a number of organizational uses, including retention of valued employees, improved scheduling, cost reductions in some instances, and improved recruitment.

Retention of valued employees. Most managers initially choose to use part-timers in order to keep a good worker who might otherwise have had to leave the organization. Retaining a trained employee who has performed well but who must work part-time is usually more cost-effective than replacing that employee with a new hire.

Improved scheduling. Standard 9–5 schedules are not always appropriate in terms of accomplishing the tasks that must be done. Some facilities or services are more effectively managed by using split shifts or operating on an extended basis; others must respond to peak periods that occur daily, weekly, seasonally, or on a fluctuating basis. Supplementing the full-time work force with regular part-timers can give the organization the flexibility it needs to match its labor supply to the demands of the work.

Cost savings. The use of part-timers can result in cost savings in several areas: If an employee wants to reduce his or her work time and the extra hours are not replaced, payroll costs are cut. If the extra hours are replaced but are worked by a less-experienced and less-costly new hire, the organization still comes out ahead in terms of payroll costs. Costs associated with absenteeism and turnover have been positively affected by the availability of regular part-time options. And if an organization's regular part-timers are able to take on a few more hours during peak periods, the organization may be able to cut back on involuntary overtime.

Improved recruitment. Although some companies report mixed results in recruiting part-timers, this may be because the conditions of employment (such as salary scale and benefits) that they are offering these employees are not sufficiently attractive. Many employers have cited significant improvements in both the number and quality of applicants when they add a regular part-time option to their full-time recruitment campaign.

Pros and Cons of Regular Part-Time

As we've seen in the preceding section, for managers, the primary benefits of being able to provide employees with reduced work-time options are the potential for retaining trained and committed workers, a better match between work load and worker availability, and improved recruitment.

Costs are a major factor in an organization's decision about the feasibility of using part-timers. Although, as noted earlier, the use of part-timers can result in cost savings in certain areas, costs may be increased in other areas—which means that management must perform a detailed analysis of costs versus benefits in considering any voluntary reduced work-time option.

Management must also consider the impact of public and private policy and the attitudes of management, unions, and employees toward the concept of voluntary part-time employment.

In the following subsections, we will take a closer look at each of these factors that significantly affect an organization's decision on whether—and how—to use part-timers. Concerns about the complications of supervising part-timers are another major consideration—one that will be discussed in a separate section later in the chapter.

Employee Retention

Losing trained personnel who are an integral part of a company's culture can be a significant expense, particularly if you add up all the relevant factors—such as downtime, if the position is not filled right away, recruitment and interviewing costs, and the initial adjustment period for the new employee. It therefore makes good sense to accommodate the trained employee who, for reasons of health or conflicting responsibilities, must work part-time, at least for a while. At all levels of responsibility and in all industries, this need to retain valued employees has provided the primary impctus for the expansion of regular part-time employment.

Common by-products of accommodating employees' needs for reduced work-time options are:

- Improved job performance
- Increased energy
- Increased motivation and commitment to the organization

Scheduling

The ability to tailor the work force to meet the precise needs of the work to be performed (which often calls for uneven and/or fluctuating coverage) is, as mentioned earlier, another primary advantage of part-time employment.

Some managers have begun to use a combination of part- and full-time employees to improve scheduling in particular areas. Transamerica Occidental Life Insurance Company uses students to staff a four-hour night shift that supplements the work of its regular clerical personnel. Employers that work with the general public—such as motor vehicle licensing departments, banks, and ticketing agencies—usually have peak hours of client demand. Many have successfully integrated part-time employees with their regular full-timers during these periods.

If flexible scheduling, geared to current demand, is the objective, Noyes Publications, a small publishing company in New Jersey, provides a good model:

> At present there are four regular part-time employees [*out of twenty-four total*] handling the billing and typing invoices. Full-time employees are never hired for these positions because the volume of the firm's incoming mail orders fluctuates throughout the year.
>
> While part-time employees generally work four to five hours a day, they are free to skip a day or two if they have an outside commitment, or if they or their manager see that there is too little

work for them to do. Unlike their full-time colleagues, they are also free to report to work anytime from 8:00 A.M. to 9:30 A.M., so their flexible hours are one of the chief benefits they receive, along with the same fringe benefits as the full-time employees. Neither turnover or last-minute cancellations have been a problem, reports Griffin [*the office manager*].[11]

As more employers recognize the value of part-time work as a management tool, some organizations have begun to create special pools designed to rehire the organization's own former employees (either retirees or workers who have left because of the pressure of family responsibilities) on a part-time, on-call basis. This practice has provided an additional resource for managers faced with sporadic or seasonal staffing needs and is very popular with the employees involved.

Recruitment

In the previous section, we mentioned the significant improvement in the number and quality of job applicants that many employers report once they broaden their recruitment campaign to actively solicit part-timers and not just full-timers. The inclusion of part-timers not only expands the pool of potential applicants but also sends a signal to applicants for full-time positions that the organization is a supportive, innovative employer—one that they would like to work for.

Recruitment campaigns focusing on part-time can also target particular segments of the labor force, such as reentry women, seniors, students, and people with health limitations for whom full-time work would be difficult or impossible. An advertisement for secretaries run by the Walgreen Company's corporate office in suburban Deerfield, Illinois, produced so many qualified applicants that the company was able to fill the open positions and then set up a substitute pool as well. A Commonwealth of Massachusetts booklet prepared for managers attests to the effectiveness of advertising:

> The results from placing a classified ad for a part-time professional can be extraordinary. One advertisement for a part-time research position drew over 50 responses; 20 of those responding were "well-qualified for the job." A two-day-a-week, six month research position drew 83 responses, ten of which received high level ratings by the three person review team. For a midlevel position, another agency received 70 responses. In each case the résumés received were so good that they were passed around the agency and more than one of the respondents were hired.[12]

This is not always the case, however. Some employers have had mixed or negative results recruiting part-time employees. Unfortunately, it is not possible to tell whether the disappointing results were because of lack of interest within a particular labor pool, the conditions of employment associated with the positions being offered, or some other reason.

Cost Implications

In order to justify expanding the availability of part-time work, managers and supervisors need detailed information about costs. The expense associated with any position can be broken down into *direct costs* (base salary and employee benefits), *indirect costs* (administrative overhead, training, supervision, and facilities), and *program costs* (those associated with absenteeism, turnover, coverage, recruitment, and productivity).

Table 3-1 shows a breakdown of the costs in each of these three categories. It can be used to compare the costs associated with a regular full-time position and the costs associated with one or more part-time options that might be used to perform the same work. (Table 3-2 is a blank copy of this form that you may wish to use to do

Table 3-1.   Cost analysis by position: example.

			Half-Time		
		Current Cost of the Position	Current Employee	New Hire	New, Less-Experienced
I.	Direct costs				
	A. Base salary	$30,000.00	$15,000.00	$15,000.00	$10,500.00
	B. Employee benefits				
	1. Statutory				
	• Social Security (7.51% of first $48,000)	2,253.00	1,126.50	1,126.50	788.55
	• Unemployment insurance (2.3% of first $7,000)	161.00	161.00	161.00	161.00
	• Worker's compensation ($.85 per $100 of compensation)	255.00	127.50	127.50	89.25
	2. Compensatory				
	• Sick leave (2 weeks)	1,153.85	576.92	576.92	403.85
	• Vacation (3 weeks—current employee; 2 weeks—new hire)	1,730.77	865.38	576.92	403.85

(Continued)

Table 3-1. *(continued)*

	Current Cost of the Position	Half-Time		
		Current Employee	New Hire	New, Less-Experienced
• Holidays (10 days)	1,153.85	576.92	576.92	403.85
• Other				
3. Suplementary				
• Insurance				
Prorated life ($10,000)	50.00	25.00	25.00	25.00
Medical/dental ($125 deductible)	1,500.00	750.00	750.00	750.00
Long-term disability	250.00	125.00	125.00	85.00
• Pension (13% salary)	3,900.00	1,950.00	1,195.00	1,365.00
• Profit sharing (5%)	150.00	75.00	75.00	52.50
• Stock purchase options				
• Tax shelter annuities				
• Tuition payments				
• Discount purchase plans				
• Other				
Total direct costs	$42,557.47	$21,359.22	$21,070.76	$15,027.85
II. Indirect costs				
A. New hire administration			$ 150.00	$ 150.00
B. Training			500.00	500.00
C. Supervision	$2,000.00	$1,000.00	1,000.00	1,200.00
D. Square footage (80 square feet)	480.00	240.00	240.00	240.00
Total indirect costs	$2,480.00	$1,240.00	$1,890.00	$2,090.00
III. Program costs				
A. Absenteeism				
B. Turnover				
C. Coverage				
D. Recruitment				
E. Production rates				
Total program costs	$0.00	$0.00	$0.00	$0.00
TOTAL COSTS	$45,037.47	$22,599.22	$22,960.76	$17,117.85

Table 3-2. Cost analysis by position: worksheet.

	Current Cost: Full-Timer	Part-Time		
		___ Hours	___ Hours	___ Hours
I. Direct costs				
A. Base salary				
B. Employee benefits				
1. Statutory				
• Social security (___% of first $_____)				
• Unemployment insurance (___% of first $_____)				
• Worker's compensation (___ per $100 of compensation)				
2. Compensatory				
• Sick leave (___ weeks)				
• Vacation (___ weeks—current employee; ___ weeks—new hire)				
• Holidays (___ days)				
• Other				
3. Supplementary				
• Insurance Prorated life ($_____) Medical/dental ($_____ deductible) Long-term disability				
• Pension (___% salary)				
• Profit sharing (___%)				
• Stock purchase options				
• Tax shelter annuities				
• Tuition payments				
• Discount purchase plans				
• Other	_____	_____	_____	_____
Total direct costs				
II. Indirect costs				
A. New hire administration				
B. Training				
C. Supervision				
D. Square footage (_____ square feet)	_____	_____	_____	_____
Total indirect costs				

(Continued)

Table 3-2. *(continued)*

	Current Cost: Full-Timer	Part-Time ___ Hours	___ Hours	___ Hours
III. Program costs				
A. Absenteeism				
B. Turnover				
C. Coverage				
D. Recruitment				
E. Production rates	_____	_____	_____	_____
Total program costs	======	======	======	======
TOTAL COSTS				

your own cost analysis.) An item-by-item analysis such as this enables managers and supervisors to pinpoint the cost impact of using part-timers for any given position and, if necessary, adjust the conditions of employment in ways that will make the use of part-timers more cost-effective for the organization.

The following subsections analyze each of the three major cost areas listed in Table 3-1 in terms of its ramifications for part-time work and suggest ways to formulate a fair but cost-effective policy on the use of part-timers. This discussion will emphasize the cost implications that are of greatest concern to managers and supervisors—fringe benefits, administrative overhead, training, supervision, space and equipment use, absenteeism and turnover, and productivity.

Direct Costs   The category of direct costs includes base salary (which involves not only the relatively simple issue of pay for regular hours worked by part-timers but the more complicated issue of pay for overtime hours that they work) and fringe benefits.

Base salary. Regular part-timers should be paid a pro rata of what a full-timer with the same qualifications would make. This establishes an equitable foundation on which to build a program of integrated full- and part-time employment options. (Paying part-timers on a pro rata basis is in contrast to the assumption prevailing among employers until the mid-1970s that part-timers were compensated at a lower rate of pay than full-timers. It was also generally assumed that part-timers should be the first tier of employees to be laid off and that they need not receive benefits. As we shall see, all three of these assumptions are now being challenged.)

The growing use of *overtime* has become a cause for concern in many organizations today. Employers are increasingly using overtime as a cost-containment tool that allows them to expand operations without expanding the labor force. Unions defend this practice because many of their members want premium overtime pay. Even though other employees may *not* want the extra hours, they, too, must work these hours if the organization regularly uses overtime in this manner. As companies downsize significantly, employee burnout is often a result.

Overtime becomes a particularly sensitive issue for part-timers when management's expectation is that part-time employees will regularly work overtime at straight pay. When this is a "hidden agenda," it undermines the working relationship of part-timers and their employer. The scheduling requirements of the position should be spelled out in the basic contract. If the requirements change and a full-time schedule (or more than a full-time schedule) is really needed, then perhaps the part-time schedule should be expanded to more hours (say, 30–40) to include a second part-timer or converted into a shared arrangement. This is fairer than expecting the incumbent employee to regularly work more hours than were originally contracted for.

Employee benefits. As part-time workers have become a more important segment of the labor force, renewed attention has been paid to the conditions of work for regular part-timers. In particular, the issue of providing fringe benefits for less than full-time employees lies at the core of the debate about how to achieve flexibility in the workplace. Although such practices as compensating part-timers at a lower rate of pay than full-timers, laying them off ahead of full-timers, and denying them benefits have not disappeared, since the late 1970s there has been a slow trend toward improving the conditions of part-time work. These improvements include providing pro rata compensation (mentioned above) and giving part-time employees the same fringe benefits that full-timers receive.

A 1985 survey by Hewitt Associates of 484 nonunion private-sector employers showed that 49 percent of the respondents provide health insurance for part-time employees working 20–29 hours, 51 percent provide sick leave, 77 percent provide paid holidays, and 75 percent provide paid vacations.[13] Although the results of a 1987 Administrative Management Society survey of benefits offered to part-timers, shown in Figure 3-2, reflect different percentages than

Figure 3-2. Benefits offered to part-time employees.

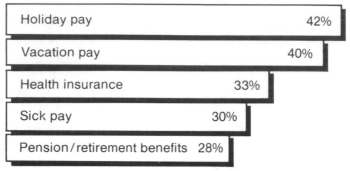

Holiday pay   42%

Vacation pay   40%

Health insurance   33%

Sick pay   30%

Pension/retirement benefits 28%

Percentages represent percent of companies.

SOURCE: Administrative Management Society, *Contract Labor Survey* (Trevose, Pa.: AMS, 1987), 10.

those found in the Hewitt Associates survey, they still indicate that significant numbers of employers *are* providing part-time employees with benefits comparable to what full-timers receive.

Mark Manin, a Massachusetts-based benefits consultant, suggests that organizations examining the issue of benefits for part-timers should keep three basic considerations in mind:

1. The question of whether to include or exclude part-time employees when it comes to a benefits program should be considered a strategic-planning issue and reflect the organization's economic environment, relevant demographic factors, and labor force needs.
2. It should be recognized that there has been increased pressure to include part-timers in benefits programs because these workers are becoming an increasingly important force in the workplace.
3. The overall trend in federal legislation is toward mandated and portable benefits, and it is reasonable to believe that legislation in this area will be forthcoming in the future.[14]

Since the cost of fixed benefits has been climbing for years, employers today are clearly concerned about containing this cost, eliminating duplication of coverage, and providing benefits that are really needed rather than frills. When it comes to part-timers, they are looking for ways to offer fringe benefits that are both equitable and cost-effective. One way to provide benefits for less than full-time workers is to prorate those benefits, in terms of either the cost or the amount of coverage. Another approach is to include these employees in flexible benefits plans. Flexible benefits, sometimes referred to as cafeteria plans, are benefits programs that give employees a choice in which benefits they will receive, within a certain value range.

Flexible benefits formulas have the potential for individualizing both the types of benefits an employee receives and the cost of those benefits. While growing interest in flexible benefits has encouraged those who advocate extending access to benefits coverage to all regular part-time employees, as of the late 1980s, the trend has not been in the direction of inclusion. The reasons are unclear, but between 60 percent and 90 percent of flexible benefits programs exclude all part-timers.[15] It may be that the shift to flexible benefits is coming at the same time as increased awareness of the need for cost containment and that the inclusion of an extra class of employee will most certainly cost more.

In the long run, however, exclusion may have a negative impact on other cost areas such as recruitment, turnover, productivity, and the organization's ability to be sufficiently flexible. As Manin[16] and others suggest, a comprehensive analysis of how a benefits strategy fits in with overall organizational objectives should be used as the basis for decisions in this area, and the current and future role of part-timers should be among the considerations.

Legislation relating to the issue of fringe benefits for part-time employees is emerging on both the state and federal levels. The Tax Reform Act of 1986 requires that employees who normally work 17.5 hours or more per week be counted in the nondiscrimination rules covering life and health benefits under Section 89 of the Internal Revenue Code. It also states that "a life or health plan could be discriminatory if the employer provided health benefit is reduced more than proportionately for employees who typically work less than 30 hours per week."[17]

In 1987, Sen. Edward M. Kennedy introduced a bill that would require employers to provide the same basic health benefits to part-time workers and their dependents as they provide to their full-time employees. In 1988 in the House, Rep. Pat Schroeder introduced the Part-Time and Temporary Employees Protection Act, which calls for inclusion for all employees on a prorata basis in whatever pension and health benefits are offered to regular full-time employees. The Schroeder bill also calls for prorating the cost of the benefits.

Various states, concerned about the growing number of people without health insurance, have also undertaken initiatives in this area. In April 1988, Massachusetts Gov. Michael Dukakis signed the country's first law guaranteeing health insurance to all residents of a state. The law will gradually introduce health care coverage for the residents of Massachusetts who are currently uninsured—both those who are working and those who are unemployed. Michigan, Maine, and Denver County, Colorado, are offering subsidies or other financial incentives to encourage small employers to begin providing health insurance. Oregon will offer tax credits to small employers that start providing coverage to previously uninsured employees; and a New Hampshire law now prohibits insurers from barring group insurance coverage to persons working 15 hours or half the normal workweek on a regular basis. It is unclear what effect legislative initiatives might have, but fairness and equity in the area of working conditions are clearly on a number of agendas.

In analyzing the cost implications to an organization of using regular part-time employees, it is helpful to look at the costs associated with a single position, as was illustrated in Table 3-1. For an employer, however, the *cumulative, or multiplier, effect* will be the most important factor. Most companies do not conduct detailed cost-benefit analyses in which they add up the costs of absenteeism or turnover and recruitment for particular positions and balance these costs off against productivity gains resulting from better scheduling or improved employee morale. Managers need to recognize the importance of attitude as it relates to the use of regular part-time, however, and push themselves to think beyond the extra administrative expense or the temptation to reduce costs by dropping a few employees from the insurance rolls. Such considerations as protecting the investment already made in current employees, avoiding the costs of recruitment, and determining the future potential of employees who may need temporary accommodation should be given equal weight in managers' assessment.

Fringe benefits differ from one company to another, but they always fall into three categories: statutory, compensatory, and supplementary. Using the cost analysis in Table 3-1, as an outline, let's consider some of the factors in each area as they relate to part-timers:

Statutory benefits. For part-timers, these benefits include Social Security, unemployment insurance, and worker's compensation insurance:

  ■ *Social Security.* This benefit is currently computed, for each employee, at 7.51 percent of income up to $48,000 a year (1989 ceiling). Employers incur extra expense only if they hire a new employee to fill the vacated hours and the total position pays more than the current ceiling.

■ *Unemployment insurance.* Although rates and limits vary from
state to state within the framework of federal legislation,
unemployment insurance is also computed on a per capita
basis. Since rates are affected by layoffs, if voluntary part-
time options are available to enable the employer to achieve
cutbacks in payroll cost and minimize layoffs, this may help to
keep the organization's "experience rating" low.

■ *Worker's compensation insurance.* While mandated, this insurance is determined by the particular policy carried by the
employer. It is usually based on a percentage of payroll, which
means that part-timers do not cost more than full-time employees.

■ *Compensatory benefits.* Wages paid for time not worked—
such as sick leave, holidays, and vacation—fall into this category. They are generally prorated for part-timers so that the
cost is comparable to the cost for full-time employees. In some
cases, employers have reported savings in this benefit area as
a result of offering part-time options. The State of California's
Department of Motor Vehicles observed that sick leave used
by its employees who had worked full-time and had reduced
their hours as part of a 1977–1979 pilot program on permanent
part-time employment dropped from 4.06 percent to 3.35 percent during the course of the project.[18] That is, for the employee working part-time and earning $15,000 a year, the
savings would be $106 a year (4.06% − 3.35% × $15,000 =
$106).

Supplementary benefits. This benefit area is more complex and less
standardized than the others. These benefits supplement an employee's income by providing some or all of the following: insurance
(medical, dental, life, long-term disability), pension, profit sharing,
stock purchase options, tax-sheltered annuities, tuition payments,
and discount purchase plans. From an employer's standpoint, the
most important, and most costly, of these benefits are medical and
dental insurance and pensions.

■ *Medical and dental insurance.* These two types of insurance
coverage are major considerations for both the employer and
the employee. Employees need access to group coverage in
order to afford health insurance. For the employee, this coverage represents one of the most costly kinds of fringe benefit.
In order to include regular part-time employees in health
insurance plans without doubling their premiums, many em-

ployers have begun to prorate the cost of health benefits according to hours worked. This kind of approach is equitable to all parties and is compatible with the concept of flexible benefits.

- *Pension plan.* After medical and dental insurance, an organization's pension plan is the most important supplementary benefit. Pensions are computed as a percentage of salary, and the cost can be automatically prorated.

Indirect Costs With respect to regular positions, indirect costs include administrative costs (both ongoing and for new hires), training, supervision, and space and equipment use.

Administrative overhead. The cost of ongoing administrative overhead is slightly higher per labor hour for part-time employees than it is for full-timers. On the other hand, the record keeping associated with adding new hires to the payroll and removing employees who have left the organization is minimized by retaining employees who would have resigned to seek part-time work elsewhere. These savings should be included in the organization's overall assessment of the impact of part-time on administrative costs.

Training. Although many employers expect training costs to be higher for part-time employees, actual experience reveals mixed results. A 1978 study of private-sector use of permanent part-time employment reported the following: "[*I*]n a majority of cases, employers' training experiences with part-time workers are the same as with full-time workers in terms of administrative cost of effort. When there are differences, costs are as likely to be lower for part-time workers as higher."[19] Another source indicates that "Twenty to thirty percent of all users have marginally higher training costs."[20] Some employers feel that it takes longer to recover their training costs because part-timers are on the job fewer hours. On the other hand, one reason for offering part-time options is to retain good employees so that training costs will not be lost permanently.

Supervision. Supervision of part-timers can be complicated by special communications needs, since these employees are not always available, and extra attention must be paid to the design of work schedules. Furthermore, if the hours originally worked by a single full-time employee are split between two part-timers, then the number of employees requiring supervision will also increase. Since most managers have had only limited experience with supervising and evaluating part-timers, many express concerns about increased demands on supervisors. Widespread use of part-time is still too new to assess how valid these concerns are, what the cost ramifications might be, or whether the problems will disappear as more managers and supervisors become comfortable with supervising employees on a variety of schedules and learn more about what kinds of part-time schedules are most appropriate to particular staffing needs.

Space and equipment. Whether or not space and equipment are properly used when regular part-time employment is expanded depends on management's willingness to analyze the needs of the tasks and schedule employees' use of space and equipment accordingly. Some employers fear that having more employees automatically means using more equipment and more space. In reality, space and equipment can be shared, and the use of both can be extended through the proper integration of a variety of schedules.

Program Costs The cost factors in this category that will be of greatest interest to most employers are the costs associated with absenteeism and turnover and the effect of part-time employment on productivity.

Absenteeism and turnover. The occurrence of absenteeism and turnover tend to decline when regular part-time options are available. If a particular job classification has exceptionally high rates of either absenteeism or turnover, it may be precisely because employees holding that position have difficulty with a full-time schedule (because of heavy pressure, tedium, or a conflict with other responsibilities)—making the availability of regular part-time positions an ideal solution.

Productivity. Part-time's impact on productivity is a human resources management cost variable. Whether or not having the option of working part-time positively affects a company's productivity is hard to prove or disprove. Part of the problem lies in the difficulty of defining *productivity,* particularly in the service industries.

Where managers and supervisors have been surveyed, their subjective opinions and anecdotal evidence seem to weigh on the positive side. Most agree that absenteeism is reduced by proper use of part-time and that part-timers are generally task-oriented and have a high level of energy and commitment. It is common to hear such comments as: "I sacrifice some convenience. I have to be a little more organized, but I get a lot more productivity"; "[B]ecause working part-time is important to her I get an unusual person for a bargain price"; and "I see part-time work as a management tool that makes people more efficient—both the part-timers and their supervisors. I use part-time to raise the quality of work in this office."[21]

With respect to the entire range of cost factors associated with the use of part-time employment, the grand total of each employer's "balance sheet" will be determined by a multitude of factors specific to the individual organization's pattern of use. With support from top management, careful planning and policy development, and effective training of supervisory personnel, the savings side should begin to expand as the organization's experience with less than full-time options grows.

Public and Private Policy Barriers

Sometimes existing policy (both the organization's own internal policies and those of the federal government) can constitute a barrier to new forms of part-time employment. This type of barrier tends to pose a problem in cases where an employer offers part-time options for older workers or even develops an on-call, part-time pool of its own retirees or other ex-employees, as Bankers Life and Casualty Company, Continental Bank, The Travelers Corporation, Corning Glass Works, Atlantic Richfield Company, and other companies have done. These pools are used for peak-period coverage, as a source of substitutes for vacationing or sick workers, or in job classifications that have high turnover or absenteeism.

However, most pension plans today contain two types of provisions that discourage senior employees' working part-time either as a way of phasing in to retirement or after retirement. First, pension benefits are generally tied not only to an employee's length of service but also to the pay level reached during the last few years of employment. It is this latter criterion that adversely affects the employee who might want to reduce work time—and pay—during the final years of a career. Employees who work fewer hours in the last several years of their work life are then penalized by a reduction in their retirement income. Second, the pension provisions of some organizations prohibit the company from making both salary and pension payments to the same employee at the same time.

Employers must eliminate these sorts of barriers if they want to facilitate phased retirement or offer attractive part-time options to their senior employees. For example, The Travelers Corporation recently changed its pension plan to permit retirees to work 960 hours annually instead of 480 hours. Chapter 5 includes two excellent models that show how senior employees can be allowed to reduce their hours and work part-time before retirement without diminishing their pensions.

In addition to the barriers so often established by the provisions of an organization's own pension plan, the federal government erects its own barrier to part-time employment for seniors in the form of the Social Security "earnings test." The earnings test now in effect places unduly restrictive limitations on the amount that retirees can earn without having the Social Security benefits taxed. There is growing support, both in the Congress and in the Department of Health and Human Services, to repeal this law. It is expected that in the near future, it will be removed as a barrier to the employment of older workers.

Management Attitudes

Some of management's negative attitudes about part-time employees have already been discussed. It should be stressed, however, that on the whole, managers who have had experience with part-timers are enthusiastic. In a 1983 study of part-time employment conducted by New York State, 214 supervisors and personnel officers were sent survey forms. Responses from 115 indicated that 65 percent of the personnel officers viewed part-time favorably, as did 71 percent of the supervisors with part-time staff and 57 percent of those without part-timers. Supervisors also reported either no difference in job performance or better job performance when part-time employees were compared to full-time employees.[22]

A very important question for department heads and supervisors is whether using part-timers will adversely affect department budgets and personnel allocations. If part-time is to be successfully integrated with full-time employment, managers should have the authority to allocate the necessary *number* of hours among both full- and part-time employees as they see fit—without worrying that the use of part-time will result in a diminished allocation.

Concerns about communication with part-time employees and having to spend extra supervisory time are also commonly expressed. These topics are discussed later, in the section entitled Special Considerations for Supervisors and Managers.

When asked what kinds of help they would like in expanding the use of part-time, managers and supervisors express a desire for top-level support, information on where and how part-time has been used successfully in other places, and supervisory training.

Union Attitudes

Until very recently, unions had a consistently negative view of part-time employment. It was perceived as being exploitive and undermining full-time employment. When job sharing emerged in the mid-

1970s, a few unions recognized it as an exception to traditional forms of part-time, in that it retained the definition of the position as being full-time and extended the benefits of full-time employment to part-time personnel. Since the mid-1970s, one labor group, Service Employees International Union (SEIU), has taken the lead in negotiating policies for part-timers and developing program approaches that protect the working conditions of part-time employees. The objective is to expand opportunities for voluntary part-time employment and to integrate part-time and full-time staff. In general, unions whose membership expresses a need for good part-time work have begun to support that demand. Those whose membership does not express such a need continue to view part-time with suspicion.

Employee Attitudes

The few polls that have dealt with the issue of part-time as an employee option have indicated that whether they currently want to work part-time or not, most employees recognize that some of their co-workers do need this option and that at some future date, they themselves may, too. Consequently, they support the development of policy that offers opportunities for voluntary, equitable part-time employment. A New York State poll of 13,812 workers in 200 agencies shows that over two thirds of the 2,947 responding employees approve the development of more part-time jobs.[23] This employee interest has been the driving force behind the evolution of new forms of regular part-time work such as job sharing and phased retirement and the V-time programs, which will be discussed in detail in subsequent chapters.

Should Your Organization Try Regular Part-Time?

The tools provided in this section can help you analyze your organization's staffing and scheduling needs and determine whether, in light of those needs, you should begin a program of regular part-time employment or expand regular part-time options if part-time is already used sporadically within your organization.

The accompanying group of profiles entitled Organizational Experience With Regular Part-Time shows how and why a program of regular part-time employment was implemented in three organizations and what impact the use of this work-time option has had. As you read these profiles, notice whether and how the experience of these companies with regular part-time might be relevant to the needs of your own organization.

ORGANIZATIONAL EXPERIENCE WITH REGULAR PART-TIME

Citibank N.A.

Description: Citibank is the worldwide financial services subsidiary of Citicorp. Headquartered in New York City, it employs 48,000 people domestically and 42,000 overseas.

Reason for Using Regular Part-Time: This work-time option has been available to nonexempt staff for many years, particularly in clerical and accounting positions. It enables management to better handle the peaks and valleys of the work load.

In the early 1980s, Citibank began offering regular part-time to professionals, or "officers," as the bank calls them. The initial group were predominantly women, who often were leaving to have children but who wanted to be able to return with the same rank and responsibilities. However, the program has also been used by men who want to reduce their hours for personal reasons as well as by employees who want to ease into retirement.

The bank benefits from this arrangement by being able to retain capable employees who might otherwise disappear for long periods of time or leave permanently.

Implementation Process: The use of part-time is described in Citibank's personnel handbook. Decisions to employ, reassign, or promote a part-time professional are tested against several criteria to decide if the overall level of responsibility for a position can be met on a part-time basis. Approvals by business managers or personnel officers are specified in the handbook.

Impact to Date: The regular part-time option meets the needs of those employees who have workday energies that they must devote to other responsibilities. Providing for this scheduling arrangement enables the bank to keep valued staff as well as adapt to changes in the economy and consequent changes in work force needs.

Citibank has found that people who have gone to part-time often return to full-time when their personal circumstances change.

SOURCE: Phone conversation with the assistant vice-president, corporate human relations (June 1988).

Levi Strauss & Co.

Description: An international apparel manufacturer employing 1,600 people at corporate headquarters in San Francisco.

Reason for Using Regular Part-Time: This option is only one of many alternative hours arrangements that have made Levi Strauss & Co. a pacesetter in the field of flexible work options. The company also offers compressed workweeks, telecommuting, phased retirement, flexitime, and summer hours, with the mutual agreement of employees and their supervisors. Regular part-time is yet another example of Levi's respectful and trusting treatment of its work force.

Implementation Process: Although the category of regular part-time is defined in the employees' personnel handbook, there is no stated policy or prescribed procedure for requesting regular part-time. Employees work out the arrangement with their manager or with the personnel department in their area. A minimum of 20 hours per week must be worked.

Sometimes, the job itself only requires part-time hours. When the job requires full-time hours, a job-sharing plan is often agreed upon.

Impact to Date: Job sharing was established in 1981. Regular part-time existed for many years before then. Most part-timers are in accounting and secretarial positions, although professional-level jobs have also been reduced to part-time or shared. Vacation and sick leave benefits are worked out proportionally. Health benefits for part-timers are the same as for full-timers.

Employees see the hours options as a recognition of their good work. Managers believe that these options contribute to productivity and good employee morale.

SOURCE: Conversations with the staff of the corporate personnel department and the manager of policy and EEO programs (June 1988).

Harbor Sweets

Description: Chocolate-making company, located in Salem, Massachusetts, with approximately 150 employees.

Reason for Using Regular Part-Time: To attract and retain committed employees and to accommodate employees' needs for flexible and reduced working arrangements. Almost all of the employees work a 20-hour schedule.

Implementation Process: There is no formal process for requesting part-time. A schedule is arranged and responsibilities agreed upon when a new employee is hired. Workers receive paid vacation and a chance to buy in a group health and disability insurance on a prorated basis, according to the number of hours they work. Employee meetings are held four or five times a year to discuss company business, and employee suggestions for improvements are encouraged and acted upon.

Impact to Date: Hiring emphasis has been on recruiting the hard-to-employ, the elderly, the handicapped, or non-English-speaking applicants and accommodating work schedules to meet their needs as well as those of the company. The result had been the formation of an effective, committed work force. Employees suggested work sharing and postponement of a bonus during an unprofitable year. The next year sales were up, and profits were shared.

President Ben Strohecker says, "Through total trust, choosing to allow people to stretch to their potential, and by letting them know it's O.K. to make a mistake, you get unbelievable results."

SOURCE: Anne Driscoll, "Candy Maker in Massachusetts Asks Even Part-Timers for Work Advice," *New York Times* (Mar. 20, 1988), 30.

Table 3-3 is a questionnaire that lists the most significant problems that organizations are usually trying to solve when they introduce or expand regular part-time options. If you answer "yes" repeatedly on this questionnaire, chances are your company would benefit from supplementing its program of full-time employment with a program of carefully selected part-time options designed to better meet its scheduling and staffing needs and the needs of its employees.

Assuming the use of regular part-timers does appear warranted, you can complete the worksheet shown in Figure 3-3. It will help you pinpoint the specific problems you wish to solve by introducing or expanding the use of regular part-time and weigh the pros and cons of such a move.

Table 3-3.   Regular part-time questionnaire.

Would Regular Part-Time Benefit Your Organization?

	Yes	No
Have good employees left the organization because part-time is not an option?		
Are some departments or job classifications experiencing above-average turnover or absenteeism?		
In order to handle the normal work load, have you had to overstaff in some areas or use an excessive number of substitutes?		
Must your organization's schedules conform to work demand rather than having all tasks performed according to a standaradized schedule?		
Is 50 percent of any department or job classification comprised of women of childbearing age?		
Is expanding coverage or extending your company's hours of operation an objective?		
If expanding coverage or extending hours of operation is an objective, would a part-time shift or the addition of some part-time personnel facilitate achieving this objective?		
Is upward mobility to the point of "plateauing" a problem in your company?		
If you are concerned about plateauing, would it help any if some of your mid- or upper-level people wanted to cut back their hours?		
Is burnout a problem for any of your company's employees?		
Would some senior employees prefer a part-time schedule?		
Are there positions for which it is difficult to recruit good applicants?		

Introducing or Expanding the Use of Regular Part-Time Employment

The steps for introducing or expanding the use of any new work-time option are basically the same. In the case of regular part-time, in addition to developing a policy and a program, management must remove barriers in current policy and find ways to deal with attitudinal inhibitors. This latter is particularly important because of the widespread bias against part-time work and part-time workers. But even companies that ostensibly have a policy against using regular part-time employees have generally made some exceptions to that rule or authorized ad hoc part-time arrangements. At some point, however, this becomes an unsatisfactory way of contracting with

Figure 3-3.   Regular part-time worksheet.

Assessing the Need for Regular Part-Time

List the main reasons why you are considering using or expanding the use of regular part-time employment:

1. _____

    _____

    _____

2. _____

    _____

    _____

3. _____

    _____

    _____

4. _____

    _____

    _____

List what you see as the advantages and disadvantages of regular part-time:

Pros: _____

    _____

    _____

    _____

(Continued)

Figure 3-3.   *(continued)*

employees, and the development of enabling policy is the logical next move.

Gain Support for the Program

The first and most important step in this process is to gain the support of top management for making the change. It is important that the move toward using regular part-time be viewed as a positive action rather than a reactive one, since policy language relating to regular part-time employment will provide the basis later on for the use of more specialized forms of regular part-time, such as job sharing, V-time, and phased retirement.

Bringing middle managers and labor representatives into the development process is a way to gain their support as well. This will be critical once the policy is developed because it will largely be implemented by middle managers and supervisors.

Set Up the Program's Administration

If this is to be an active, companywide program, appoint a coordinator to provide information and technical assistance to managers and interested employees. It is essential in the initial stages to have someone responsible for seeing that the pieces fall into place. Depending on the size of the organization and how supportive or resistant the company culture is expected to be, forming a task force might also be considered.

Design the Program

Designing a program for the use of regular part-time employment is a two-step process, involving the removal of barriers in existing policies and union contracts and the creation of an effective new supporting policy on regular part-time. We will now consider each of these steps, together with the policy issues that must be addressed in each one.

Eliminate Current Barriers The first step in designing the program should be to review current personnel policies and union contracts to identify and eliminate any internal constraints on the use of regular part-time schedules. The following policy issues often create obstacles and must be addressed in order to enable the organization to use regular part-time arrangements:

Head count. This system, which requires counting each part-time employee the same as a full-timer against personnel authorizations, hampers supervisors who want to use regular part-time assignments. A system of full-time equivalency allows for more flexibility; it expresses department allocations in terms of the number of hours worked rather than the number of persons doing the work. Some companies have reinterpreted their head count policy, authorizing the use of "half-heads"; others have begun to reexamine the appropriateness of this kind of policy in light of current staffing and scheduling needs.

Compensation. In general, a policy that calls for disparate levels of compensation between part-timers and full-timers in the same job classification and with the same level of skill and experience presents an obstacle to using regular part-time as an employment option. (See the earlier subsection entitled Direct Costs for a detailed analysis of how fringe benefits can be handled equitably for regular part-time employees.)

Reductions in force. In many organizations, policy dictates that during a work force reduction, all part-timers must be laid off first, regardless of length of service, special qualifications, or other considerations. If an organization wants to encourage the use of reduced work-time options, this policy should be changed so that part-timers are laid off according to the same formula used for reducing the number of full-time employees.

Impact on retirement income. As noted earlier in the chapter, in order for part-time to be a viable option for current senior employees, policy should be developed to ensure that retirement income will not be negatively affected if employees reduce their work time before retirement.

Barriers to working part-time after retirement (for example, provisions that prohibit a company from making both salary and pension payments to the same employee at the same time) should also be examined to eliminate potential problems in setting up a part-time pool of the organization's retirees.

Create New Policy   The second step in designing the program is to formulate new policy that supports the use of regular part-time as an employment option. The following are some of the issues that must be addressed:

Voluntary nature of part-time employment. Policy and procedure language should clearly state that part-time is not mandatory and that full-timers are protected against involuntary conversion of their jobs to part-time.

Budget policy. Developing policy that details how an expanded use of part-time will affect supervisors' budgets is a critical question. This relates to the issue of head count but also includes such questions as whether caps will be set on the number of positions that can be restructured and what will happen to percentages of work hours left over if employees work more than half-time but less than full-time.

Eligibility. The issue of who and how many is one of the important questions that employers raise about regular part-time. Will regular part-time be an option in all departments and for all job classifications, including supervisory ones?

Most organizations retain the stereotype of part-time employment as an appropriate mode for low-level or peripheral employees but make it a rule that supervisory positions cannot be worked on a part-time basis. They cling to the idea that managerial, professional, and highly trained technical employees should make a commitment of *more* than full-time. The debate rages: Should exempt-level personnel, particularly those in supervisory capacities, be allowed to work on less than a full-time basis?

As experience grows, attitudes change, and the trend today is in favor of options and flexibility. In New York State, where various kinds of regular part-time work have been pioneered since the mid-1970s, as many as one fourth of the part-time employees have supervisory responsibilities. Other employers, too, have used both part-time and job sharing successfully in supervisory positions.

Priscilla H. Claman's 1980 study of part-time employment concerned specifically with the performance of part-time supervisors defines three models of part-time supervision:

1. The "consultant" model, in which supervisors advise and coach their employees instead of keeping a close watch on them.
2. Part-time supervisors of part-time personnel, where the work group often functions as a specialized unit tangential to the primary function of the organization.
3. First-line supervisors of full-time personnel.

The study concluded that part-time supervisors functioned well where the first two models were used but that job sharing was probably a better arrangement for first-line supervisors whose subordinates were on full-time schedules.[24] Recognizing the need for part-time options in higher-level jobs, some employers, such as the Federal Reserve Bank and Ameritech Corporation, have developed job-sharing and part-time options specifically for their managerial and professional staff.

Probationary period. If the part-timer is a new hire, either the probationary period can be the same as for a full-timer, or if there would appear to be insufficient time to evaluate the employee's ability because of fewer hours on the job, a longer period may be stipulated.

Seniority. A formula for accrual of seniority by part-timers needs to be defined.

Reversibility and other changes in work schedule. As we've noted, most employees who request a reduction from a full- to a part-time schedule, as well as many applicants who are only interested in part-time when they first start working for an organization, want a less than full-time job because of a temporary need, such as caring for young children, the desire to gain new skills or finish their education, illness, or burnout. A procedure for returning to or moving toward full-time should be established. It probably will not be possible to make such a change in status "on demand," but establishing a preferred list and an application process assures that the employee is viewed as being a full-fledged worker on a part-time schedule, not as a different category of worker.

Supervisors may feel that the department needs more work hours than the part-time arrangement provides. Rather than authorizing supervisors to arbitrarily require part-timers to work more hours, some organizations define a process that attempts to accommodate the part-time arrangement either through job sharing or by filling the hours some other way. Justification of the need for increased hours from a program standpoint is another way of ensuring that there is a legitimate reason for the proposed increase.

Refer to Table 3-4, which is a program design checklist. It provides an overview of the key design issues associated with the introduction or expansion of part-time options and can be used to record your progress in dealing with each of these issues.

Develop Resource Materials

The organization needs to develop one set of resource materials targeted toward managers and supervisors and another targeted toward the company's employees and applicants.

Table 3-4.   Program design checklist: regular part-time.

Key Design Issues	Notes
Eliminating current barriers	
☐ Head count	
☐ Compensation	
☐ Reductions in force	
☐ Impact on retirement income	
Creating new policy	
☐ Voluntary nature of part-time employment	
☐ Budget policy	
☐ Eligibility	
☐ Probationary period	
☐ Seniority	
☐ Reversibility and other changes in work schedule	

Guidelines for managers and supervisors. Because of long-held negative stereotypes about part-timers, it is particularly important that the guidelines developed for managers and supervisors reflect top management's support and encouragement for utilizing part-time options—hopefully at all levels. Explicit, written guidelines provide a valuable resource for middle-level management. (Sample policy language is shown in Figure 3-4.)

Guidelines for managers and supervisors should include an introduction that gives an overview of standard part-time employment and its variations: job sharing, phased or partial retirement, V-time, leave time, and work sharing. This section should include information on the advantages that accrue to the organization from widening the types of available work schedule (such as increased flexibility and improved employee morale) and the benefits that managers and supervisors can expect (such as a recruitment edge, retention of good employees, and decreased absenteeism).

Managers' and supervisors' rights should be clearly articulated. They should be reassured that using part-time employees will not

Figure 3-4. Sample policy on regular part-time employment.

Full-Time Employees

Full-time employees:

- Are hired to fill a position that requires at least 40 hours' work per week.
- Receive a weekly salary, subject to withholding, according to company policy and the current salary structure and ranges.
- Are eligible for benefits and for participation in company plans, as outlined in the "Key to Employee Benefits" booklet and the benefits policies.

Part-Time Employees

Part-time employees:

- Are hired to fill a position that requires 20 or more hours but less than 40 hours work per week (accumulating at least 1,000 hours worked per year).
- Receive a prorated salary, based on the number of hours worked and subject to withholding, according to company policy and the current salary structure and ranges.
- Are eligible for benefits and for participation in company plans, as outlined in the "Key to Employee Benefits" booklet and the benefits policies.

SOURCE: *Survey of Private Sector Work and Family Policy* (San Francisco: New Ways to Work, 1986), 28–29.

adversely affect their department's personnel allocations or budget. Their rights in terms of approving or disapproving a request, terminating or reversing the arrangement if it is unsatisfactory, and increasing hours if the agreed-upon arrangement is insufficient should be described in detail.

Employee rights should also be discussed. It should be stressed that these workers are regular employees on a part-time schedule; they should not be viewed as second-class employees because of their reduced hours. Reinforce the fact that although a part-time schedule does affect salary, leave, and other kinds of employment conditions that relate to the number of hours worked, it does not affect status and tenure-related issues.

A step-by-step procedure for responding to requests for a reduced schedule should be provided. The example that follows is not intended to be specific to a particular organization's needs but is presented for guideline purposes only.

1. *Request information from personnel.* The personnel department should be able to provide policies and procedures relating to regular part-time employment.

2. *Ask the employee to submit the request in writing.* The request should include a suggested beginning date, an estimate of how long the employee would like to work part-time, and a suggested scheduling arrangement. If the employee is interested in job sharing, this information should be included.

3. *Meet with the employee and discuss the request.* Try to surface any potential problem areas; for example, if the employee is a supervisor, what does the record show about supervisory problems that might be even worse with a reduced schedule? Or can the employee's strengths overcome possible difficulties associated with supervising on a part-time basis? Discuss the time frame for the decision and any next steps.

4. *Decide.* Proceed as follows in making the decision:

- Talk with other supervisors of part-time employees and current part-timers. They will be able to offer practical advice that may be of considerable help. Remember that the single most important factor in the successful use of any form of part-time is the support of the immediate supervisor.
- Determine whether the needs of the position in question could best be served by having one or more part-timers working

independently or whether a job-sharing arrangement would be preferable.

■ Consider the potential for success in terms of the employee's past performance (experience indicates that employees who are effective workers as full-timers are also effective as part-timers) and his or her reasons for wanting to reduce work time (if the reasons are work-related—for example, a poor match between skills and job requirements or a personality problem—reducing the schedule may not have the desired effect; if the reason is stress, outside pressures, illness, or a need to branch out, part-time may well alleviate the difficulty).

Information materials for employees and applicants. Resource materials must also be developed for employees and applicants interested in working less than full-time. They will be interested in such issues as:

■ *Eligibility*. Who is eligible to request a part-time schedule?
■ *Financial impact*. Can the employee afford to work part-time? Financial impact worksheets—including information on compensation, fringe benefits, taxes, and retirement benefits—can help employees make this assessment and help managers promote the program. One employer's resource materials provide a breakdown of how various time reductions would affect an employee's gross and net pay. It covers such fine points as the fact that because an employee's taxes would drop with a 10 percent time reduction, a 10 percent cut in gross pay would result in less than a 10 percent reduction in net pay. (Sample financial impact worksheets are presented in Chapter 6.)
■ *Job-related impact*. What effect will the reduced schedule have on the worker's employment status and chances for advancement?
■ *Process*. How does a full-time employee apply for or request a reduced schedule?

An information sheet or booklet outlining the questions and answers relating to these issues is particularly helpful if part-time is going to be actively promoted as an employment option.

Announce the Program

Management should open channels of communication as soon as policy has been established. Many good policies on regular part-time are seldom used because employees don't know they are there. If regular part-time is to serve as a means of enabling an organization to respond flexibly to changing conditions, it must be perceived as an integral component of the organization's human resources policy.

An announcement is also essential to forestall employee apprehensions about why the policy is being introduced. Management will have to stress that this is a voluntary employee option, designed to respond to the changing needs of the work force as well as the changing needs of the organization.

Promote the Program

Traditional management attitudes about part-time employment have a mirror image in employees' perceptions of working part-time. Even those workers who would prefer a part-time schedule are often skeptical about the possible negative effects that reducing work time temporarily may have on their career advancement and job security. Most accept the fact that they will probably be "on hold," or slowed down in their advancement within the organization, while they are working fewer hours, but they need assurance that they will not be shelved for good. Middle managers and supervisors must provide this assurance.

If the company has an employee newsletter, it can be used to describe success stories and promote the regular part-time program on an ongoing basis.

Evaluate the Program

Although few organizations have bothered to conduct an evaluation of their reduced work-time programs, this can be very helpful in identifying what is effective and what isn't, where the cost savings are and how they can be enhanced, how supervisors and employees feel about regular part-time and what improvements they might suggest, and so forth.

Fine-Tune the Program

Any human resources program has glitches when it is new. As these become apparent, either through the evaluation process or from day-to-day observation, they must be dealt with. A process for fine-tuning should be agreed upon at the outset.

Table 3-5 lists some typical problems that arise when an organization uses part-timers, together their solutions that have been found to be effective.

Table 3-5. Examples of problems with regular part-time and their solutions.

Problem Indicators	Possible Solutions
Coverage is inadequate during peak hours, mornings, or late afternoons.	Arrange for coverage by a co-worker or subordinate; consider filling the remainder of the job; change the employee's schedule.
Coverage is too heavy during slow periods.	Review work scheduling; determine whether work flow patterns should or can be changed. Revise employee schedules, taking the unit's peak work load into consideration.
There is not enough time to meet with the staff as a group.	Set a core time each week when all staff members are on the job.
A co-worker resents that the part-time employee leaves "early."	Be sure that the schedule is not leaving the work unit short of staff during busy hours; make necessary schedule adjustments. Explain that the employee is following the approved schedule. Remind co-workers that part-time employees receive only a percentage of full-time pay and accruals.
Co-workers complain that when answering the employee's telephone, they never know when to say he or she will be in.	Post the part-time employee's schedule in a convenient location (near the telephone) so co-workers can tell callers when the employee will be in.
The employee feels left out of the mainstream of the unit's functions. The employee feels that he or she is uninformed on agency or office policy, procedures, or happenings that full-time employees take for granted.	Be sure that the employee works with other employees on projects or assignments. Look for patterns in meeting schedules, office communications, and informal networks that isolate the employee. Make sure that the part-time employee is properly oriented to the job, agency, and people.
A co-worker complains about handling calls and problems when the part-time employee is out.	Review the co-worker's decisions about what needs to be handled immediately and what can wait for the part-time employee. Set guidelines in this area. Determine whether the schedule arrangement (such as two workdays followed by three days off) is causing problems. Consider ways to distribute urgent matters more equitably. Consider that the

SOURCE: Adapted with permission from *Part-Time Schedules: A Guide for NYS Supervisors and Managers* (Albany: New York State Department of Civil Service, 1985), 31–32.

(Continued)

Table 3-5. *(continued)*

Problem Indicators	Possible Solutions
	absence of full-time employees from the office might be contributing to the problem. Change the part-time employee's schedule.
The part-time employee isn't taken seriously.	Convey by attitude, words, and assignments that the employee is a valuable and respected part of the unit. Be sure that people deal with the part-time employee on matters under his or her jurisdiction; don't let people go around the employee. See whether anything in the employee's behavior is contributing to the image.

Special Considerations for Supervisors and Managers

The key to successful use of regular part-time is the manager. A New York State Department of Civil Service publication on part-time employment notes:

> As fiscal resources diminish and pressures for productivity and quality of worklife increase, managers must find better ways to manage two of their most valuable resources: people and time. One way that production and workforce satisfaction can be increased is by increasing the options for linking people and time.[25]

For managers and supervisors, this means learning more about redesigning work schedules, supervising a work unit that encompasses a variety of full and reduced schedules, and evaluating workers based on how they are performing within this context. For most managers today, this is a new and relatively untapped area of expertise—but one that it is vital for them to master if their organizations are to become truly flexible.

Managers and supervisors will require training to develop this sort of expertise. Most of them, as noted, have little experience in using part-time schedules or supervising part-time employees in anything other than low-level positions. Those who have not had direct experience with part-timers generally have negative attitudes about part-time work and part-time workers and seldom think of reduced work-time schedules as a potentially powerful management tool.

Because the role of the supervisor is critical to the successful use of part-time employment, training in this area can be absolutely essential to integrating full- and part-time scheduling arrangements, especially if long-range plans include using specialized forms of regular part-time such as job sharing, phased retirement, work sharing, or V-time. Areas in which training is particularly important are:

- Management's objectives in expanding the use of reduced work time.
- Previous experience with part-time in other similar companies or in other departments within the organization.
- Redesigning work schedules and channels of communication.
- Personnel policy issues relating to part-timers.
- Fiscal policies relating to the use of part-timers.
- Supervising and evaluating part-timers.

The balance of this section examines several of these key issues in greater detail.

Analyzing job/task and work flow. Setting up a work schedule properly from the start based on an analysis of job/task and work flow is critical to being able to manage a part-time employee and evaluate his or her performance, particularly if the part-time employee was previously a full-timer. Too often, employers have authorized a reduction in schedule hoping that the same amount of work could be accomplished in fewer hours. The result is generally failure—or a totally burned out employee. For their part, in their desire for a reduced schedule, employees sometimes "bite off more than they can chew," promising to accomplish in 20 hours what can only be done in 30. Work schedules should be carefully discussed before a part-time arrangement is agreed upon or failure will have been built in from the outset.

Even if a schedule is initially successful, it may have to be redesigned at some point because of changes in the work load or flow. What started out as a part-time schedule might come to make more sense as a full-time shared position. Or 25 hours a week might become more appropriate than 20 or 30.

A supervisor considering a request that would leave part of a job title vacant must make a variety of decisions: what percentage of full-time is appropriate to the needs of the employee and those of the department; how the new schedule will fit with other employees' work flow; which tasks will be prioritized in the new schedule, which can be completed by someone else, which will not be done or will be postponed or rescheduled; and what kind of part-time schedule would work best. Part-timers can be scheduled in various ways, including: a half-day every day, covering mornings, afternoons, peak hours, or a combination of these; two and a half days each week; two full days one week and three full days the next; one week on and one week off; two weeks on and two weeks off. Whatever schedule is initially agreed upon, it should be evaluated at the end of a trial period and rearranged if necessary.

Designing good channels of communication. Not only designing but *using* good channels of communication is another important aspect of managing a mix of part- and full-time employees. With expanded use of flexible full- and part-time schedules, opportunities for communication between co-workers and between supervisor and subordinates are less frequent. Communication is also the key to successful coordination of activities and must be actively encouraged. Posting daily schedules can be very helpful, particularly if employees do a lot of off-site work or if schedules vary from week to week. Setting meeting dates well in advance so that notices of them do not fall through the cracks can also be important. Part-time employees often find that it is helpful to their job performance for their co-workers or supervisor to be able to contact them during nonwork hours if the situation demands it. This should be defined as a privilege, however, and it is one that should not be abused by those at the workplace.

Evaluating part-time employees. Evaluation of part-timers should take the same form as evaluation of full-timers. Their accomplishments should not be compared to those of a full-timer in the same position, however, but should instead be assessed in light of the way tasks and objectives were quantified at the beginning. If this was done correctly, then evaluation should flow easily from that projection; if not, the projection can be adjusted.

The evaluation of part-timers not only will involve an assessment of their activities and accomplishments but also will require greater emphasis on their ability to communicate and coordinate with co-workers than would be the case with the evaluation of full-time employees.

Summary

Permanent, or regular, part-time employment is a reduced work-time arrangement in which the part-time worker is regarded as a full-fledged employee of the organization, entitled to job security and other rights and benefits available to full-timers.

The sharp increase in the use of regular part-time since the mid-1970s can be attributed both to the economy's shift from a production orientation to a service orientation and to the radical change in the employment needs of women, many of whom work in service industries. Offering a program of voluntary regular part-time options is one way for employers to respond to the needs of these employees, who might otherwise be forced to leave the organization or who might not seek employment with the organization in the first place because they require a less than full-time schedule. Another reason for the rise in part-time employment is that part-time can enable an employer to respond flexibly to staffing and scheduling problems, such as peak-time work loads.

The increase in the use of part-timers, particularly in the retail and service sectors of the economy, has included an increase in the number of managerial and professional-level employees who choose reduced work-time options. This is in contrast to the traditional perception of part-time as a scheduling alternative appropriate only for low-level job classifications.

An organization's decision to use part-time workers is generally prompted by several considerations. Offering part-time schedules can enable the organization to attract a higher quality of job applicants and retain trained employees who might otherwise leave the organization in search of reduced hours. Part-time can give the company the flexibility it needs to respond to the demands of its work without over- or understaffing. And in some situations, the move toward part-time can reduce costs.

In assessing the advantages and disadvantages of permitting the use of part-time schedules, an organization must weigh a variety of factors. Part-time, as noted, normally results in the retention of valued employees and provides the organization with an effective tool for tailoring its labor supply to meet staffing and scheduling demands. Part-time also normally results in an improvement in the quality and quantity of job applicants, although some employers have reported little success in this area.

The costs of a move toward part-time will vary according to the decisions that each individual employer makes in structuring its program of reduced work-time options. The employer will have to carefully analyze direct and indirect costs and program costs to determine the impact of converting selected positions to a part-time schedule. Once the cost impact has been determined, it may then be necessary for the employer to adjust various aspects of the conditions of employment in order to design a program for using part-time that meets the needs of employees at a cost that is attractive to the organization.

The company considering regular part-time will have to investigate and deal with whatever barriers to this form of employment may exist both within the organization's own policies and in the regulations of government agencies. The attitudes of the major parties affected by the decision on part-time (management, unions, and employees) must also be taken into account.

The standard eight-step process for introducing a change in work-time practices applies to the introduction of regular part-time, with special emphasis on the following areas: Since part-time employees have traditionally been regarded as second-class workers, care must be taken to gain support from all levels of management for the concept of part-timers as full-status workers on a less than full-time schedule. (Resource materials directed both toward managers and supervisors and toward employees and applicants are an essential component of the effort to gain broad-based support for the use of regular part-time.) Failure to achieve this fundamental consensus could doom the program at the outset. Designing a program for regular part-time will involve the elimination of internal constraints on the use of this option, followed by the development of a comprehensive new policy that addresses the entire range of issues associated with regular part-time.

It is important that supervisors and managers be adequately prepared to cope with the special demands of supervising and managing part-timers. Training should particularly emphasize such areas as how to analyze the requirements of a position, and design a part-time work schedule (or a combination of part-time schedules) that will enable those requirements to be met and how managers and supervisors can establish good channels of communication between themselves and their part-timers and between the full- and part-time employees who report to them.

In short, providing the employer has "done its homework"—by carefully analyzing the cost implications and other key issues and developing widespread support for the program—offering reduced work-time alternatives on a regular basis can be a cost-effective move that brings a number of benefits for both employer and employees.

CHAPTER 4

Job Sharing

J ob sharing is a form of regular part-time work in which two people voluntarily share the responsibilities of one full-time position, with salary and benefits prorated. Relatively unheard of in the private sector until the late 1970s, job sharing has been growing on a case-by-case basis, and in 1986, several independent surveys of private-sector organizations showed that between 11 and 18 percent of the respondents reported having job-sharers.[1]

Origins of Job Sharing

The term job sharing was first coined in the mid-1960s. This option was devised as a way to create more part-time opportunities in career-oriented job categories in which the positions could not be reduced in hours or split into two part-time jobs. It represents an attempt to bring regular part-time into parity with regular full-time employment. When a position is defined as a full-time job that is, temporarily, being filled by two people instead of one, it is assumed that the conditions of employment (such as rate of pay, fringe benefits, and seniority) remain the same as for other positions in the same classification. As more employees express an interest in reducing work time at some point in their careers and as employers become interested in offering reduced work time as an employee option or benefit, the issue of improving the conditions of part-time employment has assumed increasing importance. Job sharing has played a significant role in making part-time work more equitable by emphasizing that it is the employees who are part-time, not the job.

Who Uses Job Sharing?

As of this writing, no comprehensive national survey of job sharing has been completed, but a variety of small, independent surveys give some sense of where, and to what extent, job sharing has come into use. A 1985 survey conducted for the American Management Association by Goodmeasure, Inc. reported that 11 percent of the respondents use job sharing. Of the user firms, 65 percent make the option available to clerical/secretarial staff, 46 percent to hourly workers, just over 25 percent to professional/technical staff, 15 percent to supervisors, 9 percent to middle managers, and 5 percent to senior managers. The survey indicated a significant growth in the number of companies using job sharing, with more than half saying that this work-time arrangement has been in place for less than five years.[2]

The survey also found a considerable difference in the extent of job sharing among various industries. Within each industry classification, the program was offered by the following portion of responding organizations: construction—4 percent; wholesale/retail trade—5 percent; finance, insurance, and real estate—12 percent; education—22 percent; and government—26 percent.[3]

The Administrative Management Society conducts regular surveys of 500 companies, and until 1988 these indicated a steady increase in job sharing. In 1981, 11 percent of the respondents reported using it; in 1985 and 1987, that number had increased to 17 percent.[4] The 1987 survey results are shown in Figure 4-1.

A 1983 survey of 260 health care organizations conducted by New Ways to Work (NWW) indicated that 52 percent of the respondents were using job sharing. A total of 28 different health care classifications have been restructured this way, including those of registered nurse, emergency room nurse, epidemiologist, and nurse anesthetist. Another NWW survey of the legal profession indicated a growing use of job sharing in both public and private law firms and agencies.[5]

In the public sector, a 1986 phone survey of the 50 states' personnel offices conducted by New Ways to Work indicated that 35 states allow state employees to share jobs. Of these, 18 states have written policies, and 12 have authorizing legislation.[6]

The federal government was an early user of job sharing. Congress passed legislation in 1978 that authorized professional-level part-time and specifically encouraged job sharing. This led to replacement of the "head count" system with one based on full-time equivalency, and all federal agencies were instructed to set up programs and procedures designed to facilitate wider use of part-time and job sharing.

Figure 4-1. Job sharing—by region.

SOURCE: Administration Management Society, *Flexible Work Survey* (Trevose, Pa.: AMS, 1987), 7.

When Is Job Sharing Most Appropriate?

Job sharing, like other forms of reduced work time, permits an organization to retain valued employees. From a manager's perspective, job sharing has some additional aspects that make it particularly effective in terms of enhancing opportunities for flexibility. These include new kinds of scheduling options that are only possible if a job is shared by two people, the potential for increasing the breadth of skills and experience in a single position, and special kinds of pairings that facilitate the achievement of human resources management objectives.

Retention of valued employees. Job sharing's unique attribute is that it is a way of allowing employees to work part-time in positions that cannot be either reduced in hours or split into two discrete part-time jobs. This is especially true in higher-level positions. For instance, when incumbents in such positions as the human resources manager at Excelan, Inc., the deputy director for legislation in the state of California's Employment Development Department, and the head of the Travelers Insurance Company's retiree job bank wanted to work part-time, job sharing was the arrangement agreed upon. Job sharing has also proved very useful in positions where continuity is necessary but, for one reason or another, turnover has been a problem. Receptionists and various types of clerical support person nel have been allowed to share jobs for this reason at Alza Corporation, Hewlett-Packard, Steelcase Inc., Quaker Oats Company, and many other companies.

By offering job-sharing options, the organization can retain the services of good workers in these types of positions who might otherwise leave in search of a suitable part-time schedule.

Improving scheduling and continuity. Having a position covered by two employees rather than one permits the employees and their supervisors to develop a variety of creative work schedules tailor-made to satisfy the requirements of both the workers and the work. Since job-sharers usually cover for each other, the organization gains needed continuity while the employees gain a built-in substitute for those times—both planned and unplanned—when they must be away from their jobs.

Increasing the breadth of skills and experience. This feature of job sharing reflects the old adage "Two heads are better than one." And in fact, pooling the skills and experience of two employees usually enhances the range of capabilities that can be applied to the work.

Achieving human resources management objectives. Job sharing offers the possibility of creatively pairing workers in ways that will enable the organization to accomplish very specific human resources objective in such areas as training, phased retirement, and upward mobility.

Pros and Cons of Job Sharing

The advantages of job sharing, as noted above, are associated with retention of good workers who need a less than full-time schedule, improvements in scheduling and continuity, expansion of the talents available within a single position, and achievement of human resources management objectives.

As we observed in Chapter 3, the adoption of any part-time scheduling arrangement requires careful management analysis of costs versus benefits. This is particularly true in the case of job sharing. Because there are so many possible permutations, the fiscal implications of job sharing are complicated and warrant more consideration. In examining the costs and savings associated with converting one or more individual positions to a job-sharing basis, the employer must look at the entire range of cost factors. In addition to the impact on administrative costs that comes from having more employees, such cost considerations as rates of turnover and absenteeism, recruitment, training, fringe benefits, and of course, the potential for increased flexibility should all be taken into account.

While it is essential to examine the ramifications of job sharing for individual positions, cumulative effect can also be important: What kinds of costs or savings might be expected if a number of positions in either the same job classification or a variety of job classifications are restructured? An analysis of job sharing's costs and benefits should include both the impact of restructuring individual positions and the impact of developing a program designed to encourage the restructuring of a range of positions. In each case, the bottom line will be defined by why and how a particular organization uses job sharing.

Management must also weight the support or opposition of supervisors, unions, and employees in making a decision on the use of job sharing.

The balance of this section examines the positive or negative ramifications of each of these factors. The later section entitled Special Considerations for Supervisors and Managers addresses another problem often cited in connection with job sharing—the inconvenience of introducing a relatively untested work arrangement that entails managing additional employees in a new way.

Scheduling and Continuity

The possibilities for designing more effective schedules and addressing continuity problems are one of job sharing's exciting features. The standard 9–5 schedule, five days a week, is not necessarily an appropriate time arrangement for all jobs any more than for all workers. As Figure 4-2 shows, job-sharers and their supervisors have redesigned work schedules in various innovative ways that take advantage of the fact that two people rather than one are filling the job. In positions where there are regular peak periods of heightened activity, where extended coverage would be an advantage, or where clients regularly require off-site meetings, having two employees who can overlap, be in two different places at the same time, or work a split shift can be a distinct advantage.

Time lost to vacations, accidents or illness, and turnover all periodically interrupt an organization's work flow. When job-sharers are allowed to trade time, they are able to fill in for each other and time and services are not lost; neither does the organization incur the cost of a substitute or temporary worker.

The possibility of sharers' trading work time, one of the unique

Figure 4-2.   Sample job-sharing schedules.

Traditional Full-Time Schedule

	Mon.	Tues.	Wed.	Thurs.	Fri.
Week 1	E1	E1	E1	E1	E1

One employee (E1) works 8 hours/day, 5 days/week
Total Hours/Week = 40; Total Hours for 2 Weeks = 80

Job Sharing Schedules

One week on/one week off

	Mon.	Tues.	Wed.	Thurs.	Fri.
Week 1	E1	E1	E1	E1	E1
Week 2	E2	E2	E2	E2	E2

Two employees (E1 and E2) work 8 hours/day for 5 days one week
and are off the next week
Total Hours/Week = 40; Total Hours for 2 Weeks = 80; Each
Employee's Hours for 2 Weeks = 40

One week on/one week off over a weekend

	Mon.	Tues.	Wed.	Thurs.	Fri.
Week 1	E1	E1	E1	E2	E2
Week 2	E2	E2	E2	E1	E1

Two employees (E1 and E2) work 8 hours/day for 5 consecutive
workdays and are off the next 5 consecutive workdays, with each 5-
day period interrupted by a weekend
Total Hours/Week = 40; Total Hours for 2 Weeks = 80; Each
Employee's Hours for 2 Weeks = 40

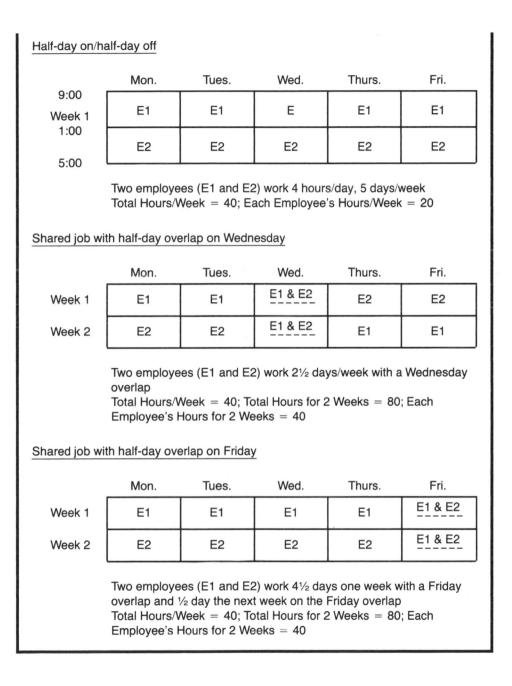

Half-day on/half-day off

	Mon.	Tues.	Wed.	Thurs.	Fri.
9:00 Week 1 1:00	E1	E1	E	E1	E1
5:00	E2	E2	E2	E2	E2

Two employees (E1 and E2) work 4 hours/day, 5 days/week
Total Hours/Week = 40; Each Employee's Hours/Week = 20

Shared job with half-day overlap on Wednesday

	Mon.	Tues.	Wed.	Thurs.	Fri.
Week 1	E1	E1	E1 & E2	E2	E2
Week 2	E2	E2	E1 & E2	E1	E1

Two employees (E1 and E2) work 2½ days/week with a Wednesday overlap
Total Hours/Week = 40; Total Hours for 2 Weeks = 80; Each Employee's Hours for 2 Weeks = 40

Shared job with half-day overlap on Friday

	Mon.	Tues.	Wed.	Thurs.	Fri.
Week 1	E1	E1	E1	E1	E1 & E2
Week 2	E2	E2	E2	E2	E1 & E2

Two employees (E1 and E2) work 4½ days one week with a Friday overlap and ½ day the next week on the Friday overlap
Total Hours/Week = 40; Total Hours for 2 Weeks = 80; Each Employee's Hours for 2 Weeks = 40

aspects of job sharing, has several important ramifications for both the manager and the employees. Organizational benefits are significant. *Continuity* can be greatly enhanced if there is agreement initially that sharers will substitute for each other whenever possible. If they are also allowed to trade time and self-schedule for personal reasons, employees are generally very receptive to assuming this kind of responsibility. The result can be a significant reduction in the amount of work time lost because of accidents or illness or an employee's need for more personal time. If one partner leaves the position, the other can provide 50 percent coverage, and often more, until a new sharer is hired.

From the employees' perspective, the ability to trade work time and arrange their own schedules allows sharers to respond to personal needs as well as work-related ones. If there is an illness in the family or a transportation problem, job sharing may enable the employee to cope without the organization's losing work time. Sharers are also able to take advantage of special opportunities such as attending a short course or seminar or traveling with a spouse.

The concept of trading work time raises the question of the obligation of partners to substitute for each other. In practice, sharers who are allowed to self-schedule for personal reasons generally are expected to fill in during each other's absences insofar as is feasible. Until recently, very few companies have had policy or contracts that cover such questions. Those that do address the issue of trading time often use language such as "sharers will substitute for each other whenever possible." Sometimes time limits are stipulated regarding how long, and to what extent, one partner will be expected to fill in for another who is absent for an extended period of time or who leaves the company's employ. Other policies permit this aspect of job sharing to be negotiated between the sharers and their direct supervisor, with the caveat that the issue of trading time and substituting be discussed and agreed upon before the arrangement begins.

Skills and Experience

In addition to creating opportunities for fine-tuning schedules, allowing two people to fill one job can greatly expand the number of skills and the types of experience available in a single job title. In many fields, work is becoming increasingly complex, and an individual in one position is often expected to demonstrate competence in a variety of areas. When two people team up to share a position, they generally offer a wider range of skills than a single incumbent.

Human Resources Management Objectives

By offering the possibility of creating "special teams," job sharing can facilitate the achievement of an assortment of objectives in the area of human resources management. The following are some examples of the types of employees who can be paired and the types of objectives that such pairings can accomplish:

- Two senior employees may share a job with each other as a way of phasing in to retirement.
- A senior employee may job-share with a younger employee, thereby enabling the older worker to train his or her replacement while phasing in to retirement.
- An employee ready for promotion can share a job half-time at a higher grade level and remain half-time at his or her current position. This option can permit an employee to advance in situations where there is no full-time opening at the higher grade level.
- An entry-level employee can share a position half-time while completing his or her education or training half-time. This way, the organization not only retains the services of the employee during the learning process but also ends up with a more-qualified employee.

Job sharing's potential for creating openings and permitting movement in a relatively static work force situation may become increasingly important as employers strive for stability along with flexibility.

Cost Implications—The Position Approach

To evaluate the overall costs—and savings—the organization must establish its objectives and define its reasons for instituting job sharing. Is job sharing being considered in response to one employee's request, because of recruitment difficulties, as an alternative to layoffs, or as a way to manage several of these problems at once? And in what areas can savings, both current and future, be projected if job sharing is instituted?

Drafting a balance sheet that shows the entire range of cost factors (direct and indirect costs and program costs) can help an employer identify all the considerations that should be included in the final equation. Tables 4-1, 4-2, and 4-3 are sample worksheets that show a comparison between the costs associated with a current full-time position and the costs associated with various types of job-sharing arrangements that might be used to accomplish the same

Table 4-1. Cost analysis by position: example of job being shared by current employee and new hire.

			Job Sharing		
		Current Cost of the Position	Current Employee	New Hire	Total
I.	Direct costs				
	A. Base salary	$30,000.00	$15,000.00	$15,000.00	$30,000.00
	B. Employee benefits				
	1. Statutory				
	• Social Security (7.51% of first $48,000)	2,253.00	1,126.50	1,126.50	2,253.00
	• Unemployment insurance (2.3% of first $7,000)	161.00	161.00	161.00	322.00
	• Worker's compensation ($.85 per $100 of compensation)	255.00	127.50	127.50	255.00
	2. Compensatory				
	• Sick leave (2 weeks)	1,153,85	576.92	576.92	1,153.84
	• Vacation (3 weeks—current employee; 2 weeks—new hire)	1,730,77	865.38	576.92	1,442.30
	• Holidays (10 days)	1,153,85	576.92	576.92	1,153.84
	• Other				
	3. Supplementary				
	• Insurance				
	Prorated life ($10,000)	50.00	25.00	25.00	50.00
	Medical/dental ($125 deductible)	1,500.00	750.00	750.00	1,500.00
	Long-term disability	250.00	125.00	125.00	250.00
	• Pension (13% salary)	3,900.00	1,950.00	1,950.00	3,900.00
	• Profit sharing (.5%)	150.00	75.00	75.00	150.00
	• Stock purchase options				
	• Tax shelter annuities				
	• Tuition payments				
	• Discount purchase plans				

| | Current Cost of the Position | Job Sharing | | |
		Current Employee	New Hire	Total
• Other				
Total direct costs	$42,557.47	$21,359.22	$21,070.76	$42,429.98
II. Indirect costs				
A. New hire administration			$ 150.00	$ 150.00
B. Training			500.00	500.00
C. Supervision	$2,000.00	$1,000.00	1,000.00	2,000.00
D. Square footage (80 square feet)	480.00	240.00	240.0	480.00
Total indirect costs	$2,480.00	$1,240.00	$1,890.00	$3,130.00
III. Program costs				
A. Absenteeism				
B. Turnover				
C. Coverage				
D. Recruitment				
E. Production rates				
Total program costs	$0.00	$0.00	$0.00	$0.00
TOTAL COSTS	$45,037.47	$22,599.22	$22,960.76	$45,559.98
DIFFERENCE				+ $522.51

work. Table 4-4 is a blank copy of this worksheet that managers may wish to use in performing their own cost analysis.

The remainder of this subsection examines the cost implications of restructuring individual jobs to a shared mode—the *position approach*. It covers direct costs (which comprise base salary, including overtime, and a variety of fringe benefits and are usually the most significant expenses that will be incurred) and indirect costs (which comprise costs in such areas as new-hire administration, training, and the use of space and equipment and are usually a less-significant expense for most employers). You may refer to Chapter 3 for a discussion of program costs (those associated with the rates of absenteeism and turnover, coverage, recruitment, and production rates), which can also be a factor.

After we consider the costs of converting individual positions to job sharing, we will turn our attention in the following subsection to some of the fiscal multiplier effects that organizations have achieved by using the *program approach*—that is, instituting job sharing on a broader basis, by restructuring one or more groups of positions.

Table 4-2.   Cost analysis by position: example of job being shared by two current employees.

		Current Cost of the Position	Job Sharing		
			Current Employee	Current Employee	Total
I.	Direct costs				
	A. Base salary	$30,000.00	$15,000.00	$15,000.00	$30,000.00
	B. Employee benefits				
	1. Statutory				
	• Social Security (7.51% of first $48,000)	2,253.00	1,126.50	1,126.50	2,253.00
	• Unemployment insurance (2.3% of first $7,000)	161.00	161.00	161.00	322.00
	• Worker's compensation ($.85 per $100 of compensation)	255.00	127.50	127.50	255.00
	2. Compensatory				
	• Sick leave (2 weeks)	1,153.85	576.92	576.92	1,153.84
	• Vacation (3 weeks)	1,730.77	865.38	865.38	1,730.76
	• Holidays (10 days)	1,153.85	576.92	576.92	1,153.84
	• Other				
	3. Supplementary				
	• Insurance				
	Prorated life ($10,000)	50.00	25.00	25.00	50.00
	Medical/dental ($125 deductible)	1,500.00	750.00	750.00	1,500.00
	Long-term disability	250.00	125.00	125.00	250.00
	• Pension (13% salary)	3,900.00	1,950.00	1,950.00	3,900.00
	• Profit sharing (5%)	150.00	75.00	75.00	150.00
	• Stock purchase options				
	• Tax shelter annuities				
	• Tuition payments				
	• Discount purchase plans				
	• Other				
	Total direct costs	$42,557.47	$21,359.22	$21,359.22	$42,718.44

	Current Cost of the Position	Job Sharing Current Employee	Current Employee	Total
II. Indirect costs				
A. New hire administration				
B. Training				
C. Supervision	$2,000.00	$1,000.00	$1,000.00	$2,000.00
D. Square footage (80 square feet)	480.00	240.00	240.00	480.00
Total indirect costs	$2,480.00	$1,240.00	$1,240.00	$2,480.00
III. Program costs				
A. Absenteeism				
B. Turnover				
C. Coverage				
D. Recruitment				
E. Production rates				
Total program costs	$0.00	$0.00	$0.00	$0.00
TOTAL COSTS	$45,037.47	$22,599.22	$22,599.22	$45,198.44
DIFFERENCE				+ $160.97

Direct Costs The cost factors in this category are base salary and any overtime that may be incurred plus fringe benefits.

Base salary. It might seem that sharing a job would have no salary-related implications. However, partners in job-sharing teams may or may not have the same level of skills and experience, so they may or may not qualify for the same salary range. Sharers' salaries should be based both on their time arrangement (such as 50-50 or 60-40) and on their individual skills and experience.

This often results in savings on the salary costs of a particular position. For example, the salary of a full-time personnel analyst with five years' experience on the job might be $35,000. If this person wishes to reduce hours and can be paired with a less-experienced new hire (who would earn $20,000 if he or she were hired full-time), the total base salary of the shared position would be only $27,500 ($17,500 [half of $35,000] + $10,000 [half of $20,000]) instead of $35,000 for the full-time services of the more-experienced employee, saving the organization $7,500. Similarly, if a senior-level teacher (who would earn $30,000 full-time) is paried with an entry-level teacher (who would earn $18,000 full-time), the combined position

Table 4-3. Cost analysis by position: example of job being shared by current senior employee and less-experienced new hire.

		Job Sharing		
	Current Cost of the Position	Older, Experienced Current Employee	Less-Experienced New Hire	Total
I. Direct costs				
A. Base salary	$30,000.00	$15,000.00	$10,500.00	$25,500.00
B. Employee benefits				
1. Statutory				
• Social Security (7.51% of first $48,000)	2,253.00	1,126.50	788.55	1,915,05
• Unemployment insurance (2.3% of first $7,000)	161.00	161.00	161.00	322.00
• Worker's compensation ($85 per $100 of compensation)	255.00	127.50	89.25	216.75
2. Compensatory				
• Sick leave (2 weeks)	1,153.85	576.92	403.85	980.77
• Vacation (3 weeks—current employee; 2 weeks—new hire)	1,730.77	865.38	403.85	1,269.23
• Holidays (10 days)	1,153,85	576.92	403.85	980.77
• Other				
3. Supplementary				
• Insurance				
Prorated life ($10,000)	50.00	25.00	25.00	50.00
Medical/dental ($125 deductible)	1,500.00	750.00	750.00	1,500.00
Long-term disability	250.00	125.00	85.00	210.00
• Pension (13% salary)	3,900.00	1,950.00	1,365.00	3,315.00
• Profit sharing (.5%)	150.00	75.00	52.50	127.50
• Stock purchase options				

	Current Cost of the Position	Job Sharing		
		Older, Experienced Current Employee	Less-Experienced New Hire	Total
• Tax shelter annuities				
• Tuition payments				
• Discount purchase plans				
• Other				
Total direct costs	$42,557,47	$21,359.22	$15,027.85	$36,387.07
II. Indirect costs				
A. New hire administration			$ 150.00	$ 150.00
B. Training			500.00	500.00
C. Supervision	$2,000.00	$1,000.00	1,200.00	2,200.00
D. Square footage (80 square feet)	480.00	240.00	240.00	480.00
Total indirect costs	$2,480.00	$1,240.00	$2,090.00	$3,330.00
III. Program costs				
A. Absenteeism				
B. Turnover				
C. Coverage				
D. Recruitment				
E. Production rates				
Total program costs	$0.00	$0.00	$0.00	$0.00
TOTAL COSTS	$45,037.47	$22,599.22	$17,117.85	$39,717.07
DIFFERENCE				− $5,320,40

would cost a school district $24,000 ($15,000 + $9,000) instead of $30,000, for a savings of $6,000.

Employers are often surprised at the notion of paying job-sharing partners at different rates. Paying at the rate that each of the job-sharers would receive if he or she were employed full-time in the same job classification is the most common policy, however, and one that sharers perceive as equitable.

Related to the issue of base salary is the issue of *overtime*. As was discussed in Chapter 3, because of growing fixed costs per

Table 4-4.   Cost analysis by position: worksheet.

	Current Cost: Full-Timer	Job sharing Employee A	Employee B	Total
I. Direct costs				
A. Base salary				
B. Employee benefits				
1. Statutory				
• Social Security (___% of first $_____)				
• Unemployment insurance (___% of first $_____)				
• Worker's compensation (___ per $100 of compensation)				
2. Compensatory				
• Sick leave (___ weeks)				
• Vacation (___ weeks—current employee; ___ weeks—new hire)				
• Holidays (___ days)				
• Other				
3. Supplementary				
• Insurance Prorated life ($_____) Medical/dental ($_____ deductible) Long-term disability				
• Pension (___% salary)				
• Profit sharing (___%)				
• Stock purchase options				
• Tax shelter annuities				
• Tuition payments				
• Discount purchase plans				
• Other	_____	_____	_____	____
Total direct costs				
II. Indirect costs				
A. New hire administration				
B. Training				
C. Supervision				
D. Square footage (_____ square feet)	_____	_____	_____	____
Total indirect costs				

	Current Cost:	Job sharing		
	Full-Timer	Employee A	Employee B	Total
III. Program costs				
A. Absenteeism				
B. Turnover				
C. Coverage				
D. Recruitment				
E. Production rates	_____	_____	_____	____
Total program costs	======	========	========	====
TOTAL COSTS				
DIFFERENCE				

employee, many employers have increased their use of overtime instead of expanding their permanent work force. Such extensive use of overtime can be quite costly for the employer and can result in increased pressure on the organization's employees, sometimes leading to burnout. Employers of job-sharers, on the other hand, are often able to reduce or eliminate the need for overtime by improving the scheduling in particular positions. Job-sharers can be scheduled to work together during periods of peak demand, or the supervisor can arrange a gap period that extends service hours without either employee's having to work more than an eight-hour day. If an employer allows sharers to trade time freely, the organization achieves increased scheduling flexibility and maximum coverage at no extra cost.

In instances where overtime is still necessary, the question arises of when job-sharers should receive premium pay. The formula preferred by advocates of job sharing derives from the concept of treating a shared job the same as any other full-time position in the same job classification. Using this rule of thumb, overtime is paid when the nonexempt sharers' combined hours total more than 40 a week. The premium pay is divided equally between them if both have worked the same number of hours in that pay period or distributed proportionally on the basis of extra hours worked if they have not.

Employee benefits. Fringe benefits differ from one company to another and, as noted in Chapter 3, fall into three categories: statutory, compensatory, and supplementary. The following material does not repeat the detailed discussion contained in Chapter 3 but instead focuses on the benefits considerations that most directly affect job sharing.

Statutory benefits. This benefits category includes Social Security, unemployment insurance, and worker's compensation insurance.

- ■ *Social Security*. Employers incur extra expense for job-sharers only when two employees share a position that pays more than $48,000. Most jobs pay less than that. For positions at or above the ceiling, the employer must contribute 7.51 percent, up to a maximum ceiling of $96,000 (double the $48,000). Job-sharers in a position paying $50,000, for instance, would cost an employer $150.20 (7.51 × $2,000 [the amount by which the combined salary exceeds the $48,000 ceiling]) more per year in Social Security than one full-time employee who held the same job.
- ■ *Unemployment insurance*. It is difficult to generalize about unemployment insurance costs associated with job sharing because the rates and limits vary from state to state. For example, on a $7,000 ceiling, an employer with a 2.3 percent rating pays $161 for a full-time employee making $30,000. If the position is shared, the employer pays double the cost— $322. It should be pointed out, however, that as with other forms of regular part-time, employers that institute job sharing or expand the practice in order to avoid layoffs may save money in the long run, because by retaining current workers, the organization minimizes unemployment insurance claims, thereby keeping its "experience rating" lower than it otherwise would be.
- ■ *Worker's compensation insurance*. This cost is usually based on a percentage of payroll, which means that no additional expense is incurred if a position is shared.

Compensatory benefits. Such fringe benefits as sick leave, vacation, and holidays are generally prorated according to the amount of time worked by each sharer, so job sharing does not automatically increase the organization's costs in this category. In fact, some employers have found that a job-sharing arrangement may cut the expense associated with illness, absence, or vacation, because the sharers can cover for each other when one partner is away from the job, reducing the need to utilize expensive substitutes or temporary agency personnel.

Supplementary benefits. As is the case with other regular part-timers, it is important for employers to extend supplementary benefits, particularly medical and dental insurance, to job-sharers. In order to do this without doubling the cost they incur, some employers pay half the health insurance amount for each job-sharer that they would normally pay for a full-time employee. The sharers are then given the option of paying the remainder. This approach often results in cost savings if sharers are covered under a spouse's policy and elect not to receive (and pay for half the cost of) this benefit from the employer. It also ensures equitable treatment in case the employee has no other access to group health insurance and must avail himself or herself of the opportunity to obtain coverage in this manner.

Indirect Costs Before restructuring a full-time position so that two people can share it, employers should review the administrative overhead costs associated with new hires as well as the costs associated with training and the use of space and equipment.

Administrative overhead. In addition to the ongoing costs of administrative overhead, the costs associated with a new hire could include recruitment of a replacement if a current full-time employee leaves. But no new-hire costs are incurred if the job-sharing team consists of two current full-timers who want to cut back their hours.

Training. If one or both sharers require specialized training that cannot be imparted by an incumbent partner, the employer will incur the cost of having both partners trained by someone else within the organization. If one partner is a current full-timer who is able to train his or her partner, the cost is limited to the time spent by both partners in the training process. If the team comprises two people currently working full-time in the same job classification as the position to be shared, then no initial training costs will be incurred.

Space and equipment. If the team members need to work together at the same time, extra space and equipment may be required. Most pairs, however, schedule their time so they can share space and equipment.

An often-overlooked cost saving in this area stems from the fact that job sharing cuts down on absenteeism and turnover. When a full-time employee is away from his or her job, the employer is paying for equipment, space, heat and lights, insurance, and even a stall in the company parking lot—all for someone who isn't there. Whether the absence results in an empty office desk, a vacant production-line work station, or an unstaffed factory punch press, the cost to the organization is considerable. In addition to the reduction in the overall rates of absenteeism and turnover, the fact that job-sharers can fill in for each other in the event that one does become sick or resign also enables the employer to better recoup its investment in space and equipment.

Cost Implications—The Program Approach

Employers that have had successful experience with a few shared positions often consider expanding the use of job sharing. They can do this either one job at a time, by focusing on a group of positions or employees, or by targeting a particular company problem. For example, an employer may decide to make a priority of job-sharing requests from employees with young children or older employees nearing retirement age. Another employer may designate certain positions, such as computer programmer or market researcher, as open to job sharing. Yet another may use the idea of two people's sharing one full-time job as a recruitment device or as a means of attempting to reduce absenteeism.

The main reason for taking a group, or program, approach rather than continuing to restructure one job at a time is to solve a problem and/or to compound the savings achieved in previous, smaller job-sharing experiments. This subsection explains some of the reasons why employers have formulated job-sharing programs and presents guidelines for doing so.

To reduce absenteeism. When employees have nonwork responsibilities that conflict with their job, the result at the workplace may be chronic or intermittent absenteeism. When the problem is generic rather than individual, it becomes an organizational concern. At least that's what Rolscreen Company, a midwestern manufacturer, thought when it realized that absenteeism on its production line was appreciably higher than the company average. An employee with good skills but a poor attendance record suggested job sharing as an option for production-line employees, almost all of whom were working mothers with young children. The company thoroughly reviewed her suggestion and then let her share her job as a pilot project. Four years later, there were 30 job-sharing teams, absenteeism had dropped from 5.8 percent to 1.2 percent, and the company had eliminated the need to overstaff the production line. (The following section of this chapter presents a detailed profile of Rolscreen's experience with job sharing.)

To improve recruitment. Advertising a job as open to either one full-time or two job-sharing applicants can both expand and enhance an organization's recruitment efforts. By offering job sharing, Fireman's Fund Insurance Companies was able to attract better applicants for hard-to-fill positions (see Figure 4-3); Walgreen's used job

Figure 4-3. Advertisement featuring job sharing as a recruitment tool.

SOURCE: *San Francisco Sunday Examiner and Chronicle* (Jan. 31, 1982), 40.

sharing successfully to recruit in a locale whose labor force had a high percentage of homemakers; New York Life Insurance Company advertised shared positions in an effort to stabilize a segment of the company's activities where there was high turnover; and Oklahoma State University has issued a brochure for job candidates featuring the benefits of its job-sharing program (see Figure 4-4).

To provide new options for senior employees. Varian Associates in Silicon Valley and the Travelers Insurance Company are two firms that offer job sharing as an option for senior employees. Varian does it in conjunction with its phased retirement program; the Travelers Insurance Company, as an option within its program of part-time employment for annuitants.

To provide released time for training. McKesson Corporation in San Francisco has been using job sharing in conjunction with its efforts to provide work experience for high school–age youth in ways that expand opportunities for its current employees as well. Each student works two hours a day, five days a week, in various departments, including office services, the mail room, documentation services, and personnel. He or she is assigned a work supervisor and trained on the job by that person. After the student is trained, the full-time employee who had been performing the tasks is free to cross-train in other departments in order to expand his or her skills and potential for advancement during the two hours that the student replacement is working.

To supplement a work-sharing strategy. If a company decides to cut back on paid hours of work during an economic downturn in order to save jobs and retain employees, voluntary job sharing is one option that may be offered. Several airlines have authorized job sharing for flight attendants and ticket personnel for this reason. (Chapter 8 discusses work sharing in detail.)

To retain valued employees. Retention of trained workers is probably the most prevalent factor in persuading employers to try job sharing for the first time. Levi Strauss, Quaker Oats, Steelcase, and others have cited the need to accommodate employees who had to reduce their work time for a while and whose positions could not be handled on a part-time basis as the reason for initially experimenting with job sharing and then formulating policy or guidelines expanding its use.

Supervisors' Attitudes

Job sharing is still a new idea, and supervisors' reactions to it vary widely. Those who have had experience with job sharing generally support it enthusiastically as an option, although they may feel that the attributes of the particular pair they supervised were the primary factor in making this scheduling alternative successful. Those lacking experience with job sharing tend to be skeptical about allowing two people to share one position.

Union Attitudes

Labor leaders tend to view job sharing more favorably than they do other forms of part-time work. This is largely because of their perception that job sharing retains the form of a full-time position and so is a way to upgrade part-time employment. As with other forms of reduced work time, unions are concerned that it be voluntary, that base salary scale and fringe benefits be maintained, that protections against speedup be instituted, and that layoffs occur according to some kind of seniority process rather than part-timers' automatically being laid off first.

Employee Attitudes

Employees in general are enthusiastic about the introduction of flexible and reduced work-time options such as job sharing. Whether or not they are interested in working that way themselves, they recognize these policies as representing the company's willingness to innovate and be supportive of employee needs. Negative attitudes may arise, however, if a particular job-sharing team does not communicate well with co-workers (a special concern in terms of scheduling arrangements) or if the option is perceived as being used in a way that reflects favoritism.

Should Your Organization Try Job Sharing?

The purpose of this section is to help you analyze job sharing in light of your organization's staffing and scheduling needs and decide whether adopting this technique would be advantageous.

First, the accompanying group of profiles ("Organizational Experience With Job Sharing") describes how and why job sharing was used in three organizations and what effect it has had. Consider the ways in which the experience of these organizations might parallel the circumstances that your own company faces.

Table 4-5 raises a series of issues that are of primary concern to organizations that institute job sharing. The more "yes" answers you

(Text continues on page 133.)

Figure 4-4.   Brochure for job candidates explaining a job-sharing program.

Job-Sharing, A Team Approach

Team
Approach

A Job-Sharing
Plan Which Works!

Office of University Personnel
407 Whitehurst Hall
Oklahoma State University

Job-sharing, the *new* way to work, is proving feasible and effective on the Oklahoma State University Campus.

Job-sharing involves two persons accepting the responsibility for one full-time position, thus giving each person that much desired commodity—*time*; time for travel, family or recreation, while still utilizing skills and knowledge of the work world.

These part-time positions are particularly beneficial for women during child-bearing years, older women not yet ready for retirement, or those who just want to keep their hand on the pulse of the work world.

Cooperation, Compatibility and *Communication* are the key factors for a successful and effective team. Job-sharers find that the flexibility of hours far out weighs the disadvantages of the lower salary.

Job-sharing is an ideal solution for many campus positions such as receptionist, file/clerk, clerk/typist and many others. Employers are seldom left stranded, as team workers cooperate when personal emergency situations arise, and they equalize staff pressure during peak activity periods.

It has been proven that not only are two heads better than one, but two persons sharing the same job can give an extension of service and often an increase in productivity of 25% or more. There is less absenteeism, tardiness and more pride in work done well. Reasons for this higher quality of work efficiency can be attributed to higher energy, enthusiasm and motivation. Together, job-sharers can frequently offer a lot more than a single employee.

Director of University Personnel Services Gene Turner says, "I'm a great believer in this program because it has worked so well for us. There are a lot of talented people who want to work less than an eight hour day. Given the options of tailoring their schedules to meet their own needs, these people are most productive, dependable and highly motivated."

SOURCE: Oklahoma State University, Stillwater, Okla.

Marita Johnson who shares receptionist duties in the Office of University Personnel Services, says "Job-sharing in the Personnel Office has provided a way to re-enter the work world which I left to raise my family and yet it provides the flexibility for my partner and me to adjust our work schedules to accomodate our interests and to meet the needs of our families. It has also brought my family closer together, because we each assume responsibility to help make each other's day a little bit better."

OKLAHOMA STATE UNIVERSITY

Marita's partner, Sandy Barth concurs by saying, "I love it. What else can I say? I have been so happy since I came to work for Personnel Services in November of 1979. My life has been so full. I loved being at home when my children were there, but when they were all in school I felt the need to be around people and to grow mentally. I wasn't sure I could work, I had been away from it for so long. The people I work with have given me a great deal of support and confidence in my self. Having a friend as a partner is another advantage. We work together setting up our schedule and we are very flexible when one of us wants to change. I feel as though I have the best of both worlds."

Potential job-sharers are encouraged to find a partner, perhaps a neighbor, bridge partner, or just a friend with whom they feel they could work successfully. However, the Office of University Personnel Services maintains a list of names of those wishing to be paired for a position on a part-time basis.

Brush-Up Programs

Brush-up programs for those wishing to re-enter the job market are available. An open-end clerical program is now being offered by Oklahoma State University and area vocational schools offer complete clerical programs as well as some adult education classes in this locale.

Those persons employed in a permanent half-time position are now eligible for sick leave and annual leave at a proportionate rate.

For more detailed information, please contact:

Employment Interviewer
Office of University Personnel
Whitehurst Hall, Room 407
Oklahoma State University
Stillwater, Oklahoma 74078
(405) 624-5373

ORGANIZATIONAL EXPERIENCE WITH JOB SHARING

Rolscreen Company

Description: Rolscreen, a midwestern manufacturer of Pella windows and patio doors, employs approximately 1,700 people. In addition to its job-sharing program, Rolscreen uses a compressed workweek and has used work sharing as an alternative to layoffs.

Reason for Using Job Sharing: Job sharing was originally tried in 1977 in response to an employee's request. Management was interested in its potential for reducing absenteeism on the production line.

Implementation Process: The job-sharing program is only open to current full-time employees in three of the company's production-line and clerical job classifications. Eligible employees are responsible for finding their own partner; the company serves a clearinghouse function by providing a mechanism for potential job-sharers to list their names and self-refer to possible partners. The sharers work out their own schedules; partial days are not allowed, however, because of the disruption they would cause in a production-line setting. Sharers are responsible for covering their own absences. Anyone joining the program must remain in it for six months; anyone dropping from the program cannot rejoin for one year.

Impact to Date: According to the company, absenteeism immediately improved by 81 percent in test group A and 31 percent in test group B. (The latter included a six-month stretch of full-time work.)

The need to overstaff in order to compensate for absenteeism was eliminated, and overtime was reduced. Also, the supervisor no longer had to take responsibility for finding replacements for absent production-line workers.

Health and dental insurance costs were doubled because the company chose to provide full benefits to job-sharers.

The program is very popular with both employees and supervisors.

SOURCE: Materials developed by Rolscreen Company, Pella, Iowa, to describe the organization's job-sharing program, 1982; *Analyzing the Cost* (San Francisco: New Ways to Work, 1981), 8.

Federal Reserve Bank of San Francisco

Description: The Federal Reserve Bank of San Francisco is one of 12 branches of the nation's central bank that serves the needs of banks, savings and loan associations, and bank holding companies in the western United States. It has 2,500 employees, a little over half of whom are based at its headquarters office in San Francisco. In addition to job sharing, virtually all departments use regular part-time employees, and approximately half of the employees are on some form of flexible schedule. Because of the difficulty in staffing the midnight shift in its round-the-clock payment services department, the bank uses a variety of schedules to expand the recruitment pool.

Reason for Using Job Sharing: A research economist whose husband was ill requested the opportunity to job-share with a returning maternity leave employee. Management wanted to be able to retain experienced staff and offer part-time options at the exempt, or professional, level. The employee's proposal was reviewed and accepted.

Implementation Process: The job-sharing option has been available since 1983 and is limited to current full-time exempt-level employees or members of the "floater" staff. Interested employees submit a proposal to their managers for approval. Sharers receive full health insurance coverage; other benefits are prorated.

Impact to Date: Employees have chosen the option in order to care for ailing family members, as a transition from maternity leave, and to pursue outside interests. Job sharing is popular with both employees and their supervisors.

No problems have been reported. Management believes that the cost of providing full health benefits is offset by the increased productivity of the job-sharers.

SOURCE: *Survey of Private Sector Work and Family Policy: San Francisco and Alameda Counties* (San Francisco: New Ways to Work, 1986), 13–14.

Northeast Utilities

Description: A utilities company headquartered in Hartford, Connecticut, with 10,000 employees.

Reason for Using Job Sharing: The organization initially used job sharing as a way to attract and retain applicants for positions as customer representatives. Later, its use was expanded in order to retain current employees who were leaving because of conflicts between 40-hour jobs and family responsibilities.

Implementation Process: The management committee authorized a job-sharing pilot project in December 1986. A maximum of 50 pairs were set up for testing purposes. All Northeast Utilities employees are eligible to apply, with the exception of workers covered by union contracts and employees in supervisory or managerial positions requiring work leadership.

Jobs may be split in any way agreed upon by the sharers and their supervisor. A common schedule has been three days on and two off one week, followed by two days on and three off the next. Other possible arrangements include two and one half days weekly; alternate days, weeks, or months; or half-days. Employees are encouraged to find their own partner, but if they cannot, the job is posted. If no in-house applicant can be found, the company advertises outside the organization.

Sharers working 20 hours a week or more receive full health insurance benefits for themselves but not for their dependents. They may purchase dependent coverage at group rates, however. Other benefits are prorated.

Impact to Date: By offering job sharing, the company succeeded in attracting a large pool of applicants who were interested in part-time employment. In addition, the company cites increased productivity, reduced use of sick leave and personal time, reduced turnover, and improved employee morale.

Northeast Utilities also notes that job sharing cuts down on the need for temporary help, since sharers may choose to work full-time when their partners are sick or on vacation. It has also reduced the need for overtime.

Northeast Utilities' management development analyst, Louise Klaber, credits the support of the CEO and the human resources manager for the program's inception. Initial acceptance was difficult and took a long time. She also noted that having a written contract is important because it reassures supervisors that they will not lose control of the situation.

SOURCE: "Benefits of Job Sharing," *Human Resource Management News* (July 25, 1987), 2; *The National Report on Work and Family,* special report no. 5 (Washington, D.C.: Buraff Publications, May 1988), 23.

have on this questionnaire, the greater the chances that job sharing would benefit your company.

If, based on your questionnaire results, it appears that job sharing is the direction in which your organization should move, you can complete the worksheet shown in Figure 4-5. It can be used to list the specific concerns that have prompted you to consider job sharing and examine the positive and negative effects that the use of this alternative work-time approach might have.

Introducing Job Sharing

In practice, job sharing has generally been introduced in an organization in an incremental way, often starting with one position that is restructured in response to a particular situation, as an exception to the general rule. If this first experience is successful, the use of job sharing is expanded—either on a case-by-case basis, to address a particular issue, or as a pilot project of some sort—and is finally incorporated as a general option. Once an organization has gotten beyond the first stage of experience, it should consider developing regulations and a set of procedures or management guidelines that will govern the use of job sharing.

Gain Support for the Program
Even if regular part-time is an accepted work mode, the introduction of job sharing as an employee option will need the support of *top management, middle management,* and *labor representatives.* Because it is a new kind of working arrangement, and experience with it is quite limited, job sharing is often viewed skeptically even by

Table 4-5. Job-sharing questionnaire.

Would Job Sharing Benefit Your Organization?

	Yes	No
Have you had to turn down employee requests for a reduced schedule because the jobs in question could not be done on a part-time basis?		
Have some of the employees whose request for a reduced schedule was turned down left your organization as a result?		
Are some departments or job classifications experiencing above-average turnover or absenteeism?		
Have you had to overstaff in some areas or use an excessive number of substitutes to compensate for turnover or absenteeism?		
Do many of your employees who have been on parental leave decide against returning to full-time work?		
If your organization's schedules must conform to work demand, could work flow be improved by having a team of job-sharers overlap during a peak period or extended coverage by creating a gap?		
Is upward mobility difficult in some departments or job classifications?		
Would some of your organization's senior employees prefer a part-time option?		

supervisors who have successfully used part-time employees. This makes support from top management at the outset particularly important. If an organization has had several positive experiences with individually negotiated job-sharing arrangements, or has conducted a successful pilot project to test job sharing at a number of different levels, this support will generally be forthcoming.

Set Up the Program's Administration

If your organization has had sufficient experience with regular part-time and with ad hoc job sharing, identifying a coordinator of the job-sharing initiative may be all that is necessary in the area of program administration. If, on the other hand, there is perceived resistance to the concept or if regular part-time is minimally used or is a newly introduced option, a task force approach may be more appropriate. In either case, one of the first steps should be to review any ad hoc or pilot project experience your company has had, identify what worked and what didn't, and research the experience of other organizations.

Figure 4-5. Job-sharing worksheet.

Assessing the Need for Job Sharing

List the main reasons why you are considering job sharing:

1. _____

_____

_____

2. _____

_____

_____

3. _____

_____

_____

4. _____

_____

_____

List what you see as the advantages and disadvantages of job sharing:

Pros: _____

_____

_____

_____

_____

(Continued)

Figure 4-5. *(continued)*

_____

_____

Cons: _____

_____

_____

_____

_____

_____

_____

Design the Program

Whatever the scope of the program that an organization decides on, this subsection provides guidelines and suggestions for (1) which areas of existing policy should be reviewed and revised if they constitute barriers to the use of job sharing and (2) how to develop new policy that will facilitate the successful introduction of job sharing as an employment option.

Eliminate Current Barriers   The first step toward eliminating current barriers is to review your organization's existing personnel policies and union contracts as they relate to job sharing and address any internal constraints that might be found. If your company now uses permanent part-time employees in responsible positions, policy language may already be in place and will need only slight adaptation to encompass job sharing.

The balance of this subsection discusses some of the major barriers to the use of job sharing that you may discover in your review of current policies and contracts.

Head count. Just as with regular part-time, the head count system is a barrier to job sharing. When organizations require each part-time employee to be counted the same as each full-time employee against personnel authorizations, the use of part-time is discouraged. For the purpose of facilitating job sharing, some employers define each partner as "half a head"; others reassess the appropriateness of the head count system and move toward a system of full-time equivalency.

Compensation. All forms of compensation normally attached to a particular position when it is held by one full-time employee should be maintained and divided between the sharers in a way that is equitable both to the employer and to the job-sharing employees. Salary scale should remain the same, and fringe benefits should be prorated based on the amount of time worked by each partner. (A detailed analysis of the compensation and benefits issue can be found in the Pros and Cons of Job Sharing section earlier in this chapter; see the subsection there entitled Cost Implications—The Position Approach.)

Reductions in force. As is the case with other forms of less than full-time work, policy dictating that during a labor force reduction, all part-timers must be laid off first—regardless of length of service, special qualifications, or other considerations—makes job sharing and other types of part-time unattractive. A problem particular to job sharing occurs when the partners have different seniority status; policy must be devised that addresses the effect of layoffs not only on each of the individual sharers but also on the future of the job-sharing team.

Impact on retirement income. Job sharing has often been discussed as a way to implement phased retirement for older workers and is generally included in policy language describing possible options for senior employees who want to work fewer hours in the period leading up to their retirement. The same problems occur as with other forms of regular part-time, however, if provision is not made to ensure that the reduced-time arrangement does not negatively impact retirement income. (For a more detailed discussion of this issue, refer to the subsection on Public and Private Policy Barriers in the section of Chapter 3 entitled Pros and Cons of Regular Part-Time.)

Create New Policy The organization needs to establish personnel policies and processes that ensure uniform treatment of job-sharers. These will support managers who are interested in experimenting with a new kind of work arrangement, assure consistent handling of different cases, and create for these employees a sense of fairness and integration into the organization's overall work force. The issues that you will need to address include:

Eligibility. Which and how many employees will you allow to job-share? Will you accept outside applications for all or part of a position? Or will you limit the option to current full-time employees? Will you exclude any job classifications from the program?

Application process. Where can an employee obtain a set of regulations governing the employment of job-sharers? Whom does the employee talk to first? What kind of preparatory work should the employee have done (such as partner identification, proposed schedule, or task analysis)? Is there a particular form to fill out? Where can it be obtained?

Compensation. How will salary be apportioned? What kinds of fringe benefits will sharers receive, and what will they cost the company? What constitutes overtime? (See the earlier subsection entitled Cost Implications—The Position Approach for a detailed analysis of compensation and suggestions for various ways to deal with these issues.)

Effect on employee status. The way compensation, fringe benefits, and other conditions of employment are handled is critical to how employees on less than full-time schedules perceive the company's fairness and their status as it relates to that of other workers. Prorating compensation and benefits according to hours worked is generally a good rule of thumb. Additional areas that should be addressed are seniority and service credit, order of layoff, probationary period, promotional opportunities, and vesting in retirement programs.

Pair formation. Must employees find their own partners and present themselves as a team? If so, must a partner be from the ranks of current employees, or can the partner who is already employed propose someone from outside the organization? Will the company help in the process (by setting up a partner-finding box in the personnel department, for example)?

Scheduling. How much trading off of work time will you allow partners? Are there any constraints that you wish to impose on the types of schedules that can be constructed? Some questions about scheduling involve policy issues that are best decided by top management; others involve decisions that may best be left to the supervisor. For instance, one reason for limiting certain types of schedules might be that your company's bookkeeping or payroll scheduling systems rules them out. In general, however, employers have found that the most effective organizational policy is one that encourages the widest possible flexibility, allowing the sharers and their supervisor to work out the details of a particular schedule within the context of company regulations.

Replacement of partners. What happens if one partner is incompetent, or the partners prove to be incompatible, or one wants to terminate the job-sharing arrangement, either to return to a full-time position within the company or to leave the company altogether? To what extent will the remaining sharer be expected to fill in until a new partner is found? Provisions must be made in advance for dealing with such problems. (The section entitled Special Considerations for Supervisors and Managers later in this chapter discusses this issue more fully.)

Conditions for reversibility. How does a job-sharer apply to return to full-time work? Will an application from a current sharer receive priority attention when the organization fills full-time openings? If so, to what extent?

New forms should be designed and current ones altered as appropriate. For example, a line might be added to the personnel request form allowing a supervisor to indicate a willingness to consider applications from job-sharing teams.

The program design checklist presented in Table 4-6 will serve as a handy reference for the main issues related to job sharing that you will have to address during the program design phase of the implementation process.

Develop Resource Materials

Managers and supervisors will require resources outlining a step-by-step process for handling job-sharing requests, and employees will require resources covering such major issues as eligibility, application procedures, and reversibility.

Guidelines for managers and supervisors. The organization should provide its managerial and supervisory personnel with detailed information on how to respond to employee requests to job-share. If such guidelines already exist covering requests to reduce a full-time position to regular part-time, a section on job sharing can simply be added. New York State, which has a very dynamic program designed to facilitate voluntary part-time and job sharing, developed an excellent booklet for its managers, from which many of the points in this subsection are drawn.[7]

In general, the process of responding to an employee request to job-share follows the steps listed below (which will, of course, be modified based on the requirements of your particular company).

Table 4-6. Program design checklist: job sharing.

Key Design Issues	Notes
Eliminating current barriers	
☐ Head count	
☐ Compensation	
☐ Reductions in force	
☐ Impact on retirement income	
Creating new policy	
☐ Eligibility	
☐ Application process	
☐ Compensation	
☐ Effect on employee status	
☐ Pair formation	
☐ Scheduling	
☐ Replacement of partners	
☐ Conditions for reversibility	

1. *Request information from personnel.* Policies and procedures from the personnel department covering part-time and job sharing should be reviewed.

2. *Ask the employee to submit the request in writing.* Such a request should include a restructured schedule, a proposal for how the job will be shared, the name of a potential partner, a suggested beginning date for the job-sharing arrangement, and if possible, an estimate of how long the employee would like to job-share. At the time the employee is asked to submit a written request, provide him or her with a checklist (such as the one shown in Table 4-7) indicating what the proposal should cover.

Table 4-7. Sample checklist for a job-sharing proposal.

Checklist for a Job-Sharing Proposal

Key Issues to be Covered in the Proposal	Notes
☐ *Advantages to the employer if the job is restructured:* for example, improved scheduling, better coverage, retention of a trained employee.	
☐ *Strengths of the particular team:* for example, combined experience, additional skills, complementary personalities.	
☐ *Proposed work plan:* how tasks and responsibilities will be divided.	
☐ *Proposed schedule:* how work time will be divided.	
☐ *Communication techniques:* how the partners will communicate with each other, with their supervisor, and with co-workers (such as a notebook, a posted schedule, or taped messages).	
☐ *Responsibilities for continuity:* for example, exchanging time, coverage during partner absence or illness, partner turnover.	
☐ *Other issues:* any cost benefits that you can identify, responses to particular concerns that your supervisor might have, examples of similar or comparable companies where job sharing has been used. Supporting information may be attached.	

3. *Meet with the employee(s).* Discuss the request, a time frame for the decision, and what the next steps might be. Open communication among all parties is important.

4. *Decide.* The following steps are suggested in making a decision to approve or turn down a job-sharing request.

■ Talk with other supervisors and employees in the company who have had experience either with part-time or with job sharing, particularly if this is the supervisor's first experience with job sharing. These contacts can offer practical advice and raise issues that should be discussed and agreed upon before the new work arrangement begins.

■ Determine whether the proposal takes advantage of the partners' individual strengths or accommodates their differing levels of skills and experience. Could this aspect of the proposal be strengthened? Table 4-8 offers an example of how the tasks within a single position might best be allocated between partners having (1) similar types and levels of skills, (2) dissimilar skills at approximately the same level, and (3) significantly different levels of skills and experience. Figure 4-6 then illustrates how a schedule could be arranged to make the best use of the talents of these three combinations of partners.

■ Consider the request's chances for success in terms of the following factors: Are one or both of the proposed job-sharers current employees? Does their previous work record indicate that they could be successful in a job-sharing arrangement? Look for compatible performance records. Since these employees will need to work together as a team, they should have demonstrated good interpersonal and communications skills. Does their proposal look as if they have thought through the problems of sharing this job? Have they put together a good plan for scheduling, communication, cooperation, and so forth? Are they willing to be flexible and responsible in terms of their time commitments so that the continuity of the job will be ensured? Does this arrangement offer advantages to the organization (such as improved scheduling, retention of good employees, implementation of affirmative action goals, cost reduction resulting from differences in salary scale, or availability of a greater range of skills)? Are there ways in which the proposal could be improved?

If the request is one you feel disposed to authorize but there are changes you would like to make in some part of the proposed arrangement, meet with the employee(s) to discuss modifying the request.

Once you have made a decision to approve or disapprove the request, notify the employee(s) and other appropriate parties (supervisor, union representative, personnel department) stating your recommen-

Table 4-8. Media specialist position restructured by task.

Task Analysis	1. Interchangeable structure for partners with similar skills		2. Equal division of responsibilities for partners with dissimilar skills		3. Unequal division of responsibilities for partners with significantly different levels of skills and experience	
	Person A	Person B	Person A	Person B	Person A	Person B
Physical						
Drafting	x	x	x		x	
Layout	x	x		x	x	
Maintaining audiovisual equipment	x	x	x			x
Maintaining media resource file	x	x		x		x
Mental						
Responsibility for completion of tasks	x	x	x	x	x	
Developing and implementing annual media budget	x	x		x	x	
Designing and editing media tools	x	x	x		x	
Writing articles, news releases	x	x		x	x	x
Designing ads for community publications	x	x	x			x
Interpersonal						
Arranging appearances of guests on media, public affairs programs	x	x	x		x	
Training and supervising media interns	x	x		x	x	
Organizing press conferences	x	x	x		x	x
Submitting weekly reports to program manager	x	x		x		x

SOURCE: Adapted from *Incorporating Sharers* (San Francisco: New Ways to Work, 1981), 14–15.

Figure 4-6. Sample scheduling options for media specialist position restructured by task.

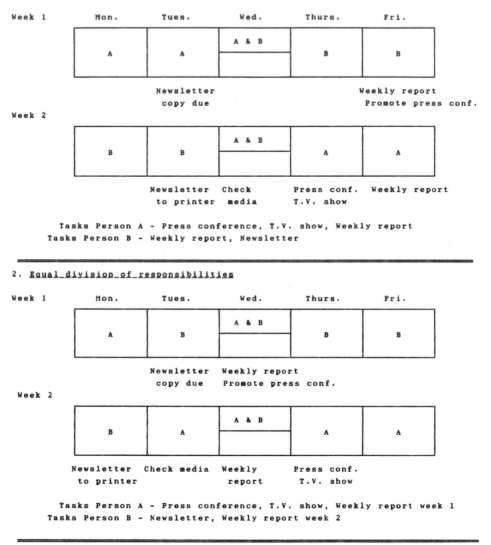

1. Interchangeable partners

Week 1	Mon.	Tues.	Wed.	Thurs.	Fri.
	A	A	A & B	B	B

Newsletter copy due   Weekly report / Promote press conf.

Week 2					
	B	B	A & B	A	A

Newsletter to printer   Check media   Press conf. / T.V. show   Weekly report

Tasks Person A - Press conference, T.V. show, Weekly report
Tasks Person B - Weekly report, Newsletter

2. Equal division of responsibilities

Week 1	Mon.	Tues.	Wed.	Thurs.	Fri.
	A	B	A & B	B	B

Newsletter copy due   Weekly report / Promote press conf.

Week 2					
	B	A	A & B	A	A

Newsletter to printer   Check media   Weekly report   Press conf. / T.V. show

Tasks Person A - Press conference, T.V. show, Weekly report week 1
Tasks Person B - Newsletter, Weekly report week 2

SOURCE: Adapted from *Incorporating Sharers* (San Francisco: New Ways to Work, 1981), 17.

3. Unequal division of responsibilities

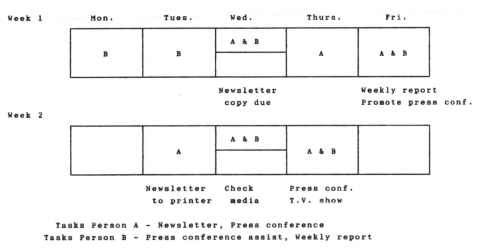

Tasks Person A - Newsletter, Press conference
Tasks Person B - Press conference assist, Weekly report

dation and your reasons for arriving at the decision. If the request to job-share has been denied, possible alternatives might be suggested.

Information materials for employees. Potential sharers must have guidelines on the following issues:

■ *Eligibility.* Are there limitations on who can job-share? Can outside applicants be considered as partners? Are any job classifications excluded?

■ *Process.* What must an interested employee do to participate in the program? Information about application procedures, proposal development (see Table 4-7), forming partnerships, and so forth should be readily available to employees. What, if any, process has the organization developed for helping employees find job-sharing partners internally? (Some employers simply set up a file box in the personnel office where prospective sharers fill out information and can self-refer to potential partners. Others have developed computerized referral systems.)

■ *Contingency planning.* Under this heading come such questions as: How can a job-sharing arrangement be reversed? How can schedules be renegotiated? Can partners trade time, and to what extent?

Figure 4-7 is a sample description of a job-sharing program. A program description such as this can serve as a useful resource for managers and supervisors as well as for interested employees.

(Text continues on page 149.)

Figure 4-7. Sample program description: job sharing.

POLICY & PROCEDURE MANUAL

PAGE: 5270
INDEX TITLE   Human Resources

SUBJECT: Job Sharing
DATE: February 1987

Policy

Recognizing the potential positive impact on recruiting, retention, attendance, productivity, and morale job sharing can offer, Presbyterian-University Hospital encourages its application where appropriate. This policy describes the characteristics of "job sharing" and the effect on benefits of those employed in this manner.

Definition

Job sharing involves two employees who would otherwise be classified as regular part-time in policy #5320, who each work at least "half time" in the same position, and who agree to combine their hours of employment to total those of a regular full-time employee (80 hours per pay period). The agreement, in writing, on Form 1083-4240-1186, which is attached to and part of this policy, indicates that these employees will arrange their own work schedule and will cover for each other's nonwork days whenever possible, even on short notice, in order to staff a regularly scheduled full-time position. (However, job-sharing partners are not required to work full-time to cover for an absence that exceeds three weeks.) Job-sharing partners may choose to work portions of a day, such as A.M. and P.M., or may work alternating days, weeks, or months, as approved by the department head.

Selection

The job-sharing position, when vacant, will be posted and filled in accordance with Selection Policy #5200. However, candidates will additionally be evaluated for their compatibility to function as a team.

Two part-time positions, totaling 80 hours per pay period, that are occupied may be combined to a full-time shared position, without posting, at the discretion of the department head. These situations should be reviewed by the Director, Division of Human Resources, approved by the Administrative Representative, and follow the other provisions of this policy.

SOURCE: Roland Rogers, Director, Division of Human Resources, Presbyterian-University Hospital (Dec. 1986). Used by permission.

Pay and Benefit Differences

Both job-sharing partners will be paid in accordance with the pay grade and salary ranges established for the position they share, even though duties may vary slightly.

Each job-sharing partner will receive an individual rate of pay and performance evaluation based on experience and performance in accordance with policy #5420, Compensation Program.

As defined in policy #5320, a regular part-time employee is one who is employed on a basis of 16 or more hours, but less than 40 hours, per week. Policy #5700, Benefit Programs, indicates that *not* all benefit programs are available to regular part-time employees. Those employed on a job-sharing basis are eligible for the following additional benefits at half the level available to full-time employees:

> Paid holidays (at 4 hours' pay), including personal holidays (16 hours' total)
> Life insurance (1,040 hours times hourly base rate; $7,500 minimum)
> Health insurance, including major medical (employee pays 50% of premium)
> Dental insurance (employee pays 50% of individual premium)

Procedures

A copy of the agreement, signed by both employees and the department head, must be on file in the employees' personnel record in Employee Records and Payroll.

For each job-sharing employee, the employment classification code (policy #5320) on the "payroll action" form (PPF), as completed by the department head, must be 6 (rather than 2 for regular part-time). Both employees must be assigned to the same position in the position control system (policy #5310).

The job-sharing agreement may be terminated on four weeks' notice by either partner or by the department head. Should a suitable replacement not be found for a terminating partner within a reasonable period (four or more weeks of active recruitment), the remaining partner may choose to work on a regular full-time basis, may resign the job-shared position, or may transfer to regular part-time status if suitable vacancies exist at that time.

(Continued)

Figure 4-7. *(continued)*

JOB-SHARING AGREEMENT

The undersigned employees and department head agree to enter into a job-sharing arrangement for the position of _____ in _____ department under the following conditions:

1. The scheduled hours (shift) and days of the week of the position are: _____

   _____

2. These employees will arrange their own work schedule to provide continuous coverage for the position. Should either employee require time off for paid or unpaid absence—such as sick leave, personal holiday, or vacation—the other employee will cover for that absence, even upon short notice, whenever possible. However, coverage is not required for absence beyond three weeks.

3. a. Methods of communication to be used by participants to coordinate the duties of the position: _____

   _____

   _____

   b. Initial schedule arrangements: _____

   _____

   _____

   c. Accommodations expected on short-term notice: _____

   _____

   _____

4. This agreement may be terminated by either employee or by the department head on four weeks' written notice to all parties. Reasons would include termination of employment, scheduling difficulties, inflexible partner, etc.

   Should a suitable replacement not be found for a terminating partner within a reasonable period (four or more weeks of active recruitment), the remaining partner may choose to work on a regular full-time basis, may resign the job-shared position, or may transfer to regular part-time status if suitable vacancies exist at that time.

_____		_____	
Employee [*signature*]	Date	Employee [*signature*]	Date
_____		_____	
Director, Division of Human Resources	Date	Department Head	Date

Form 1083-4240-1186

Announce the Program

Once the program is designed and the policy is approved, the job-sharing option should be announced to managers, supervisors, and employees.

Promote the Program

If the job-sharing program is to be used, however, and not just gather dust in the company's policy and procedure manual, it must be actively promoted. And because this working arrangement is new, its use must be promoted both to employees and to managerial and supervisory personnel. This can be done in a variety of ways—for example, through newsletter stories about successful teams, in management directives, or on company bulletin boards.

The need to promote the program actively is one reason why the company should name a coordinator with ongoing responsibilities for supervising the job-sharing program and encouraging its use.

Evaluate the Program

After the program has been in place for from 6 to 12 months, it should be evaluated. This can be done by surveying all or some of the job-sharers' supervisors and the job-sharing employees themselves to obtain their reactions to the existing program and suggestions for improvements. Some key questions might be: How are the processes working? What kinds of problems have been identified? What additional resources are needed?

Fine-Tune the Program

The information obtained during the evaluation should be used to fine-tune the job-sharing program. This is a process that should be repeated periodically during the first five years of the program in order to apply generally what individual managers, supervisors, and sharers have learned.

Table 4-9 will give you an idea of some of the problems you can expect to find after a job-sharing program has been in effect for a period of time and what types of solutions have proved effective. A number of problem indicators and possible solutions shown in Table 3-5 on regular part-time employees are also applicable to the job-sharing experience.

Special Considerations for Supervisors and Managers

Job sharing is still a new employment option in most organizations. For supervisors, it generally represents a departure from normal procedures and requires the development of some new attitudes and management skills in the following key areas:

Supervisory support. The most critical factor in the successful use of job sharing is the support of the immediate supervisor. If the supervisor has been involved in, or was responsible for, the decision to authorize the job-sharing arrangement, then initial support can be assumed, and positive experience with job sharing will increase the supervisor's support for future shared arrangements.

Communication. During the first three months of the job-sharing arrangement, establishing good habits of communication—between the sharers, between the sharers and their supervisor, and between the sharers and their co-workers—will be a primary objective and is an area that the supervisor should be sensitive to. Logs and posted schedules are essential tools. If problems arise, they should be dealt with immediately, before negative feelings—particularly on the part of co-workers, clients, or other departments—develop.

The balance in the sharers' partnership. The potential for an imbalance in the sharers' partnership is another important issue to which the supervisor must be sensitive. One partner may start to become dominant—especially if the sharing was initiated by an employee who formerly held the job full-time. This kind of imbalance is easier to correct at the outset than if it becomes an established way of relating.

Duplication of effort. Excessive overlap is something to watch

Table 4-9. Examples of job-sharing problems and their solutions.

Problem indicators	Possible solutions
Coverage is too heavy during slow periods and insufficient during peak activity.	Review work scheduling; determine whether work flow patterns should or can be changed. Revise employee schedules, taking the unit's peak work load into consideration.
Job-sharers don't have time to coordinate.	Arrange the schedule so job-sharers have overlapping time. Consider increasing emphasis on logs, memos, and other written communication.
It is hard to know who is in. Job-sharers have been informally swapping time.	Maintain a calendar with the employees' schedules. Have employees swap times only with your knowledge and approval.
One job-sharer appears to be pulling more weight than the other.	Adjust assignments if one job-sharer is getting higher-priority assignments. Review job responsibilities with each job-sharer; summarize responsibilities in writing. See whether changes would improve the less-dominant job-sharer's skills in handling the assignments.
One job-sharer appears to complete assignments too slowly.	Handle as for a full-time employee. Discuss assignments and establish reasonable deadlines. Review what part of the assignment each job-sharer is responsible for. See whether one job-sharer's delays are causing the other to miss deadlines. Distribute the work differently.
One job-sharer spends time chatting with co-workers and socializing. The other job-sharer is resentful.	Discuss behavior standards and expectations. Sometimes schedule arrangements cause unequal time for socializing. For example, if one job-sharer works full days and has a lunch break while the other works half-days with no lunch break, the socializing time is inequitable. Meet with the job-sharing team to work out differences.
One job-sharer feels that the other is getting the choice, more interesting assignments.	Considering each person's strengths and weaknesses, balance work assignments fairly. Reward or praise job-sharers equally for equal performance. Ask the job-sharers to talk over their differences and recommend their own solution.

SOURCE: Adapted with permission from *Part-Time Schedules: A Guide for NYS Supervisors and Managers* (Albany: N.Y. State Dept. of Civil Service, 1985, 31–32.

out for. Some job-sharing employees, anxious to share equally and enjoying each other's company and support, experience difficulty in letting go of the need to be at every meeting and to participate in all major functions associated with the position. They lose sight of the fact that such overlapping coverage will limit what they are able to accomplish.

Division of work. When two people share the responsibilities of one full-time job, the tasks can be split between the two of them in several different ways (as was illustrated earlier in Table 4-8 and Figure 4-5):

- The sharers can be jointly responsible for the entire job. In this case, the employees are considered interchangeable, and there is no division of any of the components of the work. Production-line workers and stenographers are examples of the types of employees who are expected to handle every part of the job while they are there.
- The sharers can be independently responsible for portions of the job. The sharers may cover phone calls and handle urgent situations for each other, but basically their responsibilities are autonomous. This model works well if the job can be divided by caseload or client base, function, or project assignments.
- The sharers can have some independent and some joint responsibilities. In a secretarial team, one partner may have stronger numerical skills while the other is a better writer. Ideally, the division of work should reflect particular strengths or differences of experience.

Evaluating sharers. Whatever the basis for the division of tasks, however, evaluations usually take place on two levels: individual performance and the ability to work as a member of a job-sharing team. Since no two people are alike, supervisors should recognize that sharers may progress at different rates. One partner may merit a salary increase while the other partner does not. As with the case of prorated salary scales, the inherent fairness of evaluating the sharers individually is generally evident and should not be considered a problem in itself. If the team has become unbalanced, an effective and perceptive evaluation may provide an incentive to improve the sharing dynamic.

Replacement of partners when a sharer wishes to end the job-sharing arrangement. Many supervisors worry about the complications that could result from incompatibility of job-sharing partners or a decision by one sharer to end the partnership because he or she wants to go back to a full-time position within the company or even leave the company.

As noted earlier, procedures for such contingencies should be discussed and decided upon in advance wherever possible. For example, many employers negotiate an agreement that if one partner decides to withdraw from the arrangement, the remaining partner will fill in to the extent possible until a replacement can be found. This ensures continuity and is one of the organizational advantages of job sharing that employers report. The same principle holds true if one partner proves to be incompetent or if the two partners prove to be incompatible.

Most employers have found that replacing partners is not difficult and that employees who want to job-share can work with a variety of types of partners. Some organizations encourage the remaining employee to find a new partner, while others prefer to use regular recruitment channels. In the latter case, it is very important, at some stage, to involve the remaining sharer in the process of interviewing for a new partner.

Developing familiarity with existing job-sharing arrangements. If a supervisor is moved into a job where job-sharers are included among his or her subordinates, the situation may require some special attention, particularly if the supervisor has had no previous experience with managing job-sharers. It will be important for the new supervisor to familiarize himself or herself with the background and current status of the arrangement. This should include such activities as reviewing the organization's policy on job sharing; looking at any written records covering each job-sharing pair, such as the initial job-sharing proposals or letters of understanding from the previous supervisor; and clarifying the current schedule (fixed hours, seasonal schedule changes, holiday arrangements, and so on) of each member of the job-sharing team.

It will be important, too, for the supervisor to talk with each of the teams about the strengths and shortcomings of the arrangement as well as expectations and previous agreements; in his or her initial meetings with the teams, the supervisor should also clarify assignments and performance criteria and discuss ways to keep the channels of communication open.

Summary

The use of job sharing, in which a single full-time position is jointly held by two part-timers, has increased steadily during the 1980s as a means of permitting less than full-time work in positions that cannot be handled on a part-time basis. The essence of the concept is that the job itself in fact requires a full-time commitment, with the associated conditions of employment (salary, fringe benefits, and so on) remaining the same as for a full-timer but divided between the two holders of the position.

Job sharing is considered a useful tool if an organization wants to stem the loss of valued employees, improve scheduling, ensure continuity, and broaden the range of skills and experience in a particular position. By carefully selecting the membership of certain job-sharing teams, an organization can also achieve objectives in the area of human resources management.

Improvements in scheduling and continuity are regarded as a major advantage of job sharing. Having two employees rather than one permits the organization to set up creative schedules in which the employees work overlapping hours, or work simultaneously in two different sites, or work a wide span of hours broken by a gap— schedules that respond to the needs of the work itself rather than being dictated by the constraints of a rigid 9–5 schedule. The presence of two employees also provides the organization with a built-in, trained substitute who can maintain the work flow during the absence of either job-sharer.

Inevitably, differences in experience, temperament, and the nature and level of skills will become evident when two employees share a single position. Rather than regarding such differences as a drawback of job sharing, the savvy supervisor will take maximum advantage of them—by dividing up the work and the schedule in ways that focus on each job-sharer's strengths and abilities. By pooling the talents of two employees, each of whom is working in the areas of his or her primary capabilities, the organization often finds itself getting more, and better-quality, work for its money than it can from a single employee.

Job sharing's role in the achievement of human resources objectives is, as noted, another positive feature of this arrangement. Many companies set up job-sharing teams with a certain very specific outcome in mind. The two part-timers sharing the position may both be phasing in to retirement; one may be training his or her replacement, perhaps in preparation for retirement or in preparation for advancement to a higher-level position; one may be training half-time at a higher level at which a full-time job opening has not yet become available. The possibilities in this area are limited only by the imagination of the company's management.

In weighing the advantages and disadvantages of using job sharing, the employer will have to take a detailed look at the costs associated with this option. Some surprises may be in store, since the organization often finds that savings in base salary result when part of a position is filled by an employee who qualifies for a lower salary range, and the use of overtime may drop sharply. When the cost of group health insurance is shared by the company and the part-time employees and other benefits are prorated, job sharing will *not* double, or even substantially increase, the organization's benefits costs. In fact, the organization sometimes reduces its benefits outlay when part-timers covered by a spouse's policy decline health insurance coverage.

Job sharing will increase the costs associated with administrative overhead somewhat because the number of employees will rise, but the cost of new-hire administration and training will increase only if the implementation of this arrangement requires hiring new employees or training one or both job-sharers. If the job-sharers' schedules are set up to enable them both to use the same space and equipment, no extra expense in this area is incurred. And in fact, the decrease in absenteeism and turnover generally associated with the use of job-sharing often offsets whatever moderate cost increases may be involved.

The employer would do well to look beyond the (often considerable) advantages of restructuring individual positions to a job-sharing mode and examine the broader potential advantages to the organization of adopting a program approach—offering the option in categories of positions or company-wide. Employers that opt for a more widespread use of job sharing usually do so because this approach will enable them to multiply the savings that can be achieved when individual positions are shared and/or solve chronic problems (such as reducing absenteeism in certain job categories, improving recruitment efforts, retaining valued employees, facilitating continuing education, and allowing senior employees to cut back their work hours prior to retirement).

The attitudes of unions, supervisors, and employees play a significant role in an employer's decision about the use of job sharing.

Since shared jobs are regarded as full-status positions that happen to be worked by part-time employees, unions are usually more receptive to this scheduling alternative than they are to other forms of part-time, providing the sharers are protected against inequities that could creep into the arrangement. Supervisors may initially be skeptical about job sharing but tend to support the option once they have had successful experience with it. Most employees regard the introduction of job sharing favorably, but care must be taken to see that the practice is handled both efficiently and equitably. If certain job-sharing teams fail to communicate well with co-workers or the sharers appear to be receiving favored treatment, the organization could lose employee support for job sharing.

In implementing job sharing, a company must focus on generating understanding of, and support for, this work-time alternative; removing any organizational barriers that may discourage the use of job sharing and defining a comprehensive new policy on its use; developing resource materials that can help both supervisors and employees systematically consider the entire range of relevant factors before they enter into a job-sharing arrangement; promoting the use of job sharing once the program is in place; and modifying the program on an ongoing basis to eliminate problems that have been noted by the involved parties and incorporate suggested improvements.

Successful implementation of a job-sharing program will require the knowledgeable and skilled participation of an organization's supervisory personnel. Supervisors have to be particularly sensitive to the following types of issues: Sharers must communicate effectively, both with each other and with their fellow employees, including the supervisor; one sharer should not become dominant, throwing the partnership out of balance; the two partners must not duplicate each other's efforts; the sharers' responsibilities should be allocated so as to focus on their respective strengths; they have to be evaluated both on their individual accomplishments and on their ability to function as part of a job-sharing team; and provisions must be in place to guarantee continuity of work when an employee leaves a shared position.

The organizational advantages of permitting not only individual jobs but entire categories of jobs to be worked on a shared basis can be considerable for the employer that has examined this scheduling option closely, selected it for the right reasons, and planned its use with care.

CHAPTER 5

Phased and Partial Retirement

*P*hased retirement is a way for individuals to retire gradually by reducing their full-time employment commitment over a set period of years. *Partial retirement* is a part-time employment arrangement for senior employees in which salary may or may not be combined with partial retirement income. It has no defined time limitation.

In 1978, management expert Peter Drucker described phased and partial retirement as "the central social issue in the United States." His was a voice expressing early concern that we develop policies that "encourage people to stay on the job and remain economically productive: rather than encourage them to retire early so that there is more room at the top."[1]

Two issues make Drucker's words particularly relevant today. The first is the cost of recent downsizing programs that focus on promoting the early retirement of senior employees. Providing health insurance for retirees has been described as a "time bomb" due to go off in many companies in the early 1990s. The second compelling reason is the specter of employee shortages in the 1990s. Older workers, who often have difficult-to-replace skills and experience, may become a sought-after human resource.

Several related trends make phased and partial employment of seniors an attractive management option. They include:

■ *The trend toward earlier and earlier retirement.* In 1986, 84 percent of all employees who retired from large companies with pension plans did so before they were 65. In 1978, only 62 percent retired "early."[2] Encouraging older workers to retain at least a partial attachment to the labor force broadens

both the employers' and the workers' options as economic and
social factors change.

■ *Older workers' interest in staying in the work force longer and
in working part-time.* A poll by the Travelers Insurance Company showed that 43 percent of that organization's 62–65-year-
old employees planned to continue working past age 65, and
85 percent of the survey respondents who were 55 or older
wanted part-time jobs.[3] A 1981 Louis Harris poll indicated that
four out of five workers from ages 55 to 64 wished to combine
part-time work and partial retirement.[4]

■ *The steady decrease in the ratio of employed workers to
retirees and their dependents.* In 1935, when Social Security
was initiated, the ratio was nine to one. In 1978, it was four to
one. Current employment policies that encourage earlier and
earlier retirement are narrowing the gap even further. It is
projected that by 2025, the ratio will be close to three to one.[5]
A shift to later or partial retirement would ease the increasing
demands on both private and public pension funds.

Origins of Phased and Partial Retirement Programs

In the early 1970s, the idea of phased retirement began to be discussed and then initiated in Europe. For the most part, the impetus
for these programs in Great Britain, Germany, France, and Belgium
came from top-level management within individual companies. The
notable exception to this pattern is Sweden, where legislation allows
eligible workers nationwide to reduce their schedule in the years
preceding their eligibility for retirement and to receive a stipend that
offsets the wages lost through cutting back on paid work time.

The reasons for the emergence of phased retirement in Europe
are complex, having to do with such factors as demographics, the
introduction of new technology, and changes in attitudes about work
and leisure. They were, however, basically grounded in a concern for
the welfare of older workers and a desire to alleviate the negative
impact of abrupt, full retirement.

In the United States, private-sector phased retirement began to
attract employers' attention for some of the same reasons, but
interest in it was slower to take hold. In 1978, amendments to the
Age Discrimination in Employment Act made most compulsory retirement before age 70 illegal. In 1987, new legislation outlawed
mandatory retirement and, effective in 1988, compelled employers to
continue contributing to pension plans for workers over age 65.

With the baby-boom generation moving into the work force and women working in unprecedented numbers, some companies began to experiment with new part-time and phased retirement options for their senior employees. (Table 5-1 shows some of the alternatives that are now available to older workers.) While the primary objective in most cases was to improve possibilities for the advancement of younger workers, accommodating the needs of senior employees was also a goal.

Who Uses Phased and Partial Retirement?

One of the most extensive users of phased retirement has been the state of California. In 1974, it passed legislation enacting the "Reduced Work Load Program" for the members of the State Teachers' Retirement System. This program allows certain teachers nearing retirement age the option of reducing their hours of employment as a means of phasing in their retirement. In order to protect the teachers' retirement income and fund the program, the legislation stipulated that "although the program involves a salary reduction corresponding to the reduced employment, it allows participants to continue earning credits for retirement benefits at the same rate as full-time employees." Teachers can choose to continue paying into the retirement fund as though they were working full-time, and the district employing them contributes on the same basis. The objectives of this innovative California program are twofold: (1) to ease the financial and psychological trauma of retirement for senior teachers and (2) to permit the earlier employment of new teachers.[6] A later section of this chapter includes a profile providing further details about the "Reduced Work Load Program."

In 1980 the faculty members of the state's university system were offered a phased retirement option. This program, in addition to offering university employees 60 years or older, who have 20 or more years of university service, the option of working part-time and phasing into retirement, also allows its participants to supplement their reduced salary base with outside earned income and/or with payments from the University of California Retirement System.

In 1984, a third program, the Partial Service Retirement program, became effective. Employees who are eligible for participation include all state miscellaneous employees 62 years or older, who have a minimum of five years of credit in the Public Employees' Retirement System (PERS). Workers must reduce their work time by at

Table 5-1. Work options available to employees 50–64 years of age and 65 years or older, by size of employer.

Working Patterns	250–300		301–500		501–1,000		1,000+		Total	
	50–64	65+	50–64	65+	50–64	65+	50–64	65+	50–64	65+
Flexible schedule of less than 40 hrs/wk	30.5%	41.1%	37.0%	45.8%	38.7%	41.7%	36.4%	38.8%	36.0%	42.2%
Regularly scheduled part-time	51.7	50.7	53.3	59.5	64.1	68.7	64.2	61.1	58.1	60.5
Seasonal or part year	33.6	21.2	35.1	36.2	32.4	30.6	41.8	40.2	35.9	33.3
Gradual retirement	25.8	24.3	19.5	18.4	17.2	14.9	19.4	19.0	20.2	18.8
Possibility of full-time	a*	94.4	a	95.8	a	89.8	a	97.1	a	94.5
Job sharing	14.6	15.7	13.6	16.9	12.4	13.6	22.4	20.5	15.7	16.9
Job transfers	67.7	59.4	78.9	75.7	78.4	67.8	87.1	77.5	78.6	71.5
Consulting	28.7	33.3	37.9	39.2	35.6	34.5	56.2	56.3	40.1	41.6
Flextime	33.6	a	33.5	a	27.6	a	39.0	a	33.6	a

*Question not asked.

SOURCE: Malcolm J. Morrison, *The Transition to Retirement: The Employee's Perspective* (Bureau of Social Science Research, Inc., 1985).

least 20 percent but not more than 60 percent. Participants may elect to receive a partial retirement allowance while they are working on a reduced schedule. Unlike most phased retirement programs, they may also opt to return to a full-time schedule at a future date. If they do withdraw from the program, however, they may not reapply for partial retirement for five years. (A brochure describing this program in more detail is shown in Figure 5-4.)

In the late 1970s and early 1980s a number of private-sector companies also began to introduce alternative employment options for their older workers. Atlantic Richfield developed a job-sharing policy as part of the company's "Senior Worker Policies and Program" unit. Levi Strauss also used job sharing to help senior employees work part-time and subsequently developed a phased retirement alternative as well. Polaroid Corporation announced a pioneering "Tapering-Off" program in which older employees could reduce the number of their work hours gradually, cutting back on a daily, weekly, or monthly basis. Varian, a California Silicon Valley electronics company, set up a phased retirement program for employees who planned to retire within three years, were 55 years of age or older, and had five years of service with the organization.

Although the programs just described are still intact, unfortunately, many other such programs were severely cut back or disappeared entirely in the early 1980s as companies concentrated on downsizing and preferred "golden handshakes" to huge numbers of senior employees. Today, however, interest in phased and partial retirement as an alternative for older workers has been renewed, in part because of the Federal Tax Reform Act of 1986, which makes early retirement a less-attractive option. According to the provisions of that legislation, the maximum annual pension that can be paid under a corporate defined-benefit pension plan to a worker retiring at age 55 has been slashed from $75,000 to $40,600. When the Social Security retirement age climbs to 67 in the year 2021, that maximum will be cut even further, to $35,500. Since existing rights are protected, the legislation will have a future, not an immediate, impact.

Renewed interest in phased retirement may also result from some of the negative experiences of companies that used aggressive early retirement programs. Many employers found that by selectively offering expensive retirement bonuses, they not only lost those employees they would have preferred to keep but also aroused resentment among workers who had to be content with the basic retirement plan. In addition to the morale issue, many companies are finding early retirement incentives overly expensive in the long run.

When Are Phased and Partial Retirement Most Appropriate?

Phased and partial retirement options are appropriate ways to *encourage employees with hard-to-replace skills or experience to extend their work life*. They are also ways to *introduce more management options* with which to deal with such issues as cost control, upward mobility, and employee burnout.

Three categories of companies tend to benefit most from offering phased and partial retirement options:

1. Those that have (1) implicit or explicit policies prohibiting or restricting layoffs and (2) an aging work force. Such employers are prime candidates for consideration of some type of phased or partial retirement program.
2. Those that have a young work force and want to recruit experienced and more senior personnel. These organizations have the added assurance that they will have fewer potential retirees at the outset of their phased or partial retirement program and consequently will have more time to resolve any administrative or operational problems.
3. Those that actively promoted early retirement and experienced negative results.

Pros and Cons of Phased and Partial Retirement

The advantages and disadvantages of phased and partial retirement programs can be asserted in terms of (1) human resources considerations and (2) cost considerations. Although the concepts of phased and partial retirement still represent a radical departure from the current policy of most private-sector organizations and experience with these options has thus far been limited, this section presents what we do know at this point about the effects of offering reduced work-time programs for older employees.

A 1981 survey of Western European personnel executives, conducted by International Management Association, identified a range of problems involving both human resources considerations and cost considerations that were judged to be major obstacles to introducing alternative work patterns, including phased retirement. These obstacles, together with the percentage of respondents identifying each obstacle as a significant problem, are:

■ Insufficient thought given to hidden extra costs (31.8 percent).

■ Inadequate commitment by top management (31 percent).

■ Insufficient thought given to solving production problems (30 percent).

■ Union opposition (29.8 percent).

■ Insufficient thought given to human problems and reactions (28.3 percent).

■ Resistance by lower and middle management (28.1 percent).

■ Lack of briefing and/or training to show employees how to take advantage of the greater flexibility (27 percent).

■ Lack of support from the work force (18 percent).[7]

Human Resources Considerations

The introduction of phased and partial retirement options generally helps employers retain workers who have special skills or long-term experience with the company. If older employees are faced with a take-it-or-leave-it choice between retiring or continuing to work full-time, some would rather retire. Reducing their hours is an attractive alternative that can induce a number of these employees to extend their work life. Phased and partial retirement can also be a way to revitalize older workers who are suffering from burnout.

A program of part-time options for workers nearing retirement age can be a valuable adjunct to an organization's overall recruitment strategy. It enables the organization to attract skilled seniors who can bring greater balance to its pool of talent and experience.

By permitting senior employees to cut back their hours, a company increases the available opportunities for upward mobility and cross training. Younger full-timers can assume responsibility for the vacated portion of these positions, which lets them phase in to a higher level and, in some instances, be trained by the incumbent.

When an organization offers attractive part-time work alternatives that meet the needs not only of older workers but often of younger ones as well, the net effect tends to be a rise in employee morale.

Employers considering the feasibility of offering their employees a partial or phased retirement option must also address such issues as administrative and managerial barriers, work force utilization, future personnel needs, and the social impact that this work-time alternative might have on the organization.

Recently, the possibility of legal challenges to early retirement plans has been added to the list of factors that an organization must weigh in deciding whether to institute some type of alternative to early retirement, such as a program of phased or partial retirement. Most lawsuits arising from early retirement programs are based on questions of age discrimination (were all employees offered the same retirement terms, or were younger ones offered a more lucrative package?) and whether or not the employees were coerced into accepting premature retirement. Not allowing employees enough time to decide about a proposed retirement package has been held to be a form of coercion in some cases.

Cost Considerations

As noted earlier, phased and partial retirement are relatively new options that have not yet been used by large numbers of organizations. Yet it is safe to say that these options, when properly introduced, can be very cost-effective. On what do we base this conclusion, given the admittedly limited experience with phased and partial retirement? This conclusion becomes evident when the cost implications of some early retirement programs—the most common alternative to phased or partial retirement—are examined.

From the 1950s until the late 1980s, early retirement was a sought-after objective for both employers and employees. Most organizations that downsized their operations in the mid-1980s actively promoted early retirement. But it turns out that pushing employees into early retirement can prove very expensive for an employer. As the cost effects of these early retirement programs come to light, they should provide an incentive for wider use of such alternatives as phased and partial retirement.

The main costs associated with early retirement programs include the prolonged expense of financing various aspects of the program (such as health insurance for younger retirees and an increase in the pension benefits being paid out by the organization) and loss of experienced and talented workers.

Health insurance for retirees is a benefit that is proving to be tremendously costly for many companies. According to a *New York Times* article, "[M]any companies have been studying their situation and finding that their unfunded liabilities for retirees will equal or exceed the complete operating profit for the year. The numbers are generally in the same range as pension liability—but unfunded."[8]

The extent of the problem involving unfunded health insurance liability often corresponds to the age of the company. New organizations often have a more favorable ratio of active employees to retirees. Digital Equipment Corporation, for example, had 110,000 active employees in 1987 and only 1,000 retirees. Bethlehem Steel Corporation, on the other hand, had 37,500 employees and 70,000 retirees. In general, a *Fortune* 500 company has approximately 3 active employees to every retired one. For a typical company, the cost of funding health insurance for retirees is estimated at from one percent to 3 percent of payroll.[9]

A hidden cost cited by employers is that of providing full health benefits for younger retired workers not yet eligible for Medicare who remain enrolled in the company's health insurance plan.

Other hidden costs include those associated with training junior employees who are unfamiliar with the duties formerly handled by early retirees and, sometimes, the cost of hiring former workers as consultants.

When benefits, pension payments, and incentive payments for early retirement are totaled, and increased expenses for training and consultants are considered, the sum constitutes a major problem area for many organizations, even when the savings from payroll reductions are taken into account. In view of the high cost of early retirement programs, it would seem appropriate for employers to ask themselves what are the cost implications of *not* offering a phased or partial retirement alternative that could enable the organization to reduce its payroll without increasing its pension payout or incurring the expense of providing medical insurance to retirees who are no longer productive workers.

And finally, employers considering the advisability of permitting senior workers to reduce their hours should examine the issues of demographics and employee morale as they affect costs. A careful look at the demographics of an organization's labor force can give management an idea of how many employees, and in what job classifications, might take advantage of phased or partial retirement options. An improvement in employee morale and commitment was mentioned in the preceding subsection as a human resources consideration. Although difficult to assess as a cost factor, employee morale should not be overlooked in terms of its undeniable effect on productivity. Phased or partial retirement is an option that many employees value, regardless of whether or not they are nearing retirement age.

Should Your Organization Try Phased or Partial Retirement?

At this point, you will want to determine whether or not yours is one of the types of organizations mentioned earlier whose needs and characteristics make it a good candidate for trying a program of phased or partial retirement options.

This section contains two profiles (see Organizational Experience With Phased and Partial Retirement), which describe what happened when two employers instituted a program of reduced work-time alternatives for senior employees. These profiles will help you start considering some of the major issues involved in offering phased or partial retirement options and identify which issues are likely to play the biggest role in your own organization's decision about these options.

Now turn to the accompanying questionnaire (Table 5-2), listing the primary concerns that lead organizations to adopt phased or partial retirement programs. If, on this questionnaire, you find yourself repeatedly indicating that your organization does face the situations described, it's a good bet that some of these problems could be resolved through the introduction of less than full-time alternatives for older employees.

Assuming your questionnaire results indicate that your organization should be seriously considering phased or partial retirement, the accompanying worksheet (Figure 5-1) can be used to list the problems you would hope to solve through the introduction of this type of option and what associated benefits and drawbacks might be expected.

Introducing Phased or Partial Retirement Options

The organization that wants to offer part-time alternatives for its older workers starts by gaining top management's support and then appointing both a task force, which will be charged with designing the program and gaining companywide support, and a project administrator. Key issues are explored and policy is established during the program design phase. Once policy is finalized, the organization develops resource materials for employees who are nearing early retirement age as well as for managers and supervisors. The program announcement must be followed by an active promotion effort, to overcome the existing bias in favor of early retirement. After the program has been in effect for a period of time, it is evaluated and modified as needed.

In this section, we will take a closer look at each of these steps in the program implementation process.

Gain Support for the Program

Since existing policy in most organizations has actively encouraged early retirement, changing this orientation will require strong support

ORGANIZATIONAL EXPERIENCE WITH PHASED
AND PARTIAL RETIREMENT

Varian Associates

Description: Varian is a high-technology manufacturer of electron tubes, analytical instruments, medical instruments, and semiconductors. It is located in Palo Alto, California, and employs approximately 15,000 in the San Francisco Bay area. Other employment options used by Varian have been work sharing as an alternative to layoffs and, occasionally, job sharing.

Reason for Using Phased Retirement: The "Retirement Transition Program" was announced in 1977 to provide an additional option for senior employees and to enable the company to retain valued workers who might otherwise have retired.

Implementation Process: Interested employees who are age 55 or older, have at least five years' regular service with Varian, and plan to retire within three years complete a Retirement Transition Program Application Form and submit it to their supervisor for approval. In some cases—for example if the employee's current job includes supervisory responsibilities—approval may require a change in job assignment.

Requests can be made for a four-day workweek, a three-day workweek, or less. The minimum work schedule allowed is 20 hours per week. During the course of the program, either the employee or the supervisor may request a change in the work schedule if the individual's situation or the company's needs change.

Participants normally retain their original job classification, although changes may sometimes be necessary. Employees continue to be eligible for merit increase consideration. Medical and dental coverage remain the same, but some other benefits (life insurance, retirement and profit sharing, paid leaves for such reasons as jury duty, and disability insurance) are prorated.

Participation in the program is limited to three years, at the end of which the employee retires. Return to full-time status will be considered if the employee's personal circumstances change substantially after entering the program and the employee requests it. The company may also ask an employee to return to full-time status for a limited period of time until a temporary emergency situation can be resolved.

Impact to Date: Although the program has not been heavily used, it has on several occasions allowed the company to retain employees with hard-to-recruit skills or experience.

SOURCE: Descriptive material from Varian Associates, Palo Alto, Calif., and telephone interview with Varian's corporate human resources staff (1988).

State of California Public School Teachers

Description: The state of California has been a pioneer in the field of alternative work time and offers a number of work-time options for state employees. The State Teachers' Retirement System's "Reduced Work Load Program" is available to public school teachers.

Reason for Using Phased Retirement: The option was introduced in order to allow teachers nearing retirement to phase out of their careers. To a lesser extent, it was intended as a way to phase in new teachers.

Implementation Process: Under the "Reduced Work Load Program," teachers 55 years of age or older who are within ten years of retirement, have worked full-time in a district for the immediately preceding five years, and have worked for a total of at least ten years can negotiate to reduce their schedule to half-time. In order to receive full retirement credit, the employee and his or her employer contribute to the retirement fund "the amount that would have been contributed if the member was employed on a full-time basis." The employee retains full health coverage and other rights and benefits, "for which he makes payments that would be required if he remained in full-time employment." Retirement income remains the same as if the employee had continued to work full-time.

Impact to Date: The program was evaluated in 1980 by the state's legislative analyst. At the time, it had been in operation five years. Employers indicated that the program had reduced their salary costs because "[T]he salaries of the participants, typically senior employees in or near the top of the salary scale, are usually more than the salaries of new employees hired on a part-time basis to replace the Reduced Work Load Program participants."

SOURCE: *The Reduced Work Load Program in the State Teachers' Retirement System* (Sacramento, Calif.: Office of the Legislative Analyst, Sept. 1980), 1–23.

Table 5-2. Phased and partial retirement questionnaire.

Would Phased or Partial Retirement Benefit Your Organization?

	Yes	No
If your organization has offered early retirement incentives in the past, have there been negative consequences, such as employee resentment or underestimated costs?		
If your company has plans to restructure its work force in the near future, will senior employees be one of the groups targeted and offered incentives to leave voluntarily?		
If there is a problem with upward mobility in some of your organization's job classifications, would it be alleviated by having some senior employees cut back their hours or share jobs?		
Have any older workers expressed an interest in reducing their schedules or phasing in to retirement?		
Do some of your company's senior employees have skills that would be difficult to replace when they retire?		
Do other organizations in your industry offer phased or partial retirement options?		
Would morale be generally enhanced if your company's employees knew that phased or partial retirement alternatives were available to them?		

from *top management*. Long-held attitudes will need to be countered and present policy and processes changed in order to introduce part-time options for senior employees in a way that will elicit significant participation. Establishment of the program will require time, commitment, and leadership from all levels of management.

Once leadership from the top has been secured, a companywide *task force* that incorporates representatives from middle management, labor, the relevant fiscal and administrative areas, and the human resources side of the organization, should be established. This is a way to ensure broad input to the change process as well as gain support. The task force should be charged with reviewing current policy, conducting research on other similar companies' programs, developing a rationale for new policy and program objectives, recommending specific policy changes, and devising a process for implementation, evaluation, and fine-tuning.

Set Up the Program's Administration

The task force should appoint a *project administrator,* both to act as staff during the development of the program and to serve as a resource to managers and employees after its inception.

Figure 5-1. Phased or partial retirement worksheet.

Assessing the Need for Phased or Partial Retirement

List the main reasons why you are considering introducing a phased or partial retirement option:

1. _____

   _____

   _____

2. _____

   _____

   _____

3. _____

   _____

   _____

4. _____

   _____

   _____

List what you see as the advantages and disadvantages of phased or partial retirement:

Pros: _____

_____

_____

_____

Cons: _____

Design the Program

The process of designing a program of phased or partial retirement includes the following tasks: reviewing existing personnel policies to identify aspects of current policy that can hinder the use of part-time employees (for a discussion of such policy barriers, refer to the subsection entitled Design the Program in the section of Chapter 3 entitled Introducing or Expanding the Use of Regular Part-Time Employment); collecting information about the policies and programs of similar companies, both in the same industry and in other industries; and defining program objectives and developing policy that will support phased or partial retirement options. The definition of program objectives and the development of policy should concentrate on the following issues:

Eligibility. How many *years of employment* will be required for eligibility? At what *age* is an employee eligible? For maximum participation rates, a lower age is preferable, but it should be assumed that some of the younger employees who reduce their hours either will want to return to full-time schedules at some point or will be preparing themselves for a transition to a new employment area. This should be taken into consideration when setting program objectives and making policy decisions about duration of enrollment and reversibility.

Effect on employee status and benefits. The fringe benefits of major concern to senior employees are *medical and dental insurance* and *pension*. Policies that prorate the cost of inclusion in the group insurance plan protect those senior employees on a part-time schedule who are not yet eligible for Medicare.

In order to protect retirement income, some formula should be devised that allows the organization and senior employees on a reduced schedule to continue contributions to the pension fund as if participants in the program were working full-time so that retirement income is not adversely affected. Such protection exists in the State of California's "Reduced Work Load Program," described earlier in the chapter. Teachers who qualify are allowed to cut back their schedule, but they and their employing school districts continue paying into the retirement fund as though they were still working full-time. An evaluation of the program by the state's legislative analyst showed that the program resulted in net savings to both the districts and the retirement fund.

The remaining status and benefit areas that will be affected are the same as for other regular part-time employees and are discussed in Chapter 3 in the sections entitled Pros and Cons of Regular Part-Time (see the Cost Implications subsection) and Introducing or Expanding the Use of Regular Part-Time Employment (see the Design the Program subsection).

Duration of enrollment. An important question related to the basic intent of the program is whether the company views it as essentially a phased retirement or a partial retirement option. If the intent is to minimize early retirement and encourage work force retention, then stipulating an earlier age with no limitation on length of time in the program and a provision for reversibility may be most appropriate. If, on the other hand, the program's objective is to encourage retirement but cushion its impact, then length of participation should be specified. Most programs limit participation to one to five years before full retirement.

Minimum and maximum time reductions. Some programs define the parameters of reduction; for example, in the California Public Employees' Retirement System, "Work time may be reduced by at least 20 percent but not more than 60 percent." Others only establish the maximum schedule reduction that will be allowed: "Employees must work a minimum of 20 hours a week."

Arrangements for work-time reduction. The range of scheduling choices within the various existing phased retirement programs include: gradually shortened workdays or workweeks; regular part-time and job sharing; and extra leave time, which can be taken in a variety of ways, such as days, weeks, or months off. Ideally, the supervisor and participating employee should have as much latitude as possible to design an appropriate schedule.

Changes in work time. Most programs allow enrolled employees to change their reduced schedule once a year, with their supervisor's approval. A common practice for employees who are phasing retirement is to increase the reduction each year until full retirement is reached.

Reversibility. Whether or not an employee can withdraw from the program and return to full-time work is a critical question. The answer is determined by what the employer hopes to achieve through the program. One program stipulates that employees who withdraw cannot reenroll for five years.

The program design issues just discussed are summarized in Table 5-3, which you can use to keep track of where you stand in addressing each of these issues.

Develop Resource Materials

A company that wants to introduce a program of phased or partial retirement options for its senior workers must develop resource materials both for managers and supervisors and for older employees. A program description, such as the one in Figure 5-2, can be a useful aid for managers and supervisors as well as for interested workers.

Resource materials for managers and supervisors. Materials designed for use by managers and supervisors should emphasize the *organization's* reasons for wanting to expand the employment options for senior workers to include phased or partial retirement. Some companies also provide managers and supervisors with materials that outline the major pros and cons of such a program from the employees' perspective. These resource materials should also identify the program coordinator, to whom specific or unusual questions should be directed.

Figure 5-3 and Table 5-4 are examples of the types of information materials that managers and supervisors find helpful. Figure 5-3 is a cover memo to managerial and supervisory personnel from a corpo-

Table 5-3.   Program design checklist: phased or partial retirement.

Key Design Issues	Notes
Eliminating current barriers	
☐ Impact on retirement income	
Creating new policy	
☐ Eligibility	
☐ Effect on employee status and benefits	
☐ Duration of enrollment	
☐ Minimum and maximum time reductions	
☐ Arrangements for work-time reduction	
☐ Changes in work time	
☐ Reversibility	

rate retirement program administrator, together with a set of guidelines for supervisors to help them deal more effectively with employees nearing retirement. (The company that developed the guidelines shown in Figure 5-3 has also prepared a very similar set of guidelines directed at the organization's older workers.) Table 5-4 shows at a glance how various time reductions affect such key issues as total workdays, vacation allowance, holidays, and pension credits.

Resource materials for employees. Having resource materials available for senior employees who are approaching *early* retirement age is extremely important if an organization wants to encourage older workers' maximum participation in a phased or partial retirement program. These information materials should cover such issues as the following:

■ *Voluntary nature of the program.* Does the older employee *have* to accept a reduced schedule? The voluntary nature of the program should be emphasized, and employees should be encouraged to think about when they want to retire or whether they want to retire at all. If workshops or counseling services are already available for senior employees, the option of

(Text continues on page 180.)

Figure 5-2.   Sample program description: phased retirement.

RETIREMENT TRANSITION PROGRAM

General

A voluntary Retirement Transition Program has been established for the
benefit of regular employees who would like to work a reduced work week
during the three year period immediately preceding their planned retirement.
The objective of the program is to broaden employment alternatives available
to employees and to provide interested employees a gradual transition from
full employment to the usual reduced activity of retirement. During this
period of reduced work schedule, employees will be permitted to continue
their participation in company benefit plans.

Job Assignments

In some cases the reduced work schedule may require a change in job
assignment. For example, under normal circumstances it would not be
possible for a supervisor to continue in this role when working less than
full time. Therefore, a condition of participation will be the availability
of a job that can be performed by an employee working less than full time.
Participation in the program will be limited to a maximum of three years.

Eligibility Requirements

The program will generally be available to any regular employee with a
minimum of 5 years of service who will have attained a minimum age of 55
at the time participation in the program commences, and who plans to retire
within three years. There may, however, be some employees occupying positions
who, due to the nature of the work requirements, cannot be accommodated by
this program.

Requests for Participation

Employees who wish to participate will indicate their interest by initiating
a written request for voluntary participation. The request will be sent to
the employee's supervisor who, in coordination with his supervisor, will
indicate the availability of a suitable job assignment before forwarding the
request to Personnel. Since it might take several months in some instances
to find replacements and suitable alternative jobs for those volunteering
for the program, requests should be initiated at least three months prior
to the date the reduced work week is desired. Alternative jobs must be
identifiable and meaningful.

Details of the administration of the program are as follows:

A.   Work Schedule

     Three months prior to the end of the quarter following or coincident
     with an employee attaining age 55, or any quarter thereafter preceding
     the date the employee requests entry into the program, an application
     for the program will be initiated by the interested employee requesting

Varian / 611 Hansen Way
Palo Alto / California 94303-0883 U.S.A.

varian

SOURCE: Varian Associates, Palo Alto. Calif. (1988).

(Continued)

Figure 5-2.   *(continued)*

a reduced work week. Requests can be made for a 4 day work week or
a 3 day work week, but schedules for as little as one-half time
(20 hours) can be requested. Twenty hours would be the minimum work
schedule allowed.

There may be special work situations when two half-time employees could
fill one job, i.e., each employee could work 20 hours. In this event
each employee might work 4 hours each day for five days, or one employee
might work two full days and then 1/2 day with the second employee
completing the work week.

During the course of the program either the employee or the supervisor
may request a change in the work schedule if the individual's situation
or the company's needs change.

B. Length of the Program

Once an employee has begun participation in the program, he/she will
continue in the program until retirement or earlier termination of
employment, but in any event the period will not exceed three years.

C. Wage and Salaries

1. Job Classifications

Participants will normally retain the job classification held prior
to participating in the program. Changes in job classifications may
sometimes be necessary, e.g., supervisors who are given non-super-
visory positions in order that they might work a reduced work schedule,
employees who accept an assignment in a lower classified position to
enable them to participate, etc. The employee's hourly equivalent
rate upon entry into the program will continue to be paid unless
the employee is assigned to a job in a lower classification.

2. Merit Increases

Employees in the program will continue to be eligible for merit
increase consideration based on performance and according to
guidelines.

3. Supervisory Positions

Employees who have been in supervisory positions will be relieved of
supervisory responsibilities prior to being placed on the reduced
work schedule and will be required to apply for the program at least
three months in advance so that plans for a replacement may be made.

4. Overtime

While overtime is not generally contemplated under the program,
the following will apply if overtime is worked:

RETIREMENT TRANSITION PROGRAM   Page 3

    a.   <u>Non-exempt employees</u>: Hours worked in excess of 8 in one day or 40 in one week will be paid at 1½ times the regular rate. Work performed on scheduled days off will not be paid for at premium rates unless it exceeds 8 hours in one day or 40 hours in one week.

    b.   <u>Exempt employees</u>: The provisions governing overtime for exempt employees on a full time work schedule will apply to exempt employees in the Retirement Transition Program (i.e., exempt employees must be scheduled to work on the sixth day for four consecutive weeks).

D.   <u>Benefit Plan Participation</u>

    1.   Employees in this program will continue to be eligible for participation in the following benefit plans on the same basis as regular employees. Where eligible earnings determine the degree of participation, the employee's participation will be based on his reduced income level.

        a. Group medical & dental insurance plan
        b. Group life insurance plan*
        c. Stock purchase plan*
        d. Cash Option Profit-Sharing plan*
        e. Retirement and Profit-Sharing plan*
        f. Service Award program
        g. Tuition refund plan
        h. Travel accident insurance
        i. Holidays (which fall on scheduled work days)
        j. Vacation (accumulation pro rated based on scheduled hours of work. Vacation may be charged on scheduled work days only)
        k. Sick leave (accumulation pro rated based on scheduled hours of work. Sick leave may be used on scheduled work days only)
        l. Leaves of absence with pay* (emergency leaves, jury duty, etc.)
        m. Short-Term Disability insurance*
        n. Long-Term Disability insurance*

E.   <u>Termination of the Program</u>

    1.   Once an employee begins participation, it is intended that he/she continue for a maximum of three years or until an earlier termination or retirement. However, as with any other employee, a participant will be subject to all conditions affecting other employees, including layoff, leaves of absence, etc.

    2.   Should an employee's personal circumstances be substantially changed after entering this program, for example, an unanticipated change which results in economic hardship, etc., return to full time status will be considered upon employee initiated request. There may also be situations when the company may request an employee to return to full time status for a limited period of time until a temporary emergency situation can be resolved.

* Level of participation in these benefits is related to eligible earnings.

6/82

Figure 5-3.   Guidelines for supervisors with employees nearing retirement age.

POLAROID CORPORATION
Cambridge, Massachusetts 02139

MEMORANDUM

To: Division Personnel Teams

From: [*Corporate Retirement Administrator*]

Date: Updated March 1983

Subject: GUIDELINES FOR SUPERVISORS WITH MEMBERS PREPARING FOR RETIREMENT

The attached guideline is one that can be helpful, not only to supervisors of members in the retirement transition period, but also to members themselves preparing for retirement. As mentioned, the transition from full-time work to full-time leisure can be very difficult to adjust to.

It is important to note that many people approaching retirement tend to change their minds a number of times relative to their decision to leave. This manifests itself in different ways with different people. Some people become indecisive, not just as to when to leave, but sometimes indecisive in day-to-day decisions they make. Such behavior should not be considered abnormal or irresponsible. It is natural under the circumstances.

It must be recognized that there are many forces acting on an individual contemplating retirement. The immediate family reacts sometimes positively with *over*encouragement, sometimes negatively with lack of support in the transition, and sometimes different members of the family will "pull" in different directions. Peers outside of the workplace can place considerable pressure for or against the individual's contemplated decision; and in the workplace itself, both from supervisors and co-workers, forces can be exerted that are disruptive to an orderly decision.

The alternatives mentioned in the guideline can eliminate much of the trauma that can be apparent in the transition.

Admittedly, there are some obvious negative aspects to these alternatives. The reduced wages in a "tapering-off" mode often are unsatisfactory to the member, and if he/she is of Social Security age, it can actually become a *disincentive,* because the member could be earning just too much to be eligible for a Social Security benefit. Of course, a member "tapering-off" can be a liability from management's viewpoint, since the member must still be carried as a *full*-head for head count purposes.*

NOTE: There is now an accounting mechanism called "Total Equivalent Head Count" that permits the recording of a part-time person based on . . . actual hours scheduled.

SOURCE: Polaroid Corporation, Cambridge, Mass. (1983).

The leave-of-absence approach requires adaptation within the department to temporarily fill the need during the member's absence, and for the member, leave without pay is often not attractive.

As cases arise in which these approaches might be a workable alternative to an abrupt retirement, please contact the Corporate Retirement Office in Cambridge for advice and counsel.

Corporate Retirement Office, [*address*]

   [*name*], Corporate Retirement Administrator—[*phone number*]
   [*name*], Corporate Retirement Associate—[*phone number*]

GUIDELINES FOR SUPERVISORS WITH MEMBERS PREPARING FOR RETIREMENT

Some people are able to adjust to an abrupt transition from full-time work to retirement.

In more and more cases, though, prospective retirees are becoming aware that the transition from full-time work, to full-time leisure is a difficult one to adjust to.

This guideline is to explain some alternatives to an abrupt retirement, that are available with departmental approval, for prospective retirees, to facilitate them in this transition.

There are two basic techniques that are becoming more and more common to facilitate a prospective retiree in the retirement decision-making process. The first is called "tapering-off," or "phased retirement," and the second is a specific leave of absence to "rehearse retirement."

I. *Tapering-off:* Stated simply, the prospective retiree reduces his/her number of hours of work. This can be done in many ways, and it is strongly recommended that the member participate in the planning phase. Some members may want to reduce the number of hours they work each day; some may want to reduce the number of days they work each week; and in some particular situations, a member may want to reduce the number of weeks worked in a month. Flexibility is the key—the member needs to go over his/her plan with the department management, and of course, concurrence with department needs, etc., must be considered.

An example of "tapering-off," but in no way stated to be a model or recommendation, could be:

"Member at age 64 reduces workdays to 4 days per week (32 hours) and continues at this level for 15 months; then reduces schedule to 3 days per week (24 hours) for another 12 months; and then retires."

Flexibility in such arrangements is urged. Some members may need a longer period of "tapering-off," and it is strongly recommended that the end date be open-

(Continued)

Figure 5-3. *(continued)*

ended. Some may reach a "plateau" that is ideal for their working situation and desire an extended period at that schedule.

We had an engineer who for five years—from age 65 to age 70—reduced the hours of work to 20 hours per week and then retired. This also, of course, met the needs of the department nicely.[*]

NOTE: In all cases of reduced work hours, the member only gets paid for the hours worked, and basically, if [*he/she*] works at least 1,000 hours/year, gets a proportionate share of any bonus or profit-sharing contribution paid, a proportionate share of holidays and vacation, and a proportionate value for life insurance and LTD [*long-term disability*]. Health insurance coverage is maintained in full. Pension credit accrues proportionately for all hours worked in a calendar year, once a minimum of 500 hours has been satisfied.

II. *Rehearsal Retirement:* Indecisiveness is a very natural trait in the retirement decision-making process. The option to take a specific leave of absence gives the member an opportunity to "rehearse retirement" without terminating. At the end of the leave, the member can either come back to the same job or decide that retirement is his/her true desire. The justification "to rehearse retirement" is considered a valid reason for a specific leave of absence (LOA-SP).

Traditionally, the length of most of these leaves will be for three months. But there is no restriction to having it for a longer period with appropriate approval. [*]

NOTE: During a leave of absence (LOA), all pay and accrual for benefits is stopped. The member continues group insurance coverage through direct payment to Polaroid. If the member returns to work, the seniority date is adjusted, and credit for all benefits commences again.

In administering or for further inquiry about these alternatives, please utilize the counsel and advice of the Corporate Retirement Office, [*address*].

[*name*], Corporate Retirement Administrator—[*phone number*]
[*name*], Corporate Retirement Associate—[*phone number*]

[*signature*]
March 1983

phased or partial retirement should be incorporated within the materials and the program format.

■ *Financial implications.* What impact will phased or partial retirement have on Social Security, taxes, and benefits, particularly health insurance and the pension plan? Special resource materials for senior employees should focus on the short- and long-range financial ramifications of cutting back their schedules to various part-time levels. (In Chapter 6, on voluntary

Table 5-4. Reduced-time chart.

% Time Worked	Reg. Hrs. on PEP*	Paid Hrs. per Yr.	Work Hrs. per Yr.	Workdays per Yr.	Work Hrs. per Mo.	Vacation Allow.†	Holiday Allow.‡	Pension Credit per Yr.	Head Count Acc't.
100%	40 hrs.	2,080	1,832	229 days	153	160 hrs.	88 hrs.	1.00	1
90%	36 hrs.	1,872	1,649	206 days	137	144 hrs.	79 hrs.	.90	9/10
80%	32 hrs.	1,664	1,466	183 days	122	128 hrs.	71 hrs.	.80	4/5
75%	30 hrs.	1,560	1,374	172 days	114	120 hrs.	66 hrs.	.75	3/4
70%	28 hrs.	1,456	1,282	160 days	107	112 hrs.	62 hrs.	.70	7/10
60%	24 hrs.	1,248	1,099	137 days	91	96 hrs.	53 hrs.	.60	3/5
50%	20 hrs.	1,040	916	114 days	76	80 hrs.	44 hrs.	.50	1/2

NOTE: Used not to baffle and confuse, but to assist in tracking time worked, etc.—basically to keep [*employees*] from cheating themselves.

*PEP = Part-time Employment Program.

†Assumes member has earned *10 extra* V-days [*vacation days*] (10 yrs. service).

‡Holiday allowance based on 11 days (full-time).

SOURCE: Polaroid Corporation, Cambridge, Mass., *Corporate Retirement Administrator*, Feb. 1983.

reduced work time, another regular part-time option, there are some sample resource materials that present this sort of highly detailed information that can let employees know exactly what they are getting into by reducing their schedules to a specified extent.)

■ *Eligibility*. Who is eligible to participate in the program, at what age, and with what length of service? Are any individuals or job classifications excluded from participation in the program?

■ *Schedule changes and reversibility*. Can an agreed-upon schedule be renegotiated, and on whose authority? How often may the schedule be changed? Is reversibility possible if the senior employee subsequently decides that full-time employment is preferable? If a worker withdraws from the phased or partial retirement program, will there be a specified time period during which he or she cannot reenroll?

■ *Application process*. How can an employee find out about the program and apply to participate? The organization should establish a procedure whereby interested employees can obtain both general information and individualized information about the program and its potential impact on them as well as procedures for submitting and reviewing applications.

Figure 5-4, which describes the Partial Service Retirement program of the state of California's Public Employees' Retirement System, is an example of the type of resource materials that employees find helpful. It provides an overview of all the key issues associated with such a program, focusing particularly on the effect that a schedule reduction will have on the employee's retirement allowance (on which the employee's pension will be based).

Announce the Program

Simply announcing that the company is now offering a phased and/or partial retirement option will not be enough to ensure participation in this kind of program. Active promotion of both the concept and the program will be needed to counter the many years of emphasis on early retirement.

Promote the Program

Leaving the work force as soon as possible has been promoted as a positive objective since the early 1950s. It will take sustained encouragement to get senior employees to recognize the benefits to them-

Figure 5-4.   Brochure for employees explaining a partial retirement program.

Introduction

The Partial Service Retirement program, which became effective January 1, 1984, allows you to reduce your worktime and receive a partial retirement allowance at the same time. The amount of your partial retirement allowance is based upon the reduction of your worktime.

For example, if you reduced your worktime by 50%, your allowance would equal 50% of what you would be entitled to if you had taken a full service retirement instead of a partial service retirement. A reduction in worktime of 30% (meaning you would work 70% of full time) would entitle you to an allowance equal to 30% of your full service retirement allowance.

Worktime may be reduced by at least 20% but not more than 60%. In other words, you must work at least 40% time but not more than 80% time to participate. **Your agency must approve the reduction in worktime you wish to choose.**

Qualifying and Applying

You must meet all of the following requirements to be eligible for partial service retirement:

- be a full-time State miscellaneous member (this includes State college employees who are PERS members),
- be age 62 or older, and
- have a minimum of five years of PERS service credit. (This includes any PERS-credited service. Service credit with another California public retirement system cannot be used to meet the five-year requirement.)

State industrial, patrol, and safety members, as well as University of California employees, are **not** eligible for this benefit.

Your Personnel Office keeps the necessary application/election form (Partial Service Retirement Application, DPA-062) if you wish to apply. **Remember: You must receive departmental approval before you can apply.**

You should submit your application/election form to PERS at least 45 to 60 days before your effective date of partial retirement. This will insure that your election will be processed in a timely manner. The effective date of your partial retirement can be the first of any pay period.

SOURCE: *Partial Service Retirement* (Sacramento: California Public Employees' Retirement System, June 1984).

(Continued)

Figure 5-4. *(continued)*

Your Allowance

There are three things you need to know to estimate your partial retirement allowance:

Service Credit

The amount of PERS-covered service you've earned. (Refer to your last PERS Annual Member Statement and add any service credit you may have earned since that time.)

Benefit Factor

This is the percent of pay to which you are entitled for each year of service. It is determined by your age at partial retirement.

Your Age	Benefit Factor
62	2.272%
62¼	2.308%
62½	2.346%
62¾	2.382%
63+	2.418%

Final Compensation

Generally, this is your average monthly payrate for the last consecutive 36 months. You may elect another 36-month period if it produces a higher average.

If your PERS service was coordinated with Social Security, you have never contributed on the first $133.33 of your monthly earnings. So when computing your allowance, you must reduce your final compensation by that same $133.33.

Once you've determined these three things, you can begin calculating your estimate. You may also contact your nearest PERS Area or Field Office for an estimate.

Step 1

Determine the highest full service retirement allowance to which you would be entitled. Multiply your:

Service Credit (X) Benefit Factor (X) Final Compensation

Example:

Nancy is applying for partial service retirement. She will be 62½ years old on the effective date of her partial retirement, with 25 years of service credit. Her final compensation is $1,500, and she **is not** coordinated with Social Security. Nancy's estimate would be as follows:

Years of Service Credit		Benefit Factor		Final Compensation		Highest Full Service Retirement Allowance
25	·(X)	2.346% (=58.65%)	(X)	$1,500	=	$879.75

Your Allowance

If she **were** coordinated with Social Security, her final compensation must include the $133.33 reduction:

   25   (X) 2.346% (=58.65%) (X) $1,366.67   = $801.55
                                     ($1,500 – $133.33)

Your Example:

Determine your highest full service retirement allowance.

Years of Service Credit		Benefit Factor		Final Compensation		Highest Full Service Retirement Allowance
_____	(X)	___% (=___%)	(X)	$_____*	=	$_____

* Do you need to reduce your final compensation for coordination with Social Security? See above.

Step 2

Now, multiply your answer in Step 1 by your reduction in worktime.

Your Highest Full Service Retirement Allowance (From Step 1)	(X)	Your Reduction Of Worktime (Percentage)	=	Your Partial Service Retirement Allowance

Example:

Nancy has been approved to reduce her worktime by 40%. By using the answer in the example in Step 1, she can estimate her partial retirement.

Highest Full Service Retirement Allowance		Reduction Of Worktime		Partial Service Retirement Allowance
$879.75	(X)	40%	=	$351.90

Your Example:

Determine your partial retirement allowance by multiplying your answer in Step 1 by your reduction in worktime.

Your Highest Full Service Retirement Allowance		Your Reduction Of Worktime		Your Partial Service Retirement Allowance
$_____	(X)	___%	=	$_____

(Continued)

Figure 5-4. *(continued)*

Other Considerations

Withdrawal and Subsequent Worktime Changes

You may end your partial service retirement and withdraw from the program, at any time, with your employer's approval. Once you withdraw, however, you cannot reapply for five years.

You must also obtain your employer's approval if you wish to make additional changes with your worktime after your partial retirement begins. Decreases in your (already) reduced worktime are possible once every fiscal year, while increases may be made only once every five years.

Allowance Adjustments

Unlike a full service retirement, there are no provisions which allow for cost-of-living increases. Your partial service retirement allowance will not be recalculated due to increases in age, salary, or service credit as long as you participate in the program. It may change, however, if you increase or decrease your worktime percentage, or if an adjustment to your allowance payable on the date you enter into partial retirement is necessary.

Changing Jobs

You may transfer from one State agency to another and continue your partial retirement as long as you remain a State miscellaneous employee and your new employer approves your continuation in the program.

Separating From Employment

If you decide to permanently separate from PERS-covered employment, you cannot continue your partial retirement. You may instead choose to apply for a full service retirement (see your "PERS State Miscellaneous" member booklet), terminate your PERS membership and receive a refund (a return of your contributions on deposit

Other Considerations

with PERS, plus interest), or leave your contributions on deposit with PERS and defer taking your full service retirement.

Entering a Full Service Retirement

You may fully retire at any time while participating in the partial retirement program; however, the duration of your partial retirement may affect the calculation and amount of your full service retirement allowance. If you choose to fully retire before earning one year of PERS service credit while participating in the program, your full service retirement allowance would be calculated differently than if you had earned more than one year's service credit. **You should be aware that it is to your advantage to fully retire after earning at least one year of service credit.** Contact your nearest PERS Area or Field Office for an estimate and explanation of your full service retirement allowance after partial retirement.

Please Note: Because your worktime has been reduced to participate in this program, it will take more than one fiscal year to earn one year of PERS service credit.

Taxes and Payroll Deductions

When you begin your partial retirement, you will receive a letter from PERS showing the amount of your contributions as well as any credited interest which has been set aside to help pay for your partial retirement allowance. You can use this information to receive a determination from either the IRS or any other tax authority as to your tax liability.

Only appropriate income taxes can be deducted from your partial retirement allowance. PERS cannot advise you about the taxability of your partial retirement allowance. You must contact your local IRS or other tax authorities for information in this area.

Other Considerations

All other deductions which you may have (health and life insurance premiums, union dues, credit union payments, deferred compensation plans, purchasing additional PERS service credit, etc.) must be taken from your State salary. If you have any questions regarding payroll deductions, ask your Personnel Office.

Health and Dental Insurance

Your health and dental plans would not be affected by your participation in the program. You should remember, however, that any premium payments will be deducted from your State salary and not your partial retirement allowance.

Social Security

You may draw Social Security benefits while receiving your partial retirement allowance; however, your earnings—the combination of your State salary and your partial retirement allowance—may cause an offset to your Social Security benefits. Contact your local Social Security office for more information.

Injury, Illness, Leaves of Absence

If you become injured or ill—during your participation in the program—and cannot perform your job, you may be eligible for a disability retirement. Obtain a copy of our separate leaflet called "Disability Retirement" for more information. If your injury or illness requires that you take a leave of absence or go on Non-Industrial Disability Insurance, you may continue your partial retirement with your employer's consent. You may remain in the program if you require other types of leave; ask your Personnel Office.

Provisions for Your Beneficiaries

Unlike a full service retirement, there are no provisions which allow you to provide benefits to someone, after your death, by reducing your partial retirement allowance

Other Considerations

and selecting a retirement option. Rather, if you should die while in the program, your beneficiaries would be eligible for the same pre-retirement death benefits as the beneficiaries of members who do not participate in the program. All death benefits are explained, in detail, in your "PERS State Miscellaneous" member booklet.

Please Note: Because a portion of your contributions is used to help pay for your partial retirement allowance, any benefit which includes a return of your contributions, plus interest, to your beneficiary will be affected.

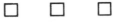

Important Numbers (Area Code 916)

If you have any questions regarding the status of your partial service retirement—after you have applied—you may call the PERS Benefits Division at 445-5030, or 485-5030 (ATSS).

TDD Interpreter Numbers

Information	445-4900
	485-4900 (ATSS)
Benefits Information	323-4290
	473-4290 (ATSS)

selves and to the organization of remaining longer in the work force. At least three areas must be addressed educationally in order to create a new orientation that will result in a successful phased or partial retirement program:

1. Managers need to understand what fiscal benefits this reduced work-time option for senior employees will bring to the organization and to society, and individual workers need to understand what ramifications this type of program has for their economic well-being.
2. The organization must counter negative myths about the capabilities of older workers. Such myths tend to support management and employee bias in favor of retiring early rather than extending work life.
3. The organization must also counter negative attitudes about part-time work and part-time workers.

Evaluate the Program

The program should be evaluated in terms of the guidelines established at the outset by the task force. One objective should be to look at participation rates; another, to look at cost, especially as it compares to previous policy initiatives (such as early retirement) relating to older workers.

Fine-Tune the Program

On the basis of the evaluation results, the program can be modified to improve its effectiveness. For example:

Problem	*Solution*
Employee participation rates are low.	Promote the program company-wide.
	Hold focus groups with senior employees to have them critique the program.
Evaluation indicates that senior employees are interested, but are concerned about making an irreversible decision to retire.	Consider adjusting program policy to allow a return to full-time employment if desired.

| Supervisors are reluctant to approve requests for participation in program. | Require written response to requests, which include a reason for the denial. |

Summary

Phased and partial retirement are employment alternatives in which older workers reduce their time commitment prior to full retirement. This reduction can take place either gradually over a specific number of years (phased retirement) or for an open-ended period of time (partial retirement). These options provide employees with a middle ground between full-time work and full retirement that can help cushion the shock of retirement while at the same time relieving employers of some of the burden of providing pension payments and health insurance for a steadily growing number of retirees. These less than full-time alternatives not only meet the needs of older employees but also provide a way for younger workers to advance.

Reduced work-time options for senior employees were first offered in Europe in the 1970s, primarily by private-sector companies. The concept gained acceptance more slowly in the United States, with phased and partial retirement programs introduced on a limited basis. But many of these programs fell victim to the wave of downsizing in the early 1980s, in which incentives were commonly offered to push older workers into an abrupt early retirement.

However, under legislation enacted in the 1970s and 1980s, employers were prohibited from compelling their older workers to retire, and the maximum pension that a company could pay to early retirees under a corporate defined-benefit pension plan was sharply reduced. These laws tended to discourage early retirement and provided a powerful incentive for both companies and older workers to seek more creative alternatives to full retirement. Coupled with the effect of this legislation was the discovery by employers that the widespread use of early retirement had a variety of negative consequences. Dismissing older workers via the "golden handshake" proved to be a costly move that often resulted in the loss of valued personnel and a drop in employee morale.

Phased and partial retirement are effective strategies for retaining senior workers whose skills and experience will be difficult to replace and for increasing the range of options available to management for coping with such problems as burnout and the need for upward mobility. These reduced work-time alternatives are most appropriate in organizations with an aging work force that have policies or practices discouraging layoffs, in organizations that want to supplement an existing predominantly young work force by recruiting more seasoned employees, and in organizations whose active use of early retirement brought negative consequences.

In considering the adoption of a program of part-time employment for senior workers, an organization should consider such advantages as the retention of skilled and experienced staff, a broadened recruitment effort, increased opportunities for upward mobility and cross training, and enhanced employee morale. The organization that offers attractive alternatives to full retirement will also not find itself the target of lawsuits arising from an overly aggressive promotion of early retirement.

Although experience with phased and partial retirement has to date been rather limited, the fact that these options are cost-effective can be deduced by examining the high cost of widespread use of early retirement. As noted above, companies that made it a practice to lure older workers into cutting short their work life quickly found themselves bereft of talent, facing morale problems that threatened to affect productivity, and saddled not only with the one-time expense of retirement incentives but also with the ongoing expense of sharply increased pension payments and unfunded liabilities for retiree health insurance. Such experience revealed the wisdom of offering employment options under which older individuals could continue to function in a part-time capacity as productive workers rather than retiring abruptly to become full-time burdens upon the corporate coffers.

The standard eight-step process for implementing an employment alternative will, in the case of phased and partial retirement, focus particularly on establishing strong support for the program at the outset, developing resource materials that fully explain the advantages of these options, and actively promoting the program's use. In all cases, this emphasis is designed to overcome the firmly entrenched assumption on the part of both managers and workers that early retirement is the only desirable goal for older employees.

A carefully designed and skillfully promoted program of reduced schedules for senior workers is, in short, a strategy whereby an organization can both recoup its investment in trained and experienced employees and combat the rising cost of pensions and retiree health benefits.

CHAPTER 6

Voluntary Reduced Work Time Programs

V-*Time* (short for *voluntary reduced work time*) programs are the newest way to offer reduced work-time options to a broad base of employees in a way that integrates part-time with full-time employment. V-Time is a time/income trade-off arrangement that allows full-time employees to reduce work hours for a specified period of time with a corresponding reduction in compensation. Although this option can be offered to individual employees on an ad hoc basis, it is most effective when offered as a formal program. V-Time differs from regular part-time employment in that there is usually a time limit on the arrangement, and a process is defined for return to full-time status.

The V-Time program design was originally developed as a way to accommodate employees who needed a temporary alternative to full-time employment. The first V-Time pilot project was implemented, however, as a joint labor-management effort to minimize layoffs. V-Time programs encompass the concept of regular part-time, including job sharing, but also provide for smaller time reductions than most part-time or job-sharing arrangements. Under a typical V-Time program:

- Reductions of work time (and pay) ranging from 2.5 percent to 5 percent, 10 percent, 20 percent, and 50 percent are offered.
- The schedule remains in force for a designated period, usually 6 or 12 months, to allow employees and employer to try out the new arrangement, with the assurance that the commitment can be either renegotiated or terminated at the end of that period.

■ All employee benefits are maintained, with some being prorated.

■ A supervisor must authorize an employee's participation in
the program.

■ The time off can be taken either on a regular basis, as a
reduced day or week, or in a block of time, such as extra leave
or days off from work.

Origins of V-Time

As noted, the original impetus for the development of V-Time programs was employees' need for a reduced work-time option that
would be available to more people because of the *smaller* increments
of reduction than are offered by traditional part-time or job sharing
and that would provide the same conditions of work as full-time
employment, coupled with a process for returning to full-time after
the need for part-time had passed. As Figure 6-1 shows, the most
popular choices of salary reduction in the New York State "Voluntary Reduction in Work Schedule Program" (formerly called the
"Voluntary Furlough Program"), which was begun in 1984, are the
10 percent and 20 percent options.

Service Employees International Union (SEIU) was the organization that designed the original V-Time program. SEIU and the

Figure 6-1.   Work/salary reductions selected under New York State's
"Voluntary Reduction in Work Schedule" program.

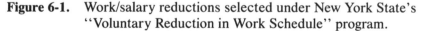

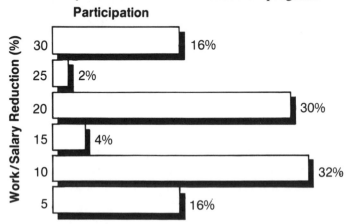

SOURCE: Employee information packet (Albany: New York State Department of
Civil Service, Apr. 1984). Used by permission.

county administration in Santa Clara, California, had since the early 1970s recognized the growing need for less than full-time work options. Previous negotiations had led to an agreement to expand traditional part-time classifications and to initiate split codes, or job sharing, for county employees. In 1975, SEIU attempted unsuccessfully to introduce a V-Time program within the county because, as Michael Baratz, executive director of the local, said, "Our people wanted more personal time." The following year, when the county announced a budget crisis and forecast a 6.5 percent reduction in staff, the union again introduced its idea of a voluntary reduced work hours program. This time, the board of supervisors lent its support to the concept as a way to minimize layoffs, and the program was begun in December 1976.

Today, more and more employees nationally are expressing a need or desire for a reduced schedule at some point in their careers. The extent of this need is still unquantified, since little research has been done in this area. Table 6-1 is from *Exchanging Earnings for Leisure: Findings of an Exploratory National Survey on Work Time Preferences*. Although this survey dates from 1978, its findings are still worth considering, since it is the only national survey of work-time preferences conducted thus far in the United States and, hence, the only truly comprehensive data we have on how many people would favor the availability of some sort of reduced work schedule.

Polls have also been conducted that seek information about the work-time preferences of particular segments of the workforce. Although less comprehensive than the Harris survey, they tend to support the same conclusion—that "prevailing work-time conditions are at variance with the preferences of today's workers."[1] During the 1980s at least four national surveys of working parents indicated the need for more work-time options.[2] The November 1988 *Better Homes and Gardens* magazine, reporting on the most recent of their polls, noted that: "As in past questionnaires, letter writers passionately and repeatedly plead for work arrangements that accommodate young families' needs: 'I would like to see more part-time jobs available for parents whereby they could work 20–30 hours a week, make a decent salary, and still be eligible for benefits. . . .' Other respondents suggest work that can be done primarily at home— maybe going into an office part of the week."[3] A 1983 report on three surveys of New York state employees and managers showed a "significant demand for part-time jobs among current full-time employees"[4] and a poll of The Travelers' senior employees also indicated considerable interest in part-time employment.[5]

Table 6-1. Stated worker preference toward exchanging portions of current income for alternative forms of free time.

Value of Tradeoff	Shorter Workday vs. Pay	Reduced Workweek vs. Pay	Added Vacation vs. Pay	Sabbatical Leaves vs. Pay	Earlier Retirement vs. Pay
Nothing for time	77.0	73.8	57.8	37.9	64.0
2% of pay for time	8.7	11.6	23.2	24.2	17.6
5% of pay for time	5.8	—	8.5	8.0	8.1
10% of pay for time	—	7.6	6.2	4.8	5.9
12% of pay for time	5.5	—	—	—	—
15% of pay for time	—	—	—	4.8	—
20% of pay for time	—	4.5	2.2	—	4.4
30% of pay for time	1.6	—	—	—	—
33% of pay for time	—	—	2.0	—	—
40% of pay for time	—	.9	—	—	—
50% of pay for time	1.5	1.6	—	—	—
Total Percent	100.0	100.0	100.0	100.0	100.0
Total Respondents	954	953	952	951	951

Note: Column spaces are frequently blank for many tradeoff options because questions dealing with different forms of free time did not always have parallel exchange options.

SOURCE: Excerpted from an Aug. 1978 survey conducted by Louis Harris and associates, as reported in *Exchanging Earnings for Leisure: Findings of an Exploratory National Survey on Work Time Preferences,* R&D Monograph 79 (Washington, D.C.: U.S. Department of Labor, Employment and Training Administration, 1980), 81.

Reduced work schedules may, as we mentioned earlier, first be tried by an organization on a case-by-case basis. However, once the organization begins to use regular part-time employment more often, the value of having a program rather than relying on individual accommodation appeals both to many managers and to employees. A program meets management's need to develop an administrative process to deal with the integration of a variety of reduced and full-time schedules as well as to plan the allocation of work time and do so in a way that ensures equity of treatment for the employees involved.

Who Uses V-Time Programs?

Two counties in northern California, Santa Clara and San Mateo, provided the first sites for V-Time programs. From there, the concept spread to state government. A California legislator used the county V-Time model as the basis for legislation entitled the Voluntary Reduced Work Time Act of 1980. It authorized state employees to request a variety of reduced work-time options. Once the legislation had passed, the state Department of Personnel Administration drew up guidelines for the establishment of agency-based programs similar to the ones offered by the two counties. In 1984, the program design was used by New York State as the basis for its "Voluntary Reduction in Work Schedule Program." Shaklee Corporation became the first private-sector user in 1983, when it introduced a V-time program for its employees. (Shaklee's experience with V-time is profiled in a later section of this chapter.)

When Is V-Time Most Appropriate?

From management's perspective, the primary reason for introducing a V-Time program is to reduce labor costs in a way that accommodates employees' needs and reinforces their commitment to the organization. By offering smaller increments of reduction along with job sharing and more traditional formats of regular part-time work, V-Time maximizes the multiplier effect of the payroll reductions. It also provides a formula for prorating the cost of health insurance and other benefits, establishing a policy context that supports the integration of full- and part-time work. As such, it represents the antithesis of the concepts embodied in the idea of contingent or "core-ring" employment.

Within particular departments, V-Time also creates some additional fiscal flexibility for management. The money saved through payroll cutbacks can be applied elsewhere or held for future use. If it is used to hire additional employees, it may be possible to obtain less-experienced personnel at lower salary rates.

Because V-Time programs offer a wider choice of time reductions under formalized conditions, they provide a broader-based and more efficient response to various kinds of need for reduced work schedules within the labor force. As with other forms of part-time, these needs include:

■ More time for family responsibilities. A number of national and organizational polls, such as the Gallup, General Mills, and New York state surveys cited earlier, have shown that flexible and reduced work-time options are of great importance

to employees with either dependent children or dependent
senior family members.
■ Time to complete or reenter education programs.
■ The desire to work part-time at the end of a career as a way of
phasing retirement.
■ Health problems that preclude full-time work.

V-Time programs can also be an important component of a *work-
sharing* strategy during economic downturns. Many companies have
found that some employees will volunteer to cut back on a portion of
paid hours in order to save jobs. Management's encouragement,
coupled with policies that protect overall employment rights, can
enable individual employees to use recessionary periods to reenter
education or training programs, catch up on domestic responsibilities, or enjoy some leisure time until the economy picks up again.
(See Chapter 8 for an in-depth discussion of work sharing.)

Pros and Cons of V-Time Programs

The advantages of introducing a V-Time program have to do with
standardizing the use of reduced schedules, making schedule cutbacks attractive to a wider range of employees, and increasing cost
savings and fiscal flexibility. The potential disadvantages have to do
with management attitudes and union attitudes.

Standardizing the use of reduced schedules. While in some organizations, employees are permitted to cut back their hours on a case-
by-case basis, management can standardize the process of accommodating employees who need reduced schedules by introducing a
V-Time program that permits such reductions under specified conditions and for a specified period of time. This eliminates many of the
inequities that inevitably result from an ad hoc management response
to requests for part-time. The range of schedule reductions is then
made available to employees on a largely voluntary basis.

Increasing the attractiveness of part-time options. Only a relatively small number of employees can contemplate the 20 percent to
50 percent work-time reductions of traditional part-time schedules.
The smaller time reductions available under a V-Time program put
time/income trade-offs within reach of more employees and therefore
enhance the organization's opportunities to reduce its payroll through
voluntary cutbacks. Because this range of scheduling options accommodates the needs and interests of such a wide variety of employees,
it is also a useful recruitment tool.

Increasing cost savings and fiscal flexibility. Offering voluntary part-time work options results in a variety of cost savings for the organization, as discussed in Chapter 3, Regular Part-Time Employment. The cost savings associated with more traditional part-time schedules can be multiplied when a company introduces a V-Time program, under which part-time can be used on a more widespread basis. When employees trade income for time, one of the primary cost reductions is a direct savings in payroll expenditures. Indirect savings may also be realized if new employees are hired at the lower end of the salary scale. Savings of this sort increase management's fiscal flexibility by making available extra dollars that can either be used to reduce the budget or be reallocated to more critical areas.

Management attitudes. A manager whose department has a heavy work load may be reluctant to approve requests for V-Time— particularly if the company has instituted a hiring freeze tied to a head count, which would prohibit extra hires, or if the department is unable to reduce its work load. Hiring temporary employees is sometimes a way to permit the use of V-Time in departments faced with this type of situation.

Union attitudes. Labor representatives are often concerned about V-Time's impact on full-time employment. They worry that jobs will be lost if schedule reductions that were originally presented as being voluntary and having a limited duration then become mandatory and permanent. Union attitudes toward V-Time, however, tend to become more favorable as positive experience with this option grows.

Should Your Organization Try V-Time?

To determine whether it would be advisable to offer a V-Time program, you will have to examine the problems faced by your organization and compare them to the types of problems most effectively solved through the use of V-Time. That's what this section is all about.

The accompanying group of profiles entitled Organizational Experience With V-Time examines V-Time programs instituted by three organizations. Notice whether, and how, the experience of these organizations parallels your own company's situation.

Table 6-2 is a questionnaire that focuses on organizational conditions pointing to the use of V-Time. Is your company currently concerned about one or more of these issues? If so, the worksheet shown in Figure 6-2 can help you analyze the need for V-Time and weigh the pros and cons of offering this scheduling arrangement.

ORGANIZATIONAL EXPERIENCE WITH V-TIME

Shaklee Corporation

Description: Shaklee, with corporate headquarters in San Francisco, is engaged in direct sales of health products. It employs approximately 500 people in the home office.

In addition to V-Time, Shaklee uses flexitime and regular part-time scheduling options.

Reason for Using V-Time: Business conditions and employee interest originally prompted the use of V-Time. In 1983, the program was suggested by employees as a way to reduce labor costs during a slight business downturn. When the program was first offered, 2 to 3 percent of the work force signed up.

Implementation Process: The provisions of the V-Time arrangement are negotiated between an interested employee and his or her manager. A written agreement is developed that indicates the number of hours the employee previously worked, defines the number of hours in the employee's reduced workweek, and specifies how fringe benefits will be affected. Typical agreements call for three- or four-day workweeks.

Sick leave and vacation pay accrual are prorated under a reduced workweek agreement. Paid holidays are reduced from 11 to 10 a year for V-Time employees. If a holiday falls on a regularly scheduled day off, the employee must work a certan number of days around the holiday in order to receive holiday pay. Rather than trying to prorate medical, dental, and vision insurance, Shaklee extends full coverage to V-Time employees. Since life insurance coverage is based on the annual salary, it is prorated.

Impact to Date: "Shaklee has gained more benefits than were perceived when this program started," according to its personnel manager. Employees on reduced workweek schedules "are at least as productive as they were before and in some cases more productive. Overall, we have found that the reduction in workweek provides some savings to the corporation. Although there is some administrative expense involved, it is minor compared to the overall dollar savings."

Users of the program have primarily been working mothers and employees who want to pursue outside interests. The option remains popular with Shaklee employees, even though only a small percentage actually takes advantage of it.

The company has had a few problems with "job definition" under the V-Time agreements. In at least one instance, the agreement was terminated because the work was not being performed satisfactorily.

SOURCE: *Survey of Private Sector Work and Family Policy: San Francisco and Alameda Counties* (San Francisco: New Ways to Work, 1986), 15.

New York State

Description: Over 200,000 employees work for the government of New York State.

Reason for Using V-Time: The state of New York has a long history of experimentation with new scheduling arrangements and has a stated objective of creating new forms of part-time work that meet employees' and the organization's needs. In 1984, in response to a survey that indicated employee interest in and need for professional-level reduced work-time options, the state of New York added a "Voluntary Furlough Program" to its existing options of regular part-time and job sharing.

Implementation Process: The V-Time option is available to the 55,000 employees represented by the Public Employees Federation and the 14,000 management/confidential employees.

Employees may choose reductions of from 5 to 30 percent in 5 percent increments. A contract is then developed between the employee and the employee's agency that defines the reduced work schedule, salary reduction, and impact on benefits.

Impact to Date: "The state saved about $4 million in reduced salaries during the first two years of the program," said Carol Schlageter, spokesperson for the program. Agency heads have the option of using the realized savings to fill other, sometimes more critical, temporary positions without increasing their budgets.

Employees use the program to phase retirement, pursue artistic interests, travel, or spend more time on family responsibilities. The most popular option, chosen by 32 percent of the employees, is a 10 percent reduction in work time and pay, with another 30 percent choosing to cut back 20 percent.

In 1985, New York State was cited by *Money* magazine in its "Ten Terrific Employers" list for being one of "a handful of employers [*that*] stand out as leaders in making the unavoidable conflict between job and family easier to bear."

SOURCE: *Go Ahead! You've Earned It!* (Albany: New York State Department of Civil Service, Governor's Office of Employee Relations, 1984); "Ten Terrific Employers," *Money* (May 1985), 144.

State of California Department of Real Estate

Description: The Department of Real Estate is located in the capital city of Sacramento and has 360 employees.

Reason for Using V-Time: The program was first introduced to avoid layoffs and then retained because employees like the option.

Implementation Process: Department employees were surveyed to determine the extent of interest in reducing work time. Of the 98 percent who returned their questionnaire, 10 percent said they were interested and 60 percent of those ultimately enrolled in the program. The program is promoted through the department newsletter and by sending written information to all employees. Employees submit a request to their supervisors; few such requests have been turned down. The most popular option had been a 10 percent time and pay reduction. Most of the civil service classes employed in the department—managers as well as nonexempt employees—have been represented in the program. Professionals have included real estate specialist I and II, real estate manager I and II, personnel analyst, and training officer.

Impact to Date: The program saved the department $37,367 the first year and $30,537 the second. The staff services manager noted that the program "required some extra work for payroll staff and unit timekeepers, but this has not been a significant problem."

SOURCE: New Ways to Work interview with staff services manager, Department of Real Estate (1984); *V-Time: A New Way to Work* (San Francisco: New Ways to Work, 1985), 10.

Table 6-2.   V-Time questionnaire.

Would V-Time Benefit Your Organization?

	Yes	No
Has the number of employee requests for reduced work schedules been growing?		
Do the demographics of your organization's labor force indicate a potential interest in a V-Time option?		
Have supervisors expressed a need for guidelines for granting requests from full-time employees to voluntarily reduce their work time?		
Does your organization or industry have peaks and valleys of labor force demand that might be smoothed out by using a wider variety of reduced time schedules?		
Is recruitment or turnover a problem that having a V-Time program might help?		

Introducing V-Time

The standard eight-step process for implementing a new work-time arrangement will in the case of V-Time focus on gaining the support of top and middle-level management, developing a program design that emphasizes parity with full-time work, and encouraging employee participation and support through an active promotion effort, backed by effective resource materials.

Gain Support for the Program

Since the concept of a V-Time program is new and relatively untested, gaining *top-level management support* is critical. If the initiative for V-Time starts with middle management, efforts must be made to gain the support of top administrators. One way is through briefings for these administrators that detail experience with existing V-Time programs or the successful use of voluntary regular part-time in peer organizations.

Middle-level management support is equally important. To obtain it, the organization should involve managers and supervisors in the design of the program so they can provide input on both policy and procedural decisions.

A major concern of department heads and supervisors is how V-Time will influence their budgets and staff allocation. Use of a full-time equivalent personnel accounting system rather than a head count system is of particular importance. An equally critical question for

Figure 6-2. V-Time worksheet.

Assessing the Need for V-Time

List the main reasons why you are considering V-Time:

1. _____

   _____

   _____

2. _____

   _____

   _____

3. _____

   _____

   _____

4. _____

   _____

   _____

List what you see as the advantages and disadvantages of V-Time:

Pros: _____

   _____

   _____

   _____

   _____

Cons: _____

many managers is whether allowing their employees to reduce work time will be taken as a signal to those who control the budget that their department can get by on less. Senior executives should reassure middle managers on this point and make them aware of their support, through either written communication, briefing sessions, or both. It also is important to assure middle managers that their department's participation in a V-Time program will not adversely affect *future* budgets—that on the contrary, V-Time can give them more flexibility because salary savings can be used somewhere else.

Whether managers will be permitted to participate in the program themselves may influence their response to employee requests and their general attitude about V-Time. Middle managers are often more supportive if the program is available to them and their peers and they see this option as applicable to all employees, not just to clerical or lower-level classifications.

If management introduces the idea of V-Time and all or part of the work force belongs to a *union,* then labor representatives should be part of the V-Time discussions from the outset of the planning process. If there is no union, employee representatives can be involved in the program's design.

In order to gain widespread support, a *task force* should be formed whose responsibilities will be to develop a policy and program and design orientation activities for all affected parties.

Set Up the Program's Administration

When introducing a V-Time program, it is important to designate a *program administrator*—someone to be in charge of the promotional campaign, application process, record keeping, and other responsibilities associated with planning and start-up. The program administrator should work with the payroll department to develop a method for handling payroll and timekeeping. Computerization of these functions has eliminated much of the complexity associated with this process once the initial format is designed.

Experience has shown that most of the time demands of setting up a V-Time program are at the front end; after the program is in operation, much less time is required. For example, the state of California Department of Real Estate's staff services manager estimates that he initially spent approximately 62 hours to plan his organization's V-Time program and advise his 360 employees about it. Currently, he spends about an hour per month on the program.

Design the Program

Once the support of top management is forthcoming, a task force has been established, and an administrator named, program design can begin. The program design phase requires that decisions be made in various areas, as explained in the following subsections.

Scope   The organization must decide whether the V-Time program will be offered first on a pilot project basis, confined to a particular department or division, or made available companywide.

Eligibility   In at least one V-Time program, only exempt-level employees are eligible to participate. This is because the program is new and the organization is unionized. The union wants to limit the program's effect until union leaders are certain that V-Time will not be used to reduce the number of full-time jobs available. In most programs, all employees are eligible but must have their supervisor's approval to enroll.

Range of Reductions to Be Offered   In general, the greater the number of choices, the greater the participation in a V-Time program. The number of increments in existing programs ranges from 3 to 12. However, the more variety there is, the more work it is to administer the program. It can be helpful for the organization to discover in advance how many and which employees might be interested in a reduced work-time option and what kind of reduction(s) would be most popular. A survey of all employees to determine their interest in V-Time can provide solid information on which to base administrative and program decisions. (A model employee survey is shown in Figure 6-3).

Figure 6-3. Sample employee survey on interest in reduced work-time options.

Reduced Work Time: Employee Survey

Section A: Background and Demographic Information

(If the surveyor wishes to obtain information about which employees, both now and in the future, are likely to want reduced work time, this section should be included. Many surveys have been conducted without collecting this information.)
Please circle the letter of one alternative for each question:

1. SEX

   a. Male
   b. Female

2. AGE

   a. Under 18
   b. 18–24
   c. 25–34
   d. 35–44
   e. 45–54
   f. 55–64
   g. 65 or over

3. MARITAL STATUS

   a. Single, never been married
   b. Married
   c. Separated, divorced, or widowed

4. FAMILY STATUS

   a. No dependents
   b. 1–2 dependents
   c. 3–5 dependents
   d. More than 5 dependents

(Continued)

Figure 6-3. *(continued)*

5. CURRENT DIVISION *(List all of your organization's divisions/departments here.)*

6. LENGTH OF TIME WORKED FOR EMPLOYER

   a. Less than one year
   b. 1–5 years
   c. 6–10 years
   d. More than 10 years

7. PRESENT SCHEDULE

   a. Full-time
   b. Part-time

8. STATUS

   a. Permanent
   b. Temporary or provisional

9. CURRENT POSITION CLASSIFICATION *(List choices or leave blank for employees to fill in.)*

Section B: Work-Time Preference

(This section is the heart of the survey. It is designed to provide information on how many people want reduced work time and the kinds of reduction they want. The surveyor may wish to state here that fringe benefits under this program will remain intact, and respondents should bear that in mind when answering the question(s). Alternatively, a question could be included that would assess the importance of benefits in determining the respondents' choice.)

10. Would you be interested, now or in the future, in reducing the amount of time you work with a commensurated reduction in pay? *(Organizations that conducted surveys indicated there was some drop-off from the number interested to the number who eventually participated.)*

    a. Yes, definitely
    b. Probably
    c. Maybe
    d. No
    If you answered no to this question, please skip all of the remaining questions.

11. Please indicate when you might be interested in reducing your time base.

    a. Immediately
    b. Within the next six months
    c. Within six months to a year
    d. Within one to three years
    e. Not for at least three years

12. Reduced work-time schedules can be arranged in various ways. Please indicate which of the following best describes what you might be interested in.

   a. Regular time off. (This means working fewer hours every day, fewer days every week, fewer weeks each month, or fewer months each year.)

   b. Irregular, but planned, time off. (This means working your full-time schedule and taking your time off in the form of occasional days off or blocks of time off—for example, adding your time onto your vacation.)

13. If your answer to question 12 was *a*, please indicate which schedule appeals to you most.

   a. Working fewer hours each day
   b. Working fewer days each week
   c. Working fewer weeks each month
   d. Working fewer months each year

14. What percentage best reflects how much time you would like to cut back?

   a. 2.5%
   b. 5%
   c. 10%
   d. 15%
   e. 20%
   f. 40%
   g. 50%

Section C: Reasons for Work-Time Preference

(This section, like section A, may not be of interest to those conducting the survey and may be omitted.)

15. If you were to exchange some of your income for reduced work time, how important would the following reasons be in your decision? (1 = very important; 2 = somewhat important; 3 = not important. Circle the number that most closely reflects your feeling.)

More time for family life and household activities	1	2	3
More time for leisure activities	1	2	3
More time for volunteer work	1	2	3
More time for furthering my education	1	2	3
More time for income-producing hobby	1	2	3
More time for a second career	1	2	3
Health benefits	1	2	3
Transition to retirement or semiretirement	1	2	3
Relief from tedious or boring nature of my job	1	2	3
Relief from stress and fatigue of my job	1	2	3

16. The following reasons migh prevent you from exchanging some of your income for reduced work time. How important would these reasons be in your decision

(Continued)

Figure 6-3. *(continued)*

not to reduce your work time? (Again, 1 = very important; 2 = somewhat important; and 3 = not important. Circle the number that most closely reflects your feeling.)			
I need a full-time income.	1	2	3
I enjoy working full-time.	1	2	3
My job is not suitable for reduced/alternative work time.	1	2	3
My productivity would decline.	1	2	3
My transportation (car pool, bus, etc.) arrangements would be affected.	1	2	3
My child care arrangements would be affected.	1	2	3
It would take longer to become eligible for promotions.	1	2	3
I feel that management would view reduced working hours negatively; I would lose status in my work group and organization.	1	2	3
I feel that it would reduce my chances for promotion.	1	2	3
I am afraid I would not be able to work full-time again if I needed to.	1	2	3
It would affect my retirement income.	1	2	3

How Reductions Can Be Taken How time off can be scheduled is particularly important to employees. For example, many would like to accumulate time and take it off in blocks rather than work fewer hours each day or week. Successful programs offer a choice of (1) working a reduced schedule (either a shorter workday or a shorter workweek) or (2) reducing pay but continuing to work full-time and taking full days or blocks of time off at a later date, with the supervisor's approval. Prospective V-Time program participants should be asked to indicate how they wish to take the time off, and supervisors should review this as part of the application.

One program makes all accumulated time off available on the starting date of the program. For example, an employee cutting back by 20 percent gets one day per week, or 52 days, off. This could conceivably be taken at the start of the program, with the employee working full-time for the rest of the year. Employees cannot carry over unused time beyond the annual termination date of the program, and an employee who withdraws from the program prior to the termination date gets his or her pay adjusted accordingly.

Enrollment Process The application form, signed by both the employee and the department head, becomes a contract between the employee and the employer. The form contains pertinent employee information (name, classification, the time reduction requested, preference for scheduling work time and time off, and the length of time that the employee wishes the reduction to be in effect (or the program termination date in cases where this is not a variable). See the sample form shown in Figure 6-4; note that this form also incorporates elements of a work-sharing program, which will be discussed in Chapter 8.

Duration of Enrollment   All V-Time programs require that an employee sign up for a specific period of time—generally 6 to 12 months—beginning with the first day of a pay period. This allows managers to plan their budgets and work needs accordingly. Programs vary, but there are two general approaches:

1. *A designated enrollment period.* During this time, an employee must decide whether to enroll, and all V-Time participants start their new schedules on the same date.
2. *Year-round enrollment.* Although some managers worry that year-round enrollment could create an administrative nightmare, one V-Time program coordinator maintains that it produces a regular flow of applicants that is more manageable than if they all started at the same time. It also provides both managers and employees with some negotiating flexibility. For example, if an employee wanted to reduce to half-time from January to March and that is a busy period for the employer, the manager could respond by saying, "I just can't afford to do it then, but if you would like to reduce from April to June, I think we could handle it."

Approval Responsibility   Supervisors generally have the responsibility for approving or denying requests for a reduced schedule. They should be aware of top management support for the program and be encouraged to give favorable consideration whenever possible. It is important for the success of the program that employee requests for participation be handled fairly and objectively. Decisions that seem arbitrary or based on favoritism will quickly foster resentment and erode morale. To ensure fairness, the organization should:

■ Establish guidelines for approving or denying requests.
■ Establish an appeal process.

Figure 6-4. Sample V-Time application form for an organization seeking to avoid layoffs.

Voluntary Reduced Workweek Request

I hereby volunteer for a reduced workweek as an alternative to layoff.

Effective the _____ (1st or 16th) of _____, 19___, I volunteer to work not less than 30 hours per week to be scheduled as indicated here:

☐ 1. 30 hour workweek: Four (4) 7½ hour days.

☐ 2. 32 hour workweek: Four (4) 8 hour days.

☐ 3. 33.75 hours (10% reduction): Five (5) 6¾ hour days.

☐ 4. 35 hour workweek: Five (5) 7 hour days.

☐ 5. 67½ hours in two workweeks: 1 scheduled day off every other week.

☐ 6. 1 scheduled day off each month.

I fully understand the effect of a reduced workweek on my salary and benefits. I also understand that in order to withdraw from the reduced workweek program, I must submit a written request to my supervisor at least two weeks in advance of the effective date of the withdrawal.

_____   _____
Employee's Name   Employee's Signature

_____   _____
Department/Division   Date

- -

I agree to the terms described above for this employee's participation in the voluntary reduced workweek program.

_____   _____
Dept. Supervisor's Signature   Date

■ Provide employees and supervisors with written information covering the guidelines and appeal process. (Examples are presented in the next subsection.)

Program Termination for Individuals Participation in the program automatically terminates when the contract period ends. The employ-

ees return to their full-time status and schedules unless both parties
agree to a renewal.

Additionally, individual participation automatically ends when
the employee is tranferred, promoted, or demoted. The employee
must renegotiate V-Time participation in terms of his or her new
status if the employee still wishes to do so and the supervisor
supports the request.

Some programs also allow either party to terminate the arrangement by giving 30 to 60 days' notice. Some require that hardship be
demonstrated before permitting the agreement to be renounced prior
to the end of the contract period.

Impact on Employee Status and Benefits   If participation in the V-
Time program is detrimental to employee benefits or status, enrollment will suffer and union support will be more difficult to secure.

The following paragraphs detail the various ways in which the
major employee status and benefits issues have been dealt with in
existing programs.

Health and dental benefits. The impact of V-Time on health and
dental benefits depends on whether current policy provides these
benefits to employees working less than full-time. As noted in Chapter 3, all employees need access to group health insurance. Prorating
the cost of this kind of benefit is viewed as equitable by most
employees and employers.

Holidays. In some organizations, part-time employees are paid
for a proportionate amount of the day, based on their time base. A
half-time employee would receive 4 hours' compensation for each
holiday in the pay period. A $^{19}/_{20}$-time employee would receive 7.6
hours' compensation for each holiday in the pay period (8
hours $\times$ $^{19}/_{20}$ = 7.6 hours). In other organizations, employees are
compensated as though they worked full-time but at a reduced hourly
rate.

Disability. Generally, these benefits are prorated according to the
employee's time base and salary. This may lower premiums as well
as benefits.

Life insurance. Since life insurance coverage is tied to salary, the
employer's cost will usually decline somewhat, as will the employee's
coverage.

Merit salary increases. A V-Time program generally has no
impact on merit raises.

Overtime. Employees must work more than 40 hours in one
workweek to qualify for overtime pay.

Probationary period. V-Time has no impact on the probationary period.

Opportunities for promotion. In some V-Time programs, qualifying experience is prorated; otherwise, there is no impact.

Order of layoff. The policy on layoffs is one key determinant of whether an employee will feel able to enroll in a V-Time program. The state of California Department of Real Estate's policy (reprinted in the next subsection) states the following provisions for handling layoffs when a V-Time program is in effect:

> If layoff becomes unavoidable, employees who participate in a voluntary reduced work time program pursuant to this article shall not routinely be subject to layoff ahead of full-time employees. Such part-time employees shall be subject to the same seniority and other layoff considerations as full-time employees in determining the order of layoff.

(See also the following discussions of retirement benefits and seniority and service credit.)

Retirement benefits. Retirement benefits can be based on either (1) contributions (V-Time participants will contribute less because the formula is generally a percentage of the monthly salary) or (2) the employees' full-time equivalent salary, using the same formula as for any other regular employee contributing to the retirement fund. (See also the following discussion of seniority and service credit.)

Seniority and service credit. In some programs, all participating employees, regardless of their individual time reductions, continue to receive one year of service credit for each 12 months that they are employed. In other programs, seniority and service credit are prorated, based on hours actually worked. For instance, an employee taking a 20 percent work-time reduction would earn 80 percent of one year of service credit for the year in which he or she participates in the program.

The following is an example of a very precise method for determining service credit used by the state of California: A full-time employee earns one tenth of a credit per qualifying (in this case monthly) pay period up to one credit per year. An employee on a reduced schedule who works the equivalent of ten qualifying pay periods per year would therefore continue to receive full retirement credit. (Although the state does not have a time base of $10/12$, this applies to time bases of $17/20$, $9/10$, or $19/20$—that is, pay reductions of up to 15 percent.) Greater time base reductions will have a negligible effect on retirement credit. (For example, $8/10$ time base earns .96 retirement service credit per year.) The months selected for a V-

Time arrangement may lessen its impact on service credit, because credit is calculated on the basis of service rendered during a state fiscal year, which runs from July 1 through June 30. Thus, a reduced work-time employee who works half-time on a V-Time agreement from April in one fiscal year through September in the next (while working full-time during the balance of those fiscal years) would receive full retirement credit for both fiscal years; if the period of the agreement were from June through November, the employee would receive full credit for the first year and .95 retirement service credit for the second year. The net effect of the foregoing method for determining service credit is that retirement benefits will be some-what less for participants who choose V-Time reductions greater than 15 percent.

If seniority accrual is prorated, V-Time participants will find themselves at the end of one year of participation with less seniority than full-time colleagues whose seniority was previously the same as theirs. Employers should keep in mind that this sort of provision may discourage the use of V-Time as an alternative to layoffs.

Sick leave. In some programs, sick leave is credited on a prorated basis on the first day of the monthly pay period following completion of a qualifying month. For example, a half-time employee receives 4 hours' sick leave credit each month; a $19/10$ employee receives 7.6 hours' credit each month (8 hours $\times$ $19/20$ = 7.6). In other programs, the amount of sick leave earned is the same as if the individual were working full-time. Compensation is based on the employee's adjusted hourly rate.

Vacation. Vacation credits can be earned according to the same formula as for service credit or according to the same formula as for sick leave.

Worker's compensation. A V-Time program generally has no impact on worker's compensation.

The major program design issues we have just discussed are summarized in Table 6-3. Figure 6-5 is a sample worksheet used to record detailed decisions about program design. A blank copy of this worksheet has also been provided (see Figure 6-6) for use in planning your own V-Time program.

Develop Resource Materials

The organization will need to create resource materials targeted toward managers and supervisors and materials targeted toward employees. Some types of resource materials can be used both with managers and supervisors and with employees.

Resource materials for managers and supervisors. These items

Table 6-3.   Program design checklist: V-Time.

Key Design Issues	Notes
Eliminating current barriers	
☐ Provisions of existing policy on part-time that might hamper V-Time	
Creating new policy	
☐ Scope	
☐ Eligibility	
☐ Range of reductions to be offered	
☐ How reductions can be taken	
☐ Enrollment process	
☐ Duration of enrollment	
☐ Approval responsibility	
☐ Program termination for individuals	
☐ Impact on employee status and benefits	

should include an explanation of the organization's objectives in introducing V-Time, an overview of the program, information on whom to contact with specific questions about implementation of the program, and guidelines for assessing employee requests for a reduced work schedule. Figure 6-7 is an example of a V-Time program description. The type of information presented in it would be useful both to managers and supervisors and to employees. Figure 6-8 is an example of a set of guidelines designed to help supervisors evaluate requests from employees to enroll in the V-Time program.

Managers particularly need to know how V-Time will affect their current and future personnel allotments and budgets. They should be advised whether or not payroll savings can be redirected toward hiring additional permanent or temporary employees or to meet some other critical need. If hiring additional employees is allowed, manag-

Figure 6-5.   Sample program design worksheet: V-Time.

■ Range of reductions will include:

  _5_ %, _10_ %, _12.5_ %, _20_ %, _30_ %, _50_ %.

■ Time off may be taken as:

  Reduced workday _____   Additional vacation _____

  Reduced workweek _____   _____

  Personal time off _____   _____

■ Enrollment will be:

  _X_ Open, all year round. _____ A _____-week period from _____
       to _____.

■ Participants will remain on the reduced schedule for:

  ☐ A fixed period set   two pay   6   12
  by management: _____ periods _____ months _____ months _____ other: _____.
  ☒ Varying periods of time agreed upon between employee and supervisor.

■ Application process tasks:

  1. Form designed   ☑ 3. Termination regulations approved ☑
  2. Criteria for handling requests   4. Approval/denial process
     written   ☑   formulated   ☑
                                          5. Appeals process designed   ☑

■ V-Time's impact on employee status and benefits will be:

  1. Health and dental plans   No impact; retain full coverage. _____

  2. Holidays   Prorated. _____

  3. Life insurance   No impact. _____

  4. Disability insurance   Based on salary; proportionately lower. _____

  5. Merit salary adjustment   No impact. _____

  6. Order of layoffs   No impact. However, seniority accrual is
                               prorated (see below). _____

SOURCE: Adapted from *V-Time: A New Way to Work* (San Francisco: New Ways to Work, 1985), 17.

(Continued)

Figure 6-5. *(continued)*

7. Overtime	Must work more than 40 hours to qualify for overtime.
8. Probationary period	No impact.
9. Promotional opportunities	No impact.
10. Retirement benefits	May be reduced as a result of reduced schedule.
11. Seniority and service credit	Based on hours actually worked.
12. Sick leave	Prorated.
13. Vacation	Prorated.
14. Worker's compensation insurance	No impact on eligibility. Benefits could be reduced.

ers should be reminded that since less-experienced workers can be hired at a lower salary rate to fill the hours no longer worked by V-Time program participants, they may also be spending less of their budgets for the same number of paid hours.

The guidelines for supervisors should cover such topics as administrative and work load considerations, scheduling of overtime, and maintaining service to the public or clients, if that is appropriate.

Resource materials for employees. Employees need overview information that details what kind of effect the program will have on their status and benefits and what the application process is. Potential participants in the program also need resource materials that help them specifically assess the financial impact of V-Time and any effect on their status and conditions of employment as a result of their participation in the program.

As noted above, employees will find it helpful to have a description of the V-Time program, such as that shown in Figure 6-7. Table 6-4 and Figure 6-9 present examples of other types of information that interested employees will need. The table shows the specific effect of various increments of work-time reduction on a given employee's monthly salary. The figure is a worksheet that employees

Figure 6-6. Sample program design worksheet: V-Time.

■ Range of reductions will include:

_____%, _____%, _____%, _____%, _____%, _____%.

■ Time off may be taken as:

_____   _____

_____   _____

_____   _____

■ Enrollment will be:

_____ Open, all year round. _____ A _____-week period from _____
        to _____.

■ Participants will remain on the reduced schedule for:

☐ A fixed period set   two pay   6   12
by management: _____ periods _____ months _____ months _____ other: _____.
☐ Varying periods of time agreed upon between employee and supervisor.

■ Application process tasks:

1. Form designed   3. Termination regulations approved ☐
2. Criteria for handling requests ☐ 4. Approval/denial process
   written   ☐   formulated   ☐
                                    5. Appeals process designed   ☐

■ V-Time's impact on employee status and benefits will be:

1. Health and dental plans   _____

2. Holidays   _____

3. Life insurance   _____

4. Disability insurance   _____

5. Merit salary adjustment   _____

6. Order of layoffs   _____

7. Overtime   _____

SOURCE: Adapted from *V-Time: A New Way to Work* (San Francisco: New Ways to Work, 1985), 18.

(Continued)

Figure 6-6.   *(continued)*

8. Probationary period _____

9. Promotional opportunities _____

10. Retirement benefits _____

11. Seniority and service
    credit _____

12. Sick leave _____

13. Vacation _____

14. Worker's compensation
    insurance _____

can use to perform an individualized calculation of their own net pay at various levels of time reduction. Detailed material such as this can enable employees to determine in advance just where they would stand financially if they were to enroll in the V-Time program.

Announce the Program

Once the program has been designed and the supporting reference materials developed, the availability of this new option should be announced to employees. But as is the case with other part-time alternatives, if the use of V-Time is to achieve the organization's objective of greater flexibility, then the program must be an active one rather than just a policy carried on the books. A concerted effort will be required to encourage employees to enroll.

Promote the Program

An employer that introduces V-Time as an alternative to layoffs wants as many workers as possible to enroll in order to achieve the maximum multiplier effect on payroll reduction. Similarly, an employer that plans to use the program to accommodate the needs of current employees or enhance recruitment will want it to be as attractive as possible. Good program design is essential, but employee interest in working less is influenced by other factors as well,

(Text continues on page 251.)

Figure 6-7. Sample program description: V-Time.

VOLUNTARY REDUCTION IN WORK SCHEDULE

Employee Packet

Contents

1–3	Memo to Employees
4–5	Voluntary Reduction in Work Schedule: Effect on Benefits and Status
6–7	VRWS Application Form: Application for Voluntary Reduction in Work Schedule (VRWS)
8–9	Schedule for VR Time Off
10–16	Examples of VRWS Work Schedule Alternatives
17	Chart of VR Time Earned by Percentage of Reduction
18–21	VRWS Planning Worksheets (2)
22–23	Worksheet to Estimate Effect of VRWS Program on Biweekly Take-Home Pay

SOURCE: *Go Ahead! You've Earned It!* (Albany: New York State Governor's Office of Employee Relations, 1984).

(Continued)

Figure 6-7. *(continued)*

DRAFT

April 5, 1984

TO: All Full-Time Annual Salaried PS&T and M/C Employees

FROM: Agency

SUBJECT: Voluntary Reduction in Work Schedules (VRWS)

As a result of an agreement between the Governor's Office of Employee Relations and the Public Employees Federation we are pleased to present a new program to all full-time annual salaried employees in the Professional, Scientific and Technical Services Unit (PS&T). The program is also being offered to all full-time annual salaried employees designated Management/ Confidential. We hope this opportunity will benefit employees, this Agency and the State as a whole. This new program is called Voluntary Reduction in Work Schedules (VRWS). It allows employees to voluntarily trade a percentage of income for an equivalent amount of time off. The program also allows flexibility in scheduling time off that will, to the extent possible, permit employees to use time off to meet their personal needs and interests. This program is being offered for Fiscal Years 1984–85 and 1985–86.

The reduced work schedule under a VRWS program could allow an employee to:

■ Take extra vacation.
■ Attend school.
■ Spend more time with family.
■ Start or continue hobbies, or pursue and develop personal interests.
■ Change the pace of his or her life.

Additionally, the employee can experience a savings on work-related expenditures such as:

■ Transportation costs.
■ Child care.
■ Lunches.
■ Work clothing.

VRWS Program

A full-time annual salaried employee may participate in a VRWS program by reducing his or her work schedule and salary a minimum of 5 percent, or

1

Figure 6-7. *(continued)*

in 5 percent increments, up to a maximum of 30 percent. In exchange for the reduction in work schedule and salary, the employee earns an equivalent amount of VR Time.

VR Time is earned and accrued each pay period on the basis of the percent reduction in work schedule. For example, an employee who elects a 10 percent reduction in work schedule will earn and accrue one day of VR Time each pay period. If the employee uses all the earned VR Time in that same pay period through a reduced daily or weekly schedule, then an even exchange is made. If the employee wishes to accrue VR Time for future use, then the employee will work the normal work schedule and accumulate the earned VR Time.

VR Time will be credited and debited as a separate entry on the employee's time card. VR Time accruals may be used in conjunction with personal and annual leave. VR Time credits may be carried over on the employee's time card past the end of the individual VRWS agreement period and past the end of the VRWS program period but must be liquidated by September 30, 1986.

During the VRWS program, the employee's paycheck is adjusted by the agreed-upon percentage, but the number of paychecks is not changed. The employee never goes off the payroll. The employee remains in active pay status for the duration of the agreement and receives paychecks each pay period at the agreed-upon temporarily reduced level.

Employees participating in this program will work a pro rata share of their normal work schedule over the duration of the agreement period. Participation in this program will not be a deterent to later career moves or considerations within the agency or the State.

Participation in the VRWS program will have little impact on status and benefits. A summary statement on the impact on status and benefits is enclosed. For purposes of salary increases and advances, the employee's basic annual salary will be treated as if it had not been reduced.

At the end of the agreement period, the employee is returned to his or her normal work schedule and pay level.

VRWS Employee Plan

Each participating employee will develop his or her individual plan for reduced work schedule and use of VR Time. The VRWS plan must specify the duration of the VRWS agreement, the percentage reduction in work schedule and salary, the amount of time earned in exchange for the reduced salary, and the schedule for use of VR Time earned.

The employee can establish a VRWS program of any number of pay periods in duration from one to the number of pay periods remaining in the VRWS program period. The VRWS agreement must begin on the first day of a pay period and end on the last day of a pay period. The employee and management may, by mutual agreement, modify the agreement or terminate the agreement early.

The VRWS plan must be consistent with agency operating needs and management must agree to the plan before it is implemented.

2

(Continued)

Figure 6-7. *(continued)*

VR Time Use Schedule

VR Time may be used on a fixed schedule or on an irregular basis. That is, a VRWS program can be implemented as a shorter workday or shorter workweek on a regular basis, as occasional days or hours off, in a block of time as an extended vacation, or as a combination of the above.

An employee's fixed schedule VR Time off, once the VRWS plan has been agreed to by management, cannot be changed without the consent of the employee except in an emergency. In the event an employee's schedule is changed without his or her consent, the employee may appeal this action through an expedited grievance procedure.

VR Time taken off on an irregular basis must be approved in advance by the employee's supervisor in the same manner as annual leave.

Comments

We believe that many employees will find VRWS an attractive program, especially since it does not require a long commitment. An important point for the employee to consider is that the percentage by which net pay is adjusted is smaller than the percentage by which gross pay is adjusted.

We encourage employees who may be considering a reduction in work schedule to fully examine the materials that follow. These materials further explain the VRWS program and will assist you in developing an individualized VRWS program:

- VRWS: Effect on Benefits and Status
- Application Form and Schedule
- Examples of VRWS Work Schedule Alternatives
- Chart of VR Time Earned by Percent of Reduction
- VRWS Planning Worksheets

3

Figure 6-7. *(continued)*

Voluntary Reduction in Work Schedule:
Effect on Benefits and Status

Annual Leave: full accruals; no change in earnings rate

Personal Leave: full credits; no change in earnings rate

Sick Leave at Full Pay: full accruals; no change in earnings rate

Holidays: no change in holiday benefit

Sick Leave at Half Pay: No impact on eligibility or entitlement. Employees who go on Sick Leave at ½ pay for 28 consecutive calendar days will have their VRWS agreement cancelled and be returned to their normal work schedule and pay base.

Workers' Compensation Leave: No impact on eligibility or entitlement. Employees who go on WCL for 28 consecutive calendar days will have their VRWS agreement cancelled and be returned to their normal work schedule and pay base.

Military Leave: no impact on eligibility or entitlement

Jury/Court Leave: no impact on eligibility or entitlement

Paid Leave Balances on Time Card: There is no requirement that leave credits be exhausted prior to the beginning of the VRWS agreement. Paid leave balances are carried forward.

Shift Pay: prorate

Inconvenience Pay: prorate

Location Pay: prorate

Geographic Pay: prorate

Pre-Shift Briefing: prorate

Salary Normal gross salary earned is reduced by percentage of voluntary reduction in work schedule; there is no effect on basic annual salary rate.

Payroll: Employee never leaves the payroll; employee remains in full payroll status with partial pay for the duration of the agreement period and receives paychecks each pay period at the agreed-upon temporarily reduced level.

Return to Normal Work Schedule: Employee will return to his or her normal work schedule upon completion of the VRWS agreement period.

Banked (Unused) VR Time Upon Return to Normal Work Schedule: VR time may be carried forward on the employee's time card after completion of the individual VRWS agreement period and past the end of the VRWS program period but must be liquidated by September 30, 1986.

Banked (Unused) VR Time Upon Separation: Unused VR Time will be paid at the full daily rate upon layoff, resignation, termination, retirement, or death.

Banked (Unused) VR Time Upon Promotion, Transfer, or Reassignment: Unused VR Time credits are carried forward on the employee's time card. Continuation of the VRWS program is at the discretion of management.

---

4   *(Continued)*

Figure 6-7. *(continued)*

Health Insurance: no effect; full coverage

Dental Insurance: no effect; full coverage

Employee Benefit Fund: no effect

Survivor's Benefit: no effect

Retirement Benefit Earnings: Will reduce final average salary if VRWS period is included in three years earnings used to calculate final average salary.

Retirement Service Credit: prorate

Social Security: no change; contribution rate set by Federal Law (6.7 percent for 1984)

Unemployment Insurance: no change

Performance Advance or Increment Advance: evaluation date is not changed; no change in eligibility

Performance Award or Lump Sum Payment: no impact; no change in eligibility

Longevity Increase: no change in eligibility

Probationary Period: no effect

Traineeship: no effect

Layoff: no impact; Seniority date for layoff purposes is not changed.

Seniority: no impact; Employee never leaves the payroll. Seniority date is not changed. Full seniority credit is earned.

Seniority for Promotion Examinations: no impact; VR time used shall be counted as time worked in determining seniority credits for promotion exams.

Eligibility for Promotion Examinations: no effect; VR time used shall be counted as time worked in determining eligibility for promotion exams.

Eligibility for Open Competitive Examinations: prorate; VR time used shall not be considered time worked for determining length of Service for *open competitive* examinations.

Overtime Work: VR time used shall not be counted as time worked in determining eligibility for overtime payments at premium rates within a workweek.

5

Figure 6-7. *(continued)*

Application for Voluntary Reduction in Work Schedule (VRWS)

Agency Code: _____   Name: _____

Agency: _____   Title: _____

Division: _____   SG: _____

Office: _____   Line No.: _____

                                        NU: _____

% Reduction in Work Schedule requested: _____ %

Number of pay periods of participation: _____ pay periods

VR Time to be earned during agreement period: _____ days

Beginning first day of pay period #_____ , (date) _____ , 19_____

Ending last day of pay period   #_____ , (date) _____ , 19_____

Normal work schedule _____ hours/week; _____ hours/pay period

Reduced AVG work schedule _____ hours/week; _____ hours/pay period

VR Time earned _____ hours/week; _____ hours/pay period

Proposed Schedule of VR Time use (You may also attach a planning worksheet):

A. ☐ Shorter workday/Normal workweek. Specify on schedule on reverse side of application.

B. ☐ Shorter workweek/Normal workday. Specify on schedule on reverse side of application.

C.* ☐ (ALTERNATIVE WORK SCHEDULE ARRANGEMENT) Longer workday/Shorter workweek. Specify on schedule on reverse side of application.

6

(Continued)

Figure 6-7.   *(continued)*

D.   ☐   Block(s) of time off. Specify on schedule on reverse side of application.
E.   ☐   Intermittent time off. Specify pattern, if any.
F.   ☐   Combination of above. Specify on schedule on reverse side of application.

_____   _____
              Employee Signature   Date
- -

☐ APPROVED   ☐ DISAPPROVED (attach written justification and transmit to
                                                      Personnel Officer)

Effective Date: _____

I agree to the proposed temporary adjustment in work schedule and understand that
this employee will work a pro rata share of his or her normal work schedule over the
duration of the agreement period.

_____   _____
              Supervisor/Date   Section Chief—Office Head/Date
- -

☐ APPROVED   ☐ DISAPPROVED   _____
                                                              Personnel Officer/Date

*Copy of this form must be sent to the Division of the Budget, Central Management
 and Budgeting Unit for employees who receive agency approval to use this scheduling option.

AGENCY TO KEEP THIS FORM ON FILE—
NEEDED FOR REPORTING PURPOSES
7

Figure 6-7. *(continued)*

Schedule for VR Time Off

Payroll Period		Thurs	Fri.	Sat.	Sun.	Mon.	Tues.	Wed.	Thurs	Fri.	Sat.	Sun.	Mon.	Tues.	Wed.
No.	Dates Covered														
1															
2															
3															
4															
5															
6															
7															
8															
9															
10															
11															
12															
13															
14															
15															
16															
17															
18															
19															
20															
21															
22															
23															
24															
25															
26															

8

(Continued)

Figure 6-7. *(continued)*

Instructions

1. In Payroll Period column, indicate beginning and ending dates of each pay period covered by the agreement.
2. For each pay period, indicate all days/time worked (include number of hours worked) and days/time not worked, that is, indicate all pass days and all VR Time off. If you plan to use other accruals in conjunction with VR schedule, these days/this time should also be included in the schedule. Use the codes listed below to indicate category of days/time.
3. Where the schedule repeats each pay period, fill out the schedule (include number of hours worked/not worked) and days off for the first pay period only and indicate "same" for subsequent pay periods.
4. For partial day absences, indicate number of hours worked/off and code for category of leave (for example, 5½-W; 2-VR)

Work/Leave Category Codes

| VR: VR Leave | AL: Annual Leave |
| W: Day Worked | X: Pass Days |

9

Figure 6-7. *(continued)*

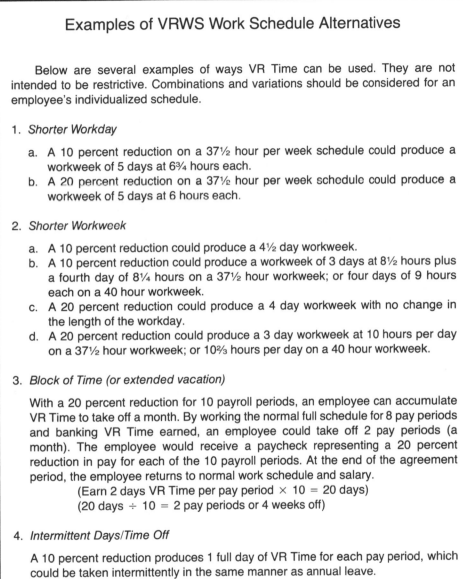

Examples of VRWS Work Schedule Alternatives

Below are several examples of ways VR Time can be used. They are not intended to be restrictive. Combinations and variations should be considered for an employee's individualized schedule.

1. *Shorter Workday*

   a. A 10 percent reduction on a 37½ hour per week schedule could produce a workweek of 5 days at 6¾ hours each.
   b. A 20 percent reduction on a 37½ hour per week schedule could produce a workweek of 5 days at 6 hours each.

2. *Shorter Workweek*

   a. A 10 percent reduction could produce a 4½ day workweek.
   b. A 10 percent reduction could produce a workweek of 3 days at 8½ hours plus a fourth day of 8¼ hours on a 37½ hour workweek; or four days of 9 hours each on a 40 hour workweek.
   c. A 20 percent reduction could produce a 4 day workweek with no change in the length of the workday.
   d. A 20 percent reduction could produce a 3 day workweek at 10 hours per day on a 37½ hour workweek; or 10⅔ hours per day on a 40 hour workweek.

3. *Block of Time (or extended vacation)*

   With a 20 percent reduction for 10 payroll periods, an employee can accumulate VR Time to take off a month. By working the normal full schedule for 8 pay periods and banking VR Time earned, an employee could take off 2 pay periods (a month). The employee would receive a paycheck representing a 20 percent reduction in pay for each of the 10 payroll periods. At the end of the agreement period, the employee returns to normal work schedule and salary.
   (Earn 2 days VR Time per pay period × 10 = 20 days)
   (20 days ÷ 10 = 2 pay periods or 4 weeks off)

4. *Intermittent Days/Time Off*

   A 10 percent reduction produces 1 full day of VR Time for each pay period, which could be taken intermittently in the same manner as annual leave.

10

(Continued)

Figure 6-7. *(continued)*

Planning Worksheet for Scheduling VR Time: Example #1

Normal Workweek: __40__ hours
Percent Reduction: __10__ %
Reduced Workweek: __36__ hours
VR Time Earned per Week: __4__ hours*
VR Time Earned per Pay Period: __8__ hours*

Month	Pay Period	VR Time Earned (In Hours)	VR Time Used (In Hours)	VR Time Balance (In Hours)	Work Schedule Plan	
APR.	1	8		8		
	2	8		16		
MAY	3	8		24		
	4	8		32	WORK NORMAL WEEK, BANK VR CREDITS	R E C E I V E .90% OF NORMAL SALARY FOR 20 DAY PERIODS
JUN.	5	8		40		
	6	8		48		
JUL.	7	8		56		
	8	8		64		
AUG.	9	8	40	32	TAKE 2 WKS. OFF USING 5 DAYS EA. BANKED VR TIME & ACCRUED A.L.	
	10	8		40		
SEP.	11	8		48		
	12	8		56	WORK NORMAL WEEK, BANK VR CREDITS	
OCT.	13	8		64		
	14	8		72		
	15	8		80		

11

Figure 6-7. *(continued)*

NOV.	16	8		88	
	17	8		96	
DEC.	18	8		104	
	19	8	80	32	TAKE 4 WEEKS OFF USING 3 WEEKS BANKED VR TIME AND 1 WEEK ACCRUED A.L.
JAN.	20	8	40	0	
	21				
FEB.	22				
	23				VR AGREEMENT ENDS, RETURN TO NORMAL WORKWEEK AND NORMAL SALARY
MAR.	24				
	25				
	26				

*See Time Equivalencies Chart for VR time earned per week and per pay period.

12

(Continued)

Figure 6-7. *(continued)*

Planning Worksheet for Scheduling VR Time: Example #2

Normal Workweek: <u>37½</u> hours
Percent Reduction: <u>20</u> %
Reduced Workweek: <u>30</u> hours
VR Time Earned per Week: <u>7½</u> hours*
VR Time Earned per Pay Period: <u>15</u> hours*

Month	Pay Period	VR Time Earned (In Hours)	VR Time Used (In Hours)	VR Time Balance (In Hours)	Work Schedule Plan	
APR.	1	15		15		
	2	15		30		
MAY	3	15		45		
	4	15		60		
JUN.	5	15		75		
	6	15		90		RECEIVE 80% OF NORMAL SALARY FOR 25 PAY PERIODS
JUL.	7	15		105	WORK NORMAL WEEK, BANK VR CREDITS	
	8	15		120		
AUG.	9	15		135		
	10	15		150		
SEP.	11	15		165		
	12	15		180		
OCT.	13	15		195		
	14	15		210		
	15	15		225		

Figure 6-7. *(continued)*

NOV.	16	15		240
	17	15		255
DEC.	18	15		270
	19	15		285
JAN.	20	15		300
	21	15	75	240
FEB.	22	15	75	180
	23	15	75	120
MAR.	24	15	75	60
	25	15	75	0
	26			

TAKE 10 WEEKS OFF
USING BANKED
VR CREDITS

VR AGREEMENT ENDS, RESUME
NORMAL WORKWEEK AND SALARY

*See Time Equivalencies Chart for VR time earned per week and per pay period.

14

(Continued)

Figure 6-7.   *(continued)*

Planning Worksheet for Scheduling VR Time: Example #3

Normal Workweek: __37½__ hours
Percent Reduction: __10__ %
Reduced Workweek: __33¾__ hours
VR Time Earned per Week: __3¾__ hours*
VR Time Earned per Pay Period: __7½__ hours*

Month	Pay Period	VR Time Earned (In Hours)	VR Time Used (In Hours)	VR Time Balance (In Hours)	Work Schedule Plan
APR.	1	7½	7½		
	2	7½	7½		
MAY	3	7½	7½		
	4	7½	7½		
JUN.	5	7½	7½		
	6	7½	7½		
JUL.	7	7½	7½		WORK COMPRESSED WEEK: 3 DAYS AT 8½ HOURS, 1 DAY AT 8¼ HOURS
	8	7½	7½		
AUG.	9	7½	7½		
	10	7½	7½		
SEP.	11	7½	7½		
	12	7½	7½		
OCT.	13	7½	7½		
	14	7½	7½		
	15	7½	7½		

15

Figure 6-7. *(continued)*

NOV.	16	7½	7½	
	17	7½	7½	
DEC.	18	7½	7½	
	19	7½	7½	RECEIVE 90% OF NORMAL PAY FOR 26 PAY PERIODS
JAN.	20	7½	7½	
	21	7½	7½	
FEB.	22	7½	7½	
	23	7½	7½	
MAR.	24	7½	7½	
	25	7½	7½	
	26	7½	7½	

*See Time Equivalencies Chart for VR time earned per week and per pay period.

16

(Continued)

Figure 6-7. *(continued)*

Voluntary Reduction In Work Schedule
(VR Time Earned in Days)

Number of Pay Periods	% Reduction Taken					
	5%	10%	15%	20%	25%	30%
1	½	1	1½	2	2½	3
2	1	2	3	4	5	6
3	1½	3	4½	6	7½	9
4	2	4	6	8	10	12
5	2½	5	7½	10	12½	15
6	3	6	9	12	15	18
7	3½	7	10½	14	17½	21
8	4	8	12	16	20	24
9	4½	9	13½	18	22½	27
10	5	10	15	20	25	30
11	5½	11	16½	22	27½	33
12	6	12	18	24	30	36
13	6½	13	19½	26	32½	39
14	7	14	21	28	35	42
15	7½	15	22½	30	37½	45
16	8	16	24	32	40	48
17	8½	17	25½	34	42½	51
18	9	18	27	36	45	54
19	9½	19	28½	38	47½	57
20	10	20	30	40	50	60
21	10½	21	31½	42	52½	63
22	11	22	33	44	55	66
23	11½	23	34½	46	57½	69
24	12	24	36	48	60	72
25	12½	25	37½	50	62½	75
26	13	26	39	52	65	78

To convert to hours: Multiply the number of days by the number of hours in a normal workday.

Figure 6-7.   *(continued)*

Planning Worksheet for Determining VR Time Needed

A. GOALS

Use this section to determine how many hours of accruals will be necessary to take a block (or blocks) of time off.

Time off desired:

Weeks

Multiply: _____ no. weeks desired

× _____ no. hours in normal workweek (37.5 or 40)

= _____ no. hours needed

OR

Days

Multiply: _____ no. days desired

× _____ no. hours in normal workday (7.5 or 8)

= _____ no. hours needed

OR

Hours per Pay Pariod

Multiply: _____ no. hours desired per pay period

× _____ no. pay periods affected (see payroll schedule)

= _____ no. hours needed

B. ACCURALS TO BE USED IN CONJUNCTION WITH VR TIME

If you plan to combine VR time earned with other leave accruals, this section should be completed. Include current leave credits and leave credits to be earned which you plan to use in conjunction with accrued VR time.

18   *(Continued)*

Figure 6-7. *(continued)*

ANNUAL LEAVE:	Current Balance	hrs.
	to Be Earned	hrs.
HOLIDAY TIME:	Current Balance	hrs.
	to Be Earned	hrs.
COMPENSATORY TIME:	Current Balance	hrs.
	TOTAL	hrs.

C. PLANNING

Use this section to determine the Voluntary Reduction in Work Schedule you need to take the desired amount of time off.

1. Time off desired (from Section A)		hrs.
2. Subract total accruals (from Section B)	—	hrs.
3. Hours of VR time needed		hrs.
4. Divide Box #3 by normal work-day (7.5 or 8) giving the number of days of VR time needed for desired time off		days

---> DAYS OF VR TIME YOU NEED TO EARN TO ACHIEVE YOUR GOAL

See chart for VR Time Earned in Days to determine the number of pay periods and percent of reduction necessary to achieve desired time off.

19

Figure 6-7. *(continued)*

Planning Worksheet for Scheduling VR Time

Normal Workweek: _____ hours

Percent Reduction: _____%

Reduced Workweek: _____ hours

VR Time Earned per Week: _____ hours*

VR Time Earned per Pay Period: _____ hours*

Month	Pay Period	VR Time Earned (In Hours)	VR Time Used (In Hours)	VR Time Balance (In Hours)	Work Schedule Plan
APR.	1				
	2				
MAY	3				
	4				
JUN.	5				
	6				
JUL.	7				
	8				
AUG.	9				
	10				
SEP.	11				
	12				
OCT.	13				
	14				
	15				

(Continued)

Figure 6-7.   *(continued)*

NOV.	16					
	17					
DEC.	18					
	19					
JAN.	20					
	21					
FEB.	22					
	23					
MAR.	24					
	25					
	26					

*See Time Equivalencies Chart for VR Time earned per week and per pay period.

21

Figure 6-7. *(continued)*

Worksheet to Estimate Effect of VRWS Program on Biweekly Take-Home Pay

1. ENTER BASIC ANNUAL SALARY --------------➤	1	$
2. ENTER % SALARY INCREASE DUE ON _____ 19___ (if applicable) (as a decimal) --------------------➤ 0.0_ Add normal amount -------------➤ 1.00 SALARY FACTOR TO BE APPLIED -------------➤	2	1.0__
3. BASIC ANNUAL SALARY INCLUDING INCREASE Multiply Box #1 by Box #2 --------------------➤ (OR use appropriate salary schedule)	3	$
4. ADD ADDITIONAL SALARY FACTORS (if applicable): a. Location Pay a _____ b. Geographic Differential b _____ c. Inconvenience Pay c _____ d. Shift Pay Differential d _____ Total Additional Salary Factors (Add a–d)------➤	4	$
5. NORMAL GROSS ANNUAL SALARY Add Box #3 and Box #4 --------------------➤	5	$
6. NORMAL BIWEEKLY GROSS—Multiply Box #5 by: .038356 for FY '84–'85--------➤	6	$
7. ADD PRE-SHIFT BRIEFING (where applicable) to Box #6	7	$
8. DETERMINE TIME TO BE WORKED (Show % amounts as decimals) Normal Time Base 1.00 8a. Subtract Reduction to Be Taken 0.__ TIME FACTOR TO BE APPLIED---------------➤	8	0.___
9. ADJUSTED BIWEEKLY GROSS Multiply Box #7 by Box #8 --------------------➤	9	$
10. BIWEEKLY DEDUCTIONS—Enter amounts only where applicable (See Payroll Office for applicable Federal, State and City Withholding Tables) a. Federal Withholding Tax a _____ b. State Withholding Tax b _____ c. City Withholding Tax c _____ d. Social Security Withholding (Multiply Box #9 by 0.067) d _____ e. Tier III NYS Retirement Contribution (Multiply Box #9 by 0.03) e _____		

22   *(Continued)*

Figure 6-7. *(continued)*

```
    f.  Other Deductions:*
        Bonds                 _____
        Retirement Loans      _____
        Health Insurance      _____
        Federated Fund        _____
        Credit Union          _____
        Union Dues            _____
        Other Insurance       _____
        _____          _____
        _____          _____

        Total Other--------≫    f _____
```

TOTAL BIWEEKLY DEDUCTIONS (Add a–f)------------≫	10	$
11. ADJUSTED BIWEEKLY NET (Subtract Box #10 from Box #9) ----------------≫	11	$

23

*Refer to paycheck stub for other biweekly deduction amounts.

Figure 6-8. Sample supervisory guidelines for handling V-Time requests.

State of California   Department of Real Estate

GUIDELINES FOR DETERMINING ADMINISTRATIVE
FEASIBILITY OF REDUCED WORK TIME REQUESTS

RE 139 (1/83)

1. *GENERAL NOTES*

State agencies and supervisors are expected to review employee requests for reduced work time positively and, whenever possible, to work out a schedule that will meet both the department's and employee's needs. In meeting this requirement, it may be necessary for supervisors to be more flexible in work scheduling than they have been in the past.

If the supervisor decides that a particular reduced work schedule is not administratively feasible, the employee who made the request for reduced work time should be provided with a written explanation for the decision via the RE 138. Before a proposed schedule is denied, however, all reasonable alternatives for backup coverage or other arrangements should be considered.

SOURCE: State of California Department of Real Estate, reprinted in *V-Time: A New Way to Work* (San Francisco: New Ways to Work, 1985), 30.

2. *SERVICE TO PUBLIC/CLIENTS*

   a. General Coverage

   Adequate scheduling and coordination of reduced work time usually will prevent a significant impact on general service to the public (e.g., public counters, general telephone inquiries, etc.). However, a reduced work time schedule that resulted in an actual disruption of service to the public or an unacceptable decline in its timeliness or quality would not be administratively feasible if the deficiency otherwise could not be corrected.

   b. Special Needs

   Reduced work time may not be feasible where an employee is the *sole* expert in an area requiring coverage during all normal working hours. The same may be the case where employees work on such an intensive one-to-one basis with special clients that assignment sharing would not be appropriate.

3. *ADMINISTRATIVE CONSIDERATIONS*

   Since reduced work-time employees would normally not all be working at the same time, the broadened supervisory span of control resulting from converting one or more full-time positions to part-time should not make a reduced work-time schedule unfeasible. However, where a supervisor already has a wide span of control for the type of work supervised, a reduced work-time schedule that resulted in the transfer of new, untrained staff could be unfeasible. However, before ruling out a reduced work-time schedule on this basis, other possibilities for managing the span of control problem within existing supervisory staffing should be fully explored.

4. *WORK LOAD CONSIDERATIONS*

   In work settings where a heavy, active work load must be accomplished, consideration must be given to high-priority work and the consequences of the effects of reduced work schedules on output before requests for reduced work time are granted.

5. *WORK LOAD AND OVERTIME*

   Participants shall not be assigned work load or mandatory overtime that is excessive in comparison to that assigned to other employees performing similar work.

6. *ADDITIONAL INFORMATION*

   If you have questions not covered by these guidelines or the Reduced Worktime Program Facts (RE 140), contact Personnel.

Table 6-4. Example of the effect of reduced work time on pay.

Associate Analyst Level
Top Step, Gross Salary $2,501

	Married, two exemptions					Single, one exemption				
	Full-Time	Percent reduction				Full-Time	Percent reduction			
		5%	10%	15%	20%		5%	10%	15%	20%
Decrease in net pay		4%	7.5%	11.5%	15.5%		3.5%	7%	10.5%	14%
Gross pay	2,501.00	2,375.95	2,250.90	2,125.85	2,000.80	2,501.00	2,375.95	2,250.90	2,125.85	2,000.80
Net pay	1,697.10	1,633.00	1,568.83	1,504.58	1,432.47	1,454.62	1,404.24	1,353.82	1,303.45	1,252.54
Withholding:										
Federal tax	466.19	427.37	388.62	349.84	317.29	624.20	577.92	531.67	485.39	439.14
State tax	70.74	63.24	55.74	48.36	42.11	155.21	141.45	127.70	113.94	100.19
Social Security	167.57	159.19	150.81	142.43	134.54	167.57	159.19	150.81	142.43	134.54
Retirement	99.40	93.15	86.90	80.64	74.39	99.40	93.15	86.90	80.64	74.39

SOURCE: State of California Employment Development Department, reprinted in *V-Time: A New Way to Work* (San Francisco: New Ways to Work, 1985), 35.

Figure 6-9. Sample worksheet for calculating the financial impact of V-Time.

MANDATORY PAYROLL DEDUCTION WORKSHEET

Employees considering reducing their time base may use this worksheet for computing mandatory deductions (state and federal withholding taxes, Social Security, and retirement) to determine their prospective net monthly salary at the reduced time base.

For easy reference in calculating your deductions, an example showing the mandatory deductions for a married employee with two exemptions and a monthly salary of $1,235.00 is provided.

1. SALARY COMPUTATION

    Example: $1,235.00   ×   85%   = $1,049.75

              Full-time monthly   % of time to   Reduced monthly
              salary rate   be worked   salary

    $ _____ × _____ = $ _____

              Full-time monthly   % of time to   Reduced monthly
              salary rate   be worked   salary

    -

2. SOCIAL SECURITY CONTRIBUTION (Omit this step if you are not a member of Social Security system.)

    Example: $1,049.75   ×   6.70%   = $70.33

              Monthly salary   Social Security   Monthly Social
                             contribution rate   Security contribution

    $ _____ ×   6.70%   = $ _____

              Monthly salary   Social Security   Monthly Social
                             contribution rate   Security contribution

    -

3. RETIREMENT CONTRIBUTION (PERS)

    If you have Social Security:

    Example: $1,049.75   − $513.00 = $536.75 × 5% = $26.83

              Monthly salary   Monthly retirement
                                                        contribution

The figures in this worksheet were developed in 1985.

SOURCE: State of California Employment Development Department, reprinted in *V-Time: A New Way to Work* (San Francisco: New Ways to Work, 1985), 42–46.

(Continued)

Figure 6-9. *(continued)*

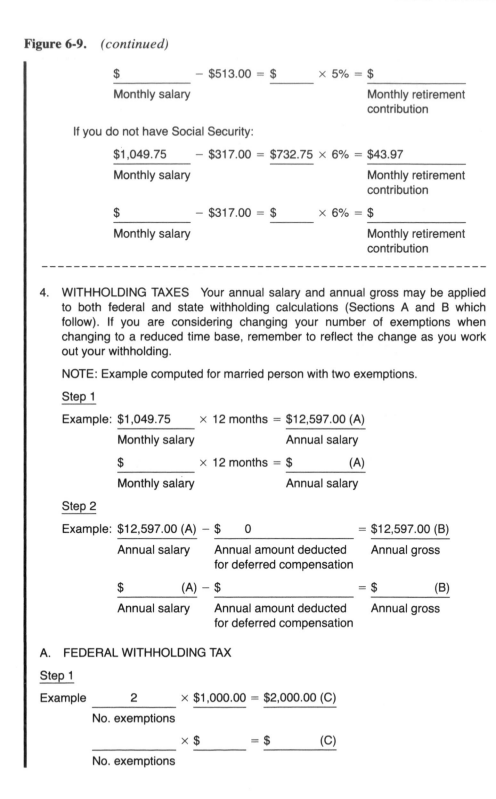

$\underline{\text{\$\qquad\qquad}}$ − \$513.00 = $\underline{\text{\$\qquad}}$ × 5% = $\underline{\text{\$\qquad\qquad}}$
Monthly salary   Monthly retirement
                                                                                            contribution

If you do not have Social Security:

$\underline{\text{\$1,049.75}}$ − \$317.00 = \$732.75 × 6% = $\underline{\text{\$43.97}}$
Monthly salary   Monthly retirement
                                                                                            contribution

$\underline{\text{\$\qquad\qquad}}$ − \$317.00 = $\underline{\text{\$\qquad}}$ × 6% = $\underline{\text{\$\qquad\qquad}}$
Monthly salary   Monthly retirement
                                                                                            contribution

---

4. WITHHOLDING TAXES   Your annual salary and annual gross may be applied to both federal and state withholding calculations (Sections A and B which follow). If you are considering changing your number of exemptions when changing to a reduced time base, remember to reflect the change as you work out your withholding.

    NOTE: Example computed for married person with two exemptions.

    <u>Step 1</u>

    Example: $\underline{\text{\$1,049.75}}$ × 12 months = $\underline{\text{\$12,597.00}}$ (A)
                Monthly salary   Annual salary

                $\underline{\text{\$\qquad}}$ × 12 months = $\underline{\text{\$\qquad}}$ (A)
                Monthly salary   Annual salary

    <u>Step 2</u>

    Example: $\underline{\text{\$12,597.00}}$ (A) − $\underline{\text{\$\quad 0 \quad}}$ = $\underline{\text{\$12,597.00}}$ (B)
                Annual salary   Annual amount deducted   Annual gross
                                              for deferred compensation

                $\underline{\text{\$\qquad}}$ (A) − $\underline{\text{\$\qquad}}$ = $\underline{\text{\$\qquad}}$ (B)
                Annual salary   Annual amount deducted   Annual gross
                                              for deferred compensation

A. FEDERAL WITHHOLDING TAX

<u>Step 1</u>

Example $\underline{\text{\quad 2 \quad}}$ × \$1,000.00 = $\underline{\text{\$2,000.00}}$ (C)
                No. exemptions

                $\underline{\text{\qquad\qquad}}$ × $\underline{\text{\$\qquad}}$ = $\underline{\text{\$\qquad}}$ (C)
                No. exemptions

Step 2

Example: $12,597.00 (B) − $2,000.00 (C) = $10,597.00 (D)

           Annual gross   Taxable wages

          $ _____ (B) − $ _____ (C) = $ _____ (D)

          Annual gross   Taxable wages

Step 3   Circle the numbers which apply to you in Table A; use them to fill in blanks for Steps 4 and 5.

TABLE A

SINGLE OR HEAD OF HOUSEHOLD

Taxable wages		Amount of tax				
Not over $1,420.00		0				
Over	Not over	(Col. 1)		(Col. 2)		(Col. 3)
$ 1,420.00	$ 3,910.00	$ 0.00	plus	14%	of excess over	$ 1,420.00
$ 3,910.00	$ 5,200.00	4 348.60	plus	16%	of excess over	$ 3,910.00
$ 5,200.00	$ 9,400.00	$ 555.00	plus	19%	of excess over	$ 5,200.00
$ 9,400.00	$14,000.00	$1,353.00	plus	24%	of excess over	$ 9,400.00
$14,000.00	$17,200.00	$2,457.00	plus	29%	of excess over	$14,000.00
$17,200.00	$22,500.00	$3,385.00	plus	32%	of excess over	$17,200.00
$22,500.00	....	$5,081.00	plus	37%	of excess over	$22,500.00

MARRIED

Taxable wages		Amount of tax				
Not over $2,400.00		0				
Over	Not over	(Col. 1)		(Col. 2)		(Col. 3)
$ 2,400.00	$ 7,650.00	$ 0.00	plus	14%	of excess over	$ 2,400.00
$ 7,650.00	$10,900.00	$ 735.00	plus	16%	of excess over	$ 7,650.00
$10,900.00	$15,400.00	$1,255.00	plus	20%	of excess over	$10,900.00
$15,400.00	$23,250.00	$2,155.00	plus	25%	of excess over	$15,400.00
$23,250.00	$28,900.00	$4,117.50	plus	31%	of excess over	$23,250.00
$28,900.00	$34,200.00	$5,869.00	plus	34%	of excess over	$28,900.00
$34,200.00	....	$7,671.00	plus	37%	of excess over	$34,200.00

Step 4

Example: $10,597.00 (D) − $7,650.00 = $2,947.00 ×   16% = $471.52 (E)

           Taxable wages   Col. 3,   Col. 2,

                          Table A   Table A

      $ _____ (D) − $ _____ = $ _____ × _____ % = $ _____ (E)

          Taxable wages   Col. 3,   Col. 2,

                        Table A   Table A

Step 5

Example: $471.52 (E) + $735.00 = $1,206.52 (F)

                   Col. 1,   Annual tax

                   Table A

(Continued)

Figure 6-9.   *(continued)*

$$\frac{\$\quad\quad(E) + \$\quad\quad}{\text{Col. 1,}\quad\quad\text{Annual tax}} = \$\quad\quad(F)$$
$$\text{Table A}$$

Step 6

Example: $\dfrac{\$1,206.52\ (F)}{\text{Annual tax}} \div 12\ \text{months} = \dfrac{\$100.54}{\text{Monthly tax}}$

$\dfrac{\$\quad\quad(F)}{\text{Annual tax}} \div 12\ \text{months} = \dfrac{\$\quad\quad}{\text{Monthly tax}}$

B.   STATE WITHHOLDING TAX

Step 1   IF ANNUAL GROSS (SEE #4 WITHHOLDING TAXES, STEP 2 [B]) IS LESS THAN OR EQUAL TO AMOUNT SHOWN IN TABLE B, NO TAX IS REQUIRED TO BE WITHHELD.
IF ANNUAL GROSS IS GREATER THAN AMOUNT IN TABLE B, PROCEED TO STEP 2.

TABLE B LOW-INCOME EXEMPTION TABLE			
SINGLE	MARRIED		HEAD OF HOUSEHOLD
	"0" or "1" exemption	"2" or more exemptions	
$5,000.00	$5,000.00	$10.000.00	$10,000.00

Step 2   Find your standard deduction in Table C.

TABLE C STANDARD DEDUCTION TABLE			
SINGLE	MARRIED		HEAD OF HOUSEHOLD
	"0" or "1" exemption	"2" or more exemptions	
$1,400.00	$1,400.00	$2,800.00	$2,800.00

Step 3

Example: $\dfrac{\$12,597.00\ (B)}{\text{Annual gross}} - \dfrac{\$2,800}{\substack{\text{Standard deduction}\\\text{per Table C}}} = \dfrac{\$9,797.00\ (C)}{\text{Taxable wages}}$

$\dfrac{\$\quad\quad(B)}{\text{Annual gross}} - \dfrac{\$\quad\quad}{\substack{\text{Standard deduction}\\\text{per Table C}}} = \dfrac{\$\quad\quad(C)}{\text{Taxable wages}}$

Step 4 Circle the numbers which apply to you in Table D; then use them to fill in the blanks on Step 5.

TABLE D

MARRIED

If the taxable wages are . . .   Computed tax is . . .

Over	But not over	(Col. 1)		(Col. 2)		(Col. 3)
$ 0	$ 5,700	$ 0.00	plus	1%	of amount over	$ 0
$ 5,700	$ 9,980	$ 57.00	plus	2%	of amount over	$ 5,700
$ 9,980	$14,260	$ 142.60	plus	3%	of amount over	$ 9,980
$14,260	$18,580	$ 271.00	plus	4%	of amount over	$14,260
$18,580	$22,860	$ 443.80	plus	5%	of amount over	$18,580
$22,860	$27,160	$ 657.80	plus	6%	of amount over	$22,860
$27,160	$31,420	$ 915.80	plus	7%	of amount over	$27,160
$31,420	$35,720	$1,214.00	plus	8%	of amount over	$31,420
$35,720	$40,000	$1,558.00	plus	9%	of amount over	$35,720
$40,000	$44,280	$1,943.20	plus	10%	of amount over	$40,000
$44,280	and over . . .	$2,371.20	plus	11%	of amount over	$44,280

SINGLE

If the taxable wages are . . .   Computed tax Is . . .

Over	But not over	(Col. 1)		(Col. 2)		(Col. 3)
$ 0	$ 2,850	$ 0.00	plus	1%	of amount over	$ 0
$ 2,850	$ 4,990	$ 28.50	plus	2%	of amount over	$ 2,850
$ 4,990	$ 7,130	$ 71.30	plus	3%	of amount over	$ 4,990
$ 7,130	$ 9,290	$ 135.50	plus	4%	of amount over	$ 7,130
$ 9,290	$11,430	$ 221.90	plus	5%	of amount over	$ 9,290
$11,430	$13,580	$ 328.90	plus	6%	of amount over	$11,430
$13,580	$15,710	$ 457.90	plus	7%	of amount over	$13,580
$15,710	$17,860	$ 607.00	plus	8%	of amount over	$15,710
$17,860	$20,000	$ 779.00	plus	9%	of amount over	$17,860
$20,000	$22,140	$ 971.60	plus	10%	of amount over	$20,000
$22,140	and over . . .	$1,185.60	plus	11%	of amount over	$22,140

UNMARRIED HEAD OF HOUSEHOLD

If the taxable wages are . . .   Computed tax is . . .

Over	But not over	(Col. 1)		(Col. 2)		(Col. 3)
$ 0	$ 5,720	$ 0.00	plus	1%	of amount over	$ 0
$ 5,720	$ 8,560	$ 57.20	plus	2%	of amount over	$ 5,720
$ 8,560	$10,710	$ 114.00	plus	3%	of amount over	$ 8,560
$10,710	$12,850	$ 178.50	plus	4%	of amount over	$10,710
$12,850	$15,000	$ 264.10	plus	5%	of amount over	$12,850
$15,000	$17,150	$ 371.60	plus	6%	of amount over	$15,000
$17,150	$19,280	$ 500.60	plus	7%	of amount over	$17,150
$19,280	$21,420	$ 649.70	plus	8%	of amount over	$19,280
$21,420	$23,570	$ 820.90	plus	9%	of amount over	$21,420
$23,570	$25,710	$1,014.40	plus	10%	of amount over	$23,570
$25,710	and over . . .	$1,228.40	plus	11%	of amount over	$25,710

Step 5

Example: $9,797.00 (C) − $5,700.00 = $4,097.00 (D) × 2% = $81.94 + $57.00 = $138.94 (E)

         Taxable wages   Col. 3,   Col. 2,   Col. 1,

                      Table D   Table D   Table D

$ _____ (C) − $ _____ = $ _____ (D) × _____ % = $ _____ + $ _____ = $ _____ (E)

         Taxable wages   Col. 3,   Col. 2,   Col. 1,

                      Table D   Table D   Table D

(Continued)

Figure 6-9. *(continued)*

Step 6   Circle your tax credit on Table E.

Step 7

Example: $138.94 (E) − $70.00   = $68.94   (F)
                        Tax credit,   Annual tax amount
                        Table E

          $ (E) − $ = $ (F)
                        Tax credit,   Annual tax amount
                        Table E

	TABLE E										
	TAX CREDIT TABLE										
MARITAL STATUS	NUMBER OF EXEMPTIONS										
	0	1	2	3	4	5	6	7	8	9	10
SINGLE	$0	$35	$46	$57	$68	$79	$90	$101	$112	$123	$134
MARRIED/ HEAD OF HOUSEHOLD	$0	$35	$70	$81	$92	$103	$114	$125	$136	$147	$158

Step 8

Example: $68.94 (F) ÷ 12 months = $5.75
          Annual tax   Monthly tax
          amount   amount

          $ (F) ÷ 12 months = $
          Annual tax   Monthly tax
          amount   amount

5. NET PAY COMPUTATION

Step 1

Example: $ 70.33 $
                               Social Security   Social Security
Note: You may have
other deductions, such   + $ 26.83   + $
as a credit union pay-   Retirement   Retirement
ment, association
dues, or insurance   + $ 100.54   + $
premium.   Federal tax   Federal tax

                            + $ 5.75   + $
                               State tax   State tax

+ $ _____	+ $ _____	
Other deductions	Other deductions	
+ $ _____	+ $ _____	
Other deductions	Other deductions	
+ $ _____	+ $ _____	
Other deductions	Other deductions	
$ 203.45	$.	
Total deductions	Total deductions	

Step 2

Example: $1,049.75	− $ 0	− $203.45	= $846.30
Monthly salary	Deferred comp.	Total deductions (from Step 1)	Net pay
$ _____	− $ _____	− $ _____	= $ _____
Monthly salary	Deferred comp.	Total deductions (from Step 1)	Net pay

chief among them the impact on the employees' finances and job future. This is where an active promotional campaign comes in.

Promotional materials should present general information about the program, including why it is being initiated, guidelines, some common questions and answers, and how to get answers to other questions. Beyond these topics, promotional materials must deal with financial considerations and the issue of the participating employees' job future if they are to encourage the fullest possible participation in the program. Employees need detailed financial impact worksheets to help them determine whether or not they can afford to work part-time and by how much they can afford to reduce their schedule. In addition, they need information to allay their fear of layoffs if cutbacks are required in either the near or long term. Such resource materials will also prove helpful to managers and supervisors in explaining the program and encouraging participation.

Briefing sessions for employees and supervisors are another helpful technique for promoting the use of V-Time. Such sessions provide a forum for management to answer questions and affirm the company's commitment to the program.

Trust between an organization and its employees is an important element. The existing level of trust will determine to a considerable extent the level of participation in the early stages of a V-Time program. A skillful promotional effort, backed by effective resource materials, can go a long way toward establishing and supporting that trust.

Evaluate the Program

The type of evaluation you conduct will depend on management's original objectives in setting up the program. Of general interest, however, will be who applied to participate in the program and how their requests were disposed of, which levels of work-time reduction were requests and which approved, what the supervisory response to the program has been, and how employees feel about V-Time. The program should be examined from a procedural and administrative standpoint as well, in order to identify any problem areas.

Fine-Tune the Program

Once the V-Time program has been evaluated, the organization must address and resolve the problems that have been identified. For example:

Problem	*Solution*
Supervisors complain that the enrollment period for the V-Time program constitutes a disruptive period every 12 months.	Consider changing to a year-round enrollment.
Employee requests for inclusion in the V-Time program remain unprocessed for long periods.	Set a time limit and state that responses to employee requests must occur within that limit.
Supervisors consider the program a drain on their resources.	Hold workshop for supervisors to discuss ways to improve the allocation of "resources" —both human and financial— as a result of the greater flexibility made possible by the V-Time program.

Summary

A voluntary reduced work time program offers regular part-time options in a way that overcomes what some employees regard as the disadvantages of more traditional part-time work. There are three main differences between regular part-time and V-Time: (1) While regular part-time work is usually open-ended, an employee enrolls in a V-Time program for a specified time period. (2) While an organization may or may not have an established procedure for a regular part-time employee to return to full-time work, such a provision is an integral part of a V-Time program, since it is expected that unless a continuation of the V-Time schedule is mutually agreed upon by the employee and his or her supervisor, the employee will resume a full-time schedule once the V-Time agreement expires. (3) And while most regular part-time work involves as much as a 20 percent to 50 percent time reduction, V-Time programs provide for a range of reductions—from as much as 50 percent to as little as 2.5 percent—making schedule cutbacks feasible for interested employees who could not handle the more substantial time (and salary) reductions of regular part-time.

V-Time programs originated at the county government level, then spread to state government and to the private sector. While experience with V-Time has to date been limited, it is clear that this work-time alternative offers a number of features that should make it increasingly attractive to employers in both the public and private sectors.

The net effect of the differences between V-Time and regular part-time is that a V-Time option will have a broader appeal to employees and be more widely used than the traditional forms of part-time. Hence, it is an especially appropriate choice for an employer that wants to offer a part-time arrangement or multiply the effect of an existing program of part-time options, either to accommodate employee needs or to meet one or more organizational objectives (such as enhancing recruitment, minimizing layoffs, or using payroll cutbacks to generate cost savings that can, if desired, be applied to meet more pressing needs).

In addition to the advantages of making part-time options more widely available, generating cost savings, and increasing the organization's fiscal flexibility, V-Time also standardizes the use of reduced schedules, eliminating the inequities often associated with ad hoc schedule cutbacks. A disadvantage of V-Time is that it can provoke concern on the part of managers and labor representatives. The former may worry that a reduced employee time commitment could leave their department unable to cope with a large, fixed work load (particularly if there are restrictions on hiring additional personnel to replace the reduced hours); the latter may worry that V-Time could eventually lead to an involuntary loss of full-time jobs.

Once an organization decides to proceed with the introduction of a V-Time program, it will concentrate on gaining the backing of top and middle-level management; designing a program that will appeal to the widest possible range of employees; and conducting a promotional campaign, backed by solid, detailed resource materials, that will encourage supervisory support and employee participation.

If faced with such problems as the need to accommodate employees seeking a temporarily reduced work schedule, broaden the organization's recruitment effort, generate cost savings, enhance fiscal flexibility, and respond to an economic downturn, an employer would do well to consider V-Time.

CHAPTER 7

Leave Time

Leave time is an authorized period of time away from work without loss of employment rights. This absence may be paid or unpaid and is usually extended and taken for such reasons as family responsibilities, health care, education, and personal or leisure time. Practically every employer with a staff of at least 100 offers paid vacations and sick leave to its regular employees. Most companies also allow unpaid leave under certain circumstances and commonly permit employees to link paid and unpaid leaves, so that they can be absent from the job for longer periods. Many, if not most, also continue benefits during paid leave.

A 1986 New Ways to Work survey of San Francisco Bay area private-sector employers showed that 82 percent in San Francisco County and 64 percent in Alameda County continue benefits during paid leave time, while only 17 percent and 18 percent, respectively, do so during unpaid periods of leave. A significant number, however (61 percent and 48 percent), continue benefits during unpaid leave time if the employee pays some or all of the cost.[1]

Origins of Expanded Leave Options

As has been the case with other aspects of work time, definitions of leave time and policies regarding it have been undergoing scrutiny and change recently, with the trend being toward creating more flexibility for both the organization and the individual employee. Since the mid-1980s, particular attention has been focused on policy development relating to two areas: (1) leave time for family responsibilities and (2) paid time off for vacation, holidays, illness or injury, and personal use. A third kind of leave, time off taken for the purpose of a sabbatical or education, has been the subject of less interest since the early 1980s, but its potential for facilitating training and continuing education, as well as alleviating burnout, makes it relevant to the interests of today's managers. This chapter provides an overview of current developments relating to each of these three kinds of leave policy.

Who Uses Expanded Leave Options?

Because the three main categories of leave time involve significantly different considerations and, as noted in the preceding section, organizational practices differ with respect to each type of leave, this section will discuss family-oriented leaves, paid time off, and sabbatical and educational leaves in separate subsections.

Family-Oriented Leaves

The type of leave about which there is the most discussion and debate today is that relating to family responsibilities. Such leaves include:

- Pregnancy disability leave
- Parental leave (including paternity leave)
- Child-care, infant-care, or primary-care leave
- Sick-child care
- Dependent senior care

Although, in the United States, the labor force participation rates of women with young children have been climbing steadily in recent years, the United States has lagged far behind other developed countries in introducing either social or organizational policy that reflects this change. According to Sheila Kamerman, professor of social policy and planning at Columbia University, and Alfred J. Kahn, authors of *The Responsive Workplace:*

> [T]he pattern in much of Europe is one in which working women, and often working parents, are permitted at least a year of unpaid, job-protected leave, in addition to a statutory paid leave, considerably longer than what is provided in the United States.[2]
>
> A glance at federal legislation covering maternity and parental leaves in a sampling of different countries is instructive:

- *Austria*. A maternity leave of 20 weeks at full salary, with up to a year off.
- *Canada*. A maternity leave of 15 weeks at 60 percent salary, with up to 41 weeks off.
- *Finland*. A maternity leave of 35 weeks at full salary.
- *France*. A maternity leave of 16 weeks at 90 percent salary.
- *Germany*. A maternity leave of 14 weeks at full salary, with up to a total of 6 months at a reduced subsidy. Job is guaranteed for 6 months.
- *Great Britain*. A maternity leave of 6 weeks at 90 percent salary, plus 12 additional weeks with a small stipend. Job is guaranteed for 40 weeks.
- *Hungary*. A maternity leave of 6 months at full salary, with a very small stipend for 2½ years more. Job is guaranteed for 3 years.
- *Italy*. A maternity leave of 22 weeks at 80 percent salary, with up to 48 weeks off.
- *Japan*. A maternity leave of 12 weeks at 60 percent salary.
- *Sweden*. A parental leave of 9 months at 90 percent salary. Job is guaranteed for 18 months. This option has been available to men since 1984.

The situation in the United States is much different: Many women still lack the right to a job-protected leave of absence when they give birth or adopt a child, and those policies that do exist vary widely in terms of such provisions as when leave can be taken, duration, and eligibility. The current policy debate in the United States does not revolve around whether or not to maintain the status quo in regard to family-oriented leave policy but rather what kind of new policy to introduce and whether a generalized approach (that is, legislation that mandates minimum requirements) or an individualized one (in which employers have total responsibility for developing the policy parameters) is most appropriate.

Since the mid-1980s, there have begun to emerge various legislative initiatives, which either mandate or encourage the development by employers of policy to address working parents' need for some flexibility in terms of time off for pregnancy and during the early weeks of an infant's life, as well as for family illness and/or crises.

Five states require employers to provide temporary disability insurance (TDI) plans: California, Hawaii, New Jersey, New York, and Rhode Island. The Federal Pregnancy Discrimination Act of 1978 made it unlawful to discriminate against a pregnant employee by treating her differently than any other temporarily disabled employee. It states that disability due to pregnancy and childbirth must be handled in the same manner as any other short-term disability. Consequently, working women in the five TDI states receive disability payments while on leave for reasons of pregnancy.

In 1987, another five states enacted a mandatory maternal or parental leave policy, bringing to 15 the number of states that have rules or laws on pregnancy leave and related issues. An additional 16 states are considering such legislation. Examples of existing state legislation include:

- *California*. In California, government code 12945(b)(2), enacted as part of the Fair Employment and Housing Act, states that covered employers—those with five or more employees—must permit women the right to "take a leave on account of pregnancy for a reasonable period of time," not to exceed four months. The "reasonable period of time" means the period during which the woman is *disabled* by pregnancy, childbirth, or related medical conditions.

   A 1987 Supreme Court decision—*California Federal Savings and Loan Association* v. *Guerra,* 107 U.S. 683 (1987)—upheld the right of states to require employers to grant special job protection to employees who are physically unable to work as a result of pregnancy and childbirth. The decision noted that federal law established a "floor not a ceiling" in efforts to redress sex-based discrimination, and it is expected that other states may now pass legislation similar to California's.

- *Connecticut*. In Connecticut, general statute 46-a-60(7)(B) states that it is illegal for an employer to "terminate a woman's employment because of her pregnancy" or to refuse an employee "a reasonable leave of absence for disability resulting from her pregnancy." Connecticut law also grants up to 24 weeks of parental leave to employees of the state government.

- *Massachusetts*. In Massachusetts, general law 149, paragraph 105D, says that a full-time employee "who is absent from such employment for a period not exceeding eight weeks for the purpose of giving birth . . . shall be restored to her previous, or a similar[,] position with the same status."

- *Montana*. In Montana, code 49-2-310, known as the Montana Maternity Leave Act, makes it unlawful for an employer to "terminate a woman's employment because of her pregnancy" or to "refuse to grant to the employee a reasonable leave of absence" for pregnancy.

■ *Minnesota*. In August 1987, Minnesota became the first state to require employers to offer leave to both the mother and the father of a newborn child. The legislation requires all companies with 21 employees or more to offer up to 6 weeks of unpaid leave to both parents.

■ *Oregon*. In Oregon, employers are required to grant up to 12 weeks of unpaid leave, split between the mother and the father only if both parents work for the same organization.

The most widely debated proposed legislation is the federal Family and Medical Leave Act—H.R. 925 (sponsored by Rep. William Clay) and S.249 (sponsored by Sen. Christopher Dodd)—originally introduced in the House and the Senate in 1986 and reintroduced in 1987. This legislation proposes a national leave policy that would provide job-protected leave for workers to meet parental responsibilities and to deal with serious health conditions. It has been strongly opposed by most employer groups and was defeated in the 100th Congress. However, it indicates a growing interest in the issue of maternity-paternity-parental leave-time policy on the part of legislators and policymakers, and its sponsors plan to reintroduce it.

As far as existing private-sector leave policy, a nationwide study of the parental leave policies of 384 companies, conducted by Catalyst, a research organization that helps corporations further the careers of women, indicated that 95 percent of the responding companies granted short-term disability leaves to their employees, with the majority providing between five and eight weeks of leave. Most gave at least some pay during the leave. More than 80 percent of the responding companies offered employees reinstatement to the same job or a comparable job after disability leave. Six percent offered the returning employee some job (but not necessarily the same job or a comparable one), while approximately 13 percent gave no guarantees at all. It was clear from the survey results that policies with regard to parental leave are in transition. Over half the respondents said that they had changed their policies in some respect within the past five years.[3]

A 1988 *Newsday* article offered the following sampling of corporate policies on parental leave, based on data from the Council on Economic Priorities:

■ *Avon Products, Inc.* Three months paid maternal disability leave; 3 months unpaid maternal leave.

- *Campbell Soup Company*. Six weeks paid maternal disability leave; up to 3 months unpaid parental leave for salaried employees.
- *Clorox Company*. Six to 8 weeks paid maternal disability leave; up to 6 months unpaid parental leave.
- *Eastman Kodak Company*. Average of 8 weeks paid maternal disability leave, up to one year in some cases; up to 4 months paid parental leave.
- *Merck & Company, Inc*. Six weeks paid maternal disability leave; up to 18 months unpaid parental leave.
- *National Westminster Bank (United States)*. Six to 8 weeks paid maternal disability leave; up to one year unpaid parental leave.
- *IBM*. Six to 8 weeks paid maternal disability leave; up to one year unpaid parental leave with option to work part-time.
- *Procter & Gamble Company*. Eight weeks paid maternal disability leave; up to 6 months unpaid parental leave.[4]

According to Sheila Kamerman and Alfred Kahn, within the corporate sector:

> Large firms and banking-financial-insurance companies are most likely to provide such leaves and are the most generous in the extensiveness of the leaves. In contrast, small employers and firms in the retail trade and service industries are least likely to provide leaves, or if permitting a leave, to guarantee the job on return.[5]

Companies are increasingly sex-blind in terms of leave policy that extends beyond the disability stage of a pregnancy. The Catalyst survey found that 37 percent of the respondents offered men unpaid leaves with a job guarantee. Although some labeled these leaves "paternity" or "parental," many such leaves were simply covered under general leave-of-absence provisions. For example, both Time Inc. and American Telephone & Telegraph Company (AT&T), have policies whereby, if both parents are employed by their respective companies, the mother and the father can take up to a year of unpaid leave between them. At AT&T, however, job and salary retention is only guaranteed for six months of that period.[6]

Adoptive parents are also benefiting from much of the new policy development. The 1984 Catalyst survey found that more than a quarter of the respondents (27.5 percent) offer adoption benefits, ranging from unpaid leave to reimbursement for adoption expenses. Many (61 percent) set an age limit of 18 for the adopted child.[7]

As the population ages, there is a growing need for time to care for elderly family members as well as young children. A 1986 Travelers Insurance Company survey of home office employees showed that approximately 20 percent of the respondents were providing an average of 10.2 hours per week of care to an older relative. A large number were in their 30s and also had young children to care for.[8] Recognizing that in addition to personal or vacation time, employees often need time to deal with family-related crises, some employers, such as Atlantic Richfield, have begun to include policy language allowing employees to use sick leave to care for sick children and other family members.

Paid Time Off

Separate from family-specific leave time, but related to it, is policy dealing with the following types of paid absences:

- Sick leave
- Holidays
- Vacation
- Personal time

Many organizations have been reevaluating their policy in these areas as a result of changes in labor force demographics. There is a growing recognition that a diverse work force has diverse needs and that the way employees use their sick leave or vacation and holiday time reflects these changed needs. This, in turn, has occasioned changes in policy. In a Conference Board report, *Corporations and Families: Changing Practices and Perspectives,* Helen Axel describes this kind of policy evolution:

> Although personnel executives say that their firms encourage (and, sometimes, require) employees to use their vacations in large pieces of time, many recognize that lifestyles or personal responsibilities do not always make long vacations possible. Most companies now permit employees to take at least some of their vacation time in small increments—days, half-days, or even (in a very limited number of instances) hours. A bank officer relates that, some years ago, her need for one afternoon off each week to care for her infant child precipitated a change in the company's vacation policy to include half-days of vacation. As frequently occurs, practice preceded policy. Until the policy was officially changed, she and her superior agreed that her absences would be shown as full days every other week.[9]

Another issue that has been reevaluated in this benefit area is the use of *sick leave* for other than employee personal illness. A study conducted for the U.S. Department of Health and Human Services indicates that management practices, in addition to demographics, affect the way sick leave is used. A major conclusion of the study is that:

> [A] significant amount of sick leave cannot be explained by personal illness or injury, care of a family member or preventive medical visit. . . . The researchers posited that there are two additional categories of sick leave use related to occurrences in the workplace—and therefore tractable by management action:
>
> ■ Time off due to real illness brought about by stress or other events or circumstances in the workplace;
> ■ "Attitudinal" use of sick leave due to conflict with co-workers, resentment of a supervisor, frustration with poor planning, and other management causes.[10]

The report also noted demographic differences in sick leave use: Younger employees were more inclined to use sick leave than were older ones, and there was a tendency toward greater use among less-experienced and less-educated employees, as well as those at lower grade levels.

The concept of "leave banks," which enable employees to pool their sick leave, is a new idea that is gaining acceptance in some areas. Teachers and police officers have pioneered the concept of establishing leave banks to help fellow employees whose sick leave allowance has been depleted by long illness. A special resolution allows Florida employees of the Internal Revenue Service to donate two years of sick leave and 35 weeks of vacation time. This leave bank was established to help a particular couple, both fellow employees, one of whom was very ill.[11]

In the early 1980s, Hewlett-Packard's reevaluation of its sick leave policy led to changes that represent a new, individualized, and more flexible approach to policy strategy in the overall area of paid time off. In 1982, Hewlett-Packard began offering a "Flexible Time Off" program, which combined vacation and sick leave time. The impetus for the program was a desire to create a more equitable policy. Previously, the company had realized that only 20 percent of the employees were responsible for using 80 percent of the sick leave time annually. Under the current plan, employees receive from 15 to 30 days off a year, depending on their length of service. This time can be used at the employees' option as either vacation time or sick leave time. They may carry over a portion of unused time off from year to year (the amount is determined by tenure) and receive a cash payout after 20 years of service. The carried-over block of time can be used for such purposes as extra vacation, temporary illness, personal business appointments, illness in the family, and problems with child care, or it may be saved for later use or a cash benefit. As the company brochure states, "[E]mployees are well able to take responsibility for the important decisions affecting their lives away from the job."[12] (Hewlett-Packard's experience with flexible time off is profiled in a later section of this chapter.)

Catalyst suggests offering flexible paid time off as part of a flexible benefits plan and describes two ways to do this: (1) making all kinds of paid time off interchangeable or (2) making paid time off interchangeable with other benefits.[13] (See Figure 7-1).

Sabbatical and Educational Leaves

Sabbaticals and *educational leave* are areas that appear at present to be "on hold" rather than subject to reexamination. In the mid-1970s, there was growing interest in the concept of sabbaticals as an employee benefit and as a way to allow employees to recoup from burnout. Interest waned in the early 1980s, but a 1986 Bureau of

Figure 7-1. Two ways to offer flexible paid time off.

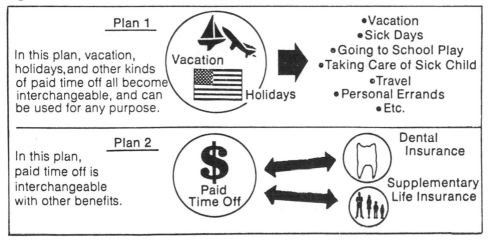

SOURCE: *Flexible Benefits: How to Set Up a Plan When Your Employees Are Complaining, Your Costs Are Rising, and You're Too Busy to Think About It* (New York: Catalyst, 1987), 47. Used by permission of Catalyst, 250 Park Avenue, New York, N.Y. 10003.

National Affairs phone survey indicated that although few companies have formal programs, "[S]abbaticals in the corporate world . . . are a somewhat rare, but prized, employee benefit, valued by both employers and employees."[14]

Sabbaticals have been kept alive even in companies facing economic problems, and the trend toward relegating them to the "back burner" may change rapidly if current policies related to downsizing and stringent cost control continue. As Dr. Jack Wood, of the department of management, University of Newcastle, New South Wales, Australia, noted in a 1987 speech entitled *The Future of Employment:*

> Terms such as "workplace stress," "burnout" and a "decline in the work ethic" have become the core of much of the recent business literature. One strategy that has been implemented in many firms to combat some of these problems in recent years is Sabbatical Leave. Varied models for Sabbatical Leave have been proposed and implemented in both the public and private sectors of industry in OECD [*Organization for Economic Cooperation and Development*] countries. The major features of some of these schemes are outlined in the following discussion and one prime benefit, the potential to create additional employment, a commonly overlooked dimension, will be emphasized.[15]

Wood goes on to describe several sabbatical programs that are self-funded by the interested employee and that enable him or her to take paid leave of up to a year. Such a program is the "Four Over Five Plan" developed for teachers in the Canadian province of Prince Edward Island. Under this plan, teachers may opt to receive 80 percent of their salary for the first four years of the plan. The deferred 20 percent is accumulated annually with interest and provides the income to finance one year's leave during the fifth year. Fringe benefits are maintained during the leave, and the teacher returns to the same position or a similar one when the leave is completed. Employment opportunities are expanded when the teachers are replaced during their absence.

Although most businesses are not able to grant many employees a year's leave because of the problems in obtaining temporary replacements, the concept of withholding salary to finance shorter periods of leave time is worth considering, particularly in light of the growing problem of employee burnout in some areas and the projected need for continuing education and training.

When Is Leave Time Most Appropriate?

Employers generally offer leave time to facilitate retraining and continuing education, enable employees to cope with stress and burnout and better manage the conflict between work and family responsibilities, and expand employment opportunities.

Retraining and continuing education. One of the most pressing problems for employers today is how to cope with the ongoing education and training requirements of our highly technical and competitive economy. Encouraging employees to assume some of the responsibilities in this area and providing leave time during which the employee's job is guaranteed are one strategy that deserves consideration.

Stress and burnout. In some organizations, work-related stress is beginning to show up as an identifiable cost in the form of increased medical insurance premiums and worker's compensation claims. Rolm Corporation (now a division of Siemans) was one of the first high-tech firms to recognize the need for "bounce-back" time. When that company devised its "Continuous Service Leave" program, under which all full-time employees with seven years' tenure were offered the chance for up to 12 calendar weeks of paid leave in addition to paid vacation, a company objective was the desire to increase productivity by allowing employees to "refresh" themselves. Employee stress and burnout is a factor in many industries, and a leave-time program is one way to combat it.

Conflict between work and family responsibilities. Leave time is generally discussed in terms of its importance as a means to help working parents adjust to the birth or adoption of a new baby. It can be equally important as an option for senior dependent care or during times of particular family stress or crisis.

Expanding employment opportunities. Leave programs have been used to spread employment, both by reducing layoffs and by creating short-term employment possibilities. For example, the state of Alaska has an "Approved Leave Without Pay" program designed to minimize layoffs, and the "Four Over Five" sabbatical program available to Prince Edward Island teachers, mentioned earlier, creates new job openings.

Pros and Cons of Leave Time

For an employer, the main advantages of offering a program of leave-time options lie in such areas as retaining valued employees, expanding work force skills, and reducing the negative effects of burnout. The disadvantages involve the issue of how to handle the work load during the employee's absence.

Employee retention. If your organization does not offer certain kinds of leave time (for example, sufficient maternity/paternity or family-care leave), it may find itself losing valued workers. And when employees leave, the company's investment goes with them.

Expansion of labor force skills. Broadening your company's educational or training leave policy can encourage employees to expand their current skills or to cross-train. Since training is increasingly expensive for many organizations, particularly those affected by constant technological changes, making it easier for employees to further their own education and training could have considerable cost impact in the future.

Combatting burnout. Employee burnout can adversely affect both quality and productivity if ways are not developed to periodically reduce its negative effects. A sabbatical or leave program is one proven strategy for revitalizing overly stressed workers.

Managing the work load. The question of how work will be handled while an employee is on leave is of particular importance to supervisors. The type of options that are available will critically influence their responsiveness, or lack thereof, to employee requests for leave time. In its survey report on the use of leaves, Catalyst listed seven ways that companies handle the responsibilities of employees who are on leave:

1. Work is rerouted to other departmental employees.
2. A replacement from within the company is obtained on a temporary basis.
3. A replacement from outside the company is hired on a temporary basis.
4. Only urgent work is rerouted to other employees, with the remainder of the work held for the leave-taker's attention upon his or her return.
5. Work is forwarded to the leave-taker at his or her home.
6. A permanent replacement is obtained, and the leave-taker is transferred to another job.
7. A permanent new replacement is hired.[16]

Figure 7-2 shows the percentage of companies that opt for each of these solutions in order to cover the responsibilities of leave-takers.

With managers, the Catalyst survey found, it is common to reroute only urgent work and, depending on the expected length of

Figure 7-2. How work is handled for nonmanagerial leave-takers.

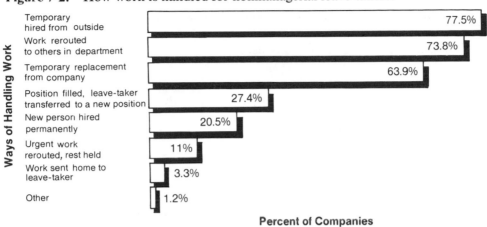

N = 337; multiple answers possible

SOURCE: *The Corporate Guide to Parental Leaves* (New York: Catalyst, 1986), 87. © 1986 by Catalyst. Used by permission of Catalyst, 250 Park Avenue, New York, N.Y. 10003.

the leave, to hold the rest or send it to the leave-taker's home.[17] Time, Inc. replaces leave-takers with people already employed by Time or substitutes who are looking for employment. These latter are assisted in finding work when the permanent employee returns. In some cases, when an employee requests a part-time schedule upon completion of maternity leave, the "temporary" replacement is interested in job sharing with the incumbent.

Should Your Organization Try Expanding Its Leave Options?

The issue of expanding your organization's leave options involves two decisions: (1) whether or not to expand those options and (2) what types of new options would be appropriate. The tools in this section can help you arrive at these decisions.

Start by referring to Organizational Experience With Leave Time, which profiles the leave programs instituted by four organizations. Two of these profiles deal with parental leave and one with flexible time off. The fourth deals with a leave option not previously mentioned in this chapter: social service leave. While programs that permit leaves for the purpose of serving community needs are seen

(Text continues on page 272.)

ORGANIZATIONAL EXPERIENCE WITH LEAVE TIME

Lotus Development Corporation

Description: A computer software company based in Cambridge, Massachusetts, with 2,000 employees worldwide.

Reason for Using Leave Time: The average age of Lotus's work force is 31, approximately half men and half women. Many of these employees are planning both careers and families, with some already facing child-raising responsibilities.

The software industry is very competitive and stressful. Lotus makes great demands on its staff in terms of long hours and working at home and therefore is willing to accommodate their personal and family needs. The company feels it is making an important statement to its employees by offering a parental leave option. It doesn't want them to quit just because they're having children and is willing to provide extra leave time and pay for it in order to retain these employees.

Implementation Process: For the primary caregiver of the child, up to four weeks of paid leave time is negotiated between the manager and the employee. When the employee returns, there is the additional option of part-time and flexitime arrangements.

The human resources department at Lotus facilitates this negotiation by interpreting the policy and providing information. A parental leave agreement is signed.

Granting leave time is a serious business consideration. Other people have to fill the gap created by the absence of the leave-taking employee. New products may be in development or about to hit the market, and the parent on leave may be indispensable. In this case, the employee may be asked to continue to do some work at home using a computer and modem.

In 1989, Lotus plans to build an on-site child-care center in its new building.

Impact to Date: The leave program, which was instituted in May 1985, is very popular with employees. There is a real sense of give and take, because employees not on leave realize that they might want to use the option themselves someday.

Lotus, which is only 6 years old, feels that it is setting the stage for other kinds of leave—including options for caregivers of AIDS patients or dying spouses.

SOURCE: Telephone interview with the human resources development staff, Lotus Development Corporation (June 1988).

National Westminster Bank PLC

Description: National Westminster Bank, located in London, is Britain's largest bank. It also has U.S. branches located in New York (Manhattan, Long Island, Brooklyn, and Queens); Westchester, Ct.; Los Angeles and San Francisco, Ca.; and Chicago, Il. The U.S. offices have a similar program available to their employees at the level described.

Reason for Using Leave Time: The leave program is designed to enable members of staff, male or female, who are potential senior management talent to take a break in their career in order to care for young children.

Implementation Process: Applicants must have completed five years' service and expect to return to work with their career commitment undiminished. Selection of participants is at the option of the bank. Throughout the period of absence, which may be up to five years, participants in the career-break scheme are expected to maintain contact with the bank on a regular basis. At a minimum, the bank requires leave-takers to participate in an annual one-day updating program, review regularly issued information packets, and attend occasional social events. Many leave-takers negotiate a regular part-time schedule, an average of six to eight weeks a year, according to Anne Watts, the bank's equal opportunities manager, in order to keep up with changes at the bank. At the end of five years, careers are resumed without loss of pay, seniority, or status.

Impact to Date: Since the program was introduced in 1981, it has attracted considerable attention and been replicated by several other banks and other types of enterprises.

SOURCE: Joann S. Lublin, "Hope for Curse of the Working Mummy," *Wall Street Journal* (Dec. 1987), 35; *Information Service News and Abstracts,* no. 91 (London: Work Research Unit. Mar.–Apr. 1988): 10–14.

Hewlett-Packard Company

Description: Hewlett-Packard, an international supplier of computers and instruments for business and medicine, employs 50,000 workers in several states and another 35,000 in other countries. Its corporate headquarters is in Palo Alto, California. Hewlett-Packard was one of the first American companies to institute a flexitime program and also uses job sharing, work sharing, and various forms of contingent employment.

Reason for Using Leave Time: The introduction of the "Flexible Time Off" program was prompted by employee suggestions and by management's perception that the old policy on time off had become inequitable. Hewlett-Packard found that 20 percent of its work force was responsible for 80 percent of the sick leave use and that employees who would have qualified for a cash payout for good attendance lost out because they left the company before becoming eligible. Management was also interested in offering employees a way to use sick leave to care for ill children or other family members.

Implementation Process: Surveys of employee attitudes and needs were conducted, and a videotape was developed to promote the plan to top management. Designing the plan, getting it approved, and then implementing it took a year and a half. "Flexible Time Off," which is a combined vacation and sick leave benefit, was first offered to all Hewlett-Packard employees in 1982.

Under the previous policy, vacation time ranged from a low of 10 days for employees with one year of service to a high of 25 days for employees who had been with the company 25 years or more. With "Flexible Time Off," the range is from 15 to 30 days, with employees enjoying the same amount of vacation time as they previously had, plus 5 additional days. Some unused time may be "banked" and carried over to another year. The amount of time that may be saved is determined by length of service. When employees leave the company, they receive the full cash value, at their current salary level, of the unused portion of banked time.

Impact to Date: Since the program went into operation, the number of sick days that employees take has dropped, and the number of vacation days that employees take has increased proportionately.

The company's perception is that employees are now able to be more honest about the reason why they are taking time off.

An employee poll showed an 88 percent positive response to the new program. Employees appreciate the fact that "Flexible Time Off" allows them to accommodate their personal needs in such areas as illness in the family, child-care problems, extra vacation, temporary illness, and personal business appointments or to save the time for later use or for a cash benefit.

Hewlett-Packard management feels that this approach to vacation and sick leave is more consistent with the company's culture than the previous rigid approach. Like the concept of flexible hours, "Flexible Time Off" allows employees discretion over how their paid time off can best be used.

SOURCE: Helen Axel, *Corporations and Families: Changing Practices and Perspectives,* research report no. 868 (New York: The Conference Board, Inc., 1985), 32; New Ways to Work conversations with the corporate human resources staff (July 1988).

Wells Fargo Bank

Description: Wells Fargo is the third largest bank in California and the ninth largest in the country in terms of assets. Its corporate offices are located in San Francisco, and it employs almost 20,000 people statewide. The bank offers various other leave options and alternative work-time options, including regular part-time and job sharing.

Reason for Using Leave Time: The "Social Service Leave" program is one of a group of corporate social responsibility programs that were developed as ways for the bank to "respond to the needs of the communities it serves." The program also gives bank employees an opportunity to help solve social problems of personal concern to themselves.

Implementation Process: Any three-year employee of the bank who is in good standing may submit a proposal for a leave of from one to six months. A selection committee chooses the participants after considering the potential impact of the applicant's goals and efforts toward solving a specific social problem. The committee also evaluates the nonprofit organization that will be the employee's work site during the leave in order to ensure that it meets certain service criteria.

The employee retains full pay and other benefits and continues to earn vacation time during the leave. Salary reviews and increases are given as scheduled. Upon returning, the employee is guaranteed the same position or a comparable one.

Impact to Date: Employees on leave have helped organize and promote recreational programs for disabled people, helped identify foster parents, and accomplished a variety of other socially beneficial objectives. Employees who have participated in the program report both gratification at the opportunity to work with a community agency and a sense of renewal after their break from their regular career.

One leave-taker came back to the bank to find that she had been promoted and made a sales team leader at a new branch bank as a result of her special project. "It was great to know that my efforts at Wells Fargo were recognized, even though I was on leave for six months!" she said.

SOURCE: Wells Fargo employee literature.

less often than programs that provide for family-oriented leaves, paid time off for a variety of personal purposes, and educational or sabbatical leaves, social service leaves are nonetheless an option that should not be overlooked by an employer that wants to encourage its workers to make a meaningful contribution to society. In reviewing the group of organizational profiles, look for parallels between the experience of these employers and the conditions facing your own company.

Table 7-1 is a questionnaire designed to help you examine your company's existing leave program and assess whether its leave options should be expanded and, if so, in what areas. If the questionnaire results indicate that the organization would benefit from offering additional leave options, the worksheet shown in Figure 7-3 can be used to help you further analyze what changes in leave policy would be appropriate.

Table 7-1. Leave-time questionnaire.

Would Expanding Leave Options Benefit Your Organization?

	Yes	No
Does your organization currently offer the following kinds of leave? • Disability • Family-related • Sick leave • Personal time off • Sabbatical • Educational/training • Other (social service, loaned employee, etc.):		
Does your organization face any of the following human resources management problems that a redefined or expanded leave policy might address? • A need for skills expansion, continuing education, or training/retraining. • Employee stress and burnout. • Conflict between work and family responsibilities. • A need to expand employment opportunities. • The loss of valued employees.		
Have employees requested leave time for circumstances that are not covered under current policy?		
Are minimum job protection and employment status guarantees incorporated into present leave policy?		

Introducing Changes in Leave-Time Policy

To expand its present policy on leave time, an organization starts by gaining support for the initiative. The effort involved in gaining support will depend on the extent of the change in leave policy that is being contemplated. The organization then sets up the program's administration, makes major decisions in the area of program design, and develops resource materials. Once the program's design and the supporting resource materials have been finalized, the program is announced and promoted to employees. After a period of operation, the program is assessed and modified as necessary. The rest of this section discusses the foregoing implementation steps in greater detail.

Gain Support for the Program

As we've seen, leave time is an area of human resources management that is undergoing considerable thought and change. Since most

Figure 7-3.   Leave-time worksheet.

Assessing the Need for Expanded Leave Options

List the main reasons why you are considering broadening your organization's current leave program:

1. _____

   _____

   _____

2. _____

   _____

   _____

3. _____

   _____

   _____

4. _____

   _____

   _____

List what you see as the advantages and disadvantages of offering an expanded program of leave options:

Pros: _____

   _____

   _____

   _____

Cons: _____

companies already have some sort of leave policy, redefining or expanding policy in this area does not entail introducing a new idea. And unlike some other work-time arrangements that cannot be introduced except through an all-or-nothing change process, leave policy can either be changed comprehensively or be changed incrementally, with different kinds of leave policy addressed individually. The degree of difficulty in gaining support for change in an organization's current leave-time policy will depend on the extent and type of change that is being contemplated.

It may, for example, represent a considerable shift in attitudinal values for a company that now has a more traditional leave policy to consider offering a parental leave that would encourage both male and female employees to take time off in order to care for newborn, adopted, or sick children or to consider replacing a program of paid time off for company-specified purposes with an annual lump-sum amount of paid time off that employees may draw on for purposes of their own choosing. As noted in the Introduction, in cases such as these involving major shifts in policy, gaining broad-based support should be a priority, and a task force can be an effective means of gaining such support.

If, on the other hand, an incremental change in existing policy is being considered, less-extensive staff commitment in this area may be sufficient.

Set Up the Program's Administration

Whether or not a task force is considered necessary, someone in the human resources management area should be identified as having responsibility for developing background information on *what other companies have done* in the area of leave policy, drafting a *proposal for new policy* related to changes in leave time, and acting as a *resource* for employees and supervisors once the changes are introduced.

Design the Program

When modifying or expanding current leave policy, the first step should be to determine what conditions may be mandated by relevant state and federal law. As we've noted, leave-time is a policy area that is evolving rapidly, and new laws are mandating changes in some cases. This is particularly true of policy pertaining to family and medical leave. In addition to determining what legal parameters have been established, the organization should consider the following issues:

Eligibility. Will a qualifying period of employment be established? Will all leave options be available to all employees, or will some restrictions or qualifications be used to establish eligibility in particular instances? Eligibility requirements might be expressed in terms of seniority or level of responsibility and need not be consistent across every aspect of leave policy.

Conditions. Can the leave be taken at any time, or must the timing be negotiated with a supervisor? Are there restrictions on what leave time may be used for? What are they? What is the maximum duration allowed? Can accrued vacation, sick leave, and compensatory time be added to the allowable leave? Does vacation and/or sick leave have to be used up either as part of any paid portion of the leave or as part of the total leave? If leave is taken for medical or pregnancy reasons, is there the possibility of a part-time transition period before the employee returns to full-time?

Effect on salary and benefits. Will employer-provided leave time be paid, partially paid, or unpaid? If disability leave will be offered, will regular compensation be continued during the disability period?

Will benefits be continued during leave? At whose expense? Will eligibility for vacation time or sabbatical consideration be affected? How will retirement benefits be continued and paid for?

Effect on employment status. Is reinstatement guaranteed? To the same position, or to a comparable or similar job? Will paid time off and/or sick leave as well as seniority continue to accrue during the leave time? Will the leave affect possibilities for advancement?

Application procedure. How does an employee apply for leave time? Who initiates the request? What kind of advance notice is necessary? Who authorizes the leave?

Disposition of work load. While the employee is on leave, will some or all of the work be rerouted? To whom? Will a replacement be obtained? From within the company or from outside? Will any work be forwarded to the leave-taker? As discussed earlier in the chapter, how an employee's work will be handled during a leave is a critical issue that will significantly affect supervisory responsiveness to requests for leave time. Procedures must be in place, or an agreement must be negotiated in advance, to ensure that the work is performed in a timely manner.

Procedure for returning to work. Upon completion of the leave, is the employee automatically reinstated to his or her former position? To an equivalent position? How does the employee arrange to return to work? Is there a form to be completed? How far in advance must the employee notify the company of his or her desire to return to work? Is part-time work possible as a transitional step? For how long?

Table 7-2 is a program design checklist that provides an overview of the design issues that are common to any program of expanded leave options. Figures 7-4 through 7-9 are worksheets that you can use to document those design decisions that are peculiar to disability leave, parental leave, family leave, paid time off, educational/training leave, and sabbatical leave.

Develop Resource Materials

The resource materials that an organization creates must meet the needs of supervisory staff as well as employees. Both groups will required detailed information about each type of leave that is available. Beyond that, supervisors must have guidelines for granting requests for leaves of various sorts and information on how to arrange for coverage of the work load during the employee's absence. Employees interested in participating in the leave program must have

Table 7-2. Program design checklist: expanded leave options.

Key Design Issues	Notes
☐ Legal requirements	
☐ Eligibility	
☐ Conditions	
☐ Effect on salary and benefits	
☐ Effect on employment status	
☐ Application procedure	
☐ Disposition of work load	
☐ Procedure for returning to work	

specific information on how taking a particular type of leave will affect them—in terms of such considerations as salary and benefits, employment status, and long-term career prospects.

Figures 7-10 and 7-11, sample policies on child-care leave and sick leave/medical appointments, illustrate the types of resource materials that supervisory personnel and employees will find helpful.

Announce the Program

When leave policy has been revised and/or expanded, employees should be notified of the changes through the usual information channels.

Promote the Program

Employees may have to be encouraged to take advantage of the new leave opportunities that have been made available. Historically, certain kinds of leave—for example, sabbaticals to relieve burnout or educational and training leaves to expand the skills of the work force—have been underutilized even though they are part of company policy. This is often due to employees' fears that the types of responsibilities they are assigned or their future prospects will be harmed if they take leave time. An effective promotional effort can counter this type of concern.

Figure 7-4.   Disability leave worksheet.

Legal requirements
_____

Eligibility
_____

Conditions
_____
Appropriate use:
_____
Duration:
_____
Other:
_____

Effect on salary and benefits
_____

Effect on employment status
_____

Application procedure
_____

Disposition of work load
_____

Procedure for returning to work
_____

Figure 7-5. Parental leave worksheet.

Legal requirements

Eligibility

Restrictions:

☐ Natural   ☐ Adopted   Maximum age of child:

Other:

Conditions

Appropriate use:

Duration:

Total: Paid: Unpaid:

When available:

   ☐ With disability insurance:

   ☐ Without disability insurance:

Other:

Effect on salary and benefits

Effect on employment status

Application procedure

```
┌─────────────────────────────────────────────────────────────┐
│ ┌───────────────────────────────────────────────────────┐   │
│ │               Disposition of work load                │   │
│ │───────────────────────────────────────────────────────│   │
│ │                                                       │   │
│ │───────────────────────────────────────────────────────│   │
│ │            Procedure for returning to work            │   │
│ │ Schedule:                                             │   │
│ │  ☐ Full-time   ☐ Part-time transitional schedule:     │   │
│ │───────────────────────────────────────────────────────│   │
│ │ Other:                                                │   │
│ │                                                       │   │
│ │                                                       │   │
│ └───────────────────────────────────────────────────────┘   │
└─────────────────────────────────────────────────────────────┘
```

Evaluate the Program

As with other work-time alternatives, a leave-time program should be evaluated after it has been in place for several months. Two issues should be particularly scrutinized:

1. Are employees using the various leave options? If not, why not?
2. Do supervisors feel that the processes established for reapportioning work are successful? If not, and if work coverage is a problem, this issue should be discussed and new strategies devised to deal with it.

Fine-Tune the Program

Following the evaluation, the organization should modify those portions of its leave policy that have been identified as problem areas. For example:

Problem	*Solution*
Evaluation indicates most first-line supervisors are reluctant to grant requests for leave.	Train/educate first-line supervisors regarding the need for this option. Emphasize "try it, you'll like it."

(Text continues on page 290.)

Figure 7-6. Family leave worksheet.

Eligibility

Conditions

Appropriate use:

☐ Parental responsibilities   ☐ Sick-child care   ☐ Family crisis
☐ Elder care   ☐ Other:

Duration:

Other:

Effect on salary and benefits

Salary:

☐ Paid   ☐ Unpaid

Other:

Effect on employment status

Application procedure

Disposition of work load

Procedure for returning to work

Figure 7-7. Paid time off worksheet.

Structured Time Off

Eligibility

Holiday:

Sick leave:

Vacation:

Conditions

Appropriate use:

Holiday:

Sick leave:

Vacation:

Duration:

Holiday:

Sick leave:

Vacation:

Other:

Holiday

Sick leave:

Vacation:

Application procedure (vacation)

Disposition of work load (sick leave, vacation)

(Continued)

Figure 7-7.   *(continued)*

Flexible Time Off
___

Eligibility
___

___

Conditions
___

Appropriate use:
___

Duration:
___

Other:
___

Figure 7-8.   Educational/training leave worksheet.

Eligibility
___

___

Conditions
___

Appropriate use:
___

Duration:
___

Restrictions:
If paid:
If unpaid:
___

Reimbursement:

☐ Fees
☐ Supplies
☐ Other:

Other:

_____

Effect on salary and benefits

_____

_____

Effect on employment status

_____
Work schedule:

_____

Seniority accrual:

_____

Salary review:

_____

Other:

_____

Application procedure

_____

_____

Disposition of work load

_____

_____

Procedure for returning to work

_____

Figure 7-9.   Sabbatical leave worksheet.

Eligibility
Conditions
Appropriate use:
Duration:
Restrictions:
If paid:
If unpaid:
Other:
Effect on salary and benefits
Effect on employment status
Application procedure
Disposition of work load
Procedure for returning to work

Figure 7-10. Sample policy on child-care leave.

OBJECTIVE

To provide employees with job protection for periods of leave following childbirth or adoption during which they may care for the child and obtain adequate day-care arrangements.

DESCRIPTION

Child-care leave

A. Child-care leave is an excused period of absence at employee request to allow a mother or father time away from work to care for a new child.
B. Child-care leave will usually follow a short-term disability leave for childbirth but may also be taken following the adoption of a child to give the parents time to adjust to the new situation and obtain child care.
C. Child-care leave is unpaid leave.
D. To begin child-care leave, employees must complete, sign, and submit to the respective group personnel manager a leave authorization stating their intended date of return to work.

Eligibility

A. Employees who have completed at least one year of service are eligible for child-care leave.
B. Child-care leave is available to both male and female employees to allow time off work with job protection during which a parent may care for a new child.
C. Female employees may only begin unpaid child-care leave after a short-term disability leave for childbirth (except in cases of adoption). Male employees may take child-care leave *upon* birth or adoption of a new child. (This leave must begin within three months of the birth or adoption.)
D. Employees are not eligible for pay during child-care leave but may use earned vacation days at the end of the disability period of leave in order to extend the paid portion of their leave.

Benefits

A. Employees should consult the personnel/benefits department prior to child-care leave for specific information. The following is only an outline concerning continuation of benefits coverage during child-care leave and is not intended to replace the plan documents as a description of available benefits.
B. Vacation does not accrue during child-care leave.
C. Profit-sharing contributions do not continue; however, service is credited for vesting purposes during approved child-care leave.

SOURCE: Adapted from *Survey of Private Sector Work and Family Policy* (San Francisco: New Ways to Work, 1986), 30–32.

(Continued)

Figure 7-10. *(continued)*

	D. Group health and life insurance continue for 30 days at company expense after child-care leave begins. After 30 days, if the employee wishes to continue this coverage, he or she must pay the entire premium.
Duration	The maximum length of time an employee can remain on leave for childbirth *and* child-care is five months (150 calendar days). This 150-day period begins on the first day away from work, whether it is short-term disability or child-care leave.
Return to work	A. An employee's own job will be held open for a total of 60 calendar days during approved leave for childbirth and child-care. (The days following childbirth that fall under the short-term disability policy will count toward this 60-day total.) B. The company guarantees reinstatement to the employee's own job for the 60-day guarantee period or to a position at a comparable level of compensation if the employee returns to work within 150 days. (Again, this includes any period of short-term disability leave following childbirth.) C. If it becomes necessary to fill the employee's job after the initial 60-day period during child-care leave, a comparable position will be sought through the respective personnel/employment group, for 30 days, as if the employee were an internal applicant. D. If no comparable job becomes available or is offered within 30 days of the date that the employee is available to return to work, the division or department that granted the leave will be required to reinstate the employee even on an overstaff basis if necessary. E. An employee who turns down a comparable position offered to provide reinstatement will be terminated as a voluntary resignation. F. Employees who fail to return to work from an approved child-care leave by the date of return indicated on the leave authorization will be terminated as voluntary resignations as of the expiration date of the leave.

Figure 7-11. Sample policy on sick leave/medical appointments.

Payment of salary for absence from work caused by illness, injury, or medical appointments of employees or their family members (e.g., child, spouse, parent, significant other) will be made on a basis that is fair and equitable both to the employee and to the company.

The company recognizes that employees may have to be absent from work from time to time because of personal illness or injury, or because of the personal illness or injury of a family member. It has established a sick leave fund to provide salary continuation during these periods.

The company regards paid sick leave as an important benefit to its employees and expects that it will be used only for bona fide illness and necessary medical appointments.

Employees become eligible for sick leave pay upon completion of the probationary period. Nonexempt full-time employees are granted up to 77 hours' (11 days') paid sick time for each year of employment, starting with the date of employment. Sick leave accrues at the rate of $1\frac{1}{12}$ days per month, and accrued sick leave may be carried forward from year to year.

Part-time employees who regularly work more than 20 hours per week are eligible for prorated sick leave according to hours scheduled to work. Accrued sick leave may be used only for bona fide absences on days a part-time employee is regularly scheduled to work.

Absences due to illness and medical appointments must be recorded on the weekly time record and are charged against accrued sick leave by the hour in quarter-hour increments. Once accrued sick leave is exhausted, no compensation will be paid for time during which the employee is absent for illness or medical appointments of for the illness or medical appointments of family members.

Employees should make every effort to schedule medical appointments before and after working hours. Medical appointments scheduled during working hours must be approved at least one day in advance by the employee's supervisor.

As an alternative to charging medical appointments against accrued sick leave, employees may arrange in advance with their supervisors to make up time of two hours or less for absences due to medical appointments.

Time may be made up either the same day the absence occurs or on days following the absence. If an employee chooses to make up time after the day the absence occurs, that time must be made up in increments of no more than one hour per day, must be productive, and must ordinarily be made up within five business days of the time the absence occurs. Premium pay will not be paid for makeup time, and all makeup time must be reported on the employee's weekly time card.

SOURCE: *Survey of Private Sector Work and Family Policy* (San Francisco: New Ways to Work, 1986), 33–34.

Problem	*Solution*
Significant percentage of maternity leave-takers do not return to their full-time positions.	Pilot-test part-time transition step.
Replacement employees are inadequately trained to assume leave-takers' work.	Assign replacements at least ten days in advance.
Employees are not requesting education or training leaves.	Run feature stories in company newsletter describing career advances of employees who have voluntarily broadened their skills base.
Department heads avoid implementation of leave option.	Tie development of leave program to evaluation.

Summary

While some of the work-time alternatives we have discussed in this book would represent a completely new undertaking for many employers, such is not the case with leave time. Most organizations already permit their employees some type of paid or unpaid absence from work during which their jobs are protected.

However, since the mid-1980s, the traditional concept of leave time has been undergoing a variety of changes. Special attention has been focused on two areas—family-related leaves and paid time off for vacation, holidays, illness or injury, and personal use. A third major category of leave time—absence for education or training or for a sabbatical—has received less attention during this period.

Family-related leaves include those taken for such purposes as pregnancy disability, birth or adoption of a child, and caring for children or family members. Many other countries in the developed world guarantee workers considerably greater protection in the areas of income and jobs during this type of absence than is typical in the United States. This situation is starting to change as various states enact legislation mandating certain levels of protection in this area. Federal legislation on family-related leaves is also being debated. Private-sector employers are increasingly offering leave opportunities, or expanding existing leave programs, to help their employees handle occasional periods during which family responsibilities must take precedence over job responsibilities.

The area of paid time off for illness or injury, holidays, vacation, and personal reasons is also undergoing changes in response to the needs of the work force for greater flexibility in the use of this time. Whereas absences with pay were once subject to many employer-mandated restrictions on the manner in which they could be taken and the purposes for which they could be used, the trend today is toward permitting employees greater freedom of choice about when and why they use their allotment of paid time off.

Although the use of sabbatical and educational leaves has not grown appreciably since the early 1980s, employers should not over-look the benefits of providing time off to workers who are suffering from burnout or who want to take advantage of training or educational opportunities. This type of leave can enable an organization to retain the services of a valued but temporarily overstressed employee and to enhance the level of education and training of its work force.

As noted, leave time is considered an effective strategy for combatting stress and burnout, facilitating employee training and continuing education, and helping employees manage conflicts between work and family responsibilities. Leaves can also be a means of increasing employment opportunities by creating temporary job openings.

The main concern regarding leaves is how the work will be handled during the employee's absence. This issue will require special attention as a company plans an expansion of its leave options. Provisions must be made to reroute the work, replace the employee temporarily or permanently, forward the work to the leave-taker, or otherwise cover the responsibilities of the position. If this issue is not effectively addressed at the outset, supervisors will be unlikely to support the leave program, and the use of leave time will prove more disruptive than helpful to the organization.

In examining its existing leave policy, a company must start by making sure its policy conforms to the provisions of any applicable state and federal legislation. Beyond that, the employer must consider its own needs in the areas of work force retention, education/ training, and job coverage as well as the needs of its employees for greater flexibility in the use of their time and greater control over their lives. Through careful planning, an organization can structure a program of paid and unpaid leaves that both employer and employees will find beneficial.

CHAPTER 8

Work Sharing

Work sharing is an alternative to layoffs in which all or part of an organization's work force temporarily reduces hours and salary in order to cut operating costs. In states where work sharing/short-time compensation enabling legislation has been passed, the cutbacks in salary can be partly recompensed by partial payments from the employing company's unemployment insurance account.

In the United States, the most common method of adjusting labor costs during economic downturns has been for employers to lay off workers. Harold Oaklander, professor of management at Pace University in New York City, noted the following in writing about work force reductions:

> In the United States today, the decision to reduce a company's workforce remains at the discretion of the employer just as it was 100 years ago. The concern of public agencies and employers has taken the form of relieving the financial consequences [*to workers*] of layoffs rather than of averting layoffs or limiting their duration. The main restrictions derived from collective agreements between unions and employers concern "selection" for layoff rather than layoff avoidance.

An alternative notion, using shorter work hours and spreading available work among more employees to reduce levels of unemployment, has been a subject of debate for some time. It was first articulated in the United States in 1887 by Samuel Gompers, president of the American Federation of Labor, when he declared, "As long as we have one person seeking work who cannot find it, the

hours of work are too long.''[1] His "share the work" approach was
fostered during the Great Depression of the 1930s by the Hoover
administration. For many workers, it came to mean "sharing the
misery" and was disavowed by workers and their representatives.
But by the mid-1970s, the destructive effects of relying on layoffs
alone to deal with economic downturns had led to a search for
alternative methods.

Origins of Work Sharing

Today, three basic types of work sharing—strategies that temporarily
reduce the number of paid hours, rather than the number of paid
employees, to adjust labor costs—are beginning to be used by companies in the United States: (1) ad hoc work sharing, (2) work sharing
in combination with short-time compensation, and (3) programs that
allow or encourage various kinds of voluntary reductions in work
time by individual employees.

Ad Hoc Work Sharing

The severity of the 1975 recession caused some employers and
policymakers to publicly question whether or not there might be a
better way than layoffs to control labor costs during economic downturns. A conference on "Alternatives to Layoffs" held in New York
City that year heard testimony from a number of employers, including
Hewlett-Packard and Pan American World Airways, Inc., that had
elected to reduce work time rather than reduce their work force as a
means of cutting back expenditures. Hewlett-Packard had instituted
a companywide four-day workweek, on alternating weeks, for a
three-month period. Pan American had developed several different
approaches, tailored to specific job classifications, which included
voluntary furloughs as well as cutbacks on work time. In the Hewlett-
Packard case, layoffs were eliminated, and at Pan American, they
were greatly minimized.[2] This kind of ad hoc work sharing has slowly
gained adherents during the last decade and has proved to be a
valuable tool for many companies.

Work Sharing With Short-Time Compensation

In Europe, another kind of work-sharing strategy was being used.
Employers there had a tradition of relying less on layoffs and more
on governmental supports and work-spreading strategies than their
U.S. counterparts. German representatives at the 1975 "Alternatives

to Layoffs'' conference told of the success of using partial unemployment insurance payments in conjunction with a reduced workweek. This kind of program had first been used in Germany in the 1920s. Its objective was to encourage organizations and workers to temporarily reduce work time with the understanding that the government would reimburse employers for providing partial compensation to employees for lost work. Conceptually, this program combined the two goals of income maintenance and job security. It was financed by a percentage payroll tax divided equally between employers and employees up to an established earnings ceiling.[3]

Similar programs were used by employers in Belgium, France, Great Britain, the Netherlands, and other Western European countries. As Eleanor Holmes Norton, chair of the New York conference, noted, the approach used unemployment insurance systems in a way that "put a premium on working."[4]

It was interest in the German model that provided the incentive for experimentation with work sharing and a complementary strategy of short-time compensation (STC), or partial unemployment insurance payments, in the United States. In 1978, California became the first state to adapt this concept for use in an American setting. The "Work Sharing Unemployment Insurance" (WSUI) program was a pilot project originally designed to mitigate expected massive layoffs in the public sector. The layoffs never materialized, however, and in 1980 and later in 1981 and 1982, during a prolonged economic downturn, users of the program were almost entirely private-sector employers. In January 1987, after several revisions and extensions, the California program became a permanent option for that state's employers.

The WSUI program is described in detail in brochures issued by the state of California (excerpts are presented in Figure 8–1). The state's employers use the form shown in Figure 8–2 to submit their work-sharing plans initially to the Employment Development Department for review and approval in order that their employees affected by cutbacks may be eligible to receive partial unemployment insurance payments. During the time that the WSUI program is in effect, companies must, on a weekly basis, provide each employee working a reduced schedule with a certification form (shown in Figure 8–3) specifying the percentage by which his or her hours and wages have been cut back during that week. The employee then submits this form to the local Employment Development Department field office to claim WSUI benefits.

In 1980, Rep. Patricia Schroeder introduced federal legislation

(Text continues on page 311.)

Figure 8-1. Description of California's work-sharing unemployment insurance program.

Work Sharing Unemployment Insurance (WSUI)

Senate Bill 1471 passed by the California State Legislature in 1978, authorized the Work Sharing Unemployment Insurance program. This legislation allows payment of work sharing unemployment insurance benefits to persons whose wages and hours are reduced as a temporary alternative to layoffs.

The program helps employers and employees avoid some of the burdens that accompany a layoff situation. For instance, if employees are retained during a temporary slowdown, employers can quickly gear up when business conditions improve. Employers are then spared the expense of recruiting, hiring and training new employees. In turn, employees are spared the hardships of full unemployment. For employers who need to reduce their work force permanently, the program can be used as a phased transition to layoff. Affected employees can continue to work at reduced levels with an opportunity to find other employment before the expected layoff.

THE ADVANTAGES OF WORK SHARING

- **It saves jobs.**

- **Almost any business or industry can participate.**

- **You keep your trained employees.**

- **It's more equitable than layoffs.**

SOURCE: *Work Sharing* (Sacramento: California Health and Welfare Agency, Employment Development Department, 1983), 1, 4–9.

Questions and Answers About Work Sharing UI

1. *Who May Participate in WSUI?*

- Any employer who has a reduction in production, services or other condition which causes the employer to seek an alternative to layoffs.

- To participate, an employer must have at least a 10 percent reduction in the work force or in a unit within the work force, and a time and wage reduction of 10 percent.

2. *How Does an Employer Participate in WSUI?*

- Employers may call or write EDD Work Sharing Unit, P.O. Box C-9640, Sacramento, CA 95823-0640. They should ask for a Work Sharing UI Plan.

- The employer sends the completed plan to EDD for approval.

- The plan requires participation of **at least two employees,** a reduction of 10 percent or more of the regular work force or work group unit, and a reduction of 10 percent or more in the wages earned and hours worked of participating employees.

- If collective bargaining agreements cover the employees, a concurrence of **each** union bargaining agent must accompany the application.

3. *How do Employees Qualify for Work Sharing UI?*

- Employees must be regularly employed by an employer whose work sharing plan has been approved by EDD.

- The employee must have qualifying wages in the base quarters used to compute a regular California Unemployment Insurance (UI) claim.

(Continued)

Figure 8-1. *(continued)*

- At least 10 percent of the employer's regular work force or unit within the work force, who are included in the approved Work Sharing Plan, must participate in each reduced work-week or in **at least** one week of a two-consecutive-week period.

  Example: A work unit includes 100 employees. In the first week, 10 employees (10 percent) are reduced and participate in the program. In the next week, only two employees participate. In **at least** one week of this two-consecutive-week period, 10 percent of the work unit participated. The requirements would not be met if five employees (5 percent) participate in each week.

- The reduction in each participating employee's **normal** workweek schedule and wages must be 10 percent or more.

- New employees hired after the Work Sharing Plan is approved may not participate in the Work Sharing Plan until such time as the employee works one complete, normal workweek (no reduction).

- Employees file initial claims for WSUI by reporting to the local EDD field office to present a certification provided by the employer. After this, transactions are ordinarily handled by mail.

4. *Is WSUI Only for the Private Sector?*

- No. The law originally was intended to help the public sector deal with expected mass layoffs following passage of Proposition 13. Since that time, many private employers have used WSUI as an option to save jobs; hence the WSUI identification with the private sector.

5. *What is the Cost to Employers Participating in WSUI?*

- Workshare benefits paid are charged to the reserve accounts of those employers who are in the claimant's base period in the same manner as any other UI benefit.

- Charges to a reserve account tend to adversely affect the reserve account balance thereby increasing the potential for a higher UI tax rate in future years.

- The Department mails a Notice of Employer Contribution Rates and Statement of Reserve Account, Form DE 2088, in February each year. This notice reflects the status of a reserve account as of the prior June 30. Any employer considering WSUI should review their latest DE 2088 to determine the probable effect on their reserve account. For additional information on reserve accounts or workshare liabilities, contact the Contribution Rate Group at

- **Direct reimbursable account** employers are billed directly for 100 percent of the WSUI costs.

6. *How Much Lead Time is Necessary to Initiate a Plan for WSUI Participation?*

- All Work Sharing Plans begin on a Sunday. An employer may choose the effective date of the plan. However, the earliest a plan may be approved is the Sunday prior to the employer's first contact with the Work Sharing UI Unit.

- If unions are involved, concurring signatures are required from each representative collective bargaining agent.

- The best answer to this question is: allow as much time as possible by starting an application as soon as you know a reduction in the work force is imminent.

(Continued)

Figure 8-1. *(continued)*

7. *What are Some Nonfiscal Merits of WSUI Participation?*

   • The outstanding feature of WSUI is: **it saves jobs.** Employees faced with layoff can, instead, work a reduced workweek with minimum salary reduction and continuation of fringe benefits.

   • WSUI gives additional time to workers to learn of other work options open to them.

8. *How Flexible is WSUI? Can it be Applied to Most Work Situations?*

   • WSUI is **extremely flexible** and can be custom-tailored to a variety of work situations.

   • Employers who are potential users of WSUI may call   for specific information regarding individual application of the program.

9. *What is the Duration of a Work Sharing Plan?*

   • A Work Sharing Plan is approved for a six-month period. If, at the end of this period, the employer is still experiencing an economic downturn, an application may be submitted for a subsequent WS Plan. Such a plan may be approved immediately after a prior plan expires provided the conditions warrant approval.

10. *Must the Reduced Weeks be Used in Consecutive Order?*

   • No. Any sequence of use is allowed. The only restriction is that at least 10 percent of the work force or of a unit within the work force covered in the plan must share in the work and wage reduction in each week, or in at least one week of a two-consecutive-week period.

11. *Can a Percentage of Employees be Rotated so that Different Employees Have Reduced Hours Each Week?*

  • Yes, so long as the 10 percent of the work force criterion is met.

12. *Can Employees be Rotated from Department to Department to Use Different Skills During Slack Periods?*

  • Employees can be rotated to meet individual needs of employers, as long as the 10 percent reduction criterion is observed.

13. *Can an Employer, Operating in Multiple Locations, have more than One Work Sharing Plan?*

  • No. Only *one* WS Plan may be approved under *one* Employer Account Number regardless of the size, structure and/or multiple locations of the employer. However, other units at the same or different location(s) may be added to an existing approved WS Plan (contact the WS Unit at for further information.)

WSUI In Other States

Programs similar to California's WSUI have been adopted by other states. Many additional states and the federal government are now actively considering work sharing legislation. Thousands of California employers have been approved to participate in WSUI.

The work sharing program provides a practical alternative to layoffs. For example, in many other states, if a business with 100 workers faces a temporary lull and must reduce its work force by 20 percent, the employer has no choice but to lay off 20 people, one out of five employees.

(Continued)

Figure 8-1. *(continued)*

Under California's WSUI program, an employer facing the same situation could file a plan with the State Employment Development Department reducing the workweek of all employees from five days to four (20 percent reduction). The employees would be eligible to receive 20 percent of their regular weekly unemployment insurance benefits.

Under this plan, everyone benefits. The employer is able to keep his work force intact during a temporary setback and no employees lose their jobs.

In cases where employers need to reduce their work force permanently, work sharing provides a means to make the transition. Affected workers can continue to work at reduced levels and a more normal income level, with the opportunity to find other employment before the expected layoff.

Several estimates have been made concerning the cost of replacing workers who move to other jobs during temporary layoffs. Some of the factors considered were: average recruitment costs; average cost of screening and selecting new workers; average training costs; and the loss of productivity during the training period. These costs totaled anywhere from $2,500 to $3,000 per employee. By using WSUI and retaining employees, these costs do not occur.

Because of WSUI's built-in flexibility and all possible variations of the program, EDD can make several suggestions concerning a program which will suit most employers' needs.

Let us help you design a program to fit your needs. Phone
        or write to:

EDD Work Sharing UI Unit
P.O. Box C-9640
Sacramento CA 95823-0640

Figure 8-2. Application for approval of a WSUl plan.

FORM DE 8686 (Front)

** EDD** Serving the People of California   First Contact Date __ JAN 27 1989__

WORK SHARING (WS) UNEMPLOYMENT INSURANCE PLAN APPLICATION

For Either: ☒ WS Plan   **OR**   ☐ Expanded WS Coverage

(Complete both sides of this form and submit in duplicate)

ENTER COMPANY INFORMATION AS SHOWN ON MOST RECENT DE 3 QUARTERLY RETURN:

1. A. Name _____

    B. Mailing Address _____

    C. Phone No. _____ D. California Employer Account No. __ __ __ __ __ __ __ __

    If name of company/subsidiary or business location where Work Sharing will occur is **different** than above, complete all items in #2, below:

2. A. Name _____

    B. Address _____ _____

    C. Phone No. _____

3. Effective date of WS Plan _____ (Earliest effective date is the Sunday prior to first contact date shown above.)

    OR

    Date of Expanded WS Coverage _____ (Sunday of the week in which first WS reductions have or will occur.)

4. Expected weekly reduction in wages and hours of affected employees _____%.

5. Specific type of business _____

6. Are any employees who will participate in this plan covered by a collective bargaining agreement?   ☐ Yes   ☐ No
    (Each applicable collective bargaining agent must complete and sign a collective bargaining concurrence statement — see reverse.)

7. Affected work unit designation (see instructions)   Bargaining Agent   No. of Employees In Unit   No. of Employees Sharing Work

    _____   _____   _____   _____

    _____   _____   _____   _____

    _____   _____   _____   _____

    _____   _____   _____   _____

                       TOTALS   _____   _____

8. Your participation in the Work Sharing program is confidential. EDD occasionally receives requests for the names of companies that would be willing to share their experiences in this program. Are you willing to have your name released for this purpose?   ☐ Yes   ☐ No

9. Please describe briefly the circumstances requiring your company's use of the Work Sharing Program to avoid a layoff:

    _____

    _____

10. If additional WS Certification forms are needed, please indicate number: _____.

11. Is this plan part of a transition to a permanent layoff or company closure?   ☐ Yes   ☐ No

12. Please indicate your payroll week ending day. _____.

FOR DEPARTMENT USE ONLY					
13. Eff. Date _____	14. W/S Ees. _____	15. % _____	16. SIC _____	17. Union (Y or N) _____	18. Status (1 or P) _____

Employment Development Department / State of California

DE 8686 Rev. 7 (6-87)   **(Complete reverse side)**

SOURCE: *Guide for Work Sharing Employers* (Sacramento: California Health and Welfare Agency, Employment Development Department, 1983), 6–9.

(Continued)

Figure 8-2. *(continued)*

FORM DE 8686 (Reverse)

A. We understand that the reserve account of a participating employer using the tax rate method will be charged in the usual manner for benefits paid under this program. In addition, it is possible that these charges may increase the employer UI contribution rate in future years.

A participating reimbursable employer will be billed quarterly for the cost of benefits in the same manner as they are currently billed for other UI benefits.

We will provide the Employment Development Department with the percentage of hour and wage reduction for each participating employee as a result of this Work Sharing Program. We understand that in order to be eligible, any employee must have worked at least one normal work week (no reduction) prior to issuance of certification forms for benefit payment.

A plan approved by the Department shall expire six months after its effective date. Expanded coverage approved to add other work units shall expire on the same date as the plan. A new plan may be approved immediately following the expiration of the previous plan if the employer finds it necessary to provide employees with continuous coverage under this program.

We have provided the information on this form so that our employees may participate in the shared work unemployment compensation benefit program, in lieu of layoff.

Employer Signature** _____ Contact Person _____

Name (Type or Print) _____ Telephone No. (___)_____

Title _____

Date _____

Signature must be of a **corporate officer, sole proprieter or **general partner.**

B. COLLECTIVE BARGAINING AGENT(S) CONCURRENCE

1. Union Name: _____ 2. Union Name: _____

   Local Number: _____   Local Number: _____

   Telephone: (___)_____   Telephone: (___)_____

   Signature: _____   Signature: _____

   Name (Type or Print): _____   Name (Type or Print): _____

   Title: _____   Title: _____

RETURN TWO COPIES OF THIS APPLICATION TO:

Employment Development Department
Work Sharing Unit
P.O. Box C-9640
Sacramento, CA 95823-0640

INSTRUCTIONS FOR COMPLETION OF WORK SHARING UNEMPLOYMENT INSURANCE PLAN APPLICATION (DE 8686)

The DE 8686 serves two (2) basic purposes:

1. To apply for a new Work Sharing (WS) Plan, and
2. To expand WS coverage by adding other work units to a previously approved WS Plan.

The Work Sharing Unit will check the appropriate block at the top of the form to identify whether your application is for a new plan, or for expanded WS coverage. If you are filing a WS Plan and later wish to add other work units, contact the WS Unit at the address provided, for an application to expand coverage.

LINE ITEM INSTRUCTIONS FOR COMPLETING WS PLAN APPLICATION (DE 8686)

Item 1: Self-explanatory.

Item 2: Complete only if the name and/or location of the affected work sharing unit(s) is different than the basic information shown in Item 1.

Item 3: WS Plans and expanded coverage always begin on Sunday. Enter the Sunday date of the week in which you expect the first reduction in hours and wages of your affected employees. The *earliest* effective date of a WS Plan is the Sunday prior to the First Contact Date, which is the date shown on the upper right corner of the form. WS Plans are approved for a six-month period. Expanded WS coverage expires on the same date as the previously approved WS Plan.

Item 4: Enter the expected percentage or reduction in the wages and hours of your participating employees.

Item 5: Enter type of business, e.g., Manufacturing — Boats, Computers, Engineering — Structural, etc.

Item 6: If "yes" block is checked, each involved bargaining agent must complete and sign Item B, Collective Bargaining Agent(s) concurrence, on the reverse side of this form.

Item 7: Enter by name the work units affected by the WS Plan (e.g., Production, Clerical, Sales, etc.). If you are not dividing your work force into units, enter "Work Force" on the first line. If the work force or units of the work force are covered by a collective bargaining agreement, enter the name of the Union(s) in the space provided. Enter, in the appropriate spaces, the total number of employees working in the affected unit and the number of those actually sharing work.

(Continued)

Figure 8-2. *(continued)*

INSTRUCTIONS FOR COMPLETION OF DE 8686 (Continued)

Item 8:   Self-explanatory.

Item 9:   Self-explanatory.

Item 10:   Please indicate the number of additional DE 4581WS cer-
                   tification forms needed to issue to your employees.

Item 11:   Self-explanatory.

Item 12:   WS Certifications are issued for seven-day periods only.
                   Please indicate your payroll week-ending date. If your
                   payroll period is other than weekly, you must use a Satur-
                   day week-ending date.

Items 13-18:   FOR DEPARTMENT USE ONLY.

                   (Now complete the reverse side of the form.)

Section A: Read the statement provided carefully. Sign where indicated
                   and complete the remaining information. *The application
                   will be returned if it is not signed by either a Corporate
                   Officer, Proprieter or General Partner.* Enter the name and
                   telephone number of your Work Share contact person.

Section B: If "Yes" block on Item 6 (six) is checked, the Collective
                   Bargaining Agent must complete and sign this section. Use
                   additional sheets if more than two (2) unions are involved.

MAILING INSTRUCTIONS

Mail *two* (2) copies of the completed form to the address provided. Within
10 days, you will receive written notification of the action taken on your
application. If your application has been approved, you will also receive
an initial supply of Work Sharing Certification forms (see pages 10-17 of
this guide for instructions on completing these forms).

Figure 8-3. Weekly work-sharing certification form.

FORM DE 4581WS (Front)

LAST NAME	FIRST NAME	SOCIAL SECURITY ACCOUNT NO.	
			Interviewer's Initial

EMPLOYER'S STATEMENT FOR THE WEEK ENDING _____.

NOTE: Issue a DE 4581WS only for the seven consecutive-day period that corresponds to your payroll week. If your payroll period is other than weekly, you must report the percentage of reduced hours and wages on a calendar week beginning Sunday and ending Saturday.

A. Complete for *FIRST* Work Sharing Week.

Base Wages _____ Wages Paid _____ Percentage of Reduction _____ %

Base Hours _____ Hours Worked _____ Percentage of Reduction _____ %

B. Complete *EACH* Week.

1. Percentage of wage reduction *due* to Work Sharing . . . . _____ %

2. Percentage of hour reduction *due* to Work Sharing . . . . _____ %

3. Was there a reduction in hours worked and wages earned among at least 10% of this employee's work unit during this week or in at least one week of this consecutive two-week period? . . . . ☐ Yes ☐ No

4. Was employee absent from work for reasons other than Work Sharing? . . . . ☐ Yes ☐ No

   If yes, was absence with your approval? _____ If not, give dates and reason _____

5. Did employee receive any sick pay? . . . . ☐ Yes ☐ No

   If yes, for what period? _____

6. Did employee refuse any work you made available during hours scheduled off due to your Work Sharing Plan? ☐ Yes ☐ No

I CERTIFY that the above information concerning the status of this company and the status/earnings of this employee for the purpose of participating in the Work Sharing Program is true and correct to the best of my knowledge.

_____ _____ _____
Name of Employer   Employer's Signature   Title

— — — — — — — — (___) _____
Employer Account No.   Employer Telephone No.

Date Issued to Employee _____
(Must be later than week ending date at top of this form)
DE 4581WS (7-83) Work Sharing Certification

SOURCE: *Guide for Work Sharing Employers* (Sacramento: California Health and Welfare Agency, Employment Development Department, 1983), 10–11.

(Continued)

Figure 8-3. *(continued)*

INSTRUCTIONS FOR COMPLETION OF FORM DE 4581WS (Front)

Employers are responsible for accurately completing the front of the DE 4581WS certifications before issuing them to their employees.

At the top of the form, enter the employee's complete name and Social Security Account Number in the appropriate spaces. In the space after EMPLOYER'S STATEMENT FOR THE WEEK ENDING, enter the date corresponding to the end of your seven-consecutive-day payroll week. **NOTE:** If your payroll period is other than weekly, e.g., monthly, you must report the percentage of reduced wages and hours in a calendar week that begins on Sunday and ends on Saturday.

Section A: Complete only on the *first* DE 4581WS issued to an employee. Base Wages/Base Hours refer to the employee's normal working situation before WS reductions. For example, if the employee normally worked five eight-hour days a week at $10.00 an hour, you would enter $400.00 wages and 40 hours. **NOTE:** Normal hours are defined as the hours the employee normally works or 40 hours, whichever is *less.*

Wages Paid/Hours Worked are the actual wages and hours of the employee in the first WS week. Using the example above, if the employee's work is reduced from five days to four days at $10.00 an hour, you would enter $320.00 paid and 32 hours worked. This is a 20 percent reduction in wages and hours, and you would enter that figure in the spaces provided for that purpose.

Section B: The numbered items in this section are to be completed on each DE 4581WS issued, *including the first one.*

Items 1 and 2—Enter only the percentage of wage and hour reduction *due* to work sharing. Additional reductions occurring for other reasons are not to be considered for completing these items. EXAMPLE: An employee's wages and hours are reduced from $400 to $320 (40 hours to 32 hours) or 20 percent due to Work Sharing. The employee is granted an additional two hours off without pay for a dental appointment. Although the total reduction in the employee's hours and wages for that week is 25 percent ($300.00 for 30 hours worked), the additional 5 percent is due to the dental appointment, *not* Work Sharing. The proper entry in Items 1 and 2 for that week would be 20 percent.

Item 3—Self-explanatory.

INSTRUCTIONS FOR COMPLETION OF FORM DE 4581WS (Front)
(Continued)

> **Item 4**—Self-explanatory. **NOTE:** A "YES" answer in this item by the employer requires a "YES" answer and the required information by the employee in Items 1 or 2 and 5 on the reverse side of the form.

> **Item 5**—Self-explanatory. **NOTE:** A "YES" answer in this item by the employer requires a "YES" answer and the required information by the employee in Items 1 and 5 on the reverse side of the form.

> **Item 6**—Self-explanatory

Complete the employer certification information at the bottom of the DE 4581WS by providing the Employer Name, California Account Number, Telephone Number, Signature and Title of authorized representative, and the date the form was issued to the employee (date issued must be *later* than the week-ending date at the top of the form).

The DE 4581WS certification may then be issued to the employee to complete the "Claimant Statement" on the reverse of the form. Employees are responsible for the completeness and accuracy of the information they provide.

Employees must report in person to an EDD office with the *first* completed and signed DE 4581WS certification. This may be done on an individual basis or, if over ten employees are involved, in accordance with any special scheduling arrangements the employer may make with the EDD office manager (the address and phone number of the nearest EDD office can be obtained from the telephone directory under "California, State of, Employment Development Department").

Subsequent DE 4581WS certifications will be mailed by the employees to the Work Sharing Unit according to instructions provided by the EDD office.

SPECIAL INSTRUCTIONS

If the employer pays wages based on piece rate, varying pay scales (shift differential, for example), or overtime worked, it will be necessary to compute the base wage for the week in order to determine the percentage of wage reduction that should be reported on the DE 4581WS certification.

The following formula should be used for that computation:

(a) Add the total wages earned during the reduced week.
(b) Divide total wages by the total number of hours worked during the week to determine the average hourly wage.

(Continued)

Figure 8-3. *(continued)*

INSTRUCTIONS FOR COMPLETION OF FORM DE 4581WS (Front)
(Continued)

(c) Multiply the average hourly wage by 40 hours (or by the number of hours normally worked before reduction, if less than 40 hours) for the base wage for the week.

(d) Subtract (a) from (c) for the amount the base wage was reduced during the week.

(e) Divide (d) by (c) for the percentage of the wage reduction for the week and enter in the appropriate section(s) on the front of the DE 4581WS.

EXAMPLE: An employee working a reduced workweek of 32 hours receives $10 for 24 hours (day shift) and $12 for 8 hours (swing shift).

(a) 24 hrs x $10 ($240) + 8 hrs x $12 ($96) = $336 total wages

(b) $336 ÷ 32 hrs = $10.50 average hourly wage

(c) $10.50 x 40 hrs = $420 base wage for week

(d) $420 (base wage) — $336 (wages earned) = $84 wage reduction

(e) $84 (wage reduction) ÷ $420 (base wages) = 20 percent reductions

When overtime is worked, it must be included in the total hours worked by the employee during the week. When this occurs, there still must be a reduction in the total hours worked, *including overtime,* of at least 10 percent. For example, for a normal 40-hour workweek, there must be a minimum reduction of four (4) hours (40 hours to 36 hours, including overtime).

Volunteer hours worked without pay by an employee must also be included as part of the total hours worked during the week. Like overtime, there still must be a reduction in the total hours worked, *including volunteer hours,* of at least 10 percent.

Additional supplies of the DE 4581WS certifications may be obtained by either writing or calling the Work Sharing Unit at the following address and phone number:

Employment Development Department
Work Sharing UI Unit
P.O. Box C-9640
Sacramento CA 95823-0640

designed to encourage states to experiment with new ways to mini-mize layoffs through work sharing and to make the issue a priority for the U.S. Department of Labor. The legislation, whose text is reprinted in Figure 8–4, was passed in 1982 as part of the Tax Equity and Fiscal Responsibility Act. The following are highlights of the guidelines that the legislation encourages states to follow in setting up a program of partial unemployment insurance compensation for workers whose employers have reduced the workweek as an alterna-tive to layoffs:

- There must be a need for the workweek to be reduced at least 10 percent before a request for STC can be considered.
- STC benefits should be a pro rata of regular unemployment insurance benefits.
- Employees should not be required to make themselves avail-able for other work or conduct a job search as a test of their eligibility to collect STC benefits.
- The total reduction in hours under STC should be no greater than the reduction in hours would have been had layoffs taken place.
- During the preceding four months, the employer's work force must not have been reduced more than 10 percent by layoffs.
- The employer must continue to provide health and retirement benefits as though the workweek had not been reduced.
- Where the work force is unionized, the union must consent to the STC plan.

Subsequent to the passage of the 1982 legislation, the Department of Labor drafted model legislation, reprinted in Figure 8–5. This model legislation, which includes policy language, is designed for use by states interested in adjusting their unemployment insurance pro-grams to enable companies facing the prospect of work-time reduc-tions to make use of STC.

Voluntary Reduced Work Time

A third work-sharing strategy has been to encourage wider use of various kinds of voluntary reduced work time arrangements—unpaid days off, shorter workweeks, sabbaticals. Originally, most reduced work-time options were introduced in order to accommodate employ-ees' needs. In a growing number of instances, this employee interest has provided a basis for cutting back budgets by allowing employees to voluntarily exchange compensation for more time off. This has been particularly true in the public sector, where cities, counties,

(Text continues on page 318.)

Figure 8-4. Text of federal legislation on work sharing supplemented by short-
time compensation.

Sec. 194. (a) It is the purpose of this section to assist States which provide partial unemployment benefits to individuals whose workweeks are reduced pursuant to an employer plan under which such reductions are made in lieu of temporary layoffs.

(b)(1) The Secretary of Labor (hereinafter in this section referred to as the "Secretary") shall develop model legislative language which may be used by States in developing and enacting short-time compensation programs, and shall provide technical assistance to States to assist in developing, enacting, and implementing such short-time compensation program.

(2) The Secretary shall conduct a study or studies for purposes of evaluating the operation, costs, effect on the State insured rate of unemployment, and other effects of State short-time compensation programs developed pursuant to this section.

(3) This section shall be a three-year experimental provision, and the provisions of this section regarding guidelines shall terminate 3 years following the date of the enactment of this Act.

(4) States are encouraged to experiment in carrying out the purpose and intent of this section. However, to assure minimum uniformity, States are encouraged to consider requiring the provisions contained in subsections (c) and (d).

(c) For purposes of this section, the term "short-time compensation program" means a program under which—

(1) individuals whose workweeks have been reduced pursuant to a qualified employer plan by at least 10 per centum will be eligible for unemployment compensation;

(2) the amount of unemployment compensation payable to any such individual shall be a pro rata portion of the unemployment compensation which would be payable to the individual if the individual were totally unemployed;

(3) eligible employees may be eligible for short-time compensation or regular unemployment compensation, as needed; except that no employee shall be eligible for more than the maximum entitlement during any benefit year to which he or she would have been entitled for total unemployment, and no employer shall be eligible for short-time compensation for more than twenty-six weeks in any twelve-month period; and

(4) eligible employees will not be expected to meet the availability for work or work search test requirements while collecting short-time compensation benefits, but shall be available for their normal workweek.

(d) For purposes of subsection (c), the term "qualified employer plan" means a plan of an employer or of an employers' association which association is party to a collective bargaining agreement (hereinafter referred to as "employers' association") under which there is a reduction in the number of hours worked by employees rather than temporary layoffs if—

(1) the employer's or employers' association's short-time compensation plan is approved by the State agency;

(2) the employer or employers' association certifies to the State agency that the aggregate reduction in work hours pursuant to such plan is in lieu of temporary

layoffs which would have affected at least 10 per centum of the employees in the unit or units to which the plan would apply and which would have resulted in an equivalent reduction of work hours;

(3) during the previous four months the work force in the affected unit or units has not been reduced by temporary layoffs of more than 10 per centum;

(4) the employer continues to provide health benefits, and retirement benefits under defined benefit pension plans (as defined in section 3(35) of the Employee Retirement Income Security Act of 1974), to employees whose workweek is reduced under such plan as though their workweek had not been reduced; and

(5) in the case of employees represented by an exclusive bargaining representative, that representative has consented to the plan.

The State agency shall review at least annually any qualified employer plan put into effect to assure that it continues to meet the requirements of this subsection and of any applicable State law.

(e) Short-time compensation shall be charged in a manner consistent with the State law.

(f) For purposes of this section, the term "State" includes the District of Columbia, the Commonwealth of Puerto Rico, and the Virgin Islands.

(g)(1) The Secretary shall conduct a study or studies of State short-time compensation programs consulting with employee and employer representatives in developing criteria and guidelines to measure the following factors:

(A) the impact of the program upon the unemployment trust fund, and a comparison with the estimated impact on the fund of layoffs which would have occurred but for the existence of the program;

(B) the extent to which the program has protected and preserved the jobs of workers, with special emphasis on newly hired employees, minorities, and women;

(C) the extent to which layoffs occur in the unit subsequent to initiation of the program and the impact of the program upon the entitlement to unemployment compensation of the employees;

(D) where feasible, the effect of varying methods of administration;

(E) the effect of short-time compensation on employers' State unemployment tax rates, including both users and nonusers of short-time compenation, on a State-by-State basis;

(F) the effect of various State laws and practices under those laws on the retirement and health benefits of employees who are on short-time compensation programs;

(G) a comparison of costs and benefits to employees, employers, and communities from use of short-time compensation and layoffs;

(H) the cost of administration of the short-time compensation program; and

(1) such other factors as may be appropriate.

(2) Not later than October 1, 1985, the Secretary shall submit to the Congress and to the President a final report on the implementation of this section. Such report shall contain an evaluation of short-time compensation programs and shall contain such recommendations as the Secretary deems advisable, including recommendations as to necessary changes in the statistical practices of the Department of Labor.

Figure 8-5. The U.S. Department of Labor's model legislative language for use by states wanting to implement short-time compensation programs.

A. *Definitions*

1. "Affected Unit" means a specified plant, department, shift, or other definable unit consisting of not less than ____ employees to which an approved short-time compensation plan applies.

2. "Fringe Benefits" include, but are not limited to, such advantages as health insurance (hospital, medical, and dental services, etc.), retirement benefits under defined benefit pension plans (as defined in Section 3(35) of the Employee Retirement Income Security Act of 1974), paid vacation and holidays, sick leave, etc., which are incidents of employment in addition to the cash remuneration earned.

3. "Short-Time Compensation" or "STC" means the unemployment benefits payable to employees in an affected unit under an approved short-time compensation plan as distinguished from the unemployment benefits otherwise payable under the conventional unemployment compensation provisions of a State law.

4. "Short-Time Compensation Plan" means a plan of an employer (or of an employers' association which association is a party to a collective bargaining agreement) under which there is a reduction in the number of hours worked by all employees of an affected unit rather than temporary layoffs of some such employees. The term "temporary layoffs" for this purpose means the separation of workers in the affected unit for an indefinite period expected to last for more than two months but not more than one year.

5. "Usual Weekly Hours of Work" means the normal hours of work for full-time and permanent part-time employees in the affected unit when that unit is operating on its normally full-time basis, not to exceed forty hours and not including overtime.

6. "Unemployment Compensation" means the unemployment benefits payable under this Act other than short-time compensation and includes any amounts payable pursuant to an agreement under any Federal law providing for compensation, assistance, or allowances with respect to unemployment.

7. "Employers' Association" means an association which is a party to a collective bargaining agreement under which the parties may negotiate a short-time compensation plan.

B. *Criteria for Approval of a Short-Time Compensation Plan*

An employer or employers' association wishing to participate in an STC program shall submit a signed written short-time compensation plan to the Director for approval. The Director shall approve an STC plan only if the following criteria are met.

1. The plan applies to and identifies specified affected units.

2. The employees in the affected unit or units are identified by name, social security number and by any other information required by the Director.

3. The usual weekly hours of work for employees in the affected unit or units are reduced by not less than 10 percent and not more than ____ percent.

4. Health benefits and retirement benefits under defined benefit pension

plans (as defined in Section 3(35) of the Employee Retirement Income Security Act of 1974), will continue to be provided to employees in affected units as though their work weeks had not been reduced.

5. The plan certifies that the aggregate reduction in work hours is in lieu of temporary layoffs which would have affected at least 10 percent of the employees in the affected unit or units to which the plan applies and which would have resulted in an equivalent reduction in work hours.

6. During the previous four months the work force in the affected unit has not been reduced by temporary layoffs of more than 10 percent of the workers.

7. The plan applies to at least 10 percent of the employees in the affected unit, and when applicable applies to all employees of the affected unit equally.

8. In the case of employees represented by an exclusive bargaining representative, the plan is approved in writing by the collective bargaining agent; in the absence of such an agent, by representatives of the employees in the affected unit.

9. The plan will not serve as a subsidy of seasonal employment during the off season, nor as a subsidy of temporary part-time or intermittent employment.

10. The employer agrees to furnish reports relating to the proper conduct of the plan and agrees to allow the Director of his/her authorized representatives access to all records necessary to verify the plan prior to approval and, after approval, to monitor and evaluate application of the plan.

In addition to the matters specified above, the Director shall take into account any other factors which may be pertinent to proper implementation of the plan.

C. *Approval or Rejection of the Plan*

The Director shall approve or reject a plan in writing within ___ days of its receipt. The reasons for rejection shall be final and nonappealable, but the employer shall be allowed to submit another plan for approval not earlier than ___ days from the date of the earlier rejection.

D. *Effective Date and Duration of Plan*

A plan shall be effective on the date specified in the plan or on a date mutually agreed upon by the employer and the Director. It shall expire at the end of the 12th full calendar month after its effective date or on the date specified in the plan if such date is earlier, provided that the plan is not previously revoked by the Director. If a plan is revoked by the Director, it shall terminate on the date specified in the Director's written order of revocation.

E. *Revocation of Approval*

The Director may revoke approval of a plan for good cause. The revocation order shall be in writing and shall specify the date the revocation is effective and the reasons therefor.

Good cause shall include, but not be limited to, failure to comply with the

(Continued)

Figure 8-5. *(continued)*

assurances given in the plan, unreasonable revision of productivity standards for the affected unit, conduct or occurrences tending to defeat the intent and effective operation of the plan, and violation of any criteria on which approval of the plan was based.

Such action may be taken at any time by the Director on his/her own motion, on the motion of any of the affected unit's employees or on the motion of the appropriate collective bargaining agent(s); provided that the Director shall review the operation of each qualified employer plan at least once during the 12-month period the plan is in effect to assure its compliance with the requirements of these provisions.

F.   *Modification of an Approved Plan*

An operational approved STC plan may be modified by the employer with the acquiescence of employee representatives if the modification is not substantial and in conformity with the plan approved by the Director, but the modifications must be reported promptly to the Director. If the hours of work are increased or decreased substantially beyond the level in the original plan, or any other conditions are changed substantially, the Director shall approve or disapprove such modifications, without changing the expiration date of the original plan. If the substantial modifications do not meet the requirements for approval, the Director shall disallow that portion of the plan in writing as specified in section E.

G.   *Eligibility for Short-Time Compensation*

1. An individual is eligible to receive STC benefits with respect to any week only if, in addition to monetary entitlement, the Director finds that:

(a) During the week, the individual is employed as a member of an affected unit under an approved short-time compensation plan which was approved prior to that week, and the plan is in effect with respect to the week for which STC is claimed.

(b) The individual is able to work and is available for the normal work week with the short-time employer.

(c) Notwithstanding any other provisions of this Act to the contrary, an individual is deemed unemployed in any week for which remuneration is payable to him/her as an employee in an affected unit for 90 percent or less than his/her normal weekly hours of work as specified under the approved short-time compensation plan in effect for the week.

(d) Notwithstanding any other provisions of this Act to the contrary, an individual shall not be denied STC benefits for any week by reason of the application of provisions relating to availability for work and active search for work with an employer other than the short-time employer.

H.   *Benefits*

1. The short-time weekly benefit amount shall be the product of the regular weekly unemployment compensation amount multiplied by the percentage of

reduction of at least 10 percent in the individual's usual weekly hours of work.

2. An individual may be eligible for STC benefits or unemployment compensation, as appropriate, except that no individual shall be eligible for combined benefits in any benefit year in an amount more than the maximum entitlement established for unemployment compensation, nor shall an individual be paid STC benefits for more than 26 weeks (whether or not consecutive) in any benefit year pursuant to a short-time plan.

3. The STC benefits paid an individual shall be deducted from the maximum entitlement amount established for that individual's benefit year.

4. Claims for STC benefits shall be filed in the same manner as claims for unemployment compensation or as prescribed in regulations by the Director.

5. Provisions applicable to unemployment compensation claimants shall apply to STC claimants to the extent that they are not inconsistent with STC provisions. An individual who files an initial claim for STC benefits shall be provided, if eligible therefor, a monetary determination of entitlement to STC benefits and shall serve a waiting week.

6. (a) If an individual works in the same week for an employer other than the short-time employer and his or her combined hours of work for both employers are equal to or greater than the usual hours of work with the short-time employer, he or she shall not be entitled to benefits under these short-time provisions or the unemployment compensation provisions.

   (b) If an individual works in the same week for both the short-time employer and another employer and his or her combined hours of work for both employers are equal to or less than 90 percent of the usual hours of work for the short-time employer, the benefit amount payable for that week shall be the weekly unemployment compensation amount reduced by the same percentage that the combined hours are of the usual hours of work. A week for which benefits are paid under this provision shall count as a week of short-time compensation.

   (c) If an individual did not work during any portion of the work week, other than the reduced portion covered by the shorttime plan, with the approval of the employer, he or she shall not be disqualified for such absence or deemed ineligible for STC benefits for that reason alone.

7. An individual who performs no services during a week for the short-time employer, and is otherwise eligible, shall be paid the full weekly unemployment compensation amount. Such a week shall not be counted as a week with respect to which STC benefits were received.

8. An individual who does not work for the short-time employer during a week, but works for another employer and is otherwise eligible, shall be paid benefits for that week under the partial unemployment compensation provisions of the State law. Such a week shall not be counted as a week with respect to which STC benefits were received.

I. *Charging Shared Work Benefits*

STC benefits shall be charged to employers' experience rating accounts in the same manner as unemployment compensation is charged under the State

(Continued)

Figure 8-5. *(continued)*

> law. Employers liable for payments in lieu of contributions shall have STC benefits attributed to service in their employ in the same manner as unemployment compensation is attributed.
>
> J.   *Extended Benefits*
>
> An individual who has received all of the STC benefits or combined unemployment compensation and STC benefits available in a benefit year shall be considered an exhaustee for purposes of extended benefits, as provided under the provisions of section ___ , and, if otherwise eligible under those provisions, shall be eligible to receive extended benefits.

school districts, and various state agencies have used voluntary reduced work time as a way to cut labor costs and minimize layoffs. However, as the Charles Schwab & Company example on page 328 illustrates, there is considerable incentive for private sector employers to use this approach, too.

Who Uses Work Sharing?

This section discusses experience to date with the three main types of work sharing: (1) ad hoc work sharing, (2) work sharing with short-time compensation, and (3) V-Time as a means of work sharing.

Ad Hoc Work Sharing

High-technology companies in Silicon Valley, California, have found ad hoc work sharing, as well as work sharing supplemented by the state's STC program, helpful in combatting the up-and-down economic swings that are prevalent in their industry. Hewlett-Packard was a pioneer in the use of ad hoc work sharing, and other employers in the field soon began to follow suit. Here are examples of how some of these Silicon Valley companies have employed ad hoc work-sharing strategies:

- ■ Hewlett-Packard cut pay for top officials by 10 percent in 1985 and reduced work time by two days a month for everyone else except sales force personnel, who were exempted from the work reduction so they could keep selling.
- ■ Monolithic Memories, Inc., a semiconductor maker with 1,300 employees, cut hourly workers back to four days' work for

four days' pay and salaried workers to five days' work for four days' pay in 1982 and again in 1985. During this period, company officers also took a 10 percent pay cut.

■ National Semiconductor Corporation shut down for 34 days in 1985.

■ Equitec cut executive salaries from 10 percent to 20 percent, with other employees losing two days of work a month from October 1985 through January 1986.

■ Intel Corporation instituted 4 percent to 8 percent pay cuts and seven days of furlough in 1985.[5]

As you may have gathered from the preceding list, 1985 was a very bad year for the semiconductor business. However, according to a 1986 report to the state of California's Office of Technology Assessment, a few companies did manage to avoid layoffs completely during that year. Advanced Micro Devices, Inc. (AMD) was one of them. According to the report:

> When the semi-conductor slump hit, the company [*AMD*] did have a somewhat leaner workforce, i.e. fewer employees per sales volume, than its competitors. In addition, for seven and a half months it cut executive salaries by 15 percent and the salaries of other professionals by 10 percent. Hourly wage workers' salaries were not cut. And all pay increases were put on hold for another six months. A hiring freeze was initiated as well and AMD lost about 1,000 employees through attrition.[6]

Like AMD, IBM uses various forms of ad hoc work sharing to buttress its employment security policy. Among the strategies IBM has employed are an 80 percent reduction in overtime, mandatory use of accrued vacation time by employees (thus creating work for 2,000 people who might otherwise have been idled), and encouragement of unpaid leaves of absence coupled with a guarantee of a job upon return.[7]

Work Sharing With Short-Time Compensation

Since 1982, 12 states have passed legislation, modeled on California's, that allows employers to use partial payments of unemployment insurance for STC in conjunction with work sharing. States offering STC as of 1988 are Arkansas, Arizona, California, Florida, Louisiana, Massachusetts, Maryland, New York, Oregon, Texas, Vermont, and Washington. Table 8–1 shows the number of employees in each of

Table 8-1. Work sharing by state: 1982–1986.

	1982	1983	1984	1985	1986
Arkansas				80	449
Arizona	19,505	5,841	2,085	20,515	11,645
California	35,252	40,887	20,963	91,203	44,709
Florida			18	8,250	3,349
Illinois			0	0	0
Louisiana					450
Maryland				2,333	1,329
New York					108
Oregon			610	3,323	473
Texas					9,619
Vermont					19
Washington			296	5,927	3,166

SOURCE: U.S. Department of Labor statistics, 1988.

these states who participated in work-sharing/STC programs between 1982 and 1986. (Note that Illinois experimented briefly with the concept of work sharing but at present does not offer the option and that as of the time the figures in Table 8–1 were compiled, the Massachusetts program had not yet begun.)

In most states, use of the STC legislation is still not widespread. If California is an example, however, the numbers are on the rise. (Note, however, the lower 1986 figure, which resulted because an improvement in the economy generally signals a decrease in the use of work sharing.)

Because work sharing with STC is new and has just begun to be studied, the data about its use are scarce. According to an evaluation of the pilot project phase of the California plan, most STC users, at least initially, were large, primarily manufacturing concerns.[8] An early survey of Oregon users showed that 70 percent of that state's labor force participation was also in manufacturing. The Oregon companies ranged in size from 3 to 1,034 employees, with an average size of 49 employees.[9]

Motorola, Inc., a major manufacturer of semiconductors, is one of the longest-term large users. Managers there have been very articulate in praising this new alternative. "It doesn't have the disabling effects financially or psychologically that being out of a job does," says Lew Hastings, Motorola legislative counsel. A 1984 study of that company's work-sharing program also showed a savings of $1,800 per worker in new-hiring and training costs.[10]

Voluntary Reduced Work Time

Both public- and private-sector employers have used voluntarily reduced work time arrangements as part of a work-sharing strategy. Corporate users have included Shaklee, Bank of America, and Charles Schwab & Company. (A profile of the Schwab program is on page 328.) Alaska offers a "Reduced Work Week as an Alternative to Layoff" program. In 1979, California passed legislation providing that "[W]henever a reduction equivalent to one percent or more of full-time equivalent jobs is contemplated in the personnel of state agencies or departments, employees in such agencies or departments shall be permitted, under certain circumstances, to voluntarily reduce their work time." (Note: In 1980, recognizing that many employees needed less than full-time schedules for personal reasons, the California state legislature passed the Reduced Work Time Act, which permanently authorizes a variety of voluntary options, including such arrangements as job sharing and four-, five-, and six-hour workdays. It retains language, however, mandating that voluntary work time cuts be offered in cases of projected reductions in force of one percent or more. The V-Time programs, which were described in detail in Chapter 6, were designed to comply with this legislation.)

When Is Work Sharing Most Appropriate?

A properly designed program of work sharing is a management strategy that can enable an employer to cut costs during downturns in the economy without the potentially crippling dislocations often caused by widespread layoffs—the loss of trained and experienced employees (which lengthens the company's turnaround time once the economy does pick up and new hires must be recruited and trained), a drop in morale on the part of the remaining employees, and a reversal of affirmative action gains.

Responding to economic fluctuations. An employer that uses layoffs as a strategy for dealing with a faltering economy will indeed cut its payroll costs. This strategy, however, is not without its price. In the short run, the employer incurs such layoff-related expenses as severance pay and retirement incentives. In the long run, the economic outlook will brighten, and the employer will find itself incurring a variety of hiring and retraining expenses (and associated delays) as it attempts to gear up its operations and regain its competitive momentum. On the other hand, the organization that cuts back paid hours and shares the remaining work when it is faced with a business slump keeps its trained and experienced staff intact, ready for an immediate response to improved conditions.

Turnaround time. The reduction of turnaround time is probably the most important reason to consider a work-sharing program. The time it takes for a company to call back laid-off workers or recruit and train new ones results in productivity losses of various kinds; lost sales, reduced market share, and customer dissatisfaction are just a few of the potential problems.

Employee morale. Widespread layoffs take their toll not only on the newly unemployed workers but also on the morale of those who stay with the company. The remaining employees, wondering which of them might be next, may experience a drop in both commitment and productivity. A work-sharing alternative to layoffs is popular with most employees because it preserves their job security and benefits and distributes the burden of cutbacks more equitably than making a small portion of laid-off workers bear the entire brunt. And combining work sharing with STC can help workers even more by cushioning the impact of their salary loss.

Affirmative action. Since women and minorities are often among the most recently hired for certain types of positions, the organization that lays off a portion of its employees in order to cut costs may find itself wiping out hard-won affirmative action gains in the process. One alternative is to use work-sharing strategies to keep the work force intact through an economic downturn, thereby preventing damage to the organization's affirmative action profile and avoiding employee lawsuits challenging the layoff procedure.

Pros and Cons of Work Sharing

When considering the use of work sharing as an alternative to layoffs, the major factors that an employer must keep in mind involve the cost implications of both strategies, their effect on productivity, the attitudes of labor and management, the effect of layoffs and work sharing on the company's affirmative action profile, the potential for legal challenges in the wake of layoffs, and the equity of both approaches.

Cost Implications
In this area, we will start by considering the costs that are sometimes reported in connection with the use of work sharing and then examine the savings that can be achieved.

Costs Work sharing is slightly more expensive on an hourly per capita basis than some of the other reduced work-time options because employers continue to pay full fringe benefits even though employees are working less than full-time.

If short-time compensation is used, work sharing may also have a negative effect on employer contributions to the unemployment insurance fund by increasing the organization's experience rating. Furthermore, if senior as well as junior employees are included in the "work group" that is eligible for STC, the average benefit payout may be raised. On the other hand, layoffs also have the same detrimental effect. Some employers have therefore designed a mixed model approach to work sharing—using STC for nonexempt employees and ad hoc work sharing for higher-level employees and some exempt workers.

In addition, some states impose a surcharge on negative-balance employers—that is, those that have contributed fewer dollars to the unemployment insurance fund than their employees have drawn in benefits. California initially had such a policy, but legislation passed in 1988 repealed the surcharge section of the Unemployment Insurance Code. This was done to make work sharing with STC more attractive to employers. Oregon, Arizona, and Florida have a surcharge provision, but Washington, which does not use the experience-rating system, does not.

The labor cost of completing the extensive documentation required in order for a company's employees to receive STC can pose a problem for small to medium-size organizations. This is unfortunate since in many states, the primary users of STC to date have been smaller companies. In some states, the staff of the administering agency facilitates the paperwork processing in order to reduce the load on participating organizations.

Savings The most obvious saving associated with a cutback in work time is a reduction in the employer's labor costs. Charles Debow, director of employee relations at Motorola's Phoenix plant, which has used work sharing with STC a number of times, estimates that from 1982 to 1986, this strategy "saved the company $7.7 million in wages."[11] And if the cutbacks take the form of intermittent shutdowns, the employer may also see a reduction in overhead costs.

With respect to unemployment insurance, both the company that lays off workers and the company that cuts back through work sharing in conjunction with STC will face a rise in costs. The difference is that while laid-off workers continue to draw unemployment insurance against their employer's account as long as they remain out of work, employees whose schedules have been reduced through work sharing will immediately stop drawing unemployment insurance once they resume a full-time schedule, thereby lowering the company's unemployment insurance outlay.

Layoff strategies can often require substantial financing, in such areas as severance pay and early retirement incentives, and can also involve the practice known as "bumping." The work-sharing approach avoids both the up-front expenses of layoffs and the longer-term costs associated with bumping, which can include distorted production scheduling, delayed start-ups, and retraining.[12]

Additional major savings are realized through the retention of trained and experienced employees, which minimizes postrecession turnaround time and avoids the cost of recruitment, training, and so on necessitated by layoff-stimulated turnover. (See also the discussion of productivity in the following subsection.)

Productivity

Because layoffs are so disruptive and painful, both to workers and to the organization, they are usually delayed as long as possible in the face of an economic downturn. Sometimes, this sort of delay can be detrimental to an organization's productivity. The various modes of work sharing provide the organization with a range of responses that can be invoked in a more timely fashion, enabling it to take earlier and less-drastic action when business begins to slack off.

Once business starts to pick up again, the organization that has employed a work-sharing strategy will find itself in a stronger position than the organization that has dismissed a portion of its work force. One aspect of the ability to resume normal operations is the retention of employees with "company-specific skills," in terms of both technological expertise and experience unique to a particular employer. Clearly, having a trained and committed work force all ready to go puts a company in a better position to produce goods or services than one that has to recall workers (many of whom may now be employed elsewhere) or recruit and train new employees. In fact, cutting down on the turnaround time needed to get back into a competitive mode following a recession is probably the greatest advantage of work sharing from an organizational standpoint.

Work sharing generally results in improved employee morale. This, in turn, is usually believed to have a positive effect on retention, recruitment, and commitment to the organization, all of which translate into productivity gains.

Labor Attitudes

Although organized labor has negotiated agreements that call for a reduction in hours, or work sharing among employees, before layoffs are permitted, labor has often been skeptical about work sharing, even when STC replaces part of the lost wages. Unions have been concerned about how and when work sharing would be used and about its impact on seniority. Since the mid-1970s, however, there has been a clause in the index of *Labor Arbitration Reports* on "work sharing to avoid layoff" that indicates growing acceptance of this practice.

In 1981, the executive council of the AFL-CIO endorsed work sharing under certain conditions. The conditions the council specified were:

1. Adequate financing of unemployment insurance trust funds.
2. Approval of the union where there is one.
3. A wage replacement level of at least two-thirds of the lost pay and workweek reductions limited to 40 percent.
4. Retention of fringe benefits.
5. Prohibition of discrimination against recently hired workers, especially minorities and women.[13]

According to AFL-CIO spokesperson John Zalusky, about 20 percent of union contracts currently provide for some form of work sharing.[14]

As Ramelle MaCoy and Martin Morand note, in their book *Short-Time Compensation*:

Layoffs threaten the union not only with short-range losses in dues income but with the demoralizing and disunifying effects on a work force in which some have lost their jobs and the rest feel threatened. Instead of focusing its energies on the causes of this affliction to the collective it represents, the union must devote its energies and resources to the impact on individuals. Its members are not all together at the workplace; they are harder to find, organize and defend.[15]

Management Attitudes

Studies done on work sharing indicate that managers like this arrangement, partly because work sharing is less disruptive than layoffs and partly because managers generally want to avoid having theirs become known as a "hire-and-fire" company. They also want to retain trained employees.

Motorola executives, looking back on their work-sharing experience, offered the following comments:

Productivity remained high during last year's cutbacks . . . because most [*workers*] stayed on the same job.

The big saving for Motorola came when semiconductor orders picked up earlier this year. . . . Recalling workers would have taken a lot longer. . . . You do a lot of wheelspinning to get [*laid-off*] people back to work.[16]

Affirmative Action Profile

Preserving affirmative action gains was one of the original objectives of advocates of work sharing. Since layoffs generally follow a "last hired, first fired" pattern, they are perceived as affecting female and minority employees disproportionately. Caught between seniority issues and the desire to preserve their hard-won affirmative action profile, many employers have found work sharing, particularly when accompanied by short-time compensation, a middle ground that allows them to achieve a number of objectives.

Legal Incentives

Increasingly, employees, either individually or en masse, are challenging the legality of layoffs and dismissals. The $13 million Atari Corporation workers' class action suit, brought by employees abruptly dismissed in 1983, was one of the most dramatic legal initiatives, but it is not unique. Trying to conduct layoffs that do not discriminate in some way against some group is an increasingly difficult process. Work sharing avoids the problems of legal challenges to the layoff procedure.

The Plant-Closing Law that became effective February 4, 1989 may also prove to be an incentive to use work sharing. It has a mass layoff provision that calls for giving employees 60 days' notice if a company dismisses at least 50 people who comprise one third of the work force or if the employer terminates 500 people.[17]

Equity

As Martin Nemirow, a social science adviser to the U.S. Department of Labor, has noted, "Equity is the major benefit of STC. The economic and social costs of full-time unemployment are distributed more evenly across all workers in a plant (or plant unit) rather than among a small minority of workers."[18]

Concurring, Morand and MaCoy note that equity can also be cost-effective:

> Few firms confronted with the necessity of laying off production workers find it feasible to lay off proportionate numbers of clerical, managerial, and supervisory personnel. In a plant of 200 employees, for example, the layoff of 40 production workers will not reduce the need for a foreman or payroll clerk. If the firm opts for STC, however, particularly if the hours reduction should take the form of a four-day week—it would be entirely possible for the firm's supervisory, managerial, and executive employees to share the reduction with the production workers and thus effect additional savings. Such a procedure would also eliminate the bitterness frequently felt by production workers because they are so frequently forced to bear the entire burden of the need for a reduction in labor costs.[19]

Should Your Organization Try Work Sharing?

We have included in this section several tools to help you determine whether or not work sharing would be an effective strategy for your own organization as it confronts periodic fluctuations in the business climate.

First, refer to the accompanying group of profiles entitled Organizational Experience With Work Sharing/STC. In it are described the work-sharing/STC programs of four companies, ranging in size from small to very large. As you read these profiles, take note of factors that might apply to your company's situation.

Table 8–2 is a questionnaire that will focus your attention on the conditions and the climate that usually exist in an organization for which work sharing would be an appropriate option. If your questionnaire results would seem to point toward work sharing, use the worksheet in Figure 8–6 to further assess this alternative.

Introducing Work Sharing

The process of introducing work sharing in an organization as an alternative to layoffs during a business slowdown consists of the following steps: Gain support from all levels of management and from labor. Set up the program's administration, which should comprise

(Text continues on page 331.)

ORGANIZATIONAL EXPERIENCE WITH WORK SHARING/STC

Humphrey, Inc.

Description: Humphrey, a manufacturer of gyroscopes and mechanical instruments, has 220 employees. Its customers are primarily the military and oil companies, so it is affected periodically by downturns in those industries.

Reason for Using Work Sharing/STC: The ability to retain skilled employees during periods of decreased demand for the company's products is the primary reason why Humphrey has used voluntary work sharing.

Implementation Process: Since departments are affected unevenly by the need for cutbacks, work sharing tends not to be implemented companywide. The workers in affected units who volunteer for work sharing generally take a 10 percent reduction in hours and pay. This has usually meant taking off one full day every other weekend. When work picks up, the employees can return to full-time status immediately.

Impact to Date: Humphrey has used work sharing three times in the last five years, and employees like the program. The company has never had a negative balance in its unemployment insurance account, so it has not experienced an increase in its tax rating as a result of the work-sharing program.

SOURCE: New Ways to Work telephone interview with the treasurer of Humphrey, Inc. (May 1988); Julie Batz, *Work Sharing: An Alternative to Layoffs* (San Francisco: New Ways to Work, 1988), 15.

Charles Schwab & Company

Description: Charles Schwab, the nation's largest discount broker, with approximately 2,300 employees, is based in San Francisco, California.

Reason for Using Voluntary Work Sharing: The work-sharing plan was devised in June 1988 as a means of cutting operating costs. This was necessary because of a downturn in the brokerage industry. The objective was to achieve a 10 percent reduction in expenses such as compensation, promotion, printing, and telecommunication while, at the same time, to retain highly trained staff.

Implementation Process: Salaries of approximately 200 managers, including the president and the chairman of the board, were temporarily reduced by 5 percent to 20 percent. In addition, employees were offered the opportunity to take sabbaticals at 25 percent of their normal pay or to temporarily cut their workweeks, take unpaid days off, or opt for early vacations. Employee requests for sabbaticals or shortened workweeks had to be approved by two supervisors.

Impact to Date: By November of 1988, Jim Wiggett, senior vice-president of human resources, estimated that "almost 100 percent" of Schwab's employees were participating in the program. He projected that the firm would save approximately $3.5 million by the end of the year as a result of the voluntary cutbacks.

SOURCE: *Schwab Plans to Implement Further Cost Reductions,* Charles Schwab news release, San Francisco, CA, June 2, 1988; Lloyd Watson, "People in Business," *San Francisco Chronicle* (November 11, 1988), B3.

Motorola, Inc.

Description: Motorola is a major manufacturer of semiconductor products. The corporate offices are in Schaumberg, Illinois, but the semiconductor production is concentrated in the Phoenix area, where 20,000 are employed. It is this facility that was the site for Motorola's initial work-sharing program.

Reason for Using Work Sharing/STC: Motorola used this option in order to retain trained employees during an economic downturn. The devastating layoffs that the company had experienced in the course of the 1975 recession prompted it to investigate how the California model of work sharing with short-time compensation might be introduced in Arizona, where Motorola is the state's largest employer. In 1981, work-sharing legislation was passed in that state, and during the 1982 recession, Motorola enrolled in the new program.

Implementation Process: The company determined the extent of the cutback that was needed and the work groups that would be affected. It presented its plan to the state's work-sharing office and, once the plan was approved, enrolled in the program. Typical cutbacks for production-line workers were half a day's work and wages per week, with a portion of the loss being made up by partial unemployment insurance payments.

Impact to Date: Motorola estimates that it saved over 1,000 jobs and $1.5 million in the fourth quarter of 1982, when the use of work sharing peaked.

Once orders picked up, the company's turnaround time was greatly enhanced because it had retained its work force, which put it in a better competitive position than companies that had used layoffs.

SOURCE: Heywood Klein, "Interest Grows in Worksharing, Which Lets Concerns Cut Workweeks to Avoid Layoffs," *Wall Street Journal* (Apr. 7, 1983), 33; correspondence with the vice-president and director of personnel administration, Motorola (June 1988).

Signetics Corporation

Description: Signetics is a semiconductor company located in Sunnyvale, California, where it has 4,000 employees. It is a subsidiary of North American Philips Corporation.

Reason for Using Work Sharing/STC: During the 1981 recession, Signetics decided to participate in the state's work-sharing/STC program as a way to reduce operating costs and avoid the pain of massive layoffs by maintaining the company's trained labor force intact during the downturn. This strategy was also seen as a way to facilitate a turnaround when business picked up again.

Implementation Process: Work sharing was structured and marketed to employees as an extended weekend. The plan called for employees to take off the last Friday of one pay period and the first Monday of the next. In advance of the long weekend, the employee relations manager distributed information about local recreation facilities and arranged for Signetics employees to get discount cards.

The logistics of signing up 4,000 employees who were working three round-the-clock shifts were simplified when Signetics persuaded the state's Employment Development Department, the agency that administers unemployment insurance, to send a representative to the company's plant to register employees.

Impact to Date: The company realized significant savings in operating costs. It not only achieved the necessary salary savings but reduced overhead costs as well. When the recession eased, Signetics had the skilled workers it needed to resume normal operations.

Signetics trained its supervisors to contain unemployment insurance costs and to respond to claims in a timely manner. Employee reaction could be summed up by the remarks of one worker who said that the work-sharing program "took very little of my time and none of my dignity."

Since 1981, Signetics has periodically used work sharing, in combination with layoffs and attrition, in order to respond to industry ups and downs.

SOURCE: Julie Batz and the staff of New Ways to Work, *Work Sharing: An Alternative to Layoffs* (San Francisco, NWW, 1988), 12.

both a task force and an administrator. Design the program, assessing the entire range of relevant issues. Develop resource materials, both for managers and for employees. Announce the program and then promote it to employees so work sharing will be seen as being of mutual benefit to labor and to the organization. Assess the effect of the program and make appropriate improvements. We will now take a closer look at each of these steps in the program implementation process.

Gain Support for the Program

For a work-sharing strategy to be effective, it must have the support of all segments of your company's work force: top management, middle management, and labor representatives. Top management's leadership is particularly important, because top management must help the organization's employees see work sharing for what it is: a way to preserve jobs during an economic downturn.

Table 8-2. Work-sharing questionnaire.

Would Work Sharing Benefit Your Organization?

	Yes	No
Does your organization's management have a cooperative working relationship with its labor force?		
Would top management fully support using work sharing as an alternative to layoffs?		
Are top managers and professional staff willing to take a pay cut to help the company during a downturn in the economy?		
Can work sharing be presented to employees as a positive, supportive measure that will save jobs?		
Or rather, will work sharing be perceived by employees as a way of exploiting them?		
Would some of your organization's employees like to volunteer to reduce their work time temporarily in order to spend more time with their families, take a training course, return to school, phase into retirement, and so on?		
Is the downturn your company faces expected to be of a short-term nature?		
Or does the downturn instead represent a more difficult, long-term problem that your company or your industry must address?		
If a prolonged downturn is anticipated, is work sharing expected to be a transition phase before layoffs?		
Does your state have legislation allowing employers to use short-time compensation under certain conditions?		

In companies that have had a history of commitment to employment security, work sharing will probably be perceived as a natural outgrowth of traditional policy. In companies that have generally used layoffs to control labor costs, it may take more effort to gain general support for work sharing, particularly from those segments of the work force who felt they were relatively secure from being laid off.

Set Up the Program's Administration
Work sharing is a fairly new concept. It often affects different departments and job classifications unevenly, so it is particularly important to use a task force when developing a work-sharing plan for the first time. Once top management and labor representatives are committed to using work sharing, broadening companywide understanding and support will be the task force's next objective.

Figure 8-6. Work-sharing worksheet.

Assessing the Need for Work Sharing

List the main reasons why you are considering work sharing:

1. _____

   _____

   _____

2. _____

   _____

   _____

3. _____

   _____

   _____

4. _____

   _____

   _____

List what you see as the advantages and disadvantages of work sharing:

Pros: _____

_____

_____

_____

_____

(Continued)

Figure 8-6. *(continued)*

_____

_____

Cons: _____

_____

_____

_____

_____

_____

The task force should also be charged with gathering background information necessary for decision making and soliciting input about the design of the work-sharing program. (See the following subsection for a discussion of the major program design issues that must be addressed.)

An administrator should be appointed to provide staff support to the task force and, once the program's design is agreed upon, to administer the work-sharing plan.

Design the Program

Before beginning to design the work-sharing program, the task force will have to compile certain background information and address several key questions. For example:

- Have other companies in your area tried work sharing? What kind of program did they use, and what was its effect?
- How long is the business slump expected to last?
- By how much will the organization need to reduce its expenditures during this period?
- What activities have to continue, and to what extent, in order to maintain the company's viability?

Once these questions have been considered, determinations can be made about the following program design issues.

Duration   Although it is impossible to predict at the outset just how long a recessionary period will last, management should establish a time period for the work-sharing plan and announce it to employees in order to reinforce the fact that this is a temporary measure. At the end of the specified period, the current plan can be evaluated and a decision made about whether conditions warrant a return to normal operating capacity or whether work sharing, perhaps in a modified form, should be continued.

Scope   Since work sharing must often be targeted, affecting particular areas of a company differently, a decision must be made about whether work sharing will be used companywide, only in designated departments or divisions, or only in designated job classifications.

Form   One key decision that must be made is what form, or combination of forms, of work sharing would effectively address the situation presently facing your organization. The task force's assessment of the probable duration of the recessionary period will be the most important factor in determining what kind and degree of work sharing will be most appropriate initially: ad hoc mandated strategies, work sharing combined with partial unemployment insurance payments (assuming your state has passed enabling legislation making short-time compensation available through the unemployment insurance system) voluntary reduced work time options, or some combination of the three.

The following are components of a work-sharing strategy that can be applied either singly or in combination:

■ *Promoting existing voluntary reduced work-time options.* These options include such strategies as a V-Time program, job sharing or regular part-time employment, unpaid leave with a guarantee of a job upon return, and phased or partial retirement.

■ *Introducing ad hoc work-sharing tactics.* These may include a wage and/or hiring freeze, furlough days, mandatory use of paid time off, elimination of banking or carryover of paid time off, one or more short plant shutdowns (for instance, between Christmas and New Year's, in the summer, or periodically).

■ *Instituting salary reductions.* Some companies have coped with business downturns by cutting salaries for a defined duration. These reductions—which are usually confined to company officers, top management, and highly paid professional staff—sometimes take the form of "five days' work for four days' pay" but have also taken the form of percentage cutbacks.

■ *Reassigning employees.* Reassignments enhance other work-sharing tactics by allocating existing human resources more efficiently. They have the added benefit of cross-training the employees involved, which broadens both the employees' options and the organization's options not only during the recessionary period but during the following economic recovery.

■ *Using short-time compensation.* If, in conjunction with a work-sharing strategy, it is possible to replace a portion of the lost wages through partial unemployment insurance payments, cost-reduction measures will become more palatable, particularly to employees in lower-paid job classifications. In those states that permit partial unemployment insurance payments to workers whose hours have been cut back, STC is usually available only for a specified period of time—for example, 20 weeks a year.

Because of the paperwork demands occasioned by the use of STC and the potentially negative effect on future unemployment insurance ratings, employers generally target the application of STC rather than making it available companywide at all levels of responsibility. In designing a work-sharing program, management and labor must carefully consider which departments or job classifications should be designated as recipients of partial unemployment insurance payments and for how long.

Although work sharing is still in its infancy as a human resources management strategy in the United States, what is known about the experience of various organizations to date suggests the following rules of thumb for determining the form that a work-sharing program should take:

■ If your company is facing a small, short-term cutback, the situation might best be dealt with through expanded use of voluntary reduced work-time arrangements such as those mentioned earlier in this section.

■ If voluntary reductions are insufficient but the cutback is perceived as being short-term and involves no more than a 20 percent reduction, then ad hoc work sharing should be considered. (It is generally felt that ad hoc work sharing can be used successfully only for reductions of 20 percent or less, and then only for a short period of time.)

■ If cutbacks of 20 to 40 percent are projected for more than a few weeks, then short-time compensation is necessary in order for employees to continue receiving a living wage. (Employers in those states that do not have STC enabling legislation might consider bringing the need for this option to the attention of the state legislature.)

The major program design issues we have just discussed are summarized in Table 8–3, which can be used to keep track of where you stand in addressing each of these issues. Table 8–4 is a sample work-sharing matrix that illustrates how one organization planned a series of targeted reductions of various types and for various durations; it compares the savings that could be achieved over a 20-week period and over the course of a year. Table 8–5 is a blank copy of this matrix that you may wish to use as an aid to planning cutbacks within your own organization.

(Text continues on page 342.)

Table 8-3. Program design checklist: work sharing.

Key Design Issues	Notes
☐ Duration	
☐ Scope	
☐ Form	
☐ Existing V-Time options	
☐ Ad-hoc work-sharing approaches	
☐ Salary reductions in selected positions	
☐ Employee reassignments	
☐ Short-time compensation	

Table 8-4. Sample work-sharing matrix.

Activity	Exempt			Nonexempt			Total Savings: 20 wks.	Total Savings: 1 yr.
	No. Emp.	For	Savings	No. Emp.	For	Savings		
Voluntary reductions								
V-time								
Job sharing								
• Technical writers (50%)	4	1 yr.	$50,000				$ 19,231	$ 50,000
• Assemblers (50%)	8	1 yr.	$52,912				$ 20,351	$ 52,912
Regular part-time								
Unpaid leave								
Phased/partial retirement								
Ad Hoc Work Sharing								
Hiring freeze								
Wage freeze								
Furlough days								
Mandatory use of paid time off								
Elimination of banking or carryover of paid time off								
Plant shutdown:								
—Christmas–New Year's								
—Summer								
• Division II (100%)	24	1 wk.	$21,000	150	1 wk.	$ 74,508	$ 95,508	$ 95,508
—Periodic								

Salary reductions:					
—Officers					
—Top mgt/professional					
• Mgt Division III (20%)	20	20 wks.	$50,000	$ 50,000	$ 50,000
—Other					
Short-Time Compensation					
(if provided for under existing state legislation)					
Companywide					
Defined work groups:					
—Headquarters staff					
—Division					
—Office					
Job classifications:					
—Clerical					
—Production					
• Division III (20%)	150	20 wks.	$765,000	$765,000	$ 765,000
—Other					
TOTAL SAVINGS				$950,090	$1,013,420

Table 8-5. Work-sharing matrix: worksheet.

Activity	Exempt			Nonexempt			Total Savings: ___ wks.	Total Savings: 1 yr.
	No. Emp.	For	Savings	No. Emp.	For	Savings		
Voluntary Reductions								
V-Time								
Job sharing								
Regular part-time								
Unpaid leave								
Phased/partial retirement								
Ad Hoc Work Sharing								
Hiring freeze								
Wage freeze								
Furlough days								
Mandatory use of paid time off								
Elimination of banking or carryover of paid time off								
Plant shutdown:								
—Christmas–New Year's								
—Summer								
—Periodic								

Salary reductions:
—Officers
—Top mgt./professional
—Other

Short-Time Compensation
(if provided for under existing
    state legislation)
Companywide
Defined work groups:
—Headquarters staff
—Division
—Office
Job classifications:
—Clerical
—Production
—Other

TOTAL SAVINGS

Develop Resource Materials

A company that plans to institute a work-sharing plan will be faced with a variety of questions and concerns on the part of management and employees. Effectively designed resource materials can do a great deal to foster understanding and acceptance of the cost-cutting measures.

Resource materials for managers. The topics of most interest to managers will be:

- How the work-sharing schedule will affect their department in terms of both finances and staffing—that is, in terms of the bottom line and the production line.
- How to encourage the use of available voluntary reduced work-time options in their departments and how to support employees who voluntarily reduce their work time beyond the mandated cuts.
- How the short-time compensation process works and what their responsibilities are in this area (assuming STC is available in your state).
- How long this phase of work sharing is expected to last.

Resource materials for employees. The topics of most interest to employees will be:

- How the various work-sharing strategies will affect them individually. For example: Will performance or salary reviews be rescheduled as a result of wage freezes? What, if any, impact will the work-sharing program have on pension fund payments?
- The projected duration of the cutbacks.
- The process for receiving partial unemployment insurance payments (if appropriate).
- The expected long-range benefits of this strategy, both to themselves and to the company.

Announce the Program

When an economic downturn threatens, rumors about layoffs and job cuts abound. In such an atmosphere of widespread concern, the work-sharing program announcement will play a critical role in determining how this cost-reduction measure will be perceived by the organization's employees. Good communication with all levels of the labor force, starting with the program announcement, is a must if work sharing is to succeed.

Information about company plans for work sharing should be imparted as soon as possible. If the organization is using this alternative to layoffs for the first time, a companywide meeting can be scheduled at which top management and members of the task force can explain the purpose of work sharing and answer employee questions from the floor about the mechanics of the program and how it will affect their unit and their own status. Employee resource materials can be distributed at this time and an announcement made about how more detailed questions will be handled. A briefing session such as this establishes an air of candor that will be helpful in the weeks to come.

Promote the Program

Although user organizations report that work sharing is very popular among employees, it is still important to promote the concept. Three points should be emphasized:

1. Work sharing is a way of providing some employment security.
2. It is more equitable than layoffs by order of seniority.
3. It will leave the company in a better competitive position when the economy recovers than it would be if layoffs had been used.

Instilling a sense of working together to get through a difficult time will create a positive dynamic that will have a carryover effect when the downturn ends.

Evaluate the Program

Unless the business slump is of very short duration, the design of the initial work-sharing program should be evaluated within six or eight weeks of the time the program is put into effect. This evaluation should focus on two areas:

1. Did the kind of cutbacks that were used achieve the desired results in the targeted areas? If not, what changes in type or degree of work sharing can be made to improve the program's effectiveness?
2. Did the use of work sharing have a positive impact on the organization's ability to resume its operations at normal capacity once economic conditions improved?

Fine-Tune the Program

Based on the results of the evaluation, the organization should take whatever measures are warranted to improve the program's effectiveness, in terms of both achieving the targeted cutbacks while the program is in effect and enhancing the organization's competitive position once the program has ended. For example:

Problem	*Solution*
Managers complain that employees must take too much time off work to deal with the registration and reporting forms required to receive Short Time Compensation.	Ask the State Employment Security Office if it will arrange to send someone on-site to handle the paperwork for your firm's employees.
The marketing department reports that the reduced schedule inhibits its ability to keep up with orders requests.	Review the situation to see if the marketing staff should resume full schedules.
Employees cannot receive Short Time Compensation because enabling legislation has not been introduced in your state.	Assign staff responsibility for developing an industry initiative to introduce STC legislation.

Summary

Work sharing is a cost-reduction strategy that a company can use to avoid laying off a portion of its work force in the face of an economic slowdown. It involves cutting back the hours and salary of some or all of the organization's staff.

There are three basic approaches to work sharing, which can be used singly or combined in a variety of ways. The first is ad hoc work sharing, in which the involved members of the labor force reduce hours and salary by a specified amount. When work sharing is combined with short-time compensation, employees receive partial unemployment insurance payments to make up for a portion of the lost wages. (This second approach is only possible in states that have passed STC enabling legislation.) And finally, the company's employees can be encouraged to reduce their hours on a voluntary basis.

Ad hoc work sharing is used by many organizations whose industries are affected by periodic swings in the economy. A case in point is high-technology companies in the computer field. During a business slowdown, some organizations elect to use ad hoc work sharing for more highly paid employees while reserving STC for lower-paid workers, thereby reducing both their companies' experience rating and future payments to the unemployment insurance fund. Twelve states currently allow partial unemployment insurance payments to employees whose hours have been reduced as part of a work-sharing program. Although experience with work sharing/STC has been limited, we do know that this approach has thus far been used most extensively in the manufacturing sector. V-Time options have been used in both the public and private sectors as a means of reducing expenditures without reducing the work force.

Work sharing is most appropriate when a company wants to respond to economic fluctuations in a way that keeps both its work force and employee morale intact, so affirmative action gains will not be jeopardized and turnaround time will be minimal.

The costs that have been reported in connection with work sharing involve such areas as the continuation of full fringe benefits for employees on a reduced schedule, a rise in the employer's experience rating if STC is used, and the paperwork burden imposed on the company in order for its employees to receive STC.

On the other hand, the organization that chooses work sharing in lieu of layoffs reduces its labor costs while avoiding such expenditures as severance pay, early retirement incentives, and the dislocations that can come when bumping occurs in conjunction with labor force reductions. Work sharing with STC offers an additional advantage, in that employees are dropped from the unemployment insurance rolls the minute they resume a full-time schedule, so the company is spared the specter of laid-off workers' drawing benefits for a potentially prolonged period of time.

The organization also realizes both savings and productivity gains by retaining its trained and experienced staff, thanks to the fact that work sharing minimizes damage to employee morale and gives the company a competitive advantage once the economy picks up and normal operations must resume.

Work sharing tends to receive a positive reception from managers, who would rather not lose their trained staff or have their company get a reputation for layoffs that could damage future recruitment prospects. It is increasingly being accepted by unions, as well, providing certain safeguards are instituted.

In addition to the advantage, mentioned above, of preserving affirmative action gains, work sharing enables the organization to cut costs in a way that does not provoke legal challenges from laid-off workers and does not unfairly impose the entire burden of the reduction on a selected few employees.

To introduce a work-sharing option, especially for the first time, an organization should focus on making sure that the program will accomplish the desired reductions in a way that does not damage the company's viability. To do this, the organization must see that work sharing is fully understood and supported by all segments of its work force, target the types of work sharing to be used, and periodically monitor the program's effectiveness in achieving its objectives.

In short, if your company is looking for a way to weather a recession with minimal disruption to its operations, a carefully selected mix of work-sharing strategies might be the way to go.

PART III

Emerging Trends

The kinds of employment alternatives described in the previous two parts represent strategies for developing more flexibility within the context of the regular work force by using a variety of flexible and reduced work-time arrangements.

Recently, in addition to new scheduling options, some employers have begun to use new staffing arrangements that incorporate a combination of regular and external employees and new technology that allows employees to work at different sites to further expand the organization's potential for flexibility. In some cases, the result has been a basic change in the employer-employee relationship, the consequences of which are still not clear.

This part will provide an overview of the two major trends that have emerged—the growing use of flexiplace and the phenomenon of the contingent work force—and will conclude with a look toward the future and the year 2000.

CHAPTER 9

Flexiplace

Increasingly, employers are finding that allowing regular employees to work at home during a part of their scheduled hours both accommodates the needs of some employees and benefits the organization. Whether the term used to describe the arrangement is *flexiplace, telecommuting* (when computer use is involved), or *working at home* or from a *satellite office,* the practice is growing. Some employees working at home are full-timers; others are on part-time schedules. Some are professionals; others, managers, clerical workers, and in some instances, production workers.

Origins of Flexiplace

Although flexiplace was among the kinds of flexible and reduced work-time options suggested by proponents of greater workplace flexibility in the early 1970s, it was not until the 1980s, with the astounding growth of personal computer use, that the arrangement received much attention as an option for regular employees. A 1984 report entitled *Telecommuting: The State of the Art and Market Trends,* issued by Electronic Services Unlimited, a New York-based consulting group, credited two reasons for telecommuting's rapid expansion: the "growth of the information society and the explosion of chip technology." The report also noted that "telecommuting is highly compatible with current life-style trends."[1]

The forces driving employee interest in flexiplace options stem from the same social, demographic, and attitudinal changes that have stimulated the need for other nonstandard work arrangements discussed in this book. With two-paycheck families the new norm, and commuter hour traffic jams common in more and more communities, working at home, either temporarily or regularly during part of the workweek, is seen by some employees as an attractive option.

Who Uses Flexiplace?

In 1981, Frank Schiff, then vice-president and chief economist for the Committee for Economic Development, gave a talk entitled *Flexiplace: An Idea Whose Time Has Come* before the Engineering Management Society's Institute of Electrical and Electronics Engineers. In it, he commented:

> Some of the best immediate possibilities for use of flexiplace exist for engineers, computer programmers and analysts, architects and designers. The concept also has considerable applicability to various kinds of white-collar and clerical jobs that already rely importantly on use of computer terminals and that frequently involve "batch" work, such as word processing, accounting, insurance analysis, processing of insurance claims, etc. Work at home also has special potential for activities that call for output at odd hours—for example, overnight typing and checking of medical reports first prepared by doctors in rough form. Eventually even various production activities in manufacturing may become candidates for "flexiplace." After all, any work that involves remote control devices could in theory be guided at a considerable distance from the place where the actual production activities take place.[2]

At the time, Schiff's comments bordered on being visionary, but much of what he projected has occurred in the intervening years. Unfortunately, we still do not know the real extent of the change in terms of the status of flexiplace options for regular employees. The Bureau of Labor Statistics gathered information in 1985 about overall trends in home-based work—that is, how many self-employed individuals, independent contractors, and employees of private- and public-sector organizations are currently working out of their home. It reported that approximately 9 million persons did at least eight hours of work per week at home.[3] A 1985 Office of Technology report, based on 1980 census information, looked primarily at the incidence of home-based office work and reported that the home is the primary workplace for 1.2 million people. The categories of employee that the report identified were: professionals and managers who do some work from the home, home-based entrepreneurs, and employees who work from their home for a single employer.[4]

Little information has been available, however, about trends in the private sector relating to the availability of off-site work, with and without a computer, for regular employees. Current estimates by experts in this field deal mostly with telecommuting. Gil Gordon, a management consultant in the field of telecommuting, estimated that as of mid-1988, there were approximately 15,000 regular employees of 500 U.S. corporations who telecommute two to four days a week.[5] Telecommuting is generally more widely used in the service sector, with insurance and telecommunications companies being among the primary user industries to date. Pioneering organizations include J. C. Penney Company, Inc., IBM, Control Data Corporation, and the Travelers Insurance Company.

Recently, there have been a number of public-sector pilot projects. In July 1987, California began a two-year project to examine the impact of telecommuting on service delivery, quality of work life for managers and employees, energy usage, and possibilities for employment of persons with disabilities. The enabling legislation also calls for consideration of "the enhancements to telecommunications and information systems now or soon to be available which may facilitate the conduct of telecommuting."

When Is Flexiplace Most Appropriate?

Flexiplace not only is a popular option among employees but also can enable employers to save on office-space costs, expand their recruitment pool, perform certain types of tasks more efficiently, improve continuity of services, extend coverage, and employ individuals who might find standard on-site, 9–5 working arrangements prohibitively difficult.

Space. In most urban areas, the cost of office space has been rising for some time. With financial management and cost containment a priority for all employers, having some employees working off-site has proved for certain organizations to be an effective way to trim the cost of office space.

Popularity with employees. Employees regard flexiplace as offering many benefits. In addition to family considerations, these benefits include not having to "dress for success"; a savings in time, since the employee does not have to spend a portion of each workday commuting, as well as increased flexibility and control when it comes to the use of time; and access to employment for those who are homebound because of a disability or some other factor.

Increasingly, in urban areas, the expense of housing and commuting are also major employee considerations. Studies by Runzheimer International, a consulting organization specializing in relocation costs, have indicated that the housing and commuting costs in and around New York City are getting to the point where "[I]t may not pay to be a commuter."[6] Washington, Boston, San Francisco, and Los Angeles also have many of the same cost pressures. To counter these costs, employers often pay higher salaries or specialized "perks" such as commuting subsidies to attract good applicants or encourage current employees to relocate. Employees who work under flexiplace arrangements, on the other hand, can reduce or eliminate commuting costs and live in less-expensive areas, farther from the employer's place of business.

Taken as a whole, these advantages of flexiplace from the employees' perspective make the arrangement a low-cost employee morale booster.

Labor force availability. Finding an adequate supply of job candidates is a problem in some areas, and flexiplace and telecommuting options allow employers to recruit from an expanded, geographically dispersed labor pool. In many areas, a related issue is lack of transit facilities, which makes working at home attractive.

Nature of the work. Flexiplace arrangements can be a more efficient way of performing some types of tasks—for example, data entry or form processing—because the work can be done at odd hours with less distraction than usually occurs in an office setting. This is true with many professional-level jobs as well.

Continuity of services. In some parts of the country, incentives for flexiplace have included the possibility of maintaining services during inclement weather, such as winter blizzards. Under such circumstances, flexiplace employees have an edge on those who must commute, in terms of both getting to the job and productivity on the job.

Extended coverage. Expanding the hours of service is also possible with flexiplace. This is particularly helpful if the organization has service operations that cover several time zones or wants to conduct an activity or offer a service that does not need to be office-based (for example, catalog shopping) during a larger portion of the workday.

Employing the hard-to-employ. Some recent applications of flexiplace or telecommuting arrangements have been aimed at bringing employment opportunities to workers with disabilities, ghetto residents, and the elderly. In 1985, a cooperative effort between Pacific Bell, the Los Angeles Urban League Training Center, Project Build, Business Services Etc., Inc., the Improvement Association of the 8th District, and the L. A. Minority Business Development Center began providing jobs for people previously considered unemployable in the Watts area of Los Angeles. The project, called JobLink Watts, pioneered the use of telecommunications to bring job opportunities from downtown Los Angeles to work centers in Watts. It trains unskilled residents and encourages the development of black-owned businesses. In addition to gaining recognition for creative, socially responsible program development, Pacific Bell has been able to demonstrate new, economical applications of its products through the project.

Overseas, 20 Japanese companies plan to sponsor a nationwide telecommuting pilot project. A major objective is to "seek out ways to ease working conditions and increase productivity of older employees" and to explore the possibility of "setting up communications bases in rural areas for use by several people."[7]

Pros and Cons of Flexiplace

The advantages and disadvantages of flexiplace involve such issues as costs versus savings, the impact of this arrangement on productivity, how to supervise and evaluate off-site workers, the need to maintain adequate contact with them, security of proprietary information, and union attitudes.

Cost considerations. Cost efficiency has been a major factor in employer receptivity to telecommuting and flexiplace arrangements. At the top of the list of incentives has been a desire to cut the rising cost of office space and overhead. In addition to rent, this includes the cost of insurance, parking, and security. Flexiplace options do reduce this type of expense, even when satellite offices are added, since these may be located in outlying areas where space is cheaper.

As noted earlier, employees like the idea of voluntary flexiplace arrangements. When this option is available, the organization will find that it can recruit from an expanded labor pool, which will include individuals who for one reason or another could not accept an on-site position, and that it can more effectively retain its existing employees, some of whom might leave the company if an off-site opportunity were not offered. By minimizing turnover, the organization saves on new-hire costs. Some companies have even been able to reduce or eliminate relocation costs by allowing employees to telecommute or work off-site when the office moves or when the employees are offered a transfer to another company location and prefer not to move.

On the expense side are the costs of purchasing and maintaining equipment for employees who are working off-site. Providing insurance for the equipment and concerns about liability and job-related employee injuries have been deterrents to the use of flexiplace arrangements in some cases. However, employers using telecommuters seem to feel that these costs are offset by the savings on space and overhead and the gains in productivity (discussed below).

Productivity. Employers that have evaluated their off-site projects report productivity gains of from 15 percent to 20 percent. Some show even higher gains, and the worst case seems to be to break even. These employers credit such gains to employees' having fewer distractions, being able to work at personal "peak" times, experiencing increased motivation because they have the desired flexibility, and working on a more continuous basis because meetings and other such duties that tend to interrupt the normal flow of work are scheduled together.[8] The possibility of extending coverage or service hours is another factor that can increase productivity.

The scheduling flexibility made possible by employee use of personal computers in their homes can also boost productivity. After-hours work on home-based personal computers is growing and is more common than full-time telecommuting in most organizations. According to a survey of 48 companies in the Pittsburgh area conducted by Professor Paul Goodman, of Carnegie-Mellon University, the practice nets companies extra time from workers. It also allows employees greater flexibility in allocating their time and enables them to work when creative insights strike.[9] For telecommuting employees who are working with data supplied by a central computer, the ability to access the information source during less-busy time periods can speed the response rate considerably.

Supervision and evaluation. A major concern for some employers has been supervising and evaluating off-site employees. Many worry about how to tell whether an employee is working when he or she is off-site and out of sight. Managing by objectives rather than by monitoring is necessary, and this requires a change in attitude and style for many managers and supervisors. The temptation for some supervisors of employees working at home with electronic equipment is to track their output by electronic monitoring. This can result in considerable stress for the employees and has become an increasingly controversial issue as more and more workers become telecommuters.

When it comes to evaluating an off-site employee's work, most employers recommend that two of the primary criteria be (1) quality of work and (2) completion of projects. The perception that it is hard to measure these factors for telecommuters represents a significant attitudinal barrier on the part of many managers with respect to off-site, computer-assisted options. However, managers in well-designed telecommuting programs have been able to evaluate performance quite adequately.

Maintaining contact with off-site employees. Retaining the connectedness of off-site workers and minimizing their sense of isolation is another issue that must be addressed. Even employees who are temperamentally suited for working on their own at home sometimes feel lonely and out of the mainstream. This problem can be addressed by scheduling regular office contact, either at the main plant or at satellite offices, and by making good use of communications vehicles such as the telephone or electronic mail.

Regular contact is important, too, in terms of retaining employee loyalty and commitment. Concerns about an erosion in employees' sense of being part of an organization have kept some employers from developing flexiplace options. However, the opposite effect seems to be true, with most companies reporting enhanced commitment as a result of their having accommodated employees' needs for flexibility, particularly when contact with the office is maintained, at least on a minimal level.

Security. Many data-processing managers worry about telecommuting employees' having unsupervised access to company data. Although there is obviously some basis for concern about compromising proprietary information and the possibility does exist, to date actual incidents have not been reported. Furthermore, since regular employees are generally able to take home software for use in their personal computers, employers should not regard the security issue as being applicable only to those employees who do most of their work off-site.

Union attitudes. Labor representatives have expressed a variety of opinions regarding flexiplace and telecommuting but tend to support such arrangements when they are offered to regular employees on a voluntary basis. Their concerns relate to changing an employee's status from regular to "independent contractor" as a condition of working from the home. (See Chapter 10, Contingent Employment.) The AFL-CIO officially opposes telecommuting on the grounds that when workers are based at home, it is difficult or impossible to enforce labor standards designed to protect them.

Should Your Organization Try Flexiplace?

In this section, you will be considering the use of flexiplace from the perspective of your own organization. Could some of the problems it faces be effectively addressed through the introduction of off-site options?

Start by referring to the accompanying group of profiles entitled Organizational Experience With Flexiplace. In it are described the flexiplace programs offered by three companies. As you read about why these programs were started, how they were implemented, and what effect they have had, be thinking in terms of the issues and strategies discussed there that might be relevant to your company's situation.

Table 9–1 is a questionnaire that raises concerns of interest to employers that could benefit from trying flexiplace. If, in reviewing the questions, you find yourself repeatedly agreeing that your organization does indeed face these conditions, then off-site arrangements might be worth a try. Figure 9–1 is a worksheet that can be used to examine flexiplace in greater detail, including the specific reasons why this option seems called for and its potential pluses and minuses.

Introducing Flexiplace

The process of introducing a program of flexiplace options starts with gaining broad-based support for this move. The program's administrative staff is then appointed, and the entire array of program design issues are addressed. The organization not only develops resource materials for both managers and employees who will be involved in the flexiplace program but also trains them in order to minimize the problems that can be associated with this arrangement and maximize its benefits. After a period of time, the program's progress is assessed, and its provisions are modified as necessary. We'll take a closer look at these steps in the following subsections.

(Text continues on page 360.)

ORGANIZATIONAL EXPERIENCE WITH FLEXIPLACE

Pacific Bell

Description: Pacific Bell, a telecommunications company, is part of the Pacific Telesis Group, which is based in San Francisco. Through its operating companies, it provides telecommunications services to 22 million people in California and Nevada.

Reason for Using Flexiplace: The "Telecommuting Project," which was begun in 1985, had two objectives: (1) to assist others in developing telecommuting programs that more effectively utilize the capacity of the public network and (2) to accommodate employees' needs for alternative work arrangements.

Implementation Process: All management employees are eligible to participate in the program on a volunteer basis, with their supervisor's concurrence.

Prospective telecommuters and their supervising manager complete a questionnaire covering such considerations as addressing the problem that prompted the telecommuting applicaton (for example, productivity or floor-space costs); identifying quantifiable business benefits/results from the off-site arrangement and determining how these will be measured; and stating the telecommuter's proposed schedule, physical work-space needs, and job responsibilities.

The prospective telecommuter and his or her manager attend a half-day orientation session at which they review task-implementation issues and a written work agreement prepared by the company's legal department.

Participants working at home get a business line specifically for telecommuting. All of their work-related telephone expenses, including toll charges, are paid for by Pacific Bell.

Impact to Date: From 500 to 1,000 employees are involved in remote work for the company, either at home, in neighborhood work centers, or at satellite offices. Pacific Bell reports that the cost of setting up and running its program has been negligible and has been outweighed by the benefits. The company cites a 20 percent increase in productivity among the telecommuters, reduced absenteeism, improved recruiting, reduced floor-space cost, and better managers. It has also, on occasion, saved on relocation costs.

SOURCE: Lynda Anapol and Leslie Crawford, "Telecommuting and Pacific Bell," *Work Times* (San Francisco: New Ways to Work, Spring 1986): 4.

J. C. Penney

Description: J. C. Penney is a national retail store chain headquartered in Dallas. Its large catalog telemarketing division employs approximately 10,000 people.

Reason for Using Flexiplace: Having a trained group of customer service representatives on-line at home enables J. C. Penney to deal with sudden "spikes" in its catalog business. The company now has a national network operations center in Brookfield, Wisconsin, so that if, for example, Richmond receives more calls than it can handle, the overflow can be transferred to Pittsburgh.

Using telecommuters also allows the company to add to its base of "associates," as J. C. Penney refers to its customer service representatives. Expanding this employee group is important, since it tends to have a high rate of turnover.

From the telecommuter's point of view, working at home can offer such advantages as saving on the cost of a second car or, for disabled individuals, the opportunity to hold down a job at all.

Implementation Process: Only employees who have already worked in a J. C. Penney catalog center for a year are entitled to convert to working on an at-home basis. The pay and benefits for off-site employees are the same as for those who work on the company's premises. In considering applications to work off-site, management looks for people who don't need a lot of supervision and are self-motivated. The key to the program's success is picking the right participants.

Before the flexiplace agreement is finalized, a management representative visits the employee's residence to ensure that adequate space (about 45 square feet) is available and that it has proper lighting and is off the major traffic pattern of the home. If the work site is acceptable, the company supplies the computer equipment and communicates daily with the telecommuter on his or her home screen.

Impact to Date: The program, instituted in 1981, has been quite successful from both the employer's and the employees' points of view. The goal is to expand the program so that there will be 24 to 48 telecommuters in each of J. C. Penney's 14 catalog centers.

SOURCE: Telephone conversation with J. C. Penney's planning and programs manager for telemarketing (June 1988).

Control Data Corporation

Description: Control Data Corporation is a multinational electronics company headquartered in Minneapolis with 32,000 employees.

Reason for Using Flexiplace: The program was originally called "Homework" and had the objective of providing people with long-term disabilities the opportunity to continue working for Control Data Corporation at home. It has since been renamed the "Alternate Work Site" program and expanded to encompass a variety of needs for a flexiplace option, not just on the part of disabled employees but on the part of any employees who prefer at-home work. Some of the employees involved in the program work at home only periodically.

Implementation Process: The "Homework" program, which was operational for two years beginning in 1978, was implemented to create a particular product. Since then, the original participants, who were disabled employees, have been integrated into the regular "Alternate Work Site" program. A former salesman is now working in telemarketing; a secretary is now working in computer programming. Some of the "Alternate Work Site" employees are at very remote locations—for example, at terminals in a mountain cabin in Oregon or in rural North Carolina. For one disabled employee in the backcountry of Missouri, the company had to run in special phone lines because all the existing ones were party lines. Using the Control Data Institute's curriculum and program, two instructors who are inmates have been teaching courses from inside Stillwater State Prison just east of St. Paul.

Impact to Date: The program has worked well, with the productivity of the "Homework" employees reported to be comparatively higher than that of their on-site counterparts.

Through the "Homework" program, some disabled people were helped to regain their full capacities. One woman who had had a stroke and another woman suffering from severe arthritis found that simply participating in productive activity led to an improvement in their health.

Some managers, particularly those who are used to managing persons rather than managing work, have difficulty supervising off-site employees.

SOURCE: Telephone conversation with the consultant, health services, Control Data Corporation (June 1988).

Gain Support for the Program

Management and union concerns about flexiplace and/or telecommuting must be addressed in order to gain support for this kind of option. One way to do this is to include on the project-planning team representatives from all areas of the organization that will be affected.

If computer or terminal use is to be a significant component of the program, then a team should also be formed to integrate the final stages of the technical implementation with the management and human resources functions.

Set Up the Program's Administration

The program's scope and its technical ramifications will determine the type and extent of the administrative staff that will be needed. At a minimum, a project administrator should be appointed. Maximum needs may extend to the appointment of a companywide project team, supported by subgroups for technical implementation and human resources implementation.

Design the Program

Before decisions can be made regarding policy and process, the primary intent and business objectives of the program must be defined and articulated. Is this going to be a telecommuting program that will focus on tasks, space configuration, and cost factors? A companywide human resources management program that will respond to employees' needs while giving the organization new options as well? A combination of the two?

Whatever the decisions regarding the program's objectives, once

Table 9-1. Flexiplace questionnaire.

Would Flexiplace Benefit Your Organization?

	Yes	No
Is the amount or cost of office space of concern in your company?		
Can you identify specific types of jobs that could be performed more efficiently off-site than on-site?		
Have some of your organization's employees requested more flexible schedules because of family responsibilities or other needs?		
Are your operations in the process of becoming decentralized?		
If decentralization is planned or underway, might some valued employees leave the company rather than relocate?		
Is the community you operate in concerned about the negative impact of heavy rush-hour traffic?		
Does your firm have a data processing backlog?		
Does your organization have trouble attracting qualified job applicants?		

those decisions are made, the following issues, which are common to any kind of off-site arrangements, must be addressed.

Scope. A fundamental question is that of the program's initial size. Does a pilot project make sense as a way to test the new program and its processes? If not, will the option be offered companywide or restricted to particular job classifications or departments? Will certain jobs be excluded?

Eligibility. Related to the question of scope is that of eligibility. Two factors should be considered when establishing policy in this area: (1) who is able to work effectively in an off-site environment and (2) the employee's relationship to the company. The consensus of most employers that offer flexiplace options is that the arrangement should be restricted to current employees who are familiar with the company's culture and committed to its goals rather than new hires.

Experience also suggests that voluntary in-house applicants should be carefully screened. Not everyone is able to work off-site. Some people can't deal with the distractions, while others are overwhelmed by the isolation. Workaholics who can't set limits tend to burn out, and "fast-trackers" worry about their careers' plateauing if they are not visible in the office. Consequently, in addition to task-related functions, the psychological makeup of the employee should be considered—including such factors as the need for self-discipline

Figure 9-1. Flexiplace worksheet.

Assessing the Need for Flexiplace

List the main reasons why you are considering flexiplace:

1. _____

   _____

   _____

2. _____

   _____

   _____

3. _____

   _____

   _____

4. _____

   _____

   _____

List what you see as the advantages and disadvantages of flexiplace:

Pros: _____

_____

_____

_____

Cons: _____

---

and motivation and the ability to work on one's own, without regular supervision or the social support of co-workers.

Legal and tax considerations. The company's tax experts, accounting advisers, and legal counsel should be consulted regarding any potential problems with zoning regulations covering at-home work, insurance considerations, and questions about employee status. The following are some tips for avoiding problems in the area of liability when an organization sets up a flexiplace program:

- If work is to be performed at home, the work area should be kept as separate as possible from the rest of the home.
- The best defense against liability problems is good education and preventive steps to identify and reduce risks.
- The company should get the facts on its state's worker's compensation statutes and look for remote-work precedents.
- A "telecommuter's agreement" should be used to spell out rights and responsibilities.
- The company should make sure that any equipment provided for the remote site is safe and working well.[10]

Compensation and benefits. The use of off-site employees involves some special considerations in the area of compensation and benefits. These are some of the issues to which the organization should be sensitive:

- Existing options regarding types of employment status, pay levels, and benefits coverage should be carefully examined to make sure telecommuters are treated fairly and equitably.
- The company should avoid taking a short-term view on salary and benefits cost control, since it may lose in the long run if it skimps in these areas.
- Creative ways should be sought to apply pay-for-performance approaches to telecommuters.
- If the company has a flexible benefits or "cafeteria compensation" plan, an attempt should be made to use it to the telecommuters' advantage or, if need be, change it to their advantage.[11]

Off-site scheduling. Regular employees who work part of the time off-site may be employed on either a full- or a part-time basis. It is important, however, that they not be scheduled to work 100 percent of their hours off-site. Some regularly scheduled time should be required in either the main office or a satellite office. Experts generally recommend that a minimum of 20 percent of employees' regularly scheduled time be on-site. It is this mandatory contact that ensures the employees' continued identification with the company's culture and community and with its overall objectives.

Establishing common-space work areas or satellite or neighborhood work centers. A variety of techniques have been developed in order to ensure that telecommuters and other off-site employees have some office "territory" to come to. Some companies provide "common-space work areas." When off-site employees return to the office, they don't have their own desk, but they do have shared desks and space in which to work among their office-based co-workers and with their home-based colleagues.

Using satellite offices, where off-site employees can work part of the time, is another way in which companies can combat the isolation factor associated with flexiplace. If the company's own program is not large enough to warrant that approach, neighborhood work centers, shared by several organizations, have begun to emerge to address the need for telecommuters' supply and support services. Both types of facility are generally less expensive than space at the main plant. Satellite offices or neighborhood work centers should be placed to minimize the need for travel, while accommodating the need that many off-site workers have for occasional access to an office environment.

Length of commitment and reversibility. Rather than leave a flexiplace arrangement open-ended, some employers ask for a specific time commitment—for example, six months or a year—after which the initial provisions of the flexiplace agreement are reviewed and reaffirmed or renegotiated. If telecommuting is involved, with a commitment in equipment from the employer, this ensures that the employee will "give it a good try." As we've noted, flexiplace is not for everyone. When valued employees find that they are unable, for whatever reason, to continue the arrangement, a process should exist for them to return to the on-site work environment.

Application process. The kind of application process that a company establishes for employees interested in a flexiplace option will depend on who is eligible to participate in this type of arrangement and what the primary objective of the program is. If the option is to be generally available within certain parameters, then a request to the immediate supervisor may be the most appropriate kind of application. In this case, the organization should develop guidelines for supervisors, similar to those presented in the chapter on job sharing, detailing how to respond to requests for off-site work. If the program is to be primarily a technically oriented telecommuting option, then a more generalized application process will be needed. For example, the Travelers Insurance Company posts its telecommuting openings along with its other job listings.

Table 9–2 is a checklist that summarizes the major program design issues we have covered in this subsection. You can use it as a handy review of these issues and to record your progress in dealing with them.

Develop Resource Materials

As is the case with most of the new employment alternatives, if optimum benefits for individual employees as well as for the organization are to be achieved, information resources must be developed for both employees and managers. Furthermore, these resource materials should be used in conjunction with a training program for employees and managers.

Resource materials for employees. Employees will be interested in resource materials that address such issues as the following:

Table 9-2. Program design checklist: flexiplace.

Key Design Issues	Notes
☐ Intent and business objectives	
☐ Scope	
☐ Eligibility	
☐ Legal and tax considerations	
☐ Compensation and benefits	
☐ Off-site scheduling	
☐ Establishing common-space work areas or satellite or neighborhood work centers	
☐ Length of commitment and reversibility	
☐ Application process	

■ Loss of living space.
■ Setting up a home office.
■ Combatting isolation.
■ Support services (machine repair, photocopying, and so on).
■ Personal financial ramifications, such as increased home costs (electricity), versus savings (commuting lunch, clothing) and tax implications, if any.
■ Dealing with distractions at home.
■ The importance of setting objectives and meeting deadlines.

Some companies, such as the Travelers Insurance Company, have developed addendums to their corporate employee handbook for telecommuters that reinforce their status as "Travelers employees first and telecommuters second."

Resources for managers. Managers will be interested in resource materials that address such issues as performance tracking; helping off-site employees set goals and timetables; and establishing and maintaining appropriate levels of communication, with regular times to review goals and progress, while recognizing that too much communication interferes with work time.

Policy guidelines relating to electronic monitoring should be developed for supervisors. Both the Computer and Business Equipment Manufacturers Association (CBEMA) and 9 to 5, an affiliate of SEIU, have issued guidelines expressing different perspectives on the issue, but with overlapping concerns.

CBEMA suggests that:

- Employees should know how, why, and when their work is being monitored.
- They should have access to their records.
- They should be measured only on organizational goals.
- Measurement statistics should be used for problem spotting and early action.
- Individual differences should be acknowledged, and workers should be able to regulate their work as much as possible.
- Rewards should be appropriate.
- Production standards should not be raised repeatedly.[12]

SEIU and 9 to 5 recommend safeguards relating to the following issues:

- *Right to know*. Ban software programs with subliminal messages. Notify workers when monitoring occurs. Give workers complete access to their files and tell them how data is collected, used, and interpreted.
- *Right to due process*. Set up grievance procedures for appeal of unfair or incorrect data and adjust pay accordingly.
- *Employee input*. Set standards or quotas with employee input so that they reflect system problems, quality of service, and workload variability.
- *Meaningful standards*. Collect productivity statistics by work group, not individual worker. Prohibit speedups. Bar use of monitoring results for discipline. Collect only data that is relevant to the work performed. Average worker performance by the month, not the week or day. Sample periodically rather than continuously. Make quantitative measures only one part of evaluations.[13]

Training. In the case of flexiplace and telecommuting options, printed resource materials are not enough. Telecommuting experts consider training—for telecommuters and other flexiplace employees as well as for their managers—to be critical to the program's success. Training topics for managers might include how to screen employees to determine who can successfully work off-site, how to manage at a distance by controlling results rather than activity levels, how to take advantage of telecommuting's flexibility and redesign schedules to increase efficiency, and how to avoid or minimize co-worker backlash.

In their book *Telecommuting*, Gil Gordon and Marcia Kelly present the following guidelines for manager training:

- Recognize and acknowledge the natural resistance of many managers to managing from a distance. It's an understandable reaction, but not a legitimate obstacle.
- Stress the difference between *close* supervision and *good* supervision.
- Stess the difference between *observing activity* and *managing for results*.
- Before managers of telecommuters can learn the specific skills they'll need, help them assess and discuss their general attitudes about remote supervision.[14]

Gordon and Kelly also indicate that managers who will be supervising off-site employees will need basic or refresher training in the following areas and that this training should focus on those aspects of these skills that are peculiar to remote supervision:

- Planning the work and breaking it into tasks.
- Delegating specific tasks to subordinates.
- Setting timetables for interim progress checks.
- Assessing progress according to time and quality criteria.
- Giving effective performance feedback on positive and negative points.[15]

Announce the Program

As with other alternative arrangements, it is important to inform your firm's employees about the flexiplace program. Whether or not they will be personally affected, either now or in the future, they can take pride in the fact that their organization is moving in new, innovative directions.

Promote the Program

As we've already noted, not everyone is able to work successfully off-site, at home. Careful screening of voluntary applicants must take place. Promotion efforts should reflect this fact. If a pilot project will be used initially, internal publicity about its progress can serve as a means of promoting awareness of the arrangement and of the constraints related to its availability.

Evaluate the Program

As is the case with the other alternative arrangements we've discussed, your flexiplace program should be evaluated after it has been in operation for a number of months to determine whether or not it is meeting its objectives and to identify and correct any problem areas. The scope and intent of the program will determine how extensive an evaluation you should undertake.

Fine-Tune the Program

After evaluation, the program should be modified as necessary to correct any problems that have been identified. For example:

Problem	*Solution*
Supervisors complain that they feel uncomfortable with employees working off-site.	Hold meetings for supervisory personnel at which they can voice their concerns. Use a facilitator who can provide information about how these problems have been handled in other firms.
Telecommuting employees complain of feeling isolated and separated from their co-workers.	Check to be certain that regular workplace contact is being maintained. Identify on-site events (social, training, and so on) that telecommuters can be encouraged to attend.
Exit interviews indicate that many employees do not know that flexiplace might have been an option for them.	Use employee communication channels to promote wider awareness of the program.

Summary

Flexiplace is an option in which regular employees work primarily off-site, either at home or from a satellite office. The practice may or may not require a computer terminal. Two factors have prompted the growing use of this arrangement: (1) the same social, demographic, and attitudinal changes that have increased the overall need for workplace flexibility and (2) technological developments in the computer field that have facilitated off-site work.

Estimates vary with respect to how widespread flexiplace is, since some reports that do include regular employees working mainly off-site lump these workers in with home-based entrepreneurs and with regular employees who work at home only on an occasional basis, and other reports focus just on off-site work that involves computer use (telecommuting). The types of work that lend themselves to being performed away from the employer's principal place of business include work that already is heavily computer-dependent, batch work, and work that must be done at odd hours.

An employer usually offers flexiplace options in order to accommodate employees' needs, save on the high cost of office space, improve employee retention and broaden the labor pool from which the company is able to recruit, ensure continuity of services, extend coverage, and provide employment opportunities for individuals such as the handicapped who might otherwise be difficult to employ. In some cases, off-site options are also offered to enhance the performance of certain types of work that are best done at unusual hours, spontaneously (when insight occurs), or without the distractions common in an office setting.

When an employer weighs the advantages and disadvantages of flexiplace, the following factors figure importantly in the decision: Flexiplace arrangements, as noted above, enable the organization to cut its expenditures for office space and sometimes for relocation, although the organization does incur the cost of purchasing, maintaining, and insuring equipment for off-site workers and must address such concerns as liability and job-related employee accidents. The employer that offers flexiplace options will normally see significant productivity gains from these workers. Supervising employees working under flexiplace arrangements does require a change in style and attitude that can at first be difficult for those managers and supervisors who are more accustomed to managing by assessing the employee's visible level of activity than to managing by assessing actual results.

Also among the pluses and minuses of off-site work are such considerations as the fact that some system must be established to ensure that the organization maintains regular contact with its off-premises workers, both to combat a potential sense of isolation and to foster loyalty and commitment to the organization. Compromising the security of proprietary information has thus far not proved to be a problem when employees are allowed to work at a distance from the main plant or office. Unions have mixed feelings about flexiplace, with some expressing concerns about its impact on the status of participating employees and others pointing out that it is difficult to enforce provisions designed to protect workers when those workers are primarily based at some location other than the employer's main premises.

When it introduces flexiplace arrangements, the organization will focus at the outset on addressing management and union concerns about the practice and on making sure that the technical aspects of the implementation process (issues associated with computer use) are well-thought-out. The program design phase will involve detailed planning around a variety of issues in order to maximize the benefits of off-site arrangements both to the employees and to the organization. Resource materials are directed at addressing the concerns that potential program participants and their supervisors will have about the impact of working outside of the employer's main premises and should be backed by a training program designed to make sure that employees can effectively work off-site and that supervisors can effectively evaluate output without the need to personally monitor input.

A decision to offer a flexiplace option would be popular with your employees and could lead to a drop in office-space costs and improvements in such areas as productivity, recruitment (which, in turn, can result in an improvement in the affirmative action profile), employee retention, and coverage, while insulating the organization from certain types of interruptions to service. So if there are jobs in your company that would lend themselves to being performed on a flexiplace basis or valued employees you might lose without such an option, this type of arrangement can be an attractive alternative to traditional 100 percent on-site work patterns.

CHAPTER 10

Contingent Employment

T he term *contingent employment* was coined in the mid-1980s to describe the growing trend toward using more nonregular part-time, temporary, and independently contracted workers. It refers primarily to the type of relationship between employer and employee rather than to the type of task performed. Full- and part-time temporary workers, consultants, independent contractors, those hired on a special project basis, and others fall into the category of contingent employee. "Uncertain of occurrence" is the way the dictionary defines *contingent,* and from the employee's perspective, this is the crux of the different between regular and contingent employment.

Origins of the Growth in Contingent Employment

The increasing interest in the use of contingent hires represents a radical departure from traditional concepts of a committed, long-term, reciprocally responsible employer/employee relationship. In part, it is an outgrowth of both employer and employee interest in greater work-time flexibility, with employees wanting more control over their time and work and employers seeking new ways to manage economic upturns and downturns.

This management strategy began to gain acceptance after the 1982 recession, partly as a reaction to the painful, widespread downsizing that occurred then. Many companies that had long-standing no-layoff polices and a strong commitment to the employment security of their workers were forced into layoffs. Since a prime objective of contingent employment is to limit a company's use of "regular" employees and deal with changing work loads by expanding the use of "peripheral" workers, contingent employment is viewed by some employers as offering relief from the pain of layoffs. It is still too soon, however, to know what its true impact will be in either this area or others.

How does this strategy work? Contingent employment is usually referred to as involving a core/ring configuration. The "core" employees are defined as the organization's regular workers. They continue to benefit from the company's traditional kinds of commitments regarding training and career development and to receive a wide range of fringe benefits. Their work is supported, and supplemented as necessary, by groups that make up the peripheral, or contingent, segment of the employer's labor force—the outer "rings." These latter workers are hired on a nonregular part-time, temporary, or contractual basis. They are often paid on a different scale than regular employees doing the same work and do not receive fringe benefits or career-oriented training from the contracting employer.

American managers have been quite receptive to this approach, since they see it as a way to control labor costs, fine-tune scheduling in some areas, and limit the possibility of extensive layoffs in the future.

Employer interest in wider use of contingent workers has coincided with some employees' desire for more flexibility and more control over their own time than they have had in traditional work settings. Some like variety in their jobs and find it by working through temporary agencies; some are independent or entrepreneurial and leave the confines of a company to start their own business; others, such as working parents, have responsibilities outside of the workplace and regard traditional schedules as too restrictive. Many of these individuals are currently finding themselves in the growing group of contingent employees.

The so-called outer rings of contingent workers fall into three categories: (1) temporary employees, (2) independent contractors, and (3) leased staff.

Temporary Employees

Temporary workers are those hired on a full- or part-time basis, either through a "temp" agency or directly by the employer.

The last two decades have seen a dramatic increase in the use of temporary workers. A 1986 Bureau of National Affairs survey indicates that the use of temporary employees that year was 400 percent higher than in 1970.[1] The increased demand for the services of temporary agencies has raised the issue of definitions. Is the term *employer* applicable to the leasing organization or to the work site? Is the term *temporary* applicable to an employee who has worked at a particular organization for a year or more?

This rise in the use of temporary workers has created changes within the temp industry as well. In order to retain skilled, reliable employees, some temp agencies have begun to offer their workers a growing array of fringe benefits, often including group health insurance. Others have specialized in professional categories of temporary employee, such as lawyers and even doctors.

As organizations have begun to think of alternative schedules as a management tool, more have begun to hire temporary employees directly. Some have created internally administered temp pools, whose members are often retirees (from the hiring company or from other companies) or former employees of the organization who left in order to care for family members. The "rehirees" bring a knowledge of company culture and procedures that outside temporaries lack. From a scheduling perspective, having a pool of on-call, temporary workers who have had company-specific training and are attuned to the organization's needs provides a valuable resource for managers faced with sporadic or seasonal staffing requirements.

As we noted in Chapter 3, employers such as Bankers Life and Casualty, Continental Bank, The Travelers Corporation, Corning Glass, and Atlantic Richfield have established pools of their own retirees that they can call on to provide peak-period coverage, serve as substitutes for vacationing or sick workers, or provide continuity in job classifications with high turnover or absenteeism. These programs are very popular with retirees, many of whom find it both financially and emotionally rewarding to be able to continue to use their skills in a known, comfortable environment. For some workers, the opportunity for a temporary job serves as a reentry period; for others, it is a way to remain partially employed after retirement. Some like the variety of experience that comes from being assigned to work in different companies or use the temporary-agency experience as a way to try out employers—sort of a probationary period in reverse. A negative aspect of the expanded use of temporary employees is the growing number of involuntary temps—workers who can find no regular employment. It is this segment of the contingent work force that appears to be growing fastest.

Independent Contractors

The catchall, somewhat gray-area term *independent contractor* refers to an individual not in the direct employ of the company to whom tasks are "contracted out." These tasks may involve such responsibilities as cleaning, clerical work, security, or even production activities. Increasingly, the term refers to an individual worker who is considered by the employer to be self-employed. This type of worker may be engaged in a wide variety of tasks. In many organizations, certain kinds of clerical jobs, particularly those related to data processing and done by telecommuting, are performed by employees who are classified as independent contractors. Growing numbers of professionals—lawyers, systems analysts, marketing consultants, computer programmers, public relations experts, and other white-collar employees—are also working this way. Like some temporary-agency workers, many enjoy the flexibility and control that come with working on their own terms. Others find that this is one way that they can remain employed in professional areas that have been downsized by corporate management.

Leased Staff

The difference between leased staff and staff hired through a temporary agency is that with a staff-leasing arrangement, an entire section of the company, rather than a few individual workers, is employed by the leasing agency. The staff of the employing company is often fired and then hired as a group by the leasing agency, which then contracts their services back to the original employer.

Staff leasing came into vogue in the mid-1970s as a way for smaller offices, such as doctors' and dentists', to avoid the time and expense of personnel administration and fringe benefits, particularly pensions. The Tax Reform Act of 1986 removed some of the incentives that had given rise to the leased-staff industry, but although a setback period was feared, the industry does not appear to have suffered.

To date, use of staff leasing is primarily confined to small and medium-size businesses, which find that the leasing agencies provide personnel at a cost of only 20 to 35 percent above gross payroll. The fringe benefits that the leasing agencies offer employees are usually greater than the small companies themselves could provide. That plus the fact that the paperwork and other functions of a personnel department are handled by the leasing agency make staff leasing attractive to many small businesses. The first organization of significant size to enter into a whole-staff leasing arrangement was Hospital

Corporation of America in January 1987.[2] Proponents claim that leasing is the wave of the future, but even some industry officials believe that it is primarily appropriate for companies with fewer than 150 employees.

Who Uses Contingent Employees?

In 1987, The Conference Board estimated that the number of contingent workers had grown 20 percent, to 34.3 million people, since the beginning of the decade. (This figure, which represents nearly one third of the work force, included all of those individuals who are self-employed and working from the home.)[3] A 1988 Administrative Management Society survey of 560 managers indicated that 39 percent of the respondents had used temporary employees more frequently in the past 12 months.[4] Figure 10–1 shows the Administrative Management Society's findings on the percentage of employers using temporary workers in each of the major regions of the United States in 1987. In that year, the number of leased employees was estimated at between 50,000 and 500,000, supplied by 353 organizations.[5] In terms of future use, some surveys project the growth of temporary and contract help at 10 to 17.7 percent a year through 1990.[6]

Figure 10-1. Use of temp help—by region.

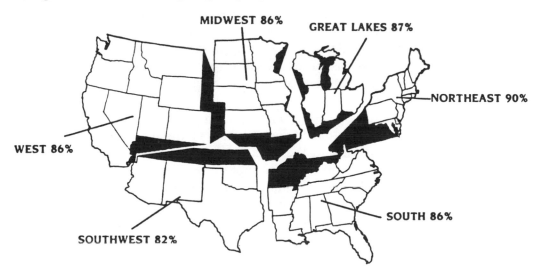

SOURCE: *1987 AMS Contract Labor Survey* (Trevose, Pa.: Administrative Management Society, 1987), 7.

Many experts see these figures as signaling a basic restructuring of the way in which employers hire, train, and use their labor force.

When Is Contingent Employment Most Appropriate?

An appropriate use of contingent employees is to complement and extend the organization's existing flexible response modes. A truly flexible company must have, at its core, a trained, committed regular work force willing to work flexibly together to achieve organizational objectives. Contingent employees can enhance the activities of such a work force if they are compensated and used appropriately and not pitted against a small, overworked, inflexible core.

Short-term needs, such as alleviating an overload of work, completing a rush order, or developing a product prototype, are sometimes met with contingent employees when there are not enough regular employees to handle the task. Well-defined projects that are of a short-term nature or require special skills are often appropriate to contingent hires as well.

Pros and Cons of Contingent Employment

The concept of restructuring an organization to reduce or limit the number of regular, or core, employees and increase the use of peripheral part-time, temporary, and contractual employees is too new for anyone to have any sense of its long-term impact on an organization. Many of the positive and negative effects can only be conjectured.

Some indicators have begun to emerge, however, and show that the areas to be scrutinized include the flexibility that contingent employment can bring to the organization; barriers to the practice that may be found in existing policy; the impact of contingent employment on labor costs, employee commitment, productivity and quality of work and service, and availability of flexible and reduced work-time schedules for regular employees; confidentiality of proprietary information; union attitudes toward this mode of work; and the ramifications, both for the organization and for society, of creating separate labor force tiers.

Flexibility. From an employer's perspective, the purpose of using a contingent employment configuration is to lower labor costs, stabilize the core of the organization, and increase its potential for a highly flexible response to future changes in labor market conditions. Although in the short run, this arrangement does give the organization rapid access to a quality talent pool, it is still too early to know what long-term effects the core/ring strategy will have on long-term flexibility.

Policy barriers. A problem area for some organizations that try to develop internally administered temporary pools is provisions in the pension program that prohibit the company from making both salary and pension payments to the same employee at the same time. To eliminate this sort of obstacle, The Travelers Corporation recently changed its pension plan to allow 960 hours of work annually instead of 480. (Some companies that do not want to change their policy rehire individual annuitants by defining them as consultants.)

As noted in Chapter 3, the Social Security "earnings test" is often a problem for older members of the temporary pool, since it places unduly restrictive limitations on how much retirees can earn each year before their Social Security benefits become subject to tax. There is growing support, both in the Congress and in the Department of Health and Human Services, to repeal this law. Expectations are that it will be removed as a barrier to the employment of seniors in the near future.

Labor costs. In the short term, use of contingent workers can indeed cut some labor costs—pay, fringe benefits, career-oriented training, overtime, and overhead—very directly. While the use of contingent workers has not yet been studied sufficiently to determine long-term cost implications with certainty, the effects of this arrangement on basic training costs, supervisory time and morale, turnover, and productivity in particular should be carefully monitored.

Many employers no longer feel able to keep sufficient numbers of full-time employees on the payroll to assure that the organization will be able to ride out fluctuations in demand for its products or services. The concept of "lean and mean," which received so much attention in the mid-1980s, was an attempt to match existing labor costs to real demand. But operating with only a minimum number of regular employees actually increases the difficulty that a company will face in dealing with fluctuations. With overtime less attractive both to the employer (because of its cost) and to many employees (because overtime provides an insufficient financial incentive to justify the infringement on their personal time), new means must be found for the organization to react to economic expansion and contraction. And if the organization relies on contingent hires, it may discover that it is training and orienting a constant procession of "new" employees who can never be built into a cohesive team.

Employee commitment. There are growing indications that for many employees—both those who work on a regular basis and those who work on a contingent basis—widespread use of a core/ring configuration can lead to a decrease in job satisfaction. This, in turn, has resulted in reduced commitment to the organization.

Contingent workers themselves, who regard their positions as being at best ephemeral, will tend to have little loyalty to the organization. And for some of their counterparts on the regular work force, equity is an issue. They resent the "peak pay" that some contingent employees earn and in certain cases perceive these employees as landing the more interesting assignments. The increased job responsibilities often associated with downsizing can result in fear of job loss as well as stress and/or burnout—all of which factors also play a significant role in the decline of satisfaction on the part of core employees.

In 1977, the Hay Group surveyed 1,600 U.S. companies and found that 88 percent of the middle managers and 72 percent of the professionals expressed satisfaction with their company.[7] A 1986 survey indicated that only 69 percent of the middle managers and somewhat over 50 percent of the professionals were satisfied.[8] In a 1987 *Wall Street Journal* article, Eli Ginsberg, of Columbia University, was quoted as saying that the erosion of morale and loyalty means that many people will manage their careers *across* companies rather than within a single company.[9] The resulting turnover will be a cost factor in itself that must be dealt with.

The full impact of contingent work on employee commitment is at present an unknown quantity and probably depends on how contingent employment is introduced within the organization and to what extent it is used. In fact, the way in which contingent workers are compensated, used, and integrated with the regular work force is a key to much of the future impact of this strategy, both on individual organizations and eventually on society in general.

In order to avoid excessive turnover and to successfully integrate contingent employees with their firm's regular work force, employers should try to take the following important measures:

1. Make flexible and reduced work-time arrangements available to regular employees. If scheduling flexibility is possible only on a contingent basis, the morale of the firm's core work force will be eroded.

2. Target segments of the labor force that are likely to prefer a contingent status. These might include students, individuals with disabilities, retirees, or workers who have temporarily left the work force because of family responsibilities.
3. Screen applicants carefully in order to ascertain whether potential employees really prefer less commitment than regular employment demands or whether they actually need full-time regular work and see this as a "foot in the door."
4. Strive for equity. Whether an employer hires directly or through an agency, it is important that fairness be a major concern. Inequality breeds divisiveness, so pay scales and benefits, including health insurance, should closely approximate those of the firm's regular employees.

Productivity and quality of work and service. Related to the issue of declining employee commitment is the question of how this erosion in loyalty will affect productivity and the quality of work and service. This is another effect of the use of contingent employment about which too little is currently known but that could have a far-reaching impact on the all-important bottom line. A union in Louisiana also raised the question of safety, charging that "inexperienced and untrained" subcontractors were working as temps at a plant that produces toxic chemicals. "With contract labor, nobody's around long enough to understand the nature of the job," asserts Tony Mazzocchi of the Labor Institute in New York.[10]

Availability of reduced work-time schedules. A possible secondary effect of the extensive use of a core/ring work force configuration, given employers' long-held negative attitudes about part-time scheduled (discussed at length in Chapter 3), would be to eliminate or greatly reduce the availability of part-time as an option for *regular* employees. If this happens, managers whose employees need reduced schedules will be adversely affected, in terms of both retention of existing employees and recruitment of new employees.

For workers, it may eventually come down to a choice between having the security of working as a "core" employee on a full-time basis or working on a much more tentative basis as a peripheral hire in order to get a part-time schedule.

Confidentiality. The issue of access to proprietary information has also been raised in high-tech companies and other organizations where competition is stiff and it is important to ensure that only employees known to be loyal to the organization have access to highly sensitive information.

Union attitudes. As might be expected, unions are very concerned about the growth of the contingent labor force. A position paper developed by SEIU for a 1987 conference entitled *Solutions for the New Workforce* notes:

> [*T*]he growing contingent workforce is a permanent phenomenon. The increase reflects a shift on the part of U.S. companies towards a human resource strategy that relies on immediate cuts in labor costs, rather than long-run productivity improvements, to restore firm profitability in the face of stiffer competition.[11]

The SEIU paper calls for new solutions, in terms of both legislation to protect the conditions of employment for all workers and workplace initiatives. Some of the latter include:

- Establishing a channel for temporaries and contract workers to become regular employees.
- Imposing restrictions on the use of temporary agencies that charge a penalty fee if the employer hires a temp worker.
- Creating regular part-time and job-sharing options that allow employees to choose reduced work hours with prorated benefits.[12]

The ramifications for the organization of creating separate labor force tiers. There is great likelihood that extensive use of contingent employees will create a labor force with two or more tiers, both within individual companies and externally, in society.

Internally, having employees who work side by side, performing the same tasks but with different conditions of work and pay scales, can have a very negative effect on morale. Companies that emulated the 1983 move by American Airlines, Inc. to a two-tier wage scale discovered considerable deleterious effects on employee morale and commitment. Many initially saved money on direct labor costs, but other problems soon emerged. New workers whose entering pay scale was lower than that of employees who were performing comparable work but who had been hired on a different basis reacted with hostility that in some cases even spilled over into customer relations. This practice also caused turnover to increase dramatically for some organizations and made recruitment more difficult. Although airlines have continued to support the two-tier concept, it has lost adherents in most other fields.[13]

Adoption of a core/ring strategy will indeed bring the organization a number of short-term benefits: The use of contingent workers forces managers to plan their labor allocation more carefully; the company may put less time and effort into hiring contingent employees than it typically expends in hiring regular employees; and the organization's output may increase rapidly thanks to the supplemental workers. The core/ring configuration therefore seems to make business sense, in terms of the organization's competitive posture and its need for profitability and growth. The problems become evident only when employers take a longer-term look at this practice and place it within a broader context.

The ramifications for society of creating separate labor force tiers. Looking beyond the implications for the organization of using a core/ring employment configuration, concerned employers must also consider the long-term impact of this practice externally, where it may have an even wider-ranging effect upon society at large. For in the process of reshaping the corporation, employers may inadvertently be reshaping American life as well.

The "rings" of contingent workers are, by definition, kept separate from the "core," with employees in the peripheral tiers having no formal means of access to the core. Since the rationale for using contingent workers is to lower labor costs, the result may be permanently lower pay scales and loss of fringe benefits as well as loss of access to training and knowledge of the industry for many members of the work force. This may happen even with highly skilled, independently contracted professionals, such as lawyers, engineers, and accountants.

For decades, the prevailing philosophy in most large U.S. companies has been that with brains, hard work, and loyalty, employees in the lower ranks could, in time, rise to the upper echelons of management. If this remains true only for those who are part of the core, then barriers will have been raised that will lead to a less-open, less-flexible, segmented employment system.

The change in management strategy represented by interest in a core/ring configuration could presage the beginning of a division of the American work force into "haves" and "have-nots": workers who have a relatively secure job, fringe benefits, and access to training and advancement opportunities, and those who have no fringe benefits or job security and are paid at a lower scale.

A system that by its nature locks many members of the work force—in this case, primarily women, minorities, and seniors—into a peripheral sphere raises troubling questions of *equity*. It also implies conditions that could pose a serious long-range threat to U.S. productivity and competitiveness. An economy such as that of the United States that thrives on diversity and creativity will not benefit from a segmented system—even though individual companies may find this approach to be cost-effective in the short run.

Employers justify the greater use of nonregular part-time, temporary, and independently contracted workers on the grounds that many individuals want more flexibility and control over their work time than regular, full-time, core-type jobs afford. Although this is true for some workers, for others the contingent status is involuntary and represents a hardship. For their own long-term self-interest, it behooves employers to carefully consider how they can build on the interest of those workers both inside and outside the organization who really want or need the independence that contingent employment may offer. Contingent workers should be hired, on equitable terms, only in cases where it would be inappropriate or impossible to fill the position or handle the situation using regular employees on reduced or flexible schedules.

The bottom line is: Although the use of contingent employees does have an important place in the future of human resources management, extensive use of it represents such a basic change from past policy that it deserves thoughtful strategic planning that emphasizes long-term objectives (both for the organization and for society) rather than immediate short-term goals.

Should Your Organization Use Contingent Employees?

In this section, you will find several tools that you can use to assess the option of contingent employment in order to determine whether it might be a wise move for your company and, if so, what type of contingent workers would be appropriate to the company's needs.

The first such tool is the accompanying group of profiles entitled Organizational Experience With Contingent Employment. In it, you will find descriptions of how two large organizations supplement their regular staff through the use of contingent workers. Do the conditions these organizations face and their reasons for trying contingent employment seem relevant to your own company's circumstances?

The questionnaire shown in Table 10–1 raises a series of issues that are usually troubling organizations that turn to the use of contingent employment. If your questionnaire results indicate that your organization is a candidate for using contingent hires, you can complete the worksheet shown in Figure 10–2 by identifying the specific problems you are trying to address and listing the options for solution, including the use of regular employees and various types of contingent workers.

ORGANIZATIONAL EXPERIENCE WITH CONTINGENT EMPLOYMENT

The Travelers Companies

Description: An insurance and financial services corporation, head-quartered in Hartford, Connecticut, with 10,000 employees in the home office and 34,000 nationwide.

Reason for Using Contingent Employees: In 1979, the corporation made a commitment to work on the issue of aging and identified economic security for the elderly as a primary concern to focus on. The company also recognized that older workers were becoming increasingly important for meeting work force needs.

Implementation Process: When the "Retiree Job Bank" program was launched in 1981, it brought back former Travelers employees to fill temporary and part-time positions. By 1985, the program was such a success and the demand for contingent workers was so great that the "Retiree Job Bank" was expanded to include retirees from other companies.

There are 750 people registered in the "Retiree Job Bank," half of them from Travelers. In any given week, 200–250 of these employees are working, filling about 60 percent of Travelers' temporary work force needs.

Impact to Date: The "Retiree Job Bank" program is cost-effective. Since Travelers hires the workers directly, it avoids temporary-agency fees, saving about $1 million a year. And the participating retirees generally earn higher pay by working directly for Travelers.

In 1985, Travelers held an "unretirement party"—a job fair that brought another 300 people into the "Retiree Job Bank" in one day. Then in September 1987, the company conducted a recruitment campaign, complete with print and radio ads, to attract retirees with keyboard skills. Travelers is now offering computer training to people in the "Retiree Job Bank," because these workers had often retired before many of the most recent technological advancements became widely used in the workplace.

SOURCE: Telephone interview with the administrator of public affairs (June 1988).

Provident Bank (Cincinnati)

Description: Provident Bank (Cincinnati) is a large midwestern financial institution.

Reason for Using Contingent Employees: The bank decided to use contingent workers during peak-time periods as a way to better match the size of its work force with the demands of its work load. This is done by assigning special part-time staff to periods of high-volume demand for services and offering premium pay in order to attract and retain them.

Implementation Process   The bank's first step was to determine the shape of the work flow—to identify the peaks and valleys of demand. A matrix was then established to set hourly wages for peak-timers. The lowest peak-time wage, which is paid to the peak-timers working the most hours per week, is slightly higher than the average wage paid to full-timers doing the same work. The highest peak-time earnings go to those employees working the fewest hours each week.

Peak-timers may be obtained by recruiting from the community at large or by contacting former employees—particularly retirees or individuals who left because of family responsibilities and may now be ready to return to the labor force on a part-time basis. As one former employee, who had left her job after her baby was born, commented when she went back to work as a peak-timer: "For me, it's just perfect. The hours are right, the money's right, and I love the job—plenty of customer contact."

Impact to Date: The bank has cut costs by assigning part-time employees to periods of peak demand and paying peak-timers higher wages without fringe benefits. According to the bank's personnel representative, this approach attracts better-qualified, more reliable applicants who stay longer.

SOURCE: Teresa Kochmar Crout, "When Paying More Costs Less," *Management World* (Feb. 1986): 14; *The Changing Workplace: New Directions in Staffing and Scheduling* (Washington, D.C.: Bureau of National Affairs, 1986), 61. Quotation in Provident Bank "Implementation Process" section is from the *Management World* article.

Table 10-1 Contingent employment questionnaire.

Would Contingent Employment Benefit Your Organization?

	Yes	No
Is work overload a problem for your organization in some departments or job classifications?		
Does your business have periods of regular peak activity?		
Have you explored all possible coverage options using regular employees?		
Do you need help covering for employees who are on vacation or on leave?		
Does your organization have any short-term needs, such as an experimental project or the expansion of a department, that need support (clerical, production) during their start-up phase?		
Does your organization have any one-time or occasional projects for which you need professional help?		

Introducing the Use of Contingent Employees

In order to introduce the use of contingent employees, the organization starts by gaining support for (1) a basic philosophy regarding the role of contingent and regular workers in the organization and (2) the appropriate use of contingent workers in conformance with that philosophy. The program's administration is then established, and program design decisions are made about such areas as the company's current practices, the extent to which staffing needs could be met using the regular work force, the functions that could best be performed by contingent employees, and policies and procedures covering the use of contingent workers.

Once the program's design is finalized, resource materials for managers are developed. The program need not be announced and promoted to employees, since unlike many of the other scheduling and staffing arrangements we have discussed in this book, contingent employment is not an employee option but rather an adjunct to overall human resources management. The program should be reviewed after an initial period, however, and fine-tuned accordingly.

The balance of this section will discuss the aforementioned steps in the program implementation process.

Figure 10-2. Contingent employment worksheet.

Assessing the Need for Contingent Employment

List the main reasons why you are considering using contingent workers:

1. _____

   _____

   _____

2. _____

   _____

   _____

3. _____

   _____

   _____

4. _____

   _____

   _____

List what you see as the advantages and disadvantages of using regular employees to perform the work. This would include such solutions as rescheduling part-timers, offering a few extra hours to regular part-timers or job-sharers, establishing a retiree/rehiree pool, and offering premium pay for peak-period work.

Solution: _____

   Pros: _____

   _____

_____

Cons: _____

_____

_____

Solution: _____

Pros: _____

_____

_____

Cons: _____

_____

_____

Solution: _____

Pros: _____

_____

_____

Cons: _____

_____

_____

List what you see as the advantages and disadvantages of using contingent workers. This would include temporary employees, independent contractors, and leased staff.

(Continued)

Figure 10-2. *(continued)*

Type of worker: _____

    Pros: _____

    _____

    _____

    Cons: _____

    _____

    _____

Type of worker:: _____

    Pros: _____

    _____

    _____

    Cons: _____

    _____

    _____

Gain Support for the Program

Before contingent employees can be used effectively, a basic philosophy regarding flexibility should have been developed and put into place with the support of top, middle, and line management. Real flexibility comes from a commitment to common organizational goals on the part of the regular, or core, employees. Once flexible scheduling options for regular employees have become an integral part of the human resources management strategy and are supported by the organization's philosophy and culture, then the use of contingent employees can be instituted as a practical addendum to the overall flexibility strategy without endangering the morale and commitment of the regular staff.

Set Up the Program's Administration

Decisions about when and how to use contingent employees should be handled within individual departments. Managers will need guidelines, however, that reflect the overall organizational philosophy about the use of contingent employees versus regular employees.

In order to develop an organizational posture on this issue, a task force should be formed and charged with drafting policy and procedure guidelines for managers. Internal focus groups can then be used to gather reaction and input before these guidelines are finalized.

Design the Program

In order to establish guidelines for managers relating to the use of contingent employees, the organization should start by reviewing current personnel policy, programs, and practices relating to:

- The availability of flexible options for regular employees (such as regular part-time, job sharing, V-Time, flexitime, and phased retirement).
- The possibility of rehiring retirees who might want to work part-time or on a short-term basis.

The organization should also consider how existing alternative scheduling options might be used more effectively to deal with the fluctuations in demand that are causing the current staffing or scheduling needs.

When the organization determines that maximum flexibility has really been achieved using the existing work force and there is still a need for additional labor hours but the situation does not warrant hiring new core employees, then a decision should be made about how contingent employees could best be used. This is done by identifying those functions that might be subcontracted as well as those functions where temporary or nonregular part-time workers might be used to complement the efforts of the existing work force until the need either has been met or is clearly long-term enough to justify expanding the regular work force.

Having identified areas where contingent workers could appropriately be used, the organization then formulates policies and procedures for hiring these supplemental workers. The following are the issues that should be addressed:

When contingent hires are appropriate. The company will need to spell out the conditions that must be satisfied before managers can resort to the use of contingent workers. It would, for instance, be appropriate to hire additional staff on a contingent basis if such strategies as offering current employees the chance to change their schedule or increase their hours and rehiring retirees had failed to completely meet the department's staffing and scheduling needs.

Criteria for selecting temporary agencies, leasing agencies, and subcontractors. The following are some pointers to keep in mind if the organization will be obtaining its contingent personnel through some type of agency rather than hiring these workers directly:

- ■ To determine the agency's ability to meet the organization's requirements, consider the agency's ethics and integrity, the geographic area it serves or could serve, the caliber of employees it provides, its capacity to meet organizationwide staffing needs, and its flexibility.
- ■ Check into the agency's reputation within your industry, and if any of your company's divisions or departments have used the agency before, by all means take that past track record into account as well.
- ■ Examine the agency's bank references, since financial stability is important in order for the agency to be able to maintain any kind of ongoing relationship, not only with your organization but with its own employees as well.
- ■ Review the agency's fees and stipulations relating to your company's hiring individuals on a regular basis after you have initially employed them through the agency as temporaries or consultants. Compare these fees and stipulations with those of other similar agencies. Avoid agencies that impose penalties for hiring temporary workers.
- ■ To minimize tension between the short-term employees and your regular staff, select a temporary, leasing, or consulting agency that provides its employees with benefits that are the same as or similar to the benefits that your organization provides to its core workers.

One of the American Management Association's *Supervisory Sense* booklets suggests that before using a temporary-help agency, the organization should get answers to the following questions:

1. Does the temporary help firm have any (or many) long-term employees with your desired qualifications who may be available on a steady basis?

2. Does the firm provide its workers with regular training to keep them abreast of the latest job developments?
3. What is the salary given to the employees? The better the salary they receive, the better chance you have of their staying longer and being more willing to take on responsibility.[14]

Authorizing the use of temporary agencies, leasing agencies, and subcontractors. Another important question that must be resolved is whether the company will choose the agencies or whether department managers will be able to select from a list of recommended agencies. If the latter, then the organization should provide managers with criteria for screening these agencies.

Hiring preference. The company should decide whether employees who have worked for it on a contingent basis will be given hiring preference if a decision is made to expand the regular work force.

The program design issues we have just discussed are summarized in checklist form in Table 10–2, which you can use to track your progress in addressing these issues.

Table 10-2. Program design checklist: contingent employment.

Key Design Issues	Notes
Reviewing current policy	
☐ Availability of flexible options for regular employees	
☐ Rehiring retirees	
Creating new policy	
☐ Improved use of existing alternative schedules	
☐ When contingent hires are appropriate	
☐ Criteria for selecting temporary agencies, leasing agencies, and subcontractors	
☐ Authorizing the use of temporary agencies, leasing agencies, and subcontractors	
☐ Hiring preference for contingent workers	

Develop Resource Materials

Resource materials for managers should provide guidance on the following topics:

■ *Identifying functions that could appropriately be performed by temporary, nonregular part-time, or independently contracted employees.*

■ *Choosing temporary employees and consultants.* Although at one time, temps were used primarily to provide clerical support, temporary workers and consultants are now available in many new areas. Managers will therefore need information about what these areas are and how these workers can best be utilized.

■ *Managing a mixed work force that consists of both core and subcontracted employees, some of whom may be working on only a short-term basis.* (For a discussion of this topic, see the final section of this chapter. Special Considerations for Supervisors and Managers.)

■ *Selecting appropriate agencies.* If the final choice of an agency is to be left to individual departments, managers should be given selection criteria as well as a list of recommended agencies.

■ *Monitoring employee morale.* When the organization is staffed by contingent as well as regular employees, managers should keep a careful watch over the morale of both groups of workers. Poor morale can have a negative impact on quality of service or production as well as on overall performance.

Evaluate the Program

The organization should set a time limit on the initial phase of using contingent employees, after which all aspects of the program should be evaluated. Particular attention should be paid to the program's effects on employee morale, ease or difficulty of supervision, quality of goods or services, and costs of turnover, training, and recruitment.

Fine-Tune the Program

Based on the evaluation results, the organization should modify its use of both regular and contingent workers in order to address whatever problems have been uncovered. For example:

Problem	*Solution*
Exit interviews indicate that regular employees feel that part-time is now an option only for "temps."	Review current policy and practice related to employee requests for a reduced schedule. Make sure supervisors understand the importance of this option in terms of retaining valued workers and providing more scheduling possibilities.
Managers in Department X report a significant increase in data entry errors. The department has recently considerably increased its use of "temp" employees.	Meet with department managers to try to determine whether there is a correlation between the two facts and, if so, what the reasons for the error increase might be.
Regular employees complain that contingent workers get all the "plum" jobs but don't carry their full share of responsibility.	Hold an employee focus group meeting to define the basis of the complaints and elicit suggestions for dealing with the problem.

Special Considerations for Supervisors and Managers

Contingent employees present an interesting challenge.* Although these workers may need help in getting motivated on the job, supervisors and managers do not have available to them the same tools that they can use to coax improved performance and output from their regular staff. They often ask themselves whether—and how—it is possible to motivate nonregular part-time workers whose employment may play only a small role in their lives and nonregular full-time workers who may know that the job is very temporary and feel that there is no chance for advancement.

The answer is that it *is* possible to motivate these workers and integrate their efforts with that of the organization's regular work force. Doing so will take both some effort on the part of supervisors

* The bulk of the material in this section is excerpted, in adapted form, from *Supervisory Sense: Supervising Part-Time and Temporary Workers* 8, no. 10 (Saranac Lake, N.Y.: American Management Association, Apr. 1988): 3–22.

and managers and an understanding of the dynamics of working with contingent employees.

Nonregular part-time and temporary positions are inherently different from regular full- or part-time employment in that the employees do not have as much emotional attachment to the job and do not invest as much of their self-identification or self-esteem in the job. In fact, the job is often chosen exclusively because of the schedule it requires or the salary it offers, and the contingent workers performing the job sometimes see themselves as merely marking time or putting in their hours. However, if the manager or supervisor does not share *or* allow this philosophy of stagnation, there is usually real potential to make the contingent position a mutually beneficial arrangement for both the organization and the employee.

Addressing the Competency Issue

Some of the most common complaints about nonregular part-time and short-term employees come from co-workers and supervisors who contend that these employees are less competent than their counterparts on the organization's regular work force and that they are not as interested in the outcome of their work. Some of these complaints may be legitimate, but fortunately, there is a great deal that the organization can do to avoid these problems. Supervisors and managers can control two factors that very directly affect competency: hiring and training.

It goes without saying that the organization should hire only those who are qualified to do the job. Although nonregular part-time or temporary positions may not hold as high a priority for the organization in terms of staffing as do positions on the regular work force, the department may have to devote *more* time to finding the right contingent employee. The hiring manager or supervisor must keep in mind that in comparison with regular full-time staffers, a full-time temp lacks both benefits and job security, and a contingent part-timer not only lacks benefits and job security but also earns considerably less. These employees may therefore need to be sold on the attributes of the actual job more persuasively than would be the case with a permanent full-timer, who may be influenced to a greater extent by the promise of a specific salary, an array of fringe benefits, and the prospect of job security. If the job itself cannot be made appealing to an applicant, then the hours or the pay may not be enough of an inducement to convince him or her to take the contingent position.

Supervisors often feel that they can get away with shortening the training period for temporary and nonregular part-time workers—

skimping on training for a full-time temp on the grounds that he or she will not be around long enough to warrant complete training or perhaps providing only half the standard amount of training for a nonregular part-timer who works half the standard number of hours. This approach is guaranteed to cause problems with quality and output down the road. The reality of the situation is that a full-time temp or nonregular part-timer needs the same amount of initial training to learn a task as a regular employee does. In fact, a part-timer may require *additional* training if, because of the part-time schedule, he or she does not put in enough hours to reinforce the initial training.

Orienting Contingent Employees to the Workplace

Once arrangements have been made for a nonregular employee to join the department, there are several things the supervisor should do before the employee gets there and once he or she arrives:

- Decide exactly what the employee will be responsible for. The supervisor should discuss this with the appropriate staff members and enlist their help in answering any questions the temp may have.
- Arrange a place for the temp to work and obtain all necessary supplies before he or she arrives.
- Contract for the amount of days that the contingent employee will be expected to work. if the supervisor wants the same employee for an extended period, he or she will have to make sure that the agency knows this and that it is cleared with the individual ahead of time.
- Give a brief tour of the work site when the employee arrives. The supervisor should be sure that the contingent employee is shown where to put his or her coat, the location of the restrooms, the cafeteria, and so forth. The tour should also include the supply room, photocopier, and any other equipment that the temp will need to use.
- Have a written list of directions for the employee to supplement the initial verbal directions. If the job includes completing specific tasks (rather than answering phones or helping other employees), it will be easier for the temp if those tasks are written down. The temp should not be expected to remember a long list of verbal instructions. Written directions may also be needed for the use of any automated equipment, even the phone system if it is at all complicated.

■ Be sure to inform the nonregular employee about company rules that may apply—for example, no personal phone calls or eating at the desk.

■ Try to assign an employee seated near the temp to answer questions and help orient the new worker. The supervisor should be sure to thank that employee for helping out.

■ Be as specific and clear as possible in giving directions. The supervisor should remember that the temp may well know nothing about the organization or the industry of which it is a part; nor will the employee know in advance how the supervisor tends to approach work. The supervisor can expect his or her words to be taken literally and should not assume that a contingent hire will necessarily do things the supervisor's way without first being told.

■ Treat the temp with the same courtesy and kindness that is shown to members of the regular work force. Even if the temp is being called in during a very hectic time for the department, the supervisor should remember that the temp may be just as sensitive to abrupt words or callous remarks as his or her colleagues on the permanent work force.

Integrating Contingent Employees Into the Work Force

The complaint that nonregular workers are not as interested in their job as members of the organization's regular staff may have some truth to it in many cases, but that does not mean that their work has to suffer or that they cannot become interested with the right type of motivation.

One of the best ways to get contingent hires interested in their job is to make an effort to include them fully in what goes on at their new workplace. They should be given copies of memos distributed when they are not present, and an attempt should be made to hold group meetings that concern them during the hours that they work. The same is true for the social occasions often celebrated at work. If they are *always* held when a nonregular part-timer is not present, this is likely to quash the employee's feelings of loyalty. These gatherings should be held when the part-timer is scheduled to work, or if that is not possible, the employee should at least be invited to attend.

There is more at stake here than just the feelings of the contingent employee. By making no effort to include the nonregular worker, the supervisor is sending a message to the regular staff that the contingent hire is not a "real" employee. If the permanent employees then act accordingly, it will serve to further alienate the temporary or nonregular part-time worker.

When deciding on the extent to which contingent workers should be kept informed about company business that may or may not directly concern them, it is probably better for the supervisor to err on the side of providing too much information rather than too little. Another way to get these peripheral workers involved is to give them a sense of what goes on during their off-hours. Even if they are immediately involved only with a specific task, it is important that they know how that task relates to the department's and the company's business as a whole.

Reducing Turnover Among Contingent Employees

If turnover is high among the organization's nonregular employees, the manager or supervisor should look into the matter. There may be steps that can be taken to reverse this trend.

In the case of nonregular part-timers, the employees are often working the reduced schedule because they have a second major responsibility—another job, child care, school. Therefore, these employees may attach greater importance to the hours that they work than do full-timers on the company's regular staff. Part-timers are less likely to be able to stay late or rearrange their schedules because it will conflict with another of their responsibilities. If the supervisor makes it a point to be aware of these conflicts, he or she can avoid requesting schedule changes that will create problems for contingent part-timers.

Sometimes, this inability to work extra hours can cause regular full-timers to resent the part-timer, which may eventually increase the turnover rate. If this is occurring, the supervisor can make sure that he or she is not inadvertently contributing to these feelings through such statements to regular staffers as, "Mary can't work late, so will you please stay?" It is better for the harmony of the work group for the supervisor to point out what a help Mary is to the department and how much she manages to accomplish in the time that she does work (doing so, of course, without making any disparaging comparisons between Mary and members of the full-time staff). The supervisor can also remind regular employees that the contingent part-timer earns considerably less than they do and receives none of the fringe benefits or job security that they enjoy.

When full- and part-time contingent workers do stay with the company for a prolonged period of time and then leave, the reason could be that the job has become boring and the person is seeking more variety. Again, this does not have to occur in most instances. Even a nonregular part-timer or a short-term full-timer can be given a variety of tasks and can be taught more about the operation once he or she has completely mastered the skills that constitute the primary job.

When contingent positions are presented as completely dead-end, employees have little incentive to stay for very long. On the other hand, when these workers are allowed to grow on the job, they can become valuable resources when permanent jobs open up in the organization. Another possibility is to redefine a contingent employee's job when he or she appears to have outgrown the original position. The manager or supervisor might even consider promoting the employee, while still maintaining the contingent status. If a nonregular position does allow for job advancement, the manager or supervisor should make sure the employee knows about this and discuss with him or her what the employee would need to accomplish in order to qualify for a promotion.

Avoiding Conflicts Between Regular and Nonregular Staffers

The best way to deal with staff conflicts is to avoid having them in the first place.

Open communication with all staff members, both regular and nonregular, is the most effective method of maintaining good employee relationships. For example, when a decision is made to hire a temporary or nonregular part-time worker, the manager or supervisor should discuss this decision with the permanent employees in the department, explaining why this new worker has been hired and what responsibilities he or she will have.

If the contingent employee is being hired to relieve some of the regular staffers of excess work, the manager or supervisor should say so. If the company believes it is more economical to hire a nonregular part-timer or a temp than to pay overtime to the regular full-timers, management should be frank about this, too.

One way for managers and supervisors to avoid conflicts arising from the use of contingent hires is to make an effort to include these workers in departmental meetings and to take into account their contributions to the department when making assignments and preparing productivity reports. The more these workers are treated as full-fledged members of the department, the more they will be accepted by the regular staff.

If conflicts do arise, and the manager or supervisor feels the need to intervene, he or she should try to address whatever issue is actually involved instead of allowing the situation to degenerate into a personality conflict. The matter should be decided based both on fairness and on what is best for the department's productivity. If necessary, the employees can be reminded that each of them should be concerned with the same thing—getting the job done efficiently and effectively.

It seems that the key to preserving harmony when the work force includes both contingent and regular employees is to make sure that each of these groups has a real appreciation for what the other group does.

In short, contingent workers can be used economically and efficiently to fill gaps in the regular work force—if they are managed wisely. It is important, however, that both the contingent workers and their managers and supervisors be serious about making their contribution a meaningful one.

Summary

Contingent employment is employment on a nonregular basis. The essence of this type of work is that contingent employees are an adjunct to an organization's regular work force; they are hired on a temporary or contractual basis, often at a different rate of pay than regular staffers, and do not receive the fringe benefits and career-oriented training that accompany permanent positions.

The increased use of contingent hires is attributable in part to the need of some employees for greater control over their schedules and their lives and in part to the need of some organizations for a means of responding effectively to fluctuations in the economy without repeatedly expanding and contracting their regular work force.

The net effect has been to create a "core/ring configuration." The core consists of the regular, or permanent, workers, who enjoy the status of full-fledged employees within the organization. The rings consist of the contingent, or peripheral, workers, whose status within the organization is strictly that of "nonemployees."

These are three main categories of contingent workers: temporary employees, independent contractors, and leased staff.

The use of temporary workers has grown considerably during the 1970s and 1980s. While an organization usually obtains these employees through a temporary-help agency, it is becoming increasingly common for organizations to save on agency fees by setting up their own temp pools.

Independent contractors are self-employed individuals hired directly by the organization to perform a wide variety of tasks. Advances in computer technology have expanded the possibilities for independent contractors to work on a telecommuting basis, and this mode of employment is increasingly being used by various types of professionals.

Staff leasing is an arrangement whereby an organization contracts with a leasing agency to hire an entire group of employees, not just one or more individual workers. The leasing agency provides fringe benefits and handles all the paperwork and administrative functions associated with these employees, thereby freeing the hiring company of these chores. Staff leasing appears to be most attractive to smaller businesses, which find it prohibitively costly to maintain an administrative staff and offer competitive benefits.

A variety of surveys have shown a marked rise in the use of contingent workers, and this growth is projected to continue. Many experts regard this trend as an indication that a major restructuring of the American work force is underway, with employers hiring, training, and using their employees differently than in the past.

Contingent employment can play an effective role in situations where an organization has already achieved maximum flexibility with its core work force but still must complete short-term tasks that are beyond the capacity or expertise of the permanent staff. In cases such as this, in which it would be inappropriate to expand the permanent staff because of the limited nature of the need for additional labor hours, the use of contingent workers is a good solution.

The advantages and disadvantages that an organization must weigh in considering contingent hires include the possible need to overcome internal policy barriers if the company wishes to employ its own retirees on a contingent basis and the enhanced flexibility that the use of nonregular workers can give the organization in meeting changes in demand for its products and services. For employers, one of the most attractive features of the use of peripheral employees is precisely the fact that it does help the company reduce its labor costs by more effectively matching labor supply with demand. But businesses may find that achieving this short-run savings takes a significant toll on the organization.

Companies that reduce their traditional level of commitment to their work force and instead rely heavily on contingent employment may in return find themselves faced with a significant decline in commitment on the part of both the permanent staff and the peripheral ranks. This decline in commitment may then be reflected in problems with productivity and quality, which can be compounded by employers that use contingent hires in lieu of offering flexible and reduced schedules to their core employees—a move that can have a negative impact on the retention and recruitment of permanent workers.

Unions tend to oppose the growing use of contingent employment, and concerns have also been raised about granting access to confidential information in the case of workers whose status is peripheral and whose loyalty is not altogether certain.

The organization that faces a decision about the use of contingent employment must look beyond the immediate need for greater flexibility, a reduction in labor costs, and an alternative to layoffs and also consider the long-term impact that the core/ring configuration may have not only on the organization but on society at large. When it sets up a two-tier labor force, in which the organization's core employees are working side by side with contingent hires, is the employer willing to run the risk of friction and resentment between these two groups and accept the consequences of having a divided staff that will never function as a fully unified team? Is the employer willing to promote the creation in American society of different classes of workers—the privileged regular employees, who enjoy the job security, benefits, and career-oriented training that come with their status as full-fledged members of the permanent work force, and the underprivileged contingent employees (often women and seniors), who may spend their working lives locked into a series of transient positions and denied access to the advantages that come with employment on a regular basis?

Enlightened employers will recognize that the overuse or misuse of contingent arrangements in a way that creates widespread hardship for employees is unjust to the individuals involved. Furthermore, they will see that limiting the country's supply of fully trained, experienced, and committed workers poses a significant long-range threat to America's productivity and competitive posture.

When it introduces the use of contingent workers, one of the organization's primary tasks is to "get its act together"—by making sure that it is gaining the maximum advantage from its core work force through flexible staffing and scheduling strategies such as we have discussed earlier in this book, and then identifying those remaining functions that can properly be performed by contingent hires. Once the organization has defined a truly appropriate role for nonregular workers, it can address such issues as evaluating temporary-help agencies and developing resource materials that will guide department managers in deciding which jobs should be filled on a contingent basis and which agency can provide the type of workers the department needs.

The organization can also at this point address the issue of how to manage a mixed labor force of regular and contingent employees, since the effective use of nonregular personnel calls for special skills and understanding on the part of the managers and supervisors to whose departments these individuals will be assigned. The contingent workers themselves must be oriented, trained, and motivated, and their colleagues on the regular work force must be helped to accept the supplemental employees, recognize their contributions, and work jointly with them to achieve organizational objectives.

In this chapter, we have not only explained what contingent employment consists of but also raised some rather critical questions about the practice. These concerns should not be taken to mean that your organization should never use contingent hires; rather, let them serve as a warning. Contingent employment is most appropriate as a *last resort*—after the organization has already achieved maximum flexibility using its regular work force. The organization runs the greatest risk of having contingent employment backfire in some of the ways that we have discussed here when it inappropriately uses this strategy as a first resort.

CHAPTER 11

Toward the Year 2000: Equiflex

In the Introduction, we looked ahead to the coming century and the kind of human resources philosophy and strategies that will be most appropriate then, as far as we can tell today. We emphasized the need for equitable flexibility (a concept that may, by that time, be known by a sobriquet such as *equiflex)*. The crux of equiflex is providing reduced and restructured work-time and work-site options at wage and prorated benefit levels that make these alternative modes truly comparable to full-time, on-site work, in order to build a stronger, more viable organization.

In the body of the book, we provided state-of-the-art guidelines about the kinds of policies and programs dealing with the flexible use of time and space that have already been implemented in some organizations. It is options like this that are expected to gain more adherents because of their potential for enhancing workplace flexibility.

Now, in this concluding chapter, we will turn our attention once again to the future—by examining some of the major trends that are expected to increase the already considerable need for innovation in the field of work-time and work-site policy and at some of the seminal ideas that may constitute the "next steps" for employers.

Major Trends Affecting the Need for Flexibility

Four trends continue to influence human resources issues in various ways:

- The globalization of the world's economy.
- The increasingly rapid pace of technological and economic change.
- Demographic changes.
- The breakdown of traditional barriers between the workplace and other aspects of workers' lives, such as family, education, and community and leisure activities.

Globalization of the World's Economy

The days when businesses operated within the boundaries of a relatively self-contained national economy are now behind us. Today's economic realities are worldwide rather than national in scope. This globalization of the world's economy is influencing the issue of work time and space in two ways:

1. Global competition has led to growing interest in cost efficiency and an awareness that what happens in distant parts of the world can have a very immediate impact on regional or local markets.
2. Many corporations have begun to do business on a multinational scale, operating within countries other than their own and employing foreign nationals. This has, of necessity, led to a tolerance for and an understanding of diversity as well as an expanding interchange of ideas between cultures. In a growing number of instances, these ideas are about work-time policy.

Because of differences in social and cultural priorities, many European and Scandinavian countries have already developed policies and programs that promote a wider range of work-time options than is typically available in the United States—particularly options that accommodate working parents and senior employees or spread employment during economic downturns. Some concepts, such as flexitime and work sharing, began in Europe and were later used in the United States; others, such as job sharing, originated in the United States but have found fertile ground abroad.

The creation in other developed countries of a context that supports interest in and experimentation with new work schedules is primarily attributable to two factors: (1) These countries have a history of conducting social and labor policy research as a basis for long-range planning, and (2) they have developed ways of delivering health insurance that do not encumber employers with that responsibility. The latter issue is of particular importance in terms of introducing new forms of regular part-time employment.

The Increasingly Rapid Pace of Technological and Economic Change

Everyone is having to learn how to deal with the quickening pace of change in the technological and economic arenas. Management guru Tom Peters' theme for the future is that managers must learn to embrace perpetual change and that the only way for a company to achieve lasting excellence will be for it to improve constantly and be responsive to changing market conditions.[1]

It is certainly true that the ability to adapt to and cope with changed conditions and make successful transitions is becoming increasingly important both for organizations and for individual employees. With new products, services, and technologies being introduced at a dizzying pace and with the deterioration of some industries and the obsolescence of some skills making dislocation and career change a reality for more and more people, education, training, and retraining have become an essential part of everyone's work life.

Within this change scenario is the related issue of workers' growing desire for more control, particularly over their time and work and over the way in which time and work relate to their life as a whole. Employers should encourage this interest. It may be the source of the energy needed for the next stage of organizational evolution. In order to reach this stage, employers must be willing to develop a context that accommodates employees' needs in ways that are constructive for both the individuals and the organization. One way to create such a context is for the organization to share responsibility with employees and allow them greater control over factors in which they have a self-interest. In so doing, businesses can both enable employees to be more productive and strengthen their commitment to the organization and its objectives. Many of the policies and programs discussed in the body of this book represent beginning steps toward this next stage of organizational evolution.

As we've seen, these initiatives were first introduced primarily as a means of responding to the needs of workers with family responsibilities, creating alternatives to layoffs, or improving employee morale. Although these are important concerns, innovative work-time options also have potentially significant ramifications for employee training that have thus far been largely overlooked but that will assume growing importance in today's climate of fast-paced change. Training employees and constantly expanding their skills in response to evolving business conditions is quite costly. If the employer must bear the entire responsibility for supplying this training and education, there is a danger that only selected or "fast-track" employees will receive this sort of attention. However, if employers encourage their workers' interest in self-management and support their taking some responsibility for broadening their own skills, particularly by offering flexible work-time options, they will reduce that cost while at the same time accommodating their employees' needs and enabling them to be more productive and of greater value to the organization.

Demographic Changes

The issues of work-time and work-site flexibility will continue to be affected by demographic changes in the work force and in the labor pool from which that work force is drawn. Women, minorities, and immigrants are expected to account for more than 80 percent of the new additions to the labor force between now and the year 2000. The pool of younger workers is shrinking, while older workers who are trained and experienced continue to retire. Given our longer life spans and the slowed pace of economic growth, these demographic changes, in combination with the effects of current private and public employment policies, threaten to overload future generations of workers with the burden of supporting too large a percentage of dependent former workers. This scenario threatens both the nation's competitive posture and its standard of living.

As we've noted throughout this book, flexible and reduced work schedules can provide new ways to manage a diverse work force, by encouraging skilled senior employees to extend their work life, accommodating experienced workers who have family responsibilities, and facilitating training and continuing education.

Integrating Work With Other Aspects of Employees' Lives

The search for ways to become more efficient has led some employers to recognize the fact that current systems often make employees less functional rather than more productive. When the balance between work and family, work and education, or work and leisure becomes stressful and that stress is ignored, the result can be absenteeism, downtime on the job, and high turnover rates. With everyone living longer than previous generations, and needing to work longer, a more flexible approach is called for—one that recognizes and supports ways in which lifelong work can be better integrated with conntinuing training and education, family responsibilities, and leisure activities.

Flexibility in the Year 2000

In his paper *Controlling Hours of Work,* R. A. Lee, of the Department of Management Studies at the University of Loughborough in Great Britain, notes:

[*T*]he accepted norm of "fixed hours" is giving way to the development of *appropriate* hours for different situations. A number of factors have stimulated progress. . . . [*T*]he strongest pressure of all comes from the need for productive performance in a time of economic stringency.[2]

The paper concludes with the following comments:

In the longer term it is tempting to foresee a society whose organizations operate a complex variety of hours patterns, these being designed to accommodate developing technologies, changing family life styles and leisure activities and to share work equitably. It is the intervening processes of change which make this optimistic future seem far away.[3]

As part of the "intervening processes of change," one of the more interesting strategies that organizations have tried is the *annual hours contract*.

Annual Hours Contracts

The idea of an annual hours contract was first articulated in the mid-1970s[4] in Scandinavia as a result of the organizational need for a more efficient way to balance labor supply and labor demand. The system was pioneered in Swedish and later in Finnish pulp and paper industry plants and then spread, in 1983, to the British paper and board industry.

The annual hours concept is relatively simple: Management and labor agree on the number of hours of work that will be needed during a given year and then design a scheduling format by which those hours will be provided. The schedule may be fixed or variable. All the hours may be scheduled at the outset, or some may be held in reserve—to be used when the employer and employees decide they are needed. The result is what British management consultant Philip Lynch has termed an "essential framework around which worktime can be arranged in whatever units or form the business requires and employees will agree to."[5]

Lynch notes that the annual hours approach offers four types of benefits:

1. It separates employee hours from production hours.
2. It enables the organization to schedule more employee hours during peak periods of activity and extend operations where needed.
3. It forces a redefinition of overtime and eliminates overtime as a means of production.

4. This new scheduling strategy can be used as a change agent—that is, as a means of creating change—within the organization.[6]

This latter point, Lynch believes, is:

the most powerful advantage of the [*annual hours*] concept. . . . The major changes that annual hours can help produce include:

- a stable earnings pattern and progress towards salaried status;
- improved work organisation and more productive work practices:
- more efficient planning and improved use of capital and labour;
- better and less costly training programmes;
- improved versatility and flexibility.[7]

Although to date most of the annual hours programs have been used in continuous-process production facilities, the annual hours concept has a much broader potential application and offers a structure within which a wide variety of full- and part-time schedules and off-site options can be applied.

As with the other new flexible scheduling options that have been described in previous chapters, considerable thinking and planning should go into changing an organization's work-hours system. Proponents of annual hours programs recommend conducting a feasibility study that focuses on the following issues:

- *The compensation system*, particularly the use of *overtime*—to determine whether the current pay system can be adapted to new work schedules and practices.
- *Work-time usage*—to see what kinds of changes might improve scheduling efficiency.
- *Production processes*—to determine whether production can be increased with the same amount of labor and capital and what impact any changes might have on labor force needs.
- *Work organization*—in terms of normal and minimum staffing levels, transferable skills, arrangements to cover for other employees, and so on.

Once the feasibility of adopting an annual hours approach has been determined and a decision has been made to use this strategy, the implementation steps are as follows:

- *Design the schedule*. Table 11-1 shows a segment of a sample annual hours schedule. It is a roster for a crew of eight people

Table 11-1.   Portion of a sample annual hours schedule.

	Crew Members							
	A	B	C	D	E	F	G	H
Week 1								
Sunday	—	5	5	—	—	5	5	—
Monday	8	8	8	8	8	8	8	—
Tuesday	8	8	—	8	8	8	8	—
Wednesday	8	—	8	8	8	8	8	8
Thursday	8	8	8	8	8	8	—	8
Friday	8	8	8	8	8	8	—	8
Saturday	5	—	—	5	5	—	—	5
Week 2								
Sunday	5	—	—	5	5	—	—	5
Monday	8	8	8	8	8	—	8	8
Tuesday	—	8	8	8	8	—	8	8
Wednesday	8	8	8	8	8	8	8	—
Thursday	8	8	8	8	—	8	8	8
Friday	8	8	8	8	—	8	8	8
Saturday	—	5	5	—	—	5	5	—
Week 3								
Sunday	—	5	5	—	—	5	5	—
Monday	8	8	8	—	8	8	8	8
Tuesday	8	8	8	—	8	8	—	8
Wednesday	8	8	8	8	8	—	8	8
Thursday	8	8	—	8	8	8	8	8
Friday	8	8	—	8	8	8	8	8
Saturday	5	—	—	5	5	—	—	5
Week 4								
Sunday	5	—	—	5	5	—	—	5
Monday	8	—	8	8	8	8	8	8
Tuesday	8	—	8	8	—	8	8	8
Wednesday	8	8	8	—	8	8	8	8
Thursday	—	8	8	8	8	8	8	8
Friday	—	8	8	8	8	8	8	8
Saturday	—	5	5	—	—	5	5	—

SOURCE: Philip Lynch, "Annual Hours: An Idea Whose Time Has Come," *Personnel Management* (Nov. 1985): 48.

who work a staggered day-shift pattern involving five-hour shifts on Saturdays and Sundays and eight-hour shifts on weekdays. The schedule rotates over a four-week period, with each worker averaging 39 hours per week.

■ *Redesign the compensation system.* If overtime has been used extensively, the organization may attempt to phase it out or redesign the pay system to offer some degree of compensation for the elimination of overtime. In addition, holiday pay and sick leave calculations must be reexamined.

Figure 11-1 is a sample annual hours wage calculation for a member of the eight-person crew whose schedule was shown in Table 11-1. In this calculation, the employee works an average of 39 hours each week but is paid for 42.75 hours because of the premium rates that apply to the weekend hours. In order to figure the average weekly worked and paid hours on an annual basis, the total number of hours that the employee is scheduled ("rostered") to work during the year (1,776) is multiplied by 42.75 ÷ 39, which converts the worked hours into paid hours by taking premium pay into account. The total time off for which the employee will be compensated (282.15 hours, which includes holidays, vacations, sick leave, and personal time), is calculated by expressing this time in weeks (6.6) and multiplying by the average weekly paid hours (42.75). By adding the total paid hours for which the employee is scheduled during the year (1,946.77) and his or her total paid hours off for the year (282.15), the company arrives at the total annual hours for which the employee will be paid (2,228.92).

■ *Develop control systems.* The organization will need some sort of system for monitoring the scheduling, to ensure that the actual worked and paid hours conform to the annual hours

Figure 11-1.   Annual hours wage calculation.

1. Weekly paid hours			
	Average worked hours per week	Premium	Average paid hours per week
Weekday:	34.0	none	34
Saturday:	2.5	× 1.5	3.75
Sunday:	2.5	× 2	5.0
Total	39.0		42.75

2. Annual rostered paid hours: 1,776 × 42.75 ÷ 39 = 1,946.77
3. Holiday paid hours: 6.6 weeks × 42.75 =   282.15

4. Total annual paid hours: 2,228.92

SOURCE: Philip Lynch, "Annual Hours: An Idea Whose Time Has Come," *Personnel Management* (Nov. 1985): 49.

plan. Some proponents of the annual hours approach suggest that an individual work-time "account" be established for each employee. Such an account starts with the employee's total targeted hours for the year, which are then debited throughout the year until the account totals zero at the end of 12 months.

■ *Redesign jobs*. One aspect of the implementation of an annual hours program is redesigning jobs in order to improve the processes for organizing work and achieve greater flexibility.

■ *Train employees and supervisors*. It is important that workers and their supervisors be trained, both in terms of any skills required to perform the redesigned jobs and in terms of handling the new scheduling arrangements.

The steps outlined above would, for most organizations, represent a radical overhaul of the existing work-hours system. In the few companies in which such a program has thus far been implemented, the benefits appear to be substantial. The research to date indicates that from the organization's perspective, these benefits include:

■ Improvement in unit costs and productivity.
■ Elimination of overtime as a means of production.
■ Enhanced ability to adapt to future technological changes and business requirements.
■ Increased flexibility with respect to both skills and hours, thanks to changed attitudes and practices.
■ Better planning and use of available time and resources.
■ Simplified and stable pay structures.
■ Better-organized and less-costly training.
■ Reduced vulnerability to strikes.
■ Improved motivation.
■ Improved administration.[8]

On the employee side, the reported benefits are:

■ Improved basic pay.
■ Increased leisure time.
■ Structured opportunities for personal development.
■ Increased job satisfaction.
■ Improved mutual support and cooperation among employees.
■ Progress toward salaried status.[9]

In looking ahead through the 1990s and beyond, annual hours systems would appear to be a promising area in need of thoughtful investigation and innovative development.

Equiflex

In the future, companies will undoubtedly use a much wider variety of work-time and work-site options such as those we have described in this book, offering their workers both full- and part-time positions as well as opportunities for leave time and off-site work.

One catalytic strategy would be using the annual hours process (which, as noted earlier in the chapter, allows for scheduling in "whatever units or form the business requires and employees will agree to") in combination with a voluntary reduced work time (V-Time) program (which is designed to respond to employees' needs for less than full-time schedules in order to balance work with other aspects of their lives). Both the annual hours and V-Time programs are examples of equitable flexibility, or equiflex, and consequently represent "win-win" situations. Taken together, they could provide a framework within which alternative work-time and work-site options could be integrated in order to achieve R. A. Lee's goal, cited at the start of this section, of "accommodat[ing] developing technologies, changing family life styles and leisure activities and . . . shar[ing] work equitably."

The accompanying profile entitled Organizational Experience With Equiflex shows how one small pediatric hospital used a creative blend of flexible scheduling options not only to meet employees' needs for a wider range of choices about when and how much they will work but to do so in a way that would help the hospital solve such serious problems as attracting and retaining qualified employees, cutting hiring-related costs, reducing turnover, staffing undesirable shifts, and encouraging employees to continue in their educational pursuits.

At the close of the 1980s, it is impossible for us to predict exactly which of the strategies we have discussed in this book will be most widely used in the coming years and in what combination these strategies will be applied. One thing, however, seems certain: By the year 2000, organizations will find that their potential for profitability is significantly affected by how skillfully they can integrate a variety of work-time and work-site options to create a climate of equitable flexibility.

ORGANIZATIONAL EXPERIENCE WITH EQUIFLEX

Children's Hospital, Stanford University

Description: Children's Hospital is a small pediatric facility that provides care for children during acute episodes of long-term catastrophic diseases such as cancer and cystic fibrosis. The hospital is located at Stanford University and has a roster of approximately 200 trained nurses, a high percentage of whom are enrolled on their own in training or advanced degree programs.

Reason for Using Equiflex: The hospital's individual scheduling system, which is currently available to nurses and some administrators, was developed to enable the facility to attract and retain exceptionally well-qualified personnel in the midst of a national nursing shortage. The equiflex options help the staff fit together the "sometimes irregular pieces of a modern lifestyle: family demands; professional requirements; personal needs for decompression, variety and even adventure."

Implementation Process: The system is run with the help of a full-time staffing "dispatcher," who uses a complicated computerized system. On a monthly basis, nurses sign an agreement specifying the number of hours they will work and the dates when they will be available. They are able to choose from a variety of flexible policies and programs, including:

- A relief-pool system, which allows nurses to work as few as 20 and as many as 40 hours a week, at times of their own choosing.
- Job-sharing arrangements.
- Leave options, which allow one nurse to work at the hospital full-time for nine months of the year and then take three months during the summer to work as a nurse on a cruise ship.
- Compressed schedules, which allow some nurses to work only weekends or evenings.

A liberal benefits policy provides full benefits starting from the first day on the job, even for part-time employees if they work at least 20 hours per week.

Impact to Date: Carol Bradshaw, director of nursing, who helped develop the plan, credits it with enabling the hospital to avoid the use of high-priced personnel agencies, costly recruiting campaigns, and cash incentives for signing contracts.

The turnover rate at Children's Hospital for 1987 was 13 percent, compared to 15 to 17 percent for other hospitals in the area. This was in spite of the fact that the hospital experiences some natural turnover because a certain percentage of the staff are spouses of students enrolled at the university and leave when their husbands or wives complete their course of study.

The hospital has also found that it is now less of a problem to staff traditionally unpopular shifts such as nights and weekends.

Bradshaw describes the spirit of the hospital's equiflex program as follows:

> It's a matter of moving pieces here and there. Here we try to treat our nurses like customers. We make them feel it's worth their while to work with us. . . . The key is to keep that subtle balance between our needs and their needs.

SOURCE: Publicity release written by Diarmuid McGuire, Children's Hospital, Stanford University, Stanford, Calif. (Oct. 8, 1987); "Children's Hospital and Nurses Both Find Relief in Flexible Scheduling Policies," *Work Times* 6, no. 3 (San Francisco: New Ways to Work, 1988), 3.

Notes

Preface

1. *Wall Street Journal* Labor Letter (Apr. 28, 1987): 1.
2. "Losing a Market to a High Wage Nation," *New York Times* (June 14, 1987): F3.

Introduction

1. Tom Peters, *Thriving on Chaos* (New York: Knopf, 1988).
2. Dana E. Friedman, *Family-Supportive Policies: The Corporate Decision-Making Process* (New York: The Conference Board, Inc., 1987), 1.
3. *New Skills Needed by Managers in Restructured Firms,* Work in America Institute Productivity Forum press release (Scarsdale, N.Y.: May 6, 1987), 2.
4. Stanley D. Nollen, *New Work Schedules in Practice,* Work in America Institute Series (New York: Van Nostrand Reinhold, 1982), 1.
5. Ibid., vii.

Part I Introduction

1. Paul Dickson, *The Future of the Workplace* (New York: Weybright and Talley, 1975), 209.

Chapter 1

1. *Monthly Labor Review* 109, no. 11 (Washington, D.C.: U.S. Department of Labor, Bureau of Labor Statistics, Nov. 1986): 18.

2. Ibid., 19.

3. *The Changing American Workplace: Work Alternatives in the 80's* (New York: AMACOM, 1985), 20.

4. "Flexitime Doubles in a Decade," *Management World* 16, no. 3 (Apr.–May 1987): 18–19.

5. Ibid., 19.

6. *The Changing Workplace: New Directions in Staffing and Scheduling* (Washington, D.C.: Bureau of National Affairs, Inc., 1986), 51.

7. Stanley D. Nollen, "Does Flexitime Improve Productivity?" *Harvard Business Review* 57 (Sept.–Oct. 1979): 12–22.

8. J. Carroll Swart, "Clerical Workers on Flexitime: A Survey of Three Industries," *Personnel* 62 (Apr. 1985): 41.

9. Ibid., 40–44.

10. Administrative Management Society, *Flexible Work Survey* (Trevose, Pa.: AMS, 1987): 4.

11. Simcha Ronen, *Flexible Working Hours* (New York: McGraw-Hill, 1981), 223.

Chapter 2

1. Herman Gadon and Allan R. Cohen, *Alternative Work Schedules: Integrating Individual and Organizational Needs* (Reading, Mass.: Addison-Wesley, 1978), 50.

2. Shirley J. Smith, "The Growing Diversity of Work Schedules," *Monthly Labor Review* 109, no. 11 (Washington, D.C.: U.S. Department of Labor, Bureau of Labor Statistics, Nov. 1986): 10.

3. *The Changing American Workplace: Work Alternatives in the 80's* (New York: AMACOM, 1985): 20.

4. Stanley D. Nollen and Virginia H. Martin, *Alternative Work Schedules,* Parts 2 and 3 (New York: AMACOM, 1978), 57.

5. Stanley D. Nollen, *New Work Schedules in Practice,* Work in America Institute Series (New York: Van Nostrand Reinhold, 1982), 68.

6. Ibid., 68.

7. Nollen and Martin, *Alternative Work Schedules,* 55.

8. Ibid., 57.

Part II   Introduction

1. *Part-Time Employment in America: Highlights of the First National Conference on Part-Time Employment* (McLean, Va.: Association of Part-Time Professionals, 1983), 36.

2. Ibid.

3. *The Changing Workplace: New Directions in Staffing and Scheduling* (Washington, D.C.: Bureau of National Affairs, 1986), 43.

Chapter 3

1. *New Work Schedules for a Changing Society* (Scarsdale, N.Y.: Work in America Institute, 1981), 31.
2. *Workforce 2000* (Washington, D.C.: U.S. Department of Labor, Employment and Training Administration, May 1987), 4.
3. Helen Axel, *Part-Time Employment: Crosscurrents of Change,* paper prepared for The Contingent Workplace conference, co-sponsored by the Graduate School and University Center of CUNY and The Woman's Bureau, Region II, U.S. Department of Labor, 1987.
4. *Part-Time Employment in America* (McLean, Va.: Association of Part-Time Professionals, Oct. 1983), 36.
5. *Part-Time Employment: Implications for Families and the Workplace* (Albany: New York State Council on Children and Families, 1983), 7.
6. *Monthly Labor Review* 109, no. 11 (Washington, D.C.: U.S. Department of Labor, Bureau of Labor Statistics, Nov. 1986): 10.
7. *New Work Schedules for a Changing Society,* 30.
8. *The Changing American Workplace: Work Alternatives in the 80's* (New York: AMACOM, 1985), 20.
9. *Survey of Private Sector Work and Family Policy: San Francisco and Alameda Counties* (San Francisco, New Ways to Work, 1986), 9.
10. *Survey on Work Time Options in the Legal Profession: San Francisco and Alameda Counties* (San Francisco: New Ways to Work, 1986), 19.
11. *Operations Report: Keeping a First-Rate but Flexible Work Force* (New York: Research Institute of America, 1986), 7.
12. Priscilla H. Claman, *It Works—Part-Time Employment in State Agencies* (Boston: Commonwealth of Massachusetts, Division of Personnel Administration, 1980), 17.
13. *Benefits for Part-Time Employees* (Lincolnshire, Ill.: Hewitt Associates, 1985), 3–4.
14. Mark Manin, "Flexible Benefits for Part-Time Employees," *Benefits News Analysis* 9, no. 3 (1987): 11–12.
15. Ibid., 12.
16. Ibid.
17. Ibid., 11–12.
18. *The Part-Time Employment Pilot Program: Final Report* (Sacramento: California State Department of Motor Vehicles, 1976), 63.
19. Stanley Nollen, B. Eddy, and V. Martin, *Permanent Part-Time Employment: The Manager's Perspective* (New York: Praeger Publishers, 1978), 70.
20. Stanley Nollen, *New Work Schedules in Practice* (New York: Van Nostrand Reinhold, 1982), 17.
21. Claman, *It Works,* 4 and 6.
22. *Part-Time Employment: Implications for Families and the Workplace,* 53.
23. Ibid., 19.
24. Claman, *It Works,* 2.
25. *Detailed Summary: Forum for Personnel Managers—Part-Time Employment: Implications for NYS Agencies,* Part-Time/Shared Job Project (Albany: New York State Department of Civil Service, 1983), 1.

Chapter 4

1. *1987 Flexible Work Survey,* AMS Business Trend Survey Series (Trevose, Pa.: Administrative Management Society, 1987), 6; *The Changing American Workplace: Work Alternatives in the 80's,* AMA Survey Report (New York: AMA-COM, 1985), 20; *The Changing Workplace: New Directions in Staffing and Scheduling* (Washington, D.C.: Bureau of National Affairs, 1986), 7; *Survey of Private Sector Work and Family Policy: San Francisco and Alameda Counties* (San Francisco: New Ways to Work, 1986), 12.
2. *The Changing American Workplace: Work Alternatives in the 80's,* 20.
3. Ibid., 42.
4. *1987 Flexible Work Survey,* 7.
5. *Job Sharing in Health Care* (San Francisco: New Ways to Work, 1984), 42; *Survey of Work Time Options in the Legal Profession: San Francisco and Alameda Counties* (San Francisco: New Ways to Work, 1986), 20.
6. *Work Times* 5, no. 2 (San Francisco: New Ways to Work, Winter 1987): 1.
7. *Part-Time Schedules: A Guide for NYS Supervisors and Managers,* Part-Time/ Shared Job Project (Albany: New York State Department of Civil Service, 1985).

Chapter 5

1. "Flexible Age Retirement: Social Issue of the Decade," *Industry Week* 197, no. 4 (Cleveland: Penton/IPC, Inc., 1978): 66.
2. *Issue Brief,* no. 68 (Washington, D.C.: Employee Benefit and Research Institute, July 1987): 8.
3. *The Travelers Pre-Retirement Opinion Survey: Report of Results* (Hartford: Travelers Insurance Company, 1981), i.
4. *Aging in the Eighties: America in Transition,* survey conducted for the National Council on the Aging, Inc. by Louis Harris and Associates, Inc., November 1981, 5.
5. *Issue Brief,* 8.
6. *The Reduced Work Load Program in the State Teachers' Retirement System* (Sacramento, Calif.: Office of the Legislative Analyst, Sept. 1980).
7. Quoted in Constance Swank, *Phased Retirement: The European Experience* (Washington, D.C.: National Council for Alternative Work Patterns, 1982), 25.
8. "Retiree Benefits Cast a Shadow," *New York Times* (July 21, 1987), Business Day section, D2.
9. "Company Liabilities Are Soaring," *New York Times* (Nov. 29, 1987), sec. 3, 2F.

Chapter 6

1. *Exchanging Earnings for Leisure: Findings of an Exploratory National Survey on Work Time Preferences,* R&D Monograph 79 (Washington, D.C.: U.S. Department of Labor, Employment and Training Administration, 1980), 2.
2. George Gallup poll conducted in conjunction with the White House Conference

on Families, 1980; *Families at Work,* General Mills, 1981; *Better Homes and Gardens* readers' polls, 1982 and 1988.

3. *Better Homes and Gardens* (November 1988), 44.

4. *Part-Time Employment: Implications for Families and the Workplace* (Albany: State of New York, 1983).

5. *The Travelers' Pre-Retirement Opinion Survey,* 1981, 13.

Chapter 7

1. *Survey of Private Sector Work and Family Policy: San Francisco and Alameda Counties* (San Francisco: New Ways to Work, 1986), 18.

2. Sheila B. Kamerman and Alfred J. Kahn, *The Responsive Workplace: Employers and a Changing Labor Force* (New York: Columbia University Press, 1987), 231.

3. *Report on a National Study of Parental Leaves* (New York: Catalyst, 1986), 34.

4. Council on Economic Priorities, as reported in Ronald E. Roel, "Parental Leave Gaining Favor," *Newsday* (June 16, 1988), 32.

5. Kamerman and Kahn, *The Responsive Workplace,* 231.

6. *Report on a National Study of Parental Leaves,* 37.

7. Ibid., 34.

8. *The Travelers Pre-Retirement Opinion Survey: Report of Results* (Hartford: Travelers Insurance Company, 1981): 13.

9. Helen Axel, *Corporations and Families: Changing Practices and Perspectives,* Report No. 868 (New York: The Conference Board, Inc., 1985), 32.

10. Work in America Institute, *World of Work Report* 11, no. 8 (Elmsford, N.Y.: Pergamon Press, Aug. 1986): 7.

11. *Work in America* 12, no. 4 (Washington, D.C.: Buraff Publications, Apr. 1987): 8.

12. Axel, *Corporations and Families,* 32.

13. *Flexible Benefits* (New York: Catalyst, 1987), 47.

14. "Daily Report for Executives" (Washington, D.C.: Bureau of National Affairs, 1986), L-1.

15. Jack Wood, *The Future of Employment,* keynote address at Australian Democrats National Conference (Cremorne, Australia: Jan. 24, 1987).

16. *Report on a National Study of Parental Leaves,* 87.

17. Ibid., 48.

Chapter 8

1. Quoted in Fred Best, *Work Sharing: Issues, Policy Options, and Prospects* (Kalamazoo, Mich.: W. E. Upjohn Institute, 1981), 3.

2. Edith F. Lynton, *Alternatives to Layoffs,* conference report (New York: Commission on Human Rights, Apr. 1975), 39, 41.

3. Ibid., 3.

4. Quoted in *Alternatives to Layoffs,* 57.

5. "HP Will Extend Cut in Work Hours," *San Francisco Chronicle* (September 24,

1985), 22; Michael Malone, "MMI Outduels the Big Boys," *San Francisco Chronicle* (May 5, 1986), 25; John Eckhouse, "National Semi Plans Furlough; LSI Sees Loss," *San Francisco Chronicle* (1985), 29; Gail E. Shares, "Equitec Cuts Costs to Halt Profit Slump," *San Francisco Chronicle* (October 8, 1985), 25.

6. Unpublished report to the state of California's Office of Technology Assessment (1986).

7. *Daily Labor Report* (Washington, D.C.: Bureau of National Affairs, Sept. 22, 1986), 3.

8. *California Shared Work Unemployment Insurance Evaluation* (Sacramento, Calif.: May 1982), 1–5.

9. Ramelle MaCoy and Martin J. Morand, *Short-Time Compensation: A Formula for Work Sharing,* Work in America Institute Series (Elmsford, N.Y.: Pergamon Press, 1984), 99.

10. Bennett Burgoon and Robert D. St. Louis, *The Impact of Work Sharing on Selected Motorola Units,* technical report 84-12 (Tempe: Arizona State University, Oct. 1984), 16.

11. "Shorter Workweeks: An Alternative to Layoffs," *Business Week* (Apr. 14, 1986), 77.

12. *New Work Schedules for a Changing Society* (Scarsdale, N.Y.: Work in America Institute, 1981), 89.

13. John Zalusky, "Short-Time Compensation," remarks to the Interstate Conference of Employment Security Agencies (Sept. 23, 1982), quoted in MaCoy and Morand, *Short-Time Compensation,* 45.

14. MaCoy and Morand, *Short-Time Compensation,* 44.

15. Ibid., 48.

16. Burgoon and St. Louis, *The Impact of Work Sharing on Selected Motorola Units,* 4.

17. Alison Leigh Cowan, "The Plant-Closing Law Reaches Into Wall Street," *New York Times* (October 27, 1988), C1.

18. Quoted in MaCoy and Morand, *Short-Time Compensation,* 166.

19. MaCoy and Morand, *Short-Time Compensation,* 26.

Chapter 9

1. *Telecommuting: The State of the Art and Market Trends* (New York: Electronic Services Unlimited, 1984), 1.

2. Frank Schiff, *Flexiplace: An Idea Whose Time Has Come,* speech to the Engineering Management Society Institute of Electrical and Electronics Engineers (New York: Engineering Management Society, 1981), 5.

3. "Work at Home: New Findings From the Current Population Survey," *Monthly Labor Review* 109, no. 11 (Nov. 1986): 31.

4. *The Changing Workplace: New Directions in Staffing and Scheduling* (Washington, D.C.: Bureau of National Affairs, 1986): 67.

5. Telephone conversation with consultant Gil Gordon, Monmouth Junction, N.J.

6. "Runzheimer Reports on Transportation," Runzheimer International, Rochester, Wisconsin.

7. *Telecommuting Review: The Gordon Report* (Monmouth Junction, N.J.: Gil Gordon Associates, Oct. 1987), 5.

8. Ibid., 8.

9. *Wall Street Journal Labor Letter* (Jan. 6, 1987), 1.

10. Adapted from Gil E. Gordon and Marcia M. Kelly, *Telecommuting* (Englewood Cliffs, N.J.: Prentice Hall, 1986), 166.

11. Ibid., 178.

12. "VDT Monitoring Sparks Work Privacy Debate," *Work in America* 12, no. 11 (Nov. 1987): 1.

13. Ibid.

14. Gordon and Kelly, *Telecommuting,* 75.

15. Ibid., 78.

Chapter 10

1. *The Changing Workplace: New Directions in Staffing and Scheduling* (Washington, D.C.: Bureau of National Affairs, 1986), 1.

2. Jeff Day, "Rent-a-Staff: A New Lease on Work?" *Across the Board* (New York: The Conference Board, July–Aug. 1987); Michael J. McCarthy, "Managing," *Wall Street Journal* (April 5, 1988), 31.

3. Michael J. McCarthy, "On Their Own in Increasing Numbers, White-Collar Workers Leave Steady Positions," *Wall Street Journal* (Oct. 13, 1987), 1, 20.

4. *1988 AMS Contract Labor Survey* (Trevose, Pa.: Administrative Management Society, 1987), 1.

5. Day, "Rent-a-Staff," 57.

6. Joani Nelson-Horchler, "The Trouble With Temps," *Industry Week* (Dec. 14, 1987), 54.

7. Amanda Bennett, "Growing Small: As Big Firms Continue to Trim Their Staffs, 2-Tier Set-Up Emerges," *Wall Street Journal* (May 4, 1987), 12.

8. Ibid.

9. Ibid.

10. Nelson-Horchler, "The Trouble With Temps," 53–57.

11. Position paper developed by Service Employees International Union for the *Solutions for the New Workforce* conference in Washington, D.C., 1987, 2.

12. Ibid., 3.

13. *Wall Street Journal* chart showing the results of a Conference Board study (July 21, 1987), 47.

14. *Supervisory Sense: Supervising Part-Time and Temporary Workers* 8, no. 10 (Saranac Lake, N.Y.: American Management Association, Apr. 1988): 8.

Chapter 11

1. Tom Peters, *Thriving on Chaos* (New York: Alfred A. Knopf, 1988).

2. R. A. Lee, "Controlling Hours of Work," *Personnel Review* 14, no. 3 (1985): 3.

3. Ibid., 11.

4. Bernhard Teriet, "Flexiyear Schedules—Only a Matter of Time?" *Monthly Labor Review* (Dec. 1977): 62–65.

5. Philip Lynch, "Annual Hours: An Idea Whose Time Has Come," *Personnel Management* (Nov. 1985): 46. Most of the detailed information about annual hours programs in this chapter was drawn from Mr. Lynch's article.

6. Ibid., 46 and 47.

7. Ibid., 47.

8. Ibid., 49.

9. Ibid.

Suggested Reading List

Chapters 1 and 2: Flexitime and Compressed Workweek

Badger, Linda K., and Marlene A. Israel. *Innovative Work Schedules and Overtime Requirements: A Survey of the Relevant Literature*. San Francisco: California Industrial Welfare Commission, Sept. 1981. 53 pages.

Concentrates on the compressed workweek and flexible scheduling and on overtime premiums as a barrier to innovation.

California Industrial Welfare Commission. *Alternatives to the Eight-Hour Day Within a Forty-Hour Week: The Four/Ten Workweek*. San Francisco: May 1985. 8 pages.

Defines and clarifies the Industrial Welfare Commission orders regarding a workweek of four days, with not more than ten hours a day.

Craddock, Suzanne, et al. "Flexitime: The Kentucky Experiments." *Public Personnel Management Journal* (Summer 1981): 244–252.

Reports on a study of the effects of flexitime on production, absenteeism, morale, and transportation in state agencies during three trial periods. The program was continued.

Latack, Janina C., and Lawrence W. Foster. "Implementation of Compressed Work Schedules: Participation and Job Redesign as Critical Factors for Employee Acceptance." *Personnel Psychology* (Spring 1985): 75–92.

Considers the effects of a 3-day, 38-hour week on information systems staff. Fatigue did not appear to be a factor.

Martin, Virginia, and David W. Jones, Jr. *The Design and Implementation of Alternative Work Schedules: Flexitime and Voluntary Staggered Hours*. Berkeley: University of California Institute of Transportation Studies, July 1980. 42 pages.

Presents detailed schedules and operating guidelines.

Mellor, Earl F. "Shift Work and Flexitime: How Prevalent Are They?" *Monthly Labor Review* (Nov. 1986): 14–21.

Includes tables showing which workers—about one in eight—have flexible schedules.

Nollen, Stanley D., and Virginia H. Martin. *Alternative Work Schedules*, parts 1, 2, and 3. AMA Survey Reports. New York: AMACOM, 1978.

Ralston, David A., and Michael F. Flanagan. "The Effect of Flexitime on Absenteeism and Turnover for Male and Female Employees." *Journal of Vocational Behavior* 26 (Apr. 1985): 206–217.

Reports that significant differences were found between men and women with respect to absenteeism but not with respect to turnover.

Ronen, Simcha. *Flexible Working Hours: An Innovation in the Quality of Work Life*. New York: McGraw-Hill, 1981.

Extensive study of the implications of flexitime, its results in a variety of organizations, and its effects on both the labor force and transportation.

―――, and Sophia P. Primps. "The Compressed Work Week as Organizational Change: Behavioral and Attitudinal Outcomes." *Academy of Management Review* 6 (Jan. 1981): 61–74.

Compiles and analyzes several recent studies, indicating favorable attitudes and somewhat ambiguous performance outcomes.

Seattle/King County Commuter Pool. *Flexible Working Hours*. Seattle: n.d.

A manual on flexitime that tells how to design and implement a program, including such topics as scheduling, solving problems, legislation, the position of unions, and sample surveys.

Silverstein, Pam, and Jozetta H. Srb. *Flexitime: Where, When, and How?* Ithaca: New York State School of Industrial and Labor Relations, Cornell University, 1979.

Swart, J. Carrol. "Clerical Workers on Flexitime: A Survey of Three Industries." *Personnel* (Apr. 1985): 40–44.

A survey of the effects of flexitime on clerical workers in banking, insurance, and utilities. It indicates that flexible schedules improve productivity and morale.

"Ten Hours a Day, Four Days a Week." *American City and County* (Oct. 1979): 77–78.

Reports that two New England public works departments find local unions receptive, employees happier, and more work done with a compressed workweek.

U.S. Congress. Public law 97-160: Federal Employees Flexible and Compressed Work Schedules Act of 1982. Washington, D.C.: Mar. 26, 1982.

Legislation that authorizes an alternative work schedules program on a permanent basis, after a successful three-year pilot project.

U.S. House of Representatives. *Flexible Compressed Work Schedules*. Committees on Post Office and Civil Service hearings: Apr. 3, 1981, and Feb. 3 and 9, 1982.

Hearings on the proposed Federal Employees Flexible and Compressed Work Schedules Act of 1982, with extensive testimony on the results of the pilot project.

Chapter 3: Regular Part-Time Employment

Alter, Joanne. *A Part-Time Career for a Full-Time You*. Boston: Houghton Mifflin, 1982.

Discusses the best part-time and shared jobs and how to get them.

Association of Part-Time Professionals. *Employee Benefits for Part-Timers*. McLean, Va., 1985. 55 pages.

———. *Part-Time Employment in America*. Highlights of the First National Conference on Part-Time Employment. McLean, Va., 1984. 83 pages.

Belous, Richard S. "The International Growth of Part-Time Employment: Estimates and Implications." Washington, D.C.: National Planning Association, 1988. 7 pages.

Discusses implications for competitiveness by U.S. firms of the growing use of part-time by European firms.

"Benefits Provided to Permanent Part-Time Employees." *IRN Perspective* (a monthly supplement to *Industrial Relations News*), (Dec. 1982).

Report on a survey of 310 employers.

Brown, Abby. "What Part-Time Professionals Think." Personnel Administrator 31, no. 8 (Aug. 1986): 33–39.

Commission of Inquiry Into Part-Time Work. *Part-Time Work in Canada*. Report to the Minister of Labour. Ottawa, Ontario, Canada: 1983. 218 pages.

Focuses on who the part-time workers are and what jobs they hold, as well as their views and those of unions and employers.

Hewitt Associates. *Benefits for Part-Time Employees*. Lincolnshire, Ill.: 1985. 24 pages.

A survey of 484 companies employing nonunion workers on part-time schedules. Includes tables comparing their benefits with those of the companies' full-time workers.

Jallade, Jean-Pierre. *Towards a Policy of Part-Time Employment*. Maastricht, Netherlands: European Centre for Work and Society, 1984.

Studies the extent and nature of part-time employment in Europe and recommends a policy to create more part-time jobs.

Kahne, Hilda. "Part-Time Work: A Hope and a Peril." In *Part-Time Work: Opportunity or Dead End?* edited by Kitty Lundy and Barbara Warme. Forthcoming from Praeger.

———. *Reconceiving Part-Time Work: New Perspectives for Older Workers and Women*. Totowa, N.J.: Rowman and Allanheld, 1985.

Describes programs that permit shorter hours and more leisure in later life and a reduced schedule for women during the child-rearing years.

Mahlin, Stewart J., and Julie Charles. "Peak-Time Pay for Part-Time Work—A Full-Time Solution to the Part-Time Problem: Pay People What They're Worth When You Need Them Most." *Personnel Journal* (Nov. 1984): 60–65.

Manin, Mark B. "Flexible Benefits for Part-Time Employees." *Benefits News Analysis* 9, no. 3 (1987): 11–12.

Analysis by a benefits consultant of why and how a company should review its benefits policies relating to part-time employees.

Nardone, Thomas J. "Part-Time Workers: Who Are They?" *Monthly Labor Review* (Feb. 1986): 13–20.

Presents a new definition of part-timers, using existing data from the Current Population Survey (a monthly survey conducted by the Department of Labor, which provides basic statistics on unemployment and the labor force) to give a more accurate estimate of the number of part-time workers.

Nollen, Stanley D., Brenda Broz Eddy, and Virginia H. Martin. *Permanent Part-Time Employment: The Manager's Perspective.* New York: Praeger Publishers, 1978.

————, and Virginia H. Martin. *Alternative Work Schedules.* Part 2, *Permanent Part-Time Employment.* AMA Survey Report. New York: AMACOM, 1978.

A careful analysis of survey responses that concentrates on short- and long-term effects as well as management problems.

Rothberg, Diane S. "Part-Time Professionals: The Flexible Work Force." *Personnel Administrator* 31, no. 8 (Aug. 1986): 28–33.

"What the Boom in Part-Time Work Means for Management." *International Management* (May 1984): 38–40.

Presents trends in Canada, Europe, and Japan, as companies and their employees find their interests starting to coincide; explains modified job sharing in Germany, among other examples.

Chapter 4: Job Sharing

Bureau of Business Practice. "Can Job Sharing Work for You?" *Employee Relations Bulletin* (Waterford, Conn.: Mar. 1982): 6.

Presents an overview of job sharing and its advantages.

Foster, Catherine. "Companies Find Job Sharing Can Be a Two-Way Benefit." *Christian Science Monitor* (Mar. 30, 1983): 23.

Includes an account of job sharing at Rolscreen in Pella, Iowa.

Lee, Patricia. "Job Sharing—A Concept Whose Time Has Come." *Office Administration and Automation* (Apr. 1984): 28.

Describes the organizational advantages of job sharing and outlines steps for introducing a job-sharing program.

Lum, Donald C. "Guest Opinion: Job Sharing." *Office Administration and Automation* (Jan. 1984): 100.

Column by a vice-president of Pfizer Inc. on job sharing as an idea that has positive results when properly administered. His opinions are based on his company's experience with secretaries.

McGuire, Nan, et al. *Job Sharing in Health Care.* San Francisco: New Ways to Work, 1984. 45 pages.

A guide for administrators and job-sharers, with case studies, cost analyses, and sample proposals.

Meier, Gretl. *Job Sharing: A New Pattern for Quality of Work and Life.* Kalamazoo, Mich.: The W. E. Upjohn Institute for Employment Research, 1979. 187 pages.

Selected interviews with job-sharers that bring out the joys and stresses of job sharing.

New York State Committee on Work Environment and Productivity. *Job Sharing in New York State: An Assessment of Implementation and Participants' Experiences.* Final report submitted by F. B. Parisky and S. L. Gardner, Oct. 1981. 105 pages.

New York State Department of Civil Service. *Part-Time Schedules: A Guide for NYS Supervisors and Managers.* Albany, N.Y.: Oct. 1985. 47 pages.

"Nine-Monther Program Helps Bank, Mothers, and College Students." *ABA Banking Journal* (Apr. 1983): 30–31.

Describes an arrangement for hiring working mothers for nine months a year and students for three months in the summer.

Olmsted, Barney. "Job Sharing: An Emerging Work Style." *International Labour Review* 118, no. 3 (May-June 1979): 283–297.

Explains the mechanics of job sharing and discusses its broader implications for society.

———, and Suzanne Smith. *The Job Sharing Handbook.* Berkeley, Calif.: Ten-Speed Press, 1985.

An essential guide to sharing the responsibilities and rewards of one full-time job. Contains checklists, questionnaires, case histories, and practical suggestions.

Chapter 5: Phased and Partial Retirement

Axel, Helen. Forthcoming publication on retiree job banks. New York: The Conference Board, Fall 1989.

Barocas, Victor S., et al. "Employee, Retiree Options for an Aging Work Force." *Business and Health* (Apr. 1985): 25–29.

Includes a discussion of retirement-oriented work options.

Blyton, Paul. "Phasing in Early Retirement." *Personnel Management* (U.K.), (Nov. 1982): 32–35.

Surveys practices in Europe and especially Britain, where phased retirement is becoming more popular.

Carlson, Elliot. "Longer Work Life? A Look at the Future of Retirement." *Modern Maturity* (June-July 1985): 22–28.

Presents arrangements for retirees to work part-time, in special programs, or as job-sharers.

Christensen, Kathleen. *Flexible Work Arrangements and Older Workers: Older Workers' Experiences With Part-Time, Temporary, Off-the-Books Jobs and Self-Employment.* New York City Center for Human Environments, Graduate School, City University of New York, May 27, 1988. 48 pages.

Drucker, Peter F. "Flexible-Age Retirement: Social Issue of the Decade." *Industry Week* (May 15, 1978): 66–71.

Discusses an issue that the author believes will be comparable to minority employment and women's rights in the 1980s and considers how benefits can be handled.

Foulkes, Fred K., and Robert D. Paul. "Company Liabilities Are Soaring." *New York Times* (Nov. 29, 1987), B2.

Looks at the cost of some companies' early retirement programs. Discusses the efforts of some organizations to contain retiree health care expenses.

Honig, Marjorie, and Gloria Hanoch. "Partial Retirement as a Separate Mode of Retirement Behavior." *Journal of Human Resources* (Winter 1985): 21–46.

A study of the various forms of partial retirement, with many detailed tables.

Jacobson, Beverly. *Young Programs for Older Workers: Case Studies in Progressive Personnel Policies*. New York: Van Nostrand Reinhold, 1980.

Discusses such topics as companies using part-time employment, phased retirement, outplacement, reentry workers, older workers, and counseling.

Jud, Robert. *The Retirement Decision: How American Managers View Their Prospects*. AMA Survey Report. New York: AMA-COM, 1981.

Presents the findings of a study in which approximately 1,200 respondents of all ages report on factors influencing their decisions about retirement age. Indicates strong respect for older managers and covers the incentives for early, deferred, or phased retirement.

McCabe, Michael. "Easing Into Retirement." *San Jose Mercury News* (Mar. 16, 1984), 4A, 4C.

Discusses flexible retirement plans at Varian, Hewlett-Packard, and Levi Strauss.

McConnell, Stephen R., et al. *Alternative Work Options for Older Workers: A Feasibility Study*. Los Angeles: University of Southern California, Ethel Percy Andrus Gerontology Center, 1980. 39 pages.

A study of older workers' interest in working beyond normal retirement age, types of retirement options, and the lack of awareness of this interest on the part of management and labor unions.

Morrison, Malcolm J. *The Transition to Retirement: The Employee's Perspective*. New York: Bureau of Social Science Research, 1985.

Paul, Carolyn E. *Expanding Part-Time Work Options for Older Americans: A Feasibility Study*. Los Angeles: Ethel Percy Andrus Gerontology Center, 1983.

Rosenberg, Gail S., and Maureen E. McCarthy. "Flexible Retirement Programs in Two U.S. Companies." *Aging and Work* (Summer 1980): 210–214.

A study of reduced workweek programs by the National Council for Alternative Work Patterns.

Smith, Suzanne. "New Law Offers Teachers Opportunity for Job Sharing, Phased Retirement." *World of Work Report* (Jan. 1980): 3–4.

Analyzes the growing advantages to teachers and school districts of California's legislation to support sharing the work load.

State of California, Legislative Analyst. *The Reduced Work Load Program in the State Teachers' Retirement System.* Sacramento, Calif.: Sept. 1980. 23 pages.

Explains the regulations for the program and its costs. Indicates a net saving to the school system.

Swank, Constance. *Phase Retirement: The European Experience.* Washington, D.C.: National Council for Alternative Work Patterns, 1982. (Available from New Ways to Work, San Francisco).

Discusses the operation, costs, and benefits of phased retirement programs in six European countries. Includes case studies and company profiles.

U.S. Congressional Budget Office. *Work and Retirement: Options for Continued Employment of Older Workers.* Washington, D.C.: 1982. 81 pages.

Considers how demographic changes will affect the labor market and the economy, the determinants of retirement decisions, and options for continued employment, such as change in income allowable under private pension plans.

"Why Late Retirement Is Getting a Corporate Blessing: As Labor Crunch Looms, Innovative Programs Keep Older Workers on the Job." *Business Week* (Jan. 16, 1984), 69 and 72.

Covers reduced hours, job changes, job sharing, "retirement rehearsal," and pension accrual after age 65.

Work in America Institute. *The Future of Older Workers in America: New Options for an Extended Working Life.* Scarsdale, N.Y.: 1980. 135 pages.

Includes a recommendation for phased retirement as a means of giving employees a taste of leisure and new activities before retirement. Describes options for job and schedule redesign, reassignment, and part-time employment.

Chapter 6:   Voluntary Reduced Work Time

Best, Fred. *Exchanging Earnings for Leisure: Findings of an Exploratory National Survey on Work Time Preferences*. R&D Monograph 79. Washington, D.C.: U.S. Department of Labor, Employment and Training Administration, 1980.

Harriman, Ann. *The Work/Leisure Tradeoff: Reduced Work Time for Managers and Professionals*. New York: Praeger Publishers, 1982.

Focuses on adapting normal organizational procedures to permit a more satisfactory allocation of time.

Moorman, Barbara, and Barney Olmsted. *V-Time—A New Way to Work: A Resource Manual for Employers and Employees*. San Francisco: New Ways to Work, 1985.

A unique book that contains detailed case histories, sample legislation, useful forms, and much more.

Olmsted, Barney. "Changing Times: The Use of Reduced Work Time Options in the United States." *International Labour Review* 122, no. 4 (July-Aug. 1983): 479–492.

Discusses the history and present status of part-time, job sharing, and voluntary reduced work time.

Chapter 7:   Leave Time

Adams, Roy J. "Education Leave: North American Development and Design Elements." *Work Times* 1, no. 2 (San Francisco: New Ways to Work, Fall 1982): 1–2, 5.

Reports primarily on developments in Canada.

Apcar, Leonard M. "More Firms Offer Sabbaticals From Jobs, but Sometimes Workers Hate to Return." *Wall Street Journal* (Mar. 26, 1985), 22.

Reports that some people worry about changed conditions on the job; some find that their appetite is whetted for more leisure.

Berman, Melissa A. "What Do Women Get?" *Across the Board* (Mar. 1987): 18–20.

Presents figures on maternity benefits gathered since the 1984 Catalyst study, which show great differences, depending on state law, size of organization, and whether a woman works in a blue-collar or white-collar job.

Best, Fred. *Flexible Life Scheduling: Breaking the Education-Work-Retirement Lockstep*. New York: Praeger Publishers, 1980.

Considers the appropriate allocation of work, income, and leisure throughout the life span.

"Changing Work Force Increases Demand for Parental Leave." *State Government News* (July 1986): 12–13, 24.

A survey of state governments that summarizes each state's policy on parental leave for its employees.

The Corporate Guide to Parental Leaves. New York: Catalyst, 1986. 147 pages.

A survey of 384 corporations and 100 recent leave-takers, with legislative guidelines and examples of company policies. Chapters tell how to write an effective policy, handle work during a temporary leave, ensure productive transitions back to work for new mothers, and develop policies for fathers and adoptive parents.

Dods, Robert A. "Is There a Sabbatical in Your Future? How One Senior Business Partner Planned His." *Business Quarterly* (Winter 1980): 30–36.

Thoughtful personal account of a travel and study leave, which includes a statement of the author's financial arrangements and his company's policy.

Erler, Gisela. "Maternity and Parental Leaves in Europe." *Work Time* (Summer 1982): 1–5.

Comparison of Austria, West Germany, Sweden, Finland, and Hungary with respect to leave policies, their acceptance by women, and the impact of paternal leaves.

Friedman, Dana E. "Liberty, Equality, Maternity!" *Across the Board* (Mar. 1987): 10–17.

Discusses the effects on corporate policies of recent court decisions and projected legislation concerning maternity benefits.

"Justices Uphold Pregnancy Leave: California Law Granting Women Their Jobs Back Is Ruled Valid." *Los Angeles Times* (Jan. 14, 1987), 1.

Explains a ruling that represents a major development in women's benefits.

Kamerman, Sheila B., et al. *Maternity Policies and Working Women*. New York: Columbia University Press, 1983.

A report on the state of maternity (and paternity) policies, including a survey of private employers and of five states that provide temporary disability insurance.

Koppman, Steve. *Time-Off for Parents: The Benefits, Costs and Options of Parental Leave*. Sacramento, Calif.: Senate Office of Research, 1987.

Krett, Karen. "Maternity, Paternity and Child Care Policies: A New Survey on Benefit Policies." *Personnel Administrator* (June 1985): 125–136.

A study in which the responses of 153 employers are analyzed by industry and company size.

Leeds, Mark H. "Maternity Leave for Fathers." *New York State Bar Journal* (Feb. 1983): 32–35: (Apr. 1983): 15–17.

Two articles that treat the issue of discrimination between the sexes in parental leave laws.

"Maternity Leave: What Some Firms Are Doing." *Of Counsel* (May 1986): 15–16.

Presents examples of the maternity leave programs of certain law firms.

Meier, Gretl S. *Worker Learning and Worktime Flexibility*. Kalamazoo, Mich.: The W. E. Upjohn Institute for Employment Research. 1983. 64 pages.

Considers how flexible work time might extend education and training opportunities, especially for women in low-status jobs.

Milofsky, David. "The Baby vs. the Corporation." *Working Woman* (June 1985): 133–134.

Discusses paternity leave as a benefit required by laws against discrimination and also expresses what such leave means to the author's feelings as a parent.

O'Malley, I. K. "Paid Educational Leave in Australia, Canada, Ireland, and the United Kingdom." *International Labour Review* (Mar.-Apr. 1982): 169–183.

Examines the policies of the four countries following the adoption of International Labor Organization Convention 140.

Rifkin, Ira. "Time Off From Job Is Pause That Refreshes." *Daily News* (Aug. 18, 1983): 1, 10.

Presents examples of companies that give sabbaticals, with details of their terms.

Shiu, Patricia. "Parental Leave Project: Final Report" (30 pages) and "Applications of ERISA Preemption Doctrine to Local and State-Enacted Parental Leave Policies" (55 pages). San Francisco: Employment Law Center, 1986. Available from Employment Law Center, 1663 Mission St., Suite 400, San Francisco 94103.

Examines the viability of a parental leave statute as state law.

Stern, David. *Managing Human Resources: The Art of Full Employment.* Boston: Auburn House, 1982.

Includes a section on sabbaticals and the use of pension funds to finance them.

Wheatly, M., and M. S. Hirsch. "Families—Maternity Leave: What the Company Owes You." *Working Woman* (June 1983): 112–114.

Presents specifics on the Pregnancy Disability Act of 1978.

Winfield, Fairlee E. *The Work and Family Sourcebook.* Greenvale, N.Y.: Panel Publishers, 1988.

Wood, Jack M. *Educational Leave and the Balance of Skills: An Australian Perspective.* Paris: Organization for Economic Cooperation and Development, Jan. 1983. 11 pages.

Maintains that Australia will fall behind the world "balance of skills" if more is not done to provide leave for continuing education and describes the extent of public- and private-sector schemes.

Zigler, Edward F., and Meryl Frank. *The Parental Leave Crisis: Toward a National Policy.* New Haven, Conn.: Yale University Press, 1988.

Chapter 8: Work Sharing

Batz, Julie, and the staff of New Ways to Work. *Work Sharing: An Alternative to Layoffs.* San Francisco: New Ways to Work, 1988. 25 pages.

Best, Fred. *Reducing Workweeks to Prevent Layoffs: The Economic and Social Impacts of Unemployment Insurance–Supported Work Sharing*. Philadelphia: Temple University Press, 1988.

————. "Short-Time Compensation in North America: Trends and Prospects." *Personnel* (Jan. 1985): 34–41.

Examines short-time compensation experience (which includes partial unemployment insurance benefits) in California, Canada, and West Germany and its impact on companies, workers, and governments.

————. *Work Sharing Issues, Policy Options and Prospects*. Kalamazoo, Mich.: The W. E. Upjohn Institute for Employment Research, 1981. 204 pages.

Principal topics include the variety of ways in which work can be shared to reduce unemployment, the economic effects of work sharing, and how work sharing can be made more attractive to workers and employers.

"Employers and Employees Benefit From Work-Sharing UI Program." *California Employer* (Mar. 1981): 2.

Presents provisions of the law and explains how it works. Notes that 1,350 employers had filed work-sharing plans.

MaCoy, Ramelle, and Martin J. Morand, eds. *Short-Time Compensation: A Formula for Work Sharing*. New York: Pergamon Press, 1984.

A Work in America Institute–sponsored study of alternatives to layoffs in Canada and West Germany and in the states of California, Oregon, and Arizona. Includes management and union viewpoints.

Meltz, Noah, Frank Reid, and Gerald S. Swartz. *Sharing the Work: An Analysis of the Issues of Worksharing and Job Sharing*. Toronto, Ontario, Canada: University of Toronto Press, 1981.

Presents a theoretical model to assess the feasibility of shared employment in the Canadian labor market, with costs and implications for workers and government. Has a good analysis of job sharing.

State of California Health and Welfare Agency, Employment Development Department. *Shared Work Unemployment Insurance Evaluation Report*. Sacramento, Calif.: May 1982.

Discusses the requirements and patterns of participation, the social gains and costs, and views and attitudes about the California shared work program.

U.S. Department of Labor, Management Relations and Cooperative Programs. *Preventing Layoffs: Developing an Effective Job Security and Economic Adjustment Program.* Washington, D.C.: 1986. 30 pages.

Focuses on how to use work- and job-sharing techniques without reducing the work force; includes case studies.

Vasche, Jon David. "Unemployment Benefits for Work Sharing." *Business Economics* (Sept. 1982): 44–49.

Analyzes the profitability of California's shared work unemployment compensation program for two representative companies, showing how the program is affected by such considerations as the company's wage structure and its policy on benefits.

"Will Plant-Closing Law Encourage More Work Sharing?" *Work Times* 7, no. 1 (Fall 1988): 1.

Chapter 9: Flexiplace

Anapol, Lynda, and Leslie Crawford. "Pioneering a New Workplace Option: Telecommuting and Pacific Bell." *Work Times* (Spring 1986): 4.

A description of Pacific Bell's in-house pilot program, in which roughly 200 Pacific Bell employees are allowed to telecommute from their homes or from "satellite" work stations.

Atkinson, William. "Home/Work." *Personnel Journal* (Nov. 1985): 105.

———. *Working at Home: Is It for You?* Homewood, Ill.: Dow Jones–Irwin, 1985.

Christensen, Kathleen E. *Impacts of Computer-Mediated Work on Women and Their Families.* New York: City College of New York, June 1985. 71 pages.

Discusses the role of technology in home-based work, the necessary safeguards, and the differences between being an entrepreneur and being an employee. The work was sponsored by the U.S. Office of Technology Assessment.

Costello, Cynthia B. *Home-Based Employment: Implications for Working Women* (Washington, D.C.: Women's Research & Education Institute, 1987). 20 pages.

Gordon, Gil. *Telecommuting Review: The Gordon Report.* Monmouth Junction, N.J. Monthly newsletter presenting information on a variety of issues related to telecommuting and flexiplace. It is an excellent resource for employers interested in telecommuting or those who already have a program up and running and want to keep abreast of new resources in this rapidly changing field.

————, and Marcia M. Kelly. *Telecommuting: How to Make It Work for You and Your Company.* Englewood Cliffs, N.J.: Prentice Hall, 1986.

Provides evaluation guidelines for the full range of remote work locations, with special attention to the pros and cons of the home as a work site. Explains remote supervision options, discusses how to determine when on-site supervision is needed, and provides a job-selection profile that helps determine which jobs will best fit into a telecommuting program.

Horvath, Francis W. "Work at Home: New Findings From the Current Population Survey." *Monthly Labor Review* (Nov. 1986): 31–35.

Study that found more than 8 million people working at least eight hours per week at home, mainly in services.

"The Portable Executive: From Faxes to Laptops, Technology Is Changing Our Work Lives." *Business Week* (October 10, 1988): 102–112.

Chapter 10:   Contingent Employment

Belous, Richard S. "Contingent Workers and Equal Employment Opportunity." Washington, D.C.: National Planning Association. Paper presented at the Industrial Relations Research Association. New York: Dec. 29, 1988.

Describes the impact of contingent employment on women and minorities.

Bennett, Amanda. "Growing Small: As Big Firms Continue to Trim Their Staffs, 2-Tier Setup Emerges." *Wall Street Journal* (May 4, 1987), 1 and 12.

Christensen, Kathleen. "Women's Labor Force Attachment in the United States: Rise of Contingent Work." Paper presented at the Israeli-American Symposium on Women and Work, sponsored by the Women's Bureau of the U.S. Department of Labor and the Israeli Ministry of Labor. Jerusalem: Nov. 12, 1986.

Fleming, John. *Work When You Want to Work: The Complete Professional Guide for the Temporary Worker*. New York: Pocket Books, 1985.

A detailed description of the temporary "work style" and how to get a temporary job.

Fowler, Elizabeth H. "Temporary Positions for Executives." *New York Times* (November 29, 1988): C19.

Describes growing use of executive-level "temps."

Granrose, Charlyn S., and Eileen Applebaum. "The Efficiency of Temporary Help and Part-Time Employment." *Personnel Administrator* (Jan. 1986): 71–83.

Analyzes costs and benefits of temporary and part-time work to organizations and employees.

Henson, Ronald C. "Coping With Fluctuating Work-Force Requirements." *Employment Relations Today* (Summer 1985): 149–156.

Discusses the reasons for needing casual, on-call, and longer-term temporaries.

Howe, Wayne J. "Temporary Help Workers: Who They Are, What Jobs They Hold." *Monthly Labor Review* (Nov. 1986): 45–47.

Concludes that "temps" are disproportionately young, female, and black, mostly in clerical and industrial-help jobs.

"In Search of a Temporary Solution." *Insight* (Oct. 6, 1986): 45.

Reports that the federal government is reviewing the rules against hiring temporary workers; some claim savings from hiring temporaries, but unions are opposed.

John, D. Geoffrey. "Staffing and Temporary Help." *Personnel Administrator* (Jan. 1987): 96–99.

Argues that effective use of temporary help can be the key to increased productivity.

Macauley, Walter W. "Developing Trends in the Temporary Services Industry." *Personnel Administrator* (Jan. 1986): 61–68.

Describes the growth of the temporary services industry, including employee leasing, franchising, and full-service agencies.

McCarthy, Michael J. "On Their Own: In Increasing Numbers, White Collar Workers Leave Steady Positions." *Wall Street Journal* (Oct. 13, 1987), 1.

Magnum, Garth, et al. "The Temporary Help Industry: A Response to the Dual Internal Labor Market." *Industrial and Labor Relations Review* (July 1985): 599–611.

Based on Commerce Department data and interviews with employers; shows how employer responses to varying work loads differ by industry, occupation, size of organization, product demand, and fringe benefits.

Olmsted, Barney. "Keeping the Solution From Becoming the Problem: Integrating Regular and "Temporary Employees." *Human Resources Professional* 1, no. 1 (November/December 1988): 28–31.

Describes problems some firms have had integrating temporary employees with regular workers. Offers suggestions based on the experiences of employers who have done it successfully.

1988 AMS Contract Labor Survey. Trevose, Pa.: Administrative Management Society.

"Special PPF Survey Report: Part-Time and Other Alternative Staffing Practices." *Bulletin to Management* 39, no. 25—part 2 (June 23, 1988). 11 pages.

U.S. Department of Labor, Women's Bureau. *Flexible Workstyles: A Look at Contingent Work*. Washington, D.C.: Sept. 1988.

Provides an overview of workplace trends from the present until the year 2000. Contains abstracts of 13 papers commissioned for a conference on contingent work sponsored by City University of New York and the Women's Bureau of the U.S. Department of Labor. Subjects covered include part-time employment, staff leasing, temporary work, independent contracting, and other pertinent issues.

Vollbrecht, Tiana. "Temps for Hire." *San Francisco Business Journal* (Oct. 1986): 27–29.

Presents interviews with staff members of several agencies in which they discuss such trends in the expanding temporary employment industry as employee leasing, worker incentives and training programs, and alternative staffing.

Wells, Amy Stuart. "Temporary Workers Going Upscale: Professionals and Businessmen Among the New Recruits." *New York Times* (Mar. 22, 1987), Careers, C17.

Reports that some professionals find the disadvantages of temporary work are balanced by the freedom, variety, and high hourly pay that go with this work style.

Chapter 11: Toward the Year 2000: Equiflex

Alternative Work Schedules: Changing Times for a Changing Workforce. The National Report on Work and Family, special report no. 5. Washington, D.C.: Buraff Publications, May 1988. 32 pages.

Presents an update of material originally published in the 1986 Bureau of National Affairs report *The Changing Workplace: New Directions in Staffing and Scheduling,* listed below.

Axel, Helen. *Corporations and Families: Changing Practices and Perspectives.* Research report no. 868. New York: The Conference Board, 1985. 51 pages.

Part 1 of this report provides background on recent trends in the family composition of the work force, an overview of the characteritics of companies particularly receptive to family-supportive programs, and some general observations about how changes in corporate policies are initiated, implemented, and evaluated. Part 2 focuses on how personnel policies, benefits, and services are being affected by these trends.

The Changing Workplace: New Directions in Staffing and Scheduling. Washington, D.C.: Bureau of National Affairs, 1986. 140 pages.

Describes why businesses and employees are seeking new work arrangements. Discusses various staffing and scheduling options and documents the increasing use of such alternatives as flexible schedules, part-time jobs, work sharing, temporary employment, and flexiplace.

Connock, Stephen. "Workforce Flexibility: Juggling Time and Task." *Personnel Management* (Oct. 1985): 36–38.

Discusses the cost-effective use of staff, by means of mobility between tasks, annual hours, and alternative forms of contract.

Flexible Benefits: How to Set Up a Plan When Your Employees Are Complaining Your Costs Are Rising, and You're Too Busy to Think About It. New York: Catalyst, 1987.

Offers comprehensive information in a nontechnical format that helps companies answer three basic questions: Will flexible benefits work for my company? How can I design a plan that does what I want and is legal? How can I communicate my plan and gauge its success?

"Flexible Working Practices." *Trade Union Report* (Stockton-on-Tees, United Kingdom: Jim Conway Memorial Foundation) 7, no. 2 (Mar. 1986): 8–17.

Reports on a trade union conference discussing the issue of flexibility in the work pace—its historical background, the reasons for its emergence, pros and cons of its various aspects, and the types of responses traditionally made by trade unions to attempts to achieve greater flexibility.

Lee, R. A. "Controlling Hours of Work." *Personnel Review* 14, no. 3 (1985): 3.

Provides an overview of the various innovations that have been introduced in the management of hours systems and some of the related research initiatives that have been undertaken. The author, a member of the department of management studies at the University of Loughborough, Great Britain, notes that "{*I*}t is surprising how little attention has been focused on {*organizational hours systems*} relative to other influence mechanisms, such as pay, job design, appraisal systems, budgets and so on."

Lynch, Philip. "Annual Hours: An Idea Whose Time Has Come." *Personnel Management* (Nov. 1985): 46–50.

An overview of annual hours contracts, a new way to organize work time that is attracting increasing interest in some industries in Great Britain.

New Work Schedules for a Changing Society. Work in America Institute Policy Study, directed by Jerome Rosow and Robert Zager. Scarsdale, N.Y.: Work in America Institute, 1981. 128 pages.

Presents recommendations concerning flexible schedules, part-time employment, job sharing, compressed workweeks, family time, and union concerns.

Nollen, Stanley D. *New Work Schedules in Practice: Managing Time in a Changing Society*. Work in America Institute Series. New York: Van Nostrand Reinhold, 1982.

Case studies of part-time, flexitime, job-sharing, and compressed workweek programs, with emphasis on management, fringe benefits, and labor's role.

Operations Report: Keeping a First-Rate but Flexible Work Force. New York: Research Institute of America, Oct. 1986. 19 pages.

Rathkey, Paul, and Andy P. Wood. *Flexibility and Working Time Options in the United Kingdom: Trends and Preferences*. Stockton-on-Tees, United Kingdom: Jim Conway Memorial Foundation, May 1988.

Paper presented at the first annual meeting of The Society for Work Options. The authors examine the issue of work-time options and preferences within the context of a changed industrial relations scene and climate in the United Kingdom. Particular attention is paid to the debate over "flexibility" as it relates to bargaining over working time.

Teriet, Bernhard. "Flexiyear Schedules—Only a Matter of Time?" *Monthly Labor Review* (Dec. 1977): 11.

A report on a new concept of allocating working hours that was being discussed in Sweden, France, and Germany: the development of a working year contract as a means of coping with variable production conditions and accommodating the interest in "new life patterns."

Woodcock, Gerry. "Achieving Annual Hours." *Industrial Society* 68 (June 1986): 12–14.

A report on how Thames Board, Workington Division, a part of Thames Group, a wholly owned subsidiary of Unilever in Great Britain, achieved an annual hours contract over an 18-month period.

Index